The La Follettes of Wisconsin

The La Follettes of Wisconsin

LOVE AND POLITICS IN PROGRESSIVE AMERICA

Bernard A. Weisberger

The University of Wisconsin Press

The University of Wisconsin Press
114 North Murray Street
Madison, Wisconsin 53715

3 Henrietta Street
London WC2E 8LU, England

2   4   6   8   10   9   7   5   3   1

Printed in the United States of America

All photographs are courtesy of the State Historical Society of Wisconsin. The negative numbers are as follows: p. 24, WHi(X313)2497E; p. 38, WHi(X28)1013; p. 40, WHi(L61)43; p. 42, WHi(X3)48658; p. 58, WHi(X3)45820; p. 61, WHi(X3)27827; p. 63, WHi(X3)13031; p. 68, WHi(L51)74; p. 71, WHi(L51)52; p. 90, WHi(X3)48646; p. 97, WHi(X3)3996; p. 100, WHi(X3)48654; p. 104, WHi(X3)48644; p. 113, WHi(X3)48485; p. 147, WHi(X3)14092; p. 152, WHi(X3) 3090; p. 220, WHi(X3)48657; p. 260, WHi(X3)48655; p. 261, WHi(X3) 48656; p. 270, WHi(X3)2068; p. 274, WHi(X3)41033; p. 284, WHi(X3)22371; p. 296, WHi(X3) 22749; p. 304, WHi(X3)14473.

Library of Congress Cataloging-in-Publication Data
Weisberger, Bernard A., 1922–
The La Follettes of Wisconsin: love and politics in
progressive America / Bernard A. Weisberger.
384 p.   cm.
Includes bibliographical references and index.
ISBN 0-299-14130-6
1. La Follette family.
2. La Follette, Robert M. (Robert Marion), 1855–1925.
3. La Follette, Belle Case, 1859–1931.   4. Progressivism (United States politics)
5. United States—Politics and government—1865–1933.
6. United States—Politics and government—1933–1945.
I. Title.
E747.W3   1994
973.9′092′2—dc20
[B]   93-32286

For all our grandchildren

Contents

Illustrations

Illustrations

Preface

I remember when I first became an admirer of Robert M. La Follette, Sr. It was 1937. I was fifteen years old and deep in Walter Millis's *Road to War*, a chronicle of how the United States got involved in what was then the one and only world war. I was strongly influenced by antiwar novels, memoirs, movies, and plays like *A Farewell to Arms, All Quiet on the Western Front,* and many others. I thought that the war itself was a cruel and meaningless slaughter and America's entry a tragedy. (I haven't changed my mind about that.) Anger and sadness swept over me when I came to the climax of the book, the rainy April night in 1917 when Woodrow Wilson read his war message to a joint session of Congress amid applause and cheers so furious that even the president later expressed surprise. But one senator did not join the hysteria. He listened in stony silence, arms folded on his chest, chewing gum — an immovable rock in the raging current. That was La Follette of Wisconsin, a hero if ever I had met one in the pages of a history book.

He seemed to me to belong to a time long gone. Like all youngsters, I made little distinction between things that happened five or fifty or five hundred years before I was born. I'm not sure that I even knew in 1937 that although La Follette was dead, one of his two sons, Robert, Jr., was in the United States Senate and the other, Philip, was governor of Wisconsin, thereby creating a one-of-a-kind brother act in American politics. Both were still young men, younger than my father.

I'm certain that I did not know that "Old Bob," my invincible war resister, had run as an independent presidential candidate in 1924 and gotten just under five million votes out of some twenty-nine million cast. One voter in six had gone for him, and that was only thirteen years earlier, very recent history. It might as well have been an official secret for all our schoolbooks had to say about it, and I had not encountered the 1924 election in any of my outside reading on current events. America's capacity to forget losers is legendary.

Not for another ten years did La Follette re-enter my awareness and then in a big way. In 1947, as a graduate student in United States history, I learned that he was one of the stars of the Progressive movement that swept the nation in the opening years of the twentieth century. In 1891, a seemingly faithful Republican, he had suddenly discovered that Wisconsin was tainted with corruption. For the next nine years he went up and down the rural byways of the state, rallying the people to join him in breaking the unholy alliance between greedy corporations and political bosses, to take back their government. He did not simply harangue listeners. He held them spellbound for hours with avalanches of facts. He told them in precise detail and hard numbers how they were being overtaxed, overcharged, and sold out, how nominating conventions were rigged, how judges were fixed and legislators bribed. He began with most of the money and respectability in the state against him, but in 1900 he won the first of three two-year terms as governor.

He gave Wisconsin a model administration, according to his lights. He pushed bills through the legislature that provided for open primary elections and fair taxation, safeguarded natural resources from land-grabbers and exploiters, and created commissions to regulate banks, insurance companies, utilities, and railroads. To these he appointed independent experts, many of them professors at the state university. He believed they would set competitive rules and rates that would bring the benefits of economic growth to the whole public instead of selected stockholders and insiders. He did not invent all of these ideas, or realize them without other people's help. They were part of the culture of reform that forward-looking, educated, "modern" men and women were beginning to share in every big city. But the fires he kindled were visible to national progressive journalists a long way off. They called his state "a laboratory of democracy." They popularized the term "the Wisconsin Idea" to describe his mixture of government by popular will and trained, disinterested intelligence.

La Follette became a national figure. Wisconsin sent him to the Senate in 1905, where he had less power but a bigger stage, and he went on battling, usually in the minority, against the monopolists and their allies in Congress to the end of his days. He made no deals and gave no quarter. He was already known as "Fighting Bob" when he threw himself in the path of the stampede to war. Only someone of absolute political fearlessness could have done it, and it cost him dearly for a time. But he came back for that last 1924 crusade as the presidential candidate of workers, farmers, and consumers who chose not to vote for Calvin Coolidge, corporate America's front man, or the Democrat John W. Davis, a conservative lawyer whose economic views were indistinguishable from Coolidge's. The next year, weary and aged far beyond his seventy years, Old Bob died of heart failure. "Young Bob," barely thirty, was chosen to fill his vacant seat. In 1930 Phil, just thirty-two, captured the Wisconsin statehouse.

The boys carried on the tradition in their fashion. During the thirties Robert, Jr., became best known in the Senate for his chairmanship of an investigating committee that revealed how employers planted thugs and spies in the workplace to break unions. Phil, as a Depression-era governor, was largely preoccupied with public works and relief measures, but he also fought hard for conservation, public power, and tight control of banks and holding companies. Both were first elected as Republicans but in political reality became supporters of the New Deal. Still, they had no love for the Democrats or for Franklin D. Roosevelt, so in 1934 they bolted and ran on the ticket of a newly created Progressive Party of Wisconsin.

But the "reign" of the second La Follette generation in the state was not to be long. In 1938 Phil tried to expand the third party into a nationwide organization, the National Progressives of America, to challenge Roosevelt. The effort was an unqualified flop, and he was badly beaten in his run for a third term. His elective career was ended at forty-one. In 1940 Bob barely won reelection to the Senate. In 1946 the Wisconsin Progressives disbanded, and Bob returned to the Republican fold, only to be beaten in the primary by Joseph R. McCarthy. He, too, still only middle-aged, was finished as a political force.

That was what I knew about the La Follettes when it was proposed to me that I undertake a biography of the family. I thought it was all there was to know. I welcomed the chance to try to answer the question of where my admired old rebel chief had gotten that remarkable courage. How had he come by and held onto his blazing integrity? And how had he passed these qualities on to his young lions? That too intrigued me as a father and a son, because I saw this as basically a story about a father and his sons. But as I dug into the material, I learned that I was completely wrong about that.

I was wrong because the books I had read rarely if ever mentioned Bob's wife and the boys' mother, Belle Case La Follette. Until recently, official history tended to overlook women. In this case it was an especially gigantic mistake, for it is impossible to understand Old Bob and Belle and their children as individuals isolated from one another.

As I worked my way deeper into an enormous archive of La Follette correspondence, I found myself in the middle of a love story. It began with a man and woman, then grew to include the family they raised. It radiated through their lives, their friendships, and their careers. It shaped the expression of their principles and explained why they clung to them with such resolve in the face of inner doubts and the world's discouragement.

Belle was no ordinary spouse. She was a law school graduate and a columnist and occasional lecturer. Besides helping Bob with his speeches, contacts, and correspondence, she wrote on behalf of sensible diet, dress, and exercise; spare-the-rod childrearing; hygienic housekeeping; and voting rights for women. She argued the case against racial segregation long before it was usual for whites to do so. She was a committed pacifist.

Belle was also a full-time wife and mother. She ran homes in Washington and Wisconsin with little help and supervised—sometimes actually conducted—the education of four children. In addition to Bob, Jr., and Phil, there were two daughters. Just as this book was going to press a member of the staff of the Wisconsin Historical Society, in the course of some photographic research, made the discovery that Fola, the La Follettes' first child and one of the story's principal characters, was in fact named Flora Dodge (La Follette) after a college classmate of her mother and father's. "Fola" was apparently a childish mispronunciation that she chose to perpetuate around the time of her own entry into the University of Wisconsin, though she is recorded as Flora both in the 1900 census and in the records of the Wisconsin Academy, the private high school that she attended. The change was permanent and total; "Flora" appears absolutely nowhere in any of the source material—published, oral, or in manuscript letters (which Fola herself preserved and arranged) that I consulted. Whether there is any significance beyond personal choice to this suppression I do not know, but no evidence suggests it. Nevertheless I insert the facts here for the record, and express my thanks to Mr. John Holzhueter, of the WHS office, for his serendipitous solution to the question (which in fact had puzzled me) of the origin of so unusual a name as "Fola." Fola went on the stage and incidentally was one of the earliest members of Actors Equity, the performers' union. She married a dramatist, campaigned in the battle for suffrage, lectured on social forces in the theater, and taught at a progressive school. The boys were born a considerable time after Fola, and finally there was Mary. She was the only one not to spend at least part of her life in some kind of work that involved addressing the public. These four were the products of a marriage based on an extraordinary matching of backgrounds, outlooks, and needs.

Bob and Belle, independent farmers' children both, met and fell in love at the University of Wisconsin, from which they were graduated in 1879. They were equally convinced that they owed something to the taxpayers of the state, who had footed the bill for their educations. But for each of them, public usefulness was much more than an obligation. It was their vocation, and democracy was their religion. To spend themselves in extending and purifying it was to live life at its highest. They thought that nothing mattered more than civic participation to right wrongs, to fight special privilege and selfishness, to enlarge the quality and not simply the rewards of self-government. They expected to teach these ideals diligently to their children, who would join them someday as comrades in arms.

They might have been impossibly self-righteous but for a sense of humor visible only to intimates and for the emotional warmth that was the glue of their lives together. Neither of them was naturally tough enough to be a full-time political crusader alone. He was sometimes moody and paranoid. She was often anxious and guilty. Each one needed the assurance of love and frequent infusions of encouragement and support. They disagreed and even quarreled occasionally but for the most part they nourished and strengthened each other in their mutual dedication. Each brought out the best qualities of the other partner.

The short answer to the question of what sustained Old Bob in his bravery was "marriage to Belle." And Belle's strength was increased by his need for her, his thankfulness that she existed. It was a perfect self-reinforcing circle of love.

As the children grew older, this circle opened to receive them. It was a wonderful parental gift, but like many such gifts it carried with it heavy burdens and the seeds of wrenching personal problems.

All of this I learned from the enormous treasure trove of their letters. Bob and Belle believed in and lived by the power and beauty of spoken and written words. Both were trained in elocution, loved to read or be read to aloud, and wrote with strength and clarity. When travel separated them they corresponded almost daily. They passed the habit on to the children. It took especially firm root in Fola and Phil, who would cover page after page. And almost all of these thousands of letters are still available, because Bob could not bear to destroy anything written by someone he loved, and Belle and the family spared him and themselves that pain by becoming compulsive savers of every scrap of writing.

The family papers contain few letters written by Bob and Belle before their adulthood, but their offspring's childhoods are well represented. The

children's letters begin with postcards or notes solemnly "dictated" by five-
and six-year-olds to amused parents or parental secretaries. They continue
through school, college, travel, marriage, and career launchings. All of the
family letters show a prodigious investment of effort. They were written
at office desks, on kitchen tables, in jerking railroad cars and lonely depots, in steamer lounges, in fleabag hotel rooms, and in sickbeds. They
bear spidery ink strokes or grayish pencil scrawls, but only rarely and late
in life the mark of a typewriter. Usually they were long, and almost always
they were full of praise for the "beloved," or "dearest," or "blessed" recipients. Passed around, folded and refolded, treasured and preserved, they
were the way the La Follettes unpacked their hearts with the private words
of devotion, conviction, consolation, and encouragement that meant everything to them.

The La Follettes saw themselves as an embattled clan forging intimate
bonds in a joint uphill battle for a better country. Sometimes the line between their inner selves, their identities within the family, and their public
lives seemed to be nearly nonexistent.

I also found in them a strange mixture of political radicalism and the
"traditional values" that conservatives now claim as their exclusive property. The La Follettes believed in reading "the classics," but doing so did
not set them apart from workers and farmers. They worshiped "Daddy"
like a patriarch but backed women's demands for equal professional and
civic rights. They loved their country but worked for the day when it would
need neither an army nor a navy. They believed in public regulation right
up to the edge of socialism, yet were dedicated to the proposition that individual hard work and responsibility were the building blocks of citizenship. They supported the idea of private property, but none of them assigned
a personal priority to accumulating very much of it. For most of their lives
they all lived on incomes that ranged from modest to inadequate.

As much as any traditionalists they believed in the objective existence
and importance of character, intelligence, reason, and duty. But they never
identified these qualities with any single group. And they never sanctified
tradition or form. As Old Bob himself put it: "Democracy is a life; and
involves continual struggle."

All of these things are better expressed in their words than mine. I have
tried to tell the story of Bob and Belle and the children here as straight-
forwardly and simply as possible and primarily out of their own pens. I
have done that partly because the story itself is as good as any novel and
partly because there are things worth learning from it. I myself think that

right now we need, and do not have, many more men and women like Bob and Belle La Follette and more families like theirs.

I do not, however, suggest that these pages contain a recipe for producing them. Even the La Follette family did not weather the storms of our time unchanged, as the narrative itself will show. One small but important evidence is in the letters themselves, the main quarry of material that I used. Those that passed among the four children (and their spouses) became less frequent and more businesslike after Belle died in 1931, just six years after Bob.

I'm not certain why the correspondence dwindled. It may be that she and Bob really kept the exchanges going by their own persistent example. With them gone, the binding love that overflowed onto paper was weakened. Or perhaps it is simply that the telephone was beginning to intrude and take over.

Perhaps the busy public lives that Phil and Bob, Jr., led took up too much energy, and they could not sit at their writing desks, "visiting" far into the night as their father had done. Perhaps the common tribulations of middle age in Depression and World War II America touched all the surviving children and quelled the high spirits that had flowed into those long messages to each other.

Or maybe the answer lies in the outside forces that abruptly broke off the "dynasty." Maybe as progressivism turned into the bureaucratic and welfare state, and the country embarked on yet another war that the La Follettes found unpalatable, the old fighting faith in "the people's" repeated struggle from adversity to triumph melted. There was no longer the impulse to write to each other as comrades in arms. A "cooler" politics made for a chillier connection among Bob and Belle's sons and daughters.

Maybe as letter writing itself in America grew more and more "old-fashioned," so did the La Follettes and their ideas. To explain that would require an excursion into the dense and tangled context of our history since the 1940s.

I offer no such explanation here, nor anything as ambitious as a theory about the rise, fall, and natural history of progressivism as the La Follettes illuminate it. Political science, sociology, and psychology can bring illumination to the story, but first it must simply be told. Here it is, for you the reader.

Acknowledgments

My specific and deep thanks go to the staffs of the Manuscript Division of the Library of Congress and of the State Historical Society of Wisconsin for their indispensable guidance through the family and personal papers of the La Follettes and their circle. The photographs were supplied by the archives of the State Historical Society of Wisconsin.

I also wish to thank those individuals who submitted to interviews, specifically, Bronson C. La Follette, Joan La Follette (Sucher), Mary Sheridan, Gordon Sinykin, and Ralph Gunn Sucher.

Special thanks to Barbara Kraft, who volunteered her formidable research skills on my behalf several times, and John M. Cooper, whose perceptive reading of the manuscript resulted in a number of truly useful suggestions. The book is better for the attention of these two good friends.

I wish also to express my gratitude to Paul Glad for sharing some of his Wisconsin research with me prior to its publication, and to E. David Cronon for efforts to track down a disputed point in the records of the University of Wisconsin.

Thanks are also due to Connie Roosevelt, whose proposal that I should write a family history launched the book; to Barbara Tischler and Byron Hollinshead for manuscript-reading and other forms of encouragement and help; to David Wigdor for arranging that one of the chapters should be presented in preliminary form at a scholarly convention; to Michael Remer for some needed special assistance at a critical point.

Finally, to family and friends for sustenance and comfort that can be neither measured nor forgotten.

The La Follettes of Wisconsin

1

Belle and Bob
(1879–1905)

The celebrating started early. News of the victory reached Madison by wire at 10:30 on the night of May 7, 1879. A waiting crowd of University of Wisconsin students surged from the telegraph office to the campus. There they built a bonfire on the baseball diamond and danced around it until after midnight, their cheers rising with the sparks that died out at treetop height, their exultant faces lit by the flickering flames. Finally the fire died down, the revelers grew tired and drifted away, and only quiet and the eternal noises of nighttime on the shore of Lake Mendota remained.

Saturday afternoon another student throng, with a brass band, was at the depot to meet the winner. Bob La Follette, a member of the senior class, stepped down from the coach into a thrilling wave of adulation. A short, slender man still a few weeks short of his twenty-fourth birthday, he was fully enjoying the role of conquering hero. They put him at the head of a long procession of carriages and pedestrians that wound its noisy way back to the university for an official reception. It was a great day in the history of the thirty-one-year-old state.[1]

The honors that Bob brought back to Wisconsin from Iowa City had been won in an interstate oratorical contest. Not basketball, football, or baseball, but public speaking was the attraction—a competition to see which collegian could present the most eloquent, convincing, and learned talk, prepared in advance, on a chosen subject. Bob had swept away half a dozen other finalists with his presentation of the character of Shakespeare's Iago.

3

He repeated it that night, "by demand of the audience," at a mass meeting held in the state capitol, but not until the president of the board of regents, two professors, and two attorneys had first made speeches in his praise. Only when the popular appetite for declamation was satisfied did the celebration end with an hour of dancing. Then there was quiet again.

That was how some Americans respected and honored the spoken word in 1879. La Follette would become a star of the last generation of American politicians to prosper by the magic of the unamplified human voice trying to move a face-to-face audience.

In the welcoming crowd was his fiancée and classmate, Belle Case. She had been the first to hear the winning speech when he read a draft of it to her as they sat under a tree on the campus one afternoon. She had been through the many repetitions and revisions in which he practiced each gesture and inflection. He consumed hours recklessly in thorough preparation, and in other extracurricular activities as well, so that his overall academic standing was endangered. It did not seem to worry him.

Belle, on the other hand, would have been very upset if it had been her own record in question. She was a model student, gifted in composition, but too shy for public speeches. She hadn't skipped a class in her four years of college. When Bob reached the statewide finals at Beloit, she faced a dilemma. Going to hear him would require leaving a recitation early in order to catch a train, and she was worried about tainting that perfect attendance record. Not to go would be disloyal to her fiancé. In the end love won and she went, but it cost her a soul-struggle that haunted her for years.[2]

Each was disciplined, principled, and dedicated, but their basic characters were refracted through different strong personalities. He was dynamic, extroverted, changeable, engrossed in the moment. She was steady, retiring, consistent, and anxious. Both challenged the world as it was, but he enjoyed the fight whereas she pressed on in the face of fear. Still, their identical ideals, their shared vision of life's purposes, held them together in a love story that only death could end, half a century later. Theirs was the kind of marriage that has become, with each passing year, almost as rare as oratory contests.

His political career was not a conventional story of temporarily triumphant reform. He fitted no particular profile but his own. It showed strong elements of egotism and theatricality, but no one could question his courage, consistency, and the blazing conviction that underlay all his specific proposals. He wanted Americans to make the realization of government by the people the highest priority in their lives, every day of their lives.

4

Belle embraced Bob's causes (plus others of her own), and their children, bred to these high standards, continued the battle to realize a dream of perfect democracy that may have been beyond the nation's readiness and will. At all events, it was a dream that time never brought to full reality.

The fire leaped, and hands applauded, the words rang, and the hope soared. Then the glow faded, the crowd went elsewhere, the night grew dark and cold. Tomorrow came, but in its hard clarity things looked somehow different than expected. Was this what progress meant?

"Greenest of all the 'plebs'"

Bob and Belle were rural Wisconsin children, apple-pie ordinary, with roots at least three generations deep in American soil. His people were Huguenots—French Protestants—by background. They made family togetherness a virtue. Bob's great-grandfather Joseph was one of three brothers (LeFollet was the name in the old country) who arrived sometime before 1750. He served as a wagoner in the Revolution. The brothers and their families settled near each other in Virginia, then moved together to Kentucky. There one of Joseph's sons, Jesse, had a farm adjoining that of Abraham Lincoln's father.

Jesse begat boys prolifically: William, Warren, Elhanan, Robert, Harvey, and Josiah, who was Robert M. La Follette's father. In the 1820s they all moved to Indiana. There, grown to young manhood, Josiah met and fell in love with Mary Ferguson. Her family was Scotch-Irish, drawn from another wave of the great Protestant exodus to the American colonies in the eighteenth century. The courtship was not smooth. She broke their engagement to marry another man in 1840, but soon experienced a loss that was not uncommon on the frontier. The man died young, leaving her pregnant with a daughter. Josiah had taken his broken heart back to Kentucky. But on hearing the news he resumed his pursuit and after five years was accepted.

Josiah and his five brothers moved collectively again around 1850, this time to Dane County in southern Wisconsin. By then his family included Mary plus her daughter by the first marriage (Ellen Buchanan) and a new son, William. In 1853 daughter Josie arrived, and on June 14, 1855, Robert Marion La Follette.

Bob would later describe himself as "one of the greenest of all the 'plebs'—a boy right from the farm."[3] He could also have claimed birth in a log cabin, but both statements leave a mistaken impression of Lincolnesque poverty at birth. Josiah was already a respected citizen of the township of Primrose, chosen as town clerk by unanimous decision of its voters, all thirty-six of them. He was promoted to assessor the following year. By 1856 he owned four hundred acres of land, eight cows and heifers, plus dairying equipment and additional livestock. The two-story, double-log home in which Mary gave birth to Bob had a stove, an oven, a cellar that would be filled with food the following winter, and even a bookcase with books. Two of the volumes were *Lives of the Presidents of the United States* and *A Practical System of Modern Geography . . . Simplified and Adapted to the Capacity of Youth,* both published in 1844.

Josiah had also accumulated the tools and lumber to convert the "double log" into a finished frame house. He was never to do so. Eight months after Bob's birth he died of pneumonia, leaving a yawning hole in the little boy's life.

Thoughts of his lost father haunted the grown man. When Mary Ferguson La Follette died in 1894, Bob had Josiah's bones dug up for reburial next to her. He took the skeleton out of the rotting coffin with his own hands and stood in the open grave amid the smells of corruption, trying to visualize the six-foot-three bearded giant who had sired him. In a private journal kept just after his college graduation Bob had already written in agony: "Oh, my idolized father, lost to me before your image was stamped on my child-mind—nothing left me but your name! What would I not give to have known the sound of your voice, to have received your approval when it was merited."[4]

The idealized father mattered to him from earliest childhood, though he was raised by another man. Even as a very little boy, he would firmly correct anyone who called him by the name of his stepfather, John Saxton. No, he insisted, "My name is La Follette." And it was no wonder, for Saxton was forced on him by the realities of life, especially for women like his mother in the 1850s. Mary La Follette, widowed a second time, could not raise her three youngest children alone, not even with the help of neighboring La Follette brothers-in-law or her son-in-law, Dean Eastman, whom Ellen Buchanan had married in 1856 at age sixteen. Respectability and necessity required a man of Mary's own. When she found him in 1862, he was the wrong one.

Saxton was a somberly clad widower seventy years old, a storekeeper and leading citizen in the nearby town of Argyle, and a Baptist deacon incorrectly reputed to be prosperous. Far from helping Mary with her financial problems, he burrowed into her estate, charging it with all the expenses of his new family down to the last penny's worth of elastic or candy for the children. She was soon forced to go to court to sell a part of her farm, and it would have happened again if a friendly judge had not made it clear to Saxton that he would not tolerate any further depredations, especially while Saxton had a business of his own.

He was a "spare-the-rod-and-spoil-the-child" disciplinarian who clashed frequently with his scrappy seven-year-old stepson. Bob spoke little of him in adult life and never mentioned him in his 1911 *Autobiography.* The silence says more than paragraphs could. His own later behavior testifies to his rage and pain under the yoke of a hard-fisted ancient who turned life and joy into darkness and mourning with mandatory Bible readings, Sundays of drawn shades and stillness, and preachments about the eternal hellfire that must be the lot of those who died unbaptized, as Josiah La Follette had. Justifiably or not, Bob's models of adult manhood were dominated by contrasting double images: on one hand, an idolized dead father rich in virtues to imitate; on the other, a despised enemy somehow married to a beloved mother. "Hyperion to a satyr" runs the phrase from *Hamlet,* in which the prince compares father to stepfather. It was La Follette's favorite play as a man. No wonder that "its language and thought," Belle said, "were a part of his life."[5]

Little Bob could not wait to escape Saxton's clutches, which circumstances fortunately made easy for him. Saxton's business lost money steadily during the 1860s, possibly because he was growing too deaf to understand his customers. After a while he folded it, tried business in another town, and finally washed up in Primrose on what remained of Josiah's old farm. By then he was too old and sick to run it, but Bob's older brother, Will, now about twenty years old and back from brief service in the Civil War, was available. Mary, faithful to her part of the bargain, nursed Saxton as he slipped toward death in 1872, as did their daughter, Josie, who would read to him from the Bible and the *Christian Standard.* For all practical purposes he was now an invalid dependent on the La Follettes of Primrose. That family consisted of Mary, Will, and Josie, but not yet Bob in any full sense.

Bob had dropped out of the family in 1868, at thirteen, choosing and getting permission to stay and continue school in Argyle. He supported himself by cutting hair in the local hotel after he talked the owner into letting him set up an improvised barber chair there. Adolescence was still an undiscovered realm, especially among working Americans. First you were a child, then a responsible man or woman.

Bob was both child and man. At three and a half he was boosted onto the teacher's desk in the newly built Primrose schoolhouse to lisp: "You'd scarce expect one of my age / to speak upon the public stage," a staple recitation for little beginners, guaranteed to bring applause and laughter. From then on he was a confirmed show-off. Public acclaim is a great balm to private hurts. As he grew older he performed, by popular request, patriotic and classical set pieces, comic songs, poems in Scottish, Irish, or Yankee dialect. His mimic's ear helped him to pick up German and the rudiments of Norwegian from immigrant neighbors.

Bob's formal schooling was indifferent. One of his schools had a hundred ungraded students in one room, tutored in all subjects by one teacher. In another the schoolmaster was a thrasher, like Saxton. But the boy picked up things quickly on his own. He played fife in a band, danced and wrestled, and learned hair cutting along with other manual skills. By the time he got to the age of independence he had the makings of a popular small-town sport—bright, well liked, slightly wild, without direction—until a first turning-point experience. One night in Argyle, when he was fifteen, he was drunk, probably not for the first time, and was caught by his teacher, Frank Higgins.

Higgins told him in no uncertain terms that he ought to be at home with his mother. In a repentant frame of mind, and perhaps feeling unthreatened now by Saxton, Bob went. It was a good time for him to return. Brother Will wanted to go west on his own. Bob took over for him and made two crops in two years, showing impressive abilities. He could plow a straight furrow, do a neat job of carpentry, judge cattle and horseflesh, and get a good price for a wagonload of produce driven in to the Madison market twenty-four miles away. Competence and perfectionism flowed unprompted from the same inner fountains. His daughter Fola would later report that he could not so much as watch calmly while someone sharpened a pencil if he thought it was not being done correctly.[6]

In 1873, he was eighteen and the unquestioned head of the household, and ambition was pushing him beyond the farm. After renting it to Dean Eastman, he drove with Mary and Josie to the outskirts of Madison in a wagon piled with their furniture, trailing a tethered cow behind. He rented a house with a barn and pasture and supported them all by scrounging and odd jobs like selling books. Meanwhile he prepared himself to enter the university through courses in private academies and a "sub-freshman" program of the university. No public high schools were available to him to do that job.

Bob's aim in this hard and bold move was not entirely clear. He left evidence with Belle that he was thinking of either a stage career or of becoming a "statesman" through the study of law. In either case he would bring strong assets. A fellow student in one of his precollege courses recalled, "[W]e had no one who could compare with him as a declaimer—he was the feature of every program."⁷

"I don't hate to do anything that needs to be done"

Belle's annals were simpler and less troubled. Her great-grandfather Case had come from Vermont, so her marriage to La Follette merged two classic streams of westward migration, one from the upland South and the other from New England. The dominating family figure of Belle's childhood memory was her grandmother Lucetta Case, who could recall her own parents' yard-by-yard struggle to Ohio through uncleared forests when she was ten years old. Lucetta's mother died not long after arrival, leaving the teen-age girl with the full burden of caring for the household and younger children. "I had no chance for an education," she lamented to Belle.

That meant, of course, no formal education. Grandmother Case "merely" knew the Bible, how to tell time by the stars and name the constellations, how to make vegetable dyes and medicinal herbs, and, of course, how to spin, weave, knit, and sew. She dipped candles, gathered sap and made maple syrup, hived bees and collected the honey, made butter and cheese, and dried fruits. "She always had such good things to eat," Belle wistfully recalled.

Grandma Case was never idle. Once when the two of them were stitching together rags for carpets, Belle innocently asked if Grandma didn't hate to sew short rags that took a long time and made only a small ball. "No, child," was the answer, "I don't hate to do anything that needs to be done."

A photograph of Belle at ten, chubby in a checked woolen dress made by her grandmother, shows her looking gravely into the camera's eye. She very much wanted the schooling that had eluded her grandmother and her mother, Mary Nesbit Case. She got the rudiments at a country school near Anson Case's farm in Baraboo. She walked two miles a day each way, fair weather or foul, never late, never absent, finishing at the head of her class. Fortunately her parents recognized that their bookish daughter deserved to go to college and become something more than another farmwife. They saved for her education, and for that reason if no other she applied herself at college in an almost driven way.

The ancestries and upbringing of Bob and Belle were, according to her, "fundamental to our lives and our understanding of each other."⁸ They culled out from the harshness and materialism (and violence) of pioneer life the positive virtues they respected: hard work and self-sufficiency. They honored these in practice and deliberately tried to pass them on by seeing to it that their own children spent plenty of time on their grandparents' farm and on one that they themselves bought in middle age. But what their son Phil remembered most in his sixties—after surviving the Great Depression—was the security. The warm kitchen stove, the well-stocked woodpile, the thick homemade quilts, the crocks of butter, jars of fruit, and sides of meat in the cellar. "What millions," he asked, "could buy that life today?"[9]

In 1875 Belle was sixteen, Bob twenty. Each was a bundle of as-yet-unjelled talents. Outwardly gregarious, inwardly hungry and self-absorbed, he required a focus that would provide a balance point. She was ready to give herself to some larger purpose, but what would it be?

For the two of them the University of Wisconsin furnished the beginnings of an answer. There they met young friends and competitors like themselves from around the state. There they grew in awareness of the economic, social, and intellectual revolutions that were hammering old certainties into dust. And there they found ideas of public usefulness that provided a mold into which their energies could be poured. That was due in good part to an extraordinary mentor, the president of the University of Wisconsin, John Bascom.

"With the bounding life of an archangel"

Bascom had been appointed by the trustees in 1874, the year before Bob and Belle's class entered. He was forty-seven years old and did not know the meaning of the word rest. He was a minister's son from upstate New York who, like Bob, had lost his father in infancy and, like Belle, was helped through college by the sacrifices of a willing family, primarily an older sister.

After graduation from Williams College, Bascom passed up the law and the ministry as possible careers in favor of becoming an educator. He returned to Williams in 1855 as an instructor in rhetoric and philosophy and began to pour out books. He was the old-fashioned kind of philosopher, prying into every specialty in search of some unifying principle. He wrote confidently and freely about psychology, political economy, esthetics, and mathematics, convinced that philosophy was at "the center of university instruction."

He had a tough-minded respect for reason but it didn't destroy, merely changed, the faith of his New England forebears. Bascom was a Christian evolutionist who married Darwinism (as a shorthand for following the evidence of science wherever it led) and God as the author of instinctive moral principle. He rejected both corrosive skepticism and bigotry. Religion was the meeting ground for philosophy's explorations in heaven and earth. "Man should walk the earth with the bounding life of an archangel," he wrote, leaving room for men and angels both.

This kind of liberalism did not endear him to conservative colleagues at Williams. His social outlook, unfurled in dozens of articles, outraged them even more. To Bascom the world might be big enough for evolution and Christ, but not for selfishness. "Society," he declared, "must be converted, as distinctly and fully converted as the individual; and the conversion of the individual will be very partial till this conversion of the community."

In practice this meant protecting the weak from the exploitive. Liberty, he argued, "stands for the use of powers, not their abuse . . . If we allow the individual to seek what he regards as his own liberty without relation to that of others . . . the commonwealth itself . . . crumbles away." So, in the teeth of a wealth-worshiping age, Bascom supported labor unions and the regulation of business. When he decided to leave for Wisconsin it was with a keen perception that his presence was becoming "less agreeable" to Williams.

Over twelve years Bascom would make it less and less agreeable to the board of regents of Wisconsin, too, but that was partly because of his constant battle to improve the quality of the university, which he judged on arrival to be in an unripe and shameful condition due to the board's neglect.

"A disgrace to the state"

The university was a curious frontierlike mixture of high ideals and pinchpenny crudeness. Founded in 1848 — the year of statehood — it aimed to be the crown of a "well-regulated system of public instruction," but the lawmakers left it to wring support money out of tiny fees, plus the interest from a small share of public land sales, plus annual appropriations usually under ten thousand dollars. New buildings had to be fought for one at a time. By 1864 the commencements were impressive-sounding occasions, commanding the attendance of the governor, the justices of the state supreme court, and other high officials and featuring addresses in Latin and German. But neither of the two dormitories had indoor plumbing, and the total number of alumni was fifty. All were men, and twenty-eight of them either were or had been in the Union Army.

Wisconsin's citizens were not sure what to expect from a university, the very idea of which was changing with the new times. Was its purpose

11

moral and traditional? To train young generations in the way they should go, armed with the wisdom of the past? Or was it to break new ground in learning? The two objectives were not always compatible, and the uncertainty was reflected in the mirrors of curriculum, faculty, and student body.

There was the matter of women, for example. The university began by admitting them only to a "normal department" for the preparation of teachers. They were not admitted to regular programs until 1870, and as late as 1877, when Belle was already a sophomore, the board of regents debated whether to end the "experiment" of coeducation. Besides the conventional doubts about the effects of college on the health and expectations of the "gentler sex," a lingering puritanism dreaded the risk of mingling boys and girls far from home. In 1878 two men and two women were expelled for "repeatedly . . . seeking each other's society." Undergraduate social rules were devised to chill the possibilities of flirtation. The library, as an instance, was open only on separate afternoons to men and women students.

Not that much time was expected to pass in the library. It was closed for three days of the week and numbered only four thousand volumes. An official visitor called it "a disgrace to the state." The impressive-sounding required program rested uneasily on such a foundation, which was hardly adequate to the "classical course" expected of all B.A. candidates until 1873—Latin, Greek, and mathematics with electives in chemistry, mechanics, physics, astronomy, political economy, international law, English literature, rhetoric, and history.

Even if new scholarly writings in these disciplines had been freely available, their use would not have been much encouraged. Classes were conducted by the traditional recitation method, which asked the students simply to repeat back memorized portions of standard texts. That was all right with some of the professors. John Sterling, for example, who taught physics, chemistry, and astronomy, was unperturbed by the absence of laboratory and research facilities. An ex-minister, he held that in scientific matters, "the testimony of the humblest Christian is worth more than the opinion of all the Darwins and Huxleys in the world." Few students would have objected to the narrow scope of instruction, either, being primarily interested in a comfortable ascent toward professional status. Homogeneous and earnest, they were likely to ask few questions and be content with traditional answers. Of the thirty-one men in the Class of 1877 eleven were bound for law, medicine, the pulpit, or business; all were American born; two-thirds were from Wisconsin and Republican; all but one were

12

Protestants. (Only five smoked and six admitted to an occasional drink.)

Bascom aimed to shake the place up, and there were already some promising openings toward making it a university rather than a rural academy. William Allen, professor of Latin and history, had done graduate work in Germany. He gave Belle, she recalled, a "first glimpse of the relation of history to life." (He was also a model scholar-activist, having served during the Civil War in the U.S. Sanitary Commission and the Freedmen's Bureau.) John B. Feuling, who taught modern languages and philology, also held a rare European doctorate. Edward A. Birge, a youthful biology instructor, introduced his students to laboratory work by insisting on minute scrutiny of the specimens he provided. Belle was so impressed that she wrote her prize-winning senior essay on the topic "Learning to See."

Bascom wanted more of this kind of education, and to get it he battled unsparingly with the politically appointed regents, harassing them for appointments and facilities plus a specific, regular share of tax moneys for higher education until they gave in. His persistence did not endear him to his official bosses who, he publicly charged, rarely had "any special knowledge of the methods of education or interest in them." He was also defiantly insensitive to Wisconsin's political niceties. Besides his forthright opposition to the worship of money and success, he was a prohibitionist in a state of beer lovers and powerful brewers and an advocate of women's rights and suffrage in advance of public opinion. "Every human being," he insisted, "has the right to the exercise of all the powers that belong to him . . . in consistency with the well-being of society." The pronoun was gender-specific but the intent was resolutely in favor of equality. He got coeducation firmly established at last. But all of his successful battles spent political capital, and in 1887, as he described it, he quit before his resignation became compulsory. He returned to a professorship at Williams and lived, unsubdued, to be eighty-seven. [10]

Bascom's involvement with Wisconsin campus life was of a direct kind that the intimate setting of a small school allowed. He taught a philosophy class required of all seniors, who also had to attend Sunday evening talks in his home and his annual baccalaureate sermon. His own son and daughter were in Belle and Bob's Class of 1879 (as were Charles Van Hise, a future president of the university, and his future wife, Alice Ring). Though some of the youngsters found him snoopy, the majority appeared to agree that his courses, taught with "healthy enthusiasm," conferred more "real mental strength" than any other part of their academic work.

Of his many convictions, the one Bascom impressed most powerfully on Bob and Belle was that the academic establishment, especially the stu-

13

dents, owed something to the taxpayers. The university, ran one of his declarations, would be "permanently great in the degree in which it understands the conditions of the prosperity and peace of the people and helps to provide them." He was "forever telling us," Bob remembered, "what the state was doing for us and urging our return obligation not to use our education wholly for our own selfish benefit." Belle's memory matched Bob's; her recollection was that "[a]gain and again he would tell us what we owed the State and impress upon us our duty to serve the State in return."[11]

To both of them, Bascom was a torch to kindling—probably *the* father-figure in Bob's life and a preacher of the secular idealism that was Belle's gospel. She was awed by him and had a "vague and general" understanding of his message; to Bob it was "concrete truth . . . whose application was plain as a pikestaff."

"The law for a profession"

The lovers met in freshman German class—he already had a smattering of the language from his friend Robert Siebecker—and what first struck Belle was La Follette's sense of humor, which he later underplayed deliberately as a public man. Whenever she saw some of the male students laughing he, sitting straight-faced in their midst, turned out to be the source of the mischief. Soon he was making her smile, too, and when they began to keep company their conversations were "lighthearted and joyous" and free from sentiment.

But Bob's easygoing facade was a deceptive defense against anxiety and struggle. He could barely afford the university, though its charges were modest enough—no tuition for state residents after 1876, and only three dollars a term for room rent. But firewood and washing and food cost money, and he had to support his mother and sister as well. So he earned his way by the kind of consuming work that became a lifetime habit. He taught in a country school, riding five miles each way every day and squeezing assignments into his sleep-fogged brain at night. His mother and Josie took in boarders and scrimped to the bone, but there was still a struggle for existence. In good Darwinian fashion it produced an evolutionary step for La Follette when it made him a journalist.

The student newspaper, the *University Press,* was then a privately published, for-profit operation. At the end of his freshman year, Bob bought it with four hundred dollars borrowed from a Madison lawyer friend. This act of small-town solidarity led to his discovery of a new aptitude. He loved running a newspaper, particularly the luxury of total control and freedom. He was editor, publisher, and owner all in one. He chose the stories to cover, gathered the information, wrote the copy, supervised layout and production, took ads, and sold subscriptions. Some customers paid in merchandise, which he then had to sell. It was a killing responsibility but at the year's end he had earned seven hundred dollars in gross profit.

In the *Press* he had a platform, a spotlight, and a chance to give discipline and muscle to his writing, which was still trimmed with Victorian nosegays. When he wrote his autobiography in 1911, he said little about his campus days except to honor Bascom and to tell the story of how he had organized an independent slate to beat an all-fraternity ticket for student government offices. That episode, possibly exaggerated, fitted his sense of being a lifelong rebel. But his editorial days may have left a deeper stamp. For years after graduation he itched to get his hands on a paper of his own again and finally did so in 1909 with *La Follette's Weekly Magazine,* even though it was a heavy drain on his time, energy, and money.

The *Press* enhanced Bob's standing on campus, especially among the serious students who followed its pages and shared his own love for telling phrases and cutting ideas. He ran essays by faculty members, exchanges of opinion, and reviews of plays and of the lectures that were both entertainment and education in Madison. And he attentively reported the debates among the campus literary societies.

The societies were more like model assemblies than social and speaking clubs. Athenaean and Hesperian were the two for men (Bob was Athenaean); Laurean (Belle's society) and Castalia were the women's counterparts. They had privately donated libraries better than the university's, where students could consult new books, government publications, periodicals, and documents in preparation for "presentations" at the Friday night meetings. In these, as many as fifteen speakers to a side were given ten minutes each to argue a position on some issue—up to six hours of speech-making by lamplight in crowded, stuffy rooms.

On special holidays the societies gave speaking "exhibitions" in the Assembly chamber of the capitol, and the event of the year was the "Joint Debate" between Athenaean and Hesperian. Only those with good academic records could take part—which eliminated Bob—and those who did worked especially hard to shine, because a noteworthy performance before a blue-ribbon audience could lay a firm foundation for a legal and political career.

Speech was nothing to be taken lightly, and it was not—not even by Bob La Follette the mischief-maker, the entertainer of his friends with dialect poems, the onetime barber boy of Argyle. In John Olin's rhetoric class, which he and Belle both attended, memorized orations were a requirement. On Belle's first try she muffed a word and slunk back to her seat "overwhelmed with a sense of disgrace." During one of Bob's presentations he forgot a line in mid-gesture. The prompter fumbled for seconds to find the place, and La Follette remained on tiptoe, arm raised, body frozen in a stretch, oblivious to the roars of laughter around him.

Everyone with an education respected the moving power of language and the attraction of drama. Celebrated orators like Robert Ingersoll enjoyed prestigious and rewarding careers in politics and at the bar. Famous actors were lionized, and genteel families amused themselves and fortified moral instruction in "playing one's part in life" by amateur theatricals at home. La Follette loved the stage and even at his busiest took time to go to Milwaukee or Chicago to see touring companies with noted stars, a practice he continued throughout his life.

Acting would have been his first choice, but genes betrayed him. He took after his undersized mother, not his tall father, and did not grow to more than five and a half feet. It cut him out of the running for important leads. He consulted John McCullough, a popular Shakespearean star, who gave him disheartening advice. "Suppose we were in *Othello*," he conjectured, "and I, as Othello, tried to throttle you as Iago. The gallery would shout: 'Leave the little fellow alone.'"

In the long run Bob was lucky. He would find in politics a different theater, one in which success also appealed to his moral sense and his practical interest in affecting the world around him. Both were powerful drives. Belle observed that while she had higher marks in some classes, like science, "his understanding . . . was practical; mine was confined to what the book said." He bore down hard on what he needed to know, and in time became exceptional in the detailed mastery of political subjects dear to him, but his effort stopped at the boundary of immediate application. As a result of that, and his outside burdens, his classwork suffered. One classmate recorded that La Follette was "just hanging on by the skin of his teeth."

Yet he kept an outward self-assurance in spite of his hard times with grades, while bookish Belle's shining record did not soothe her inner doubts. Professors Carpenter and Olin both told her she had writing talents. "I did not take these suggestions as seriously then," she mused toward the end of her life, "as I would if I were beginning over again." But she was perseverant enough to win declamation prizes herself. Bob reported one of her talks at a literary society exhibition with a combination of journalistic and lover's verve:

16

The audience were on the *qui vive* as the president announced the next orator's subject—"Children's Playthings"—and Miss Case, of the Laurean Society, took the stage. She fully sustained her reputation as a writer of uncommon merit. Gracefully, and in a clear ringing voice heard easily in every part of the Assembly Chamber, she pronounced an oration that for force and originality of thought and finish of composition was probably not equalled during the evening. She clearly showed how all the best natural impulses are cramped and stifled at the very beginning of life by substituting silly artificial baubles as children's playthings, for real animated living things; . . . that if children had living objects with which to amuse themselves and were not forced to supply with a strained imagination the animation that companionship craves, the mind would grow and develop together into a perfect unit and the other faculties would not be dwarfed by, and subject to, a wild imagination—an imagination that is the source of much injurious reading, that leads to the formation of erroneous, hurtful ideas of the world and results in the whole manhood and womanhood being spent in considering misspent childhood.

Bob's own talk at the same "Ex" was on "The Stage," and he used it to argue that the drama was "an art above painting and sculpture" in power and influence, and a medium of "often arousing people to the appreciation of their political state of affairs." Belle's talk signaled a lifelong interest in education and, despite its utilitarian dismissal of "silly baubles" and "strained imagination," was notable mostly for the earnest horror with which she considered a misspent childhood reading the wrong books.

He was no less a moralist in his fashion. The theme of the following year's prizewinning oration on Iago was that Iago was a case of intellect divorced from conscience, and therefore run wild.

What he lacks in emotion he has gained in intellectual acuteness but the result is deformity . . . His reasoning power is abnormally developed; but he has no feeling, no sympathy, no affection, no fear. His is the cold passion of intellect whose icy touch chills the warm life in all it reaches . . . His contempt for all good is supreme. The emotions are the native soil of moral life. From the feelings are grown great ethical truths one by one, forming at last the grand body of moral law. But Iago is emotionally a cipher, and his poverty of sentiment and wealth of intellect render him doubly dangerous.

"The grand body of moral law" was out there, palpable and needing enactment in human affairs. To be insensitive to it, however brilliant, was to be, like Iago, more devil than human. (La Follette contrasted him with Shakespeare's other great villain, Richard III, who was passionate and violent, stung by conscience at the end of his life, and driven to expiate the moral law by his death on the battlefield.)[12]

Belle and Bob suited each other in the earnestness that they would take together into a world that, by and large, shared their premises. He proposed to her at the end of the junior year. She was at first hesitant, wanting to keep the friendship light and unencumbered, even questioning his seriousness. "How could I be sure he was not joking?" she told their children later. In fact, he overpowered her slightly. He had been the leader and coach, she the acolyte, and she had enough independence left to be afraid of losing it. But, she recorded, "he had his own way as he usually did."

Marriage could not take place right after commencement. It would have to wait until earning power was established. They talked of career alternatives, dismissed the idea of teaching literature that they both loved, and had no problem in deciding realistically that agriculture had its social virtues but was more of a passport to hard work for a meager living than to fulfillment of higher purposes. Law seemed an obvious answer. An ambitious young man with a silver tongue and a good head for detail could make it a stepping-stone to reputation, advancement, and income. Besides, a courtroom was itself a wonderful theater, as any trial buff and generations of lawyers-turned-writers can testify.

So Belle went off to teach school at nearby Spring Green, and Bob began to prepare himself for a career at the bar. The idea of living close to the soil wasn't entirely forgotten. "The most practical and ideal plan," Belle said, "was the law for a profession and at some time a farm for a home." Practical idealists both, they went forth from Bascom's campus to serve together.

Becoming a lawyer was not hard for him. He attended one term at the university's recently established school of law (whose professors were mainly local judges) and got enough additional training in a Madison attorney's office to pass the bar exam at the end of seven months. Only six months after that, in the summer of 1880, he ran for the office of district attorney of Dane County and won. It was a headfirst splash into political waters from which he would never emerge for the rest of his life.

Naturally it would be Republican politics for La Follette. He had been born into a Republican family the year after the party's birth in Ripon, Wisconsin. By 1880, in his own words, "It had fought a desperate war for a great and righteous cause. It had behind it the passionate enthusiasm of a whole generation . . . It was the party of Lincoln and Grant and Sherman." As the party of patriotism, it drew thousands of young strivers automatically into its ranks. "We may never see its like again in this country," was Bob's adult verdict. His lifelong war with conservative Republicanism began, at least, as a lover's quarrel.[13]

In his autobiography he claimed that his motive for running was financial—the job paid eight hundred dollars a year—but that his candidacy furnished an eye-opening initiation into politics. Soon after announcing, he was summoned to see the county's Republican boss, Elisha W. Keyes, who bluntly said, "You are fooling away your time, sir." Keyes, "absolute dictator in his own territory," expected would-be officeholders to clear their plans with him, and he already had another candidate in mind. La Follette thereupon went out on his own, mobilized a network of friends to work for him, and captured both the nomination and the election.

The inspiring story, however, may say more about La Follette's state of mind in 1911, when he wrote the autobiography, than about Dane County in 1880. Keyes was actually on the way out as a party kingmaker. Nor does the evidence show that Bob ran an antimachine campaign. What he promised the voters was to run the office more cheaply than his predecessors, and his one reported campaign speech was apparently an appeal for the national Republican ticket, since it ended with a boilerplate appeal "to old soldiers and young men to reclaim the country from threatened rebel domination, and not to allow the fruits of the war to go unplucked."[14] The trademark he established in his first campaign was not independence so much as hard, grass-roots-level work as he canvassed the countryside tirelessly by horse and buggy, organizing networks of friends to get out the vote for him.

"Face to face with my old enemy"

But Keyes may have served a need for antagonism smoldering within the young lawyer.[15] The evidence is in La Follette's own hand. For a month, beginning in the fall of 1879, he kept a revealing diary that he called "Private Journal and Night Thoughts." Journal-keeping was an enterprise that the culture encouraged for a serious young man, especially a lonesome and lovesick young man.

Belle naturally figured often in those private musings, but so did a haunting dark streak, invisible to those who saw La Follette only in public. One weekend she visited, and they had a quarrel of some kind. There was an exchange of letters, and hers plunged him into gloom. "Oh, how she has misunderstood me and how much pain her words cost me," he wrote. "I know she did not mean to hurt me but it seemed like the black days of the past and it brings me face to face with my old enemy. I had thought him well out of my way but he came, dark counselor that he is, with a power that I had nearly forgotten." That mood did not last long, for the next Friday evening he took the train to Spring Green, groped his way through a fog to her boarding house, and found that "she was 'herself' again and made the old house merry with her laughter." He wanted to con-

19

tinue the discussion, but she insisted on joking, and "so I at last gave it up and had a lovely time." But the dark counselor was back forty-eight hours later, a gloomy November day that reminded him of some unexplained episode a year earlier, "the darkest day I have known." And just three weeks thereafter, when the north wind howled outside the window, Bob was "unconsciously and helplessly given over to thoughts of the past. It is on such nights as this that my thoughts go out over the long dark road—over the high bleak prairies, where the uninterrupted wind flies apace with the messengers of the mind . . . until in imagination I am standing beside my father's grave . . . How altered [would] have been the whole course of my life had it not received this cruel stroke."

But the journal entry did not end on that self-pitying note. Instead, the firm, expressive handwriting went on: "And still there are some things, many things that I would not have altered . . . Out of the responsibilities and cares and privations and struggles of the past I have gathered much good—the very flints I have been dashed against have brought forth living fire from the steel of my nature—have taught me the value of antagonisms!"[16]

What he meant was clear. His depressions were unavoidable, but they drove him to resistance in the form of action and hope. "Out of that day of clouds and fogs and shadow and suspense," he had written of an earlier attack, "out of that day of doubt and despair came my life." Gloom was his inner enemy. But hard knocks, physical illness, and, above all, political opponents were external adversaries. They could be overcome, and to challenge them gave life acceptable meaning.

Attaching modern clinical names like "manic-depressive" or "paranoid" to these traits far outruns the evidence. And reducing the man to labels in the effort to grasp him trivializes both biography and the standards of definition used by serious psychologists—to say nothing of the independent value and historical context of La Follette's ideas. But La Follette's inner storms cannot be overlooked in any story of his life. It was in the glare of their lightnings that he saw the human landscape around him.

As a lawyer he was fearful of slipping into professional admiration of courtroom cleverness on either side of a case. Nor did he adopt the potentially humane relativism of the adversary system at its best, which assumes that exact truth is unreachable and a lawyer's job is therefore to be the client's best possible advocate and hope that some form of justice prevails in the long run. In his first private case he got a tramp exonerated from a charge of shooting a constable by proving, through a doctor's testimony, that the wound was too small to have been made by the defendant's gun. Congratulations on the victory left him suspicious: "I have been many times complimented for getting him acquitted by . . . Col. Keyes and others but I do not like the way they bestow their praise. They seem to consider that I did a smart thing—that I was sharp in the management of the matter . . . but they don't seem to think that I did it all because I thought he was innocent—that I was simply fighting a fight for the truth . . . This must be my rule in all my work and will give the approval of my conscience and my little girl."

In those early youthful days Bob saw Belle as his "little girl" and as an antidote to a professional cynicism that he feared. Lawyers, dealing regularly in the mucky gutters of deceit and greed, are not apt to hold idealistic views of "human nature" for long. La Follette was afraid of his ideals corroding, of perhaps becoming an Iago, brilliant but empty of feeling or principle. In those night thoughts of his twenty-fifth year of life, he thought he saw safety in the vine-covered cottage of marriage as sentimental fiction painted it. In the throes of missing Belle, he wrote:

Oh hasten, time, when I can see her the center of a home into which shall flow plenty from my own hands, over which shall hover happiness wooed thither by the loving content that glorifies the perfect home. Yes, yes, the life, the honest, happy life, revolving within the home . . . When the whole being grows more and more noble and generous and tender and true because all its surroundings invite and nourish just that growth . . . And in this home I may only find a little harbor for a little rest each day. Mine must be a life of warfare—giving and taking blows— to deal in disputes—to sound the hollows of horrible crime, listen to the tale misery tells, and study to know all the ingenious devices which assure man's meanness to man. This is in part the life of the lawyer.

La Follette did not invent these pieties or the idea of home as a place where a "true woman" created a haven for her male and saved him from moral collapse in a brutal and competitive world. The idea was widely cherished in middle-class Victorian America and was so ingrained that leading male citizens of every political shade and attitude were apt to share it. Certainly the one sure way to political ostracism was openly to defy it.

For Bob, however, it became a guiding abstraction rather than a reality as his career carried him into heavy travels, with only intermittent visits home. Belle believed in the ideal, too, but did not fit with total comfort into its presumed role for a wife of someone with no interests beyond kitchen and nursery. Both of them would show signs of the strain created by the discord between ideal and actuality.

Bob's misgivings about the coarsening effects of the law on his sensibilities did not block him from becoming a first-class practitioner. He was relentless in building a solid case, and he could also woo juries with any orator in the state. By the end of 1881 his future looked secure enough for them to marry. The ceremony took place on the last day of the year at Belle's home. A Unitarian minister officiated, but only the immediate families were present and the word "obey" was dropped from the vows.

Fola was born just under nine months later—on September 10, 1882. Whether she was intentionally conceived is slightly unclear, because there would not be another child for thirteen more years and that was definitely by design, at least according to Belle's recall in the 1920s. "I made up my mind," she wrote then (referring to the 1890s), "that we would have more children and raise the family we had always planned." In any case, Fola's birth was a joy to them both and left Belle unwavering in her conviction that "the supreme experience in life is motherhood." But she promptly added: "I am sure there is no inherent conflict in a mother's taking good care of her children, developing her talents, and continuing to work along lines adapted to motherhood and homemaking."[17]

Belle meant it, obviously, because in the fall of 1883 she too enrolled in the university's law school. The first woman graduate, she completed the course in 1885 without fanfare and without hanging out a shingle.[18] Her motives seem to have been mixed. Developing her talents was important to her, but her law degree made her better able to support her husband's work. "Different types of women meet life's obligations according to their different standards," she later wrote to a magazine editor who asked for a piece on career choice. "The woman who is consciously striving to help her husband" but whose contribution consists in planning a dinner or joining a church "really lives outside her husband's life work." Such a woman would "have different experiences from the coeducated woman in perfect sympathy and full understanding, who sees first of all his life work as the big thing, whose first effort is to direct support, not from the outside, but from within." Not for a long time, if ever, did Belle clearly separate her own growth from the job of supporting Bob's career.[19]

Their early married life set lasting patterns. He was still in demand locally as an "elocutionist." He gave speeches at Fourth of July celebrations and readings at church benefits, a small, dapper figure in a Prince Albert and white vest, charming the audiences that he needed as much as he needed resistance and combat. He read poems in comic dialect, like *Darius Green and His Flying Machine,* and thrillers like *Sheridan's Ride* and *Curfew Must Not Ring Tonight.* And he read Shakespeare to small-town men and women who had not yet found out that such "high culture" as *Hamlet, King Lear, Macbeth, The Merchant of Venice,* and *The Taming of the Shrew* was supposed to be beyond them. The readings made him better known and helped him politically and professionally. He was careful not to overemphasize the comic side, and grew sideburns and a temporary moustache to make himself look less boyish.

In their home at night, with Belle's help he sweated over case preparation and scholarly legal volumes that he had missed in his brief training. They furnished their modest home with the books they both loved, Goethe and Schiller in German, and volumes of Cooper, George Eliot, Washington Irving, and Walter Scott. And they passed through the usual adjustment period of newlyweds.

Belle described those days in the biography of Bob that she began in 1925. Her narrative keeps him in the foreground and is almost completely uncritical, but a careful reader catches asides and silences that tell more than she may have intended. She says that they rarely quarreled, but "at times one or the other or both may have been deeply hurt, as happens in making life's adjustments; but we did not nurse the sense of wrong, nor did we discuss it. We treated it as we would physical pain—a cut or burn which it was useless to think much about and would heal in time."

Bob was generally cheerful even in the face of "professional checks." But the "old enemy" of his night thoughts was not vanquished by marriage, as Belle learned. "Only a few times did he ever yield to depression," she recorded. "And those were dark days."[20]

"Like a continuation school for us"

In 1882 Bob was reelected as district attorney. In 1884 an old mentor, Judge George E. Bryant, proposed that his young friend run for the House seat in Wisconsin's Third Congressional District. La Follette secured the nomination and just beat out his Democratic opponent by 495 votes. At twenty-nine he became the youngest member of the Forty-ninth Congress. He would repeat his victory in 1886 and 1888.[21]

Serving in the House meant spending six winters and three springs in Washington. Under the system existing until 1936, in even-numbered years Congress met from the first Monday in December until March 4 of the following year. The alternate-year "long" sessions continued until business was done, usually by June, leaving the lawmakers free to escape Washington's heat and to campaign for the autumn elections.

La Follette's service was not especially noteworthy. His oratorical talents had limited scope, since the 332-member House had been forced (unlike the Senate) to put strict time limits on individual speeches. He voted faithfully for the tariff, which was on the way to becoming Republican

The pre-Progressive La Follette was an eloquent, earnest, and conventional Republican.

holy writ, and for most measures endorsed by the leadership or especially popular in Wisconsin, such as a tax on oleomargarine. He showed some signs of independence when he dug in his heels against a grab of Menominee Indian reservation land by the Chicago, Milwaukee and St. Paul Railroad and against party-endorsed bills for shipping subsidies and a Nicaraguan interoceanic canal. These did not interfere with his general reputation as a "regular" who was rewarded with a promotion in his third term from the Indian Affairs Committee to the more prestigious tax-writing Committee on Ways and Means.[22]

But simply being in the capital was a transforming experience for the two young westerners, for Belle went with him to share boardinghouse life. Neither had ever been east of Chicago before. Washington was just coming into its own as a modern capital, with wealthy senators building and tastefully furnishing permanent homes in town and a population of well-educated civil servants staffing the growing number of bureaus. It was a place to meet aging lions and rising stars like Ohio's Representative William McKinley and the dudish young civil service commissioner from New York, Theodore Roosevelt, whose first meeting with Belle was mortifying. Gesturing broadly at a crowded reception, he knocked a cup of coffee all over her white dress.[23]

Belle was put off at first by the rigid routine of obligatory calls on other official wives in order of seniority, but she "proceeded to do this social 'stunt' religiously" and "[f]ortunately . . . did not take it too seriously," though her soul was offended by a social life "too much influenced by women without any special occupation, whose thoughts were centered on society, dress, cards, and gossip." Bob also hated engagements where a politician could be trapped for an entire evening by rattlebrains.[24]

But at their second session in town—this time accompanied by Fola and Bob's mother—they found a boardinghouse whose woman owner was a suffragist and the organizer of a literary club. On the five thousand dollar annual salary, a very decent sum for the 1880s, they treated themselves to feasts of theater provided by the touring companies that stopped in Washington. They heard comedy and opera by Gilbert and Sullivan, Wagner, and Verdi, and they saw plays starring the likes of Ada Rehan, Helena Modjeska, Sarah Bernhardt, and Edwin Booth. For Booth they had to travel up to Baltimore, because he could not bring himself to perform in Washington after his younger brother's assassination of Lincoln. "Our Washington experience outside Congress was like a continuation school for us," said Belle. Madison, population ten thousand, had been a step up from the unpaved villages of their childhood, and Washington was a gigantic boost in sophistication. In their last year there they lived on the site of one of the present Senate office buildings (at Second and B, N.E.), and Fola's playground was the Capitol park. She rejected kindergarten with five-year-old firmness, and Belle willingly taught her at home instead.

The "continuation school" offered new political lessons, too. Bob had to enlarge his old Dane County support network into a team covering a congressional district that embraced five counties. He got the clerks of those five to send him lists of voters in the preceding election, by townships. These he forwarded to friends in each township who would fill in all they knew— interests, occupations, family and personal history—about at least twenty-five "active Republicans" and fifteen "fair-minded Democrats" considered community leaders. Bob saw to it that these target voters (and others) got copies of speeches on topics of concern to them, public documents, free garden seeds, and anything else dispensed by the federal government.

But these activities ate away at his resources. He began a lifelong pattern of putting personal funds into his campaigns, which led to a debt-burdened existence. The postage for constituent mailings was free, but the reprints from the *Congressional Record* had to be paid for by the congressman ordering them. Bob sent out "hundreds of thousands" of them, and his bills from the Government Printing Office were among the reasons "why I found myself so poor when I left Congress." Poor and tired, too, because the perks of incumbency did not then include offices or staffs, except for committee chairmen. He and Belle spent long evenings up to their knees in sacks of reprints to be addressed by hand, learning how to build a "machine" with their own sweat.[25]

At campaign time back home he went out to the countryside to meet the recipients. Belle went along to jog his memory and to heed Bryant's advice that "the good people of the district like to see a Congressman accompanied by his wife." Their education in practical politics continued on long days of clopping along rural roads behind a horse's rump on the way to speaking engagements or hanging about depots waiting for trains — opportunities for handshaking and making new friends. His own spontaneity and warmth made his constituency intensely personal, and on the stump he had a knack of shifting out of formality at the beginning of a speech and dropping into "a heart-to-heart way of talking." He could go on for hours with the crowd urging him to continue, while Belle, to everyone's amusement, sat behind him shaking her head and tugging at his coat-tails to call it a night.[26]

All of it turned out to be in vain in his fourth campaign of 1890, when he was defeated in a stunning upset. He had won reelection easily in 1886 and again in 1888, when he had lined up with Republican supporters of William D. Hoard, who backed Wisconsin dairy farmers and was subsequently elected governor. It was therefore a confident La Follette who faced the voters in 1890. But the year turned out to be disastrous for the Republicans both in the nation at large, where they lost control of the House of Representatives, and in Wisconsin, where Democrats captured all the state offices, including that of treasurer—which turned out to be pivotal in the La Follette story. But no one could foresee that development on election day, when Bob ate supper at home and then whistled and strummed a guitar before going down to headquarters for the returns. At eleven he came back and shouted up the stairs to Belle, who had gone to bed "Well, Belle, [Allen] Bushnell is elected to Congress from the Third District and I am elected to practice law." He ran seven hundred votes ahead of the ticket but it was not enough. The Democratic flood washed away every Republican seat in the House except that of the La Follettes' good friend Nils P. Haugen.

It was the sixth straight election in which La Follette had run, and the first he had lost. Yet the defeat was the making of him.

"Our life will never be the same"

According to their own testimony, Bob and Belle returned to Madison somewhat deflated but apparently ready to say good-bye to politics. He admitted to "bitter disappointment" at losing his seat and later blamed it on the opposition of the state bosses. The question that lingers is why he did not simply bide his time, cultivate his Republican friends in Wisconsin, and try for Congress again in 1892. He had good friends in high places, including the former Speaker of the House, Thomas B. Reed, and a future president, William McKinley. The answer may well have been financial. He could still inspire lines waiting to get into the courtroom when he took on a case, and with a good set of partners the return to full-time law work offered an attractive prospect of money. Belle, back to earth, decided on enlarging the family and for the first time took note of the shabbiness of their surroundings. They bought furniture, acquired debts, and settled in to await the prosperity and honor that would rightfully accrue to a luminary of the Madison bar.

But only six months after the final gavel of the Fifty-first Congress, Bob was "forced" into the fight for good government when, as he insisted all his life, Philetus Sawyer offered him a bribe.

Sawyer was a seventy-five-year-old self-made lumber millionaire from Oshkosh. He was also a United States senator and one of the three Republican bosses in the state, the other two being John C. Spooner and Henry C. Payne. He was unpolished, undevious, and unapologetic for his success and power—a prototype of the gruff men at the top of the business heap a century ago, before education and professional management and public relations moved in to smooth the edges. He and La Follette had exchanged words in Washington when Bob voted against a ship subsidy bill that Sawyer supported. The old man had come over to the House in a rage and shouted at La Follette, "You are a bolter, sir; you are a bolter." La Follette reminded him that under the rules a senator had no business on the House floor and that he would have the Speaker run him out if he did not leave on his own.

Sawyer did go and, what was more, with surprising graciousness apologized to his exceedingly junior antagonist the next day saying, "You have a perfect right to vote as you please." Even La Follette admitted that Sawyer had a "blunt, frank, simple way" about him and that he merely "regarded Congress as a useful agency for the promotion of business enterprises in which he and his friends were . . . interested."27

But it was another story, according to La Follette, when on September 17, 1891, he met Sawyer in Milwaukee at the old man's request through a note sent a couple of days earlier. In a corner of the second-floor parlor of Plankinton House, Sawyer unburdened his mind. The Democratic sweep of the preceding November was threatening him with personal disaster.

A time-honored graft of the Republican state administrations had been the practice of allowing the state treasurer to deposit public funds in banks of his choosing. The choice always lit on friendly Republican bankers, and in exchange the treasurer kept the interest, using it as a party slush fund. But now the incoming Democratic administration had launched a suit to recover the money against five previous treasurers and also against the rich Republican bondsmen who guaranteed their financial liability. As one of those bondsmen, Sawyer stood to lose as much as $300,000.

One of Sawyer's cases was due to come up in the Circuit Court of Dane County before Judge Robert Siebecker, a friend from Bob's boyhood who had become his law partner and, by marrying Josie La Follette, his brother-in-law.

In La Follette's version of the interview, Sawyer said that the cases were causing him considerable anxiety. "Now I came down here to see you alone," said the old man. "No one knows I am to meet you here. I don't want to hire you as an attorney in the cases, La Follette, and don't want you to go into court. But here is fifty dollars. I will give you five hundred more, or a thousand [or five hundred more *and* a thousand, La Follette could not remember which] when Siebecker decides the cases right."

La Follette sprang to his feet, crying, "Senator Sawyer, you can't know what you are saying to me. If you struck me in the face you could not insult me as you insult me now."

"Wait—hold on!" Sawyer broke in, trying to clarify—or to change, depending on whom one believes—what he had said. He protested that he was just offering La Follette a retainer to take the case. "No," the other insisted, "you don't want to employ me as an attorney. You want to hire me to talk to the Judge about your case off the Bench." The argument continued for a bit, with Sawyer trying to placate the furious attorney, saying, "[P]erhaps I don't understand court rules" and asking if he might at least pay La Follette for the trip from Madison. "Not a dollar, sir," snapped Bob, and flung out through the crowded lobby, pursued part of the way by Sawyer.

When he got home, shaken, he announced to Belle: "Something has happened. Our life will never be the same."[28]

To see the next year through La Follette's eyes is to hold the skeleton key that opens doors to the rest of his life. He believed that he had been placed in an agonizing dilemma. His conscience (and Belle's) demanded that as a member of the bar, if nothing else, he should inform the court that an effort to corrupt it was afoot. But he knew that blowing the whistle on Sawyer would embarrass the Republican party which, despite the recent loss, still was the dominant power in Wisconsin. The scandal could take good men down along with bad ones, and the party would punish La Follette by destroying him professionally. Friends with whom he talked it over urged him to forget principle and keep his mouth shut.

He took the problem to a discreet, older federal judge who said what La Follette wanted to hear. "You must tell Judge Siebecker. You cannot permit him to sit on the case without telling him all about it." Bob did tell him, and Siebecker announced forthwith that he could not adjudicate the case. He gave no reason, but the lawsuits were an ongoing sensational story, and reporters, smelling something suspicious, leaped in and began pumping their sources. Late in October a Chicago paper's headline blazed: BRIBERY THEIR GAME. *Persons Interested in the Wisconsin State Treasury Suits Attempt Desperate Means.*

No names were mentioned but Sawyer, according to Bob, sent an emissary to set up a new meeting between the two. Bob answered that he would never have any communication with Sawyer again as long as he lived. Then Sawyer, in advance of any accusation, went public with a story of injured innocence. He had offered a retainer and been ridiculously misunderstood. He had not even known that La Follette and Siebecker were related. Responding, Bob at last went public with his version, and the damage was done.

Without a fly on the wall to testify there is no way, under strict rules of evidence, to know what was actually said or intended at the Plankinton. But whatever his failings, La Follette was never known to lie whereas Sawyer was a businessman in an age of rough play. The subsequent judgment on the matter of former Speaker of the House Thomas B. Reed — a good Republican but a hard-boiled observer of the human animal — is worth citing: "You never can tell about those old commercial fellows."[29]

Throughout the winter the Republican state press lashed out at La Follette as a liar and a spoiler. "No one can ever know what I suffered," he wrote in 1911 as he summoned up his haunting memories of that bleak season. Acquaintances shunned him. Death threats came in the mail. He kept an imperturbable face in public but depression engulfed him at home. Belle feared that he might not come struggling up from the blackness this time. And then, in the icy solitude, as if to a born-again convert, light came. "I went back over my political experiences. I thought over many things that had occurred during my service in the House. I began to understand their relation. I had seen the evils singly . . . But I had [now] been subjected to a terrible shock that opened my eyes, and I began to see really for the first time."

What Bob saw was a pattern. In the rush to develop state and nation, "corporations and individuals allied with corporations were invited to come in and take what they would" so long as they made factories, railroads, and towns spring out of the emptiness. Inevitably they had taken too much and bought or bludgeoned the political order into consent. "The experiences of my Congressional life now came back to me with new meaning—the Ship Subsidy bill, . . . the Railroad Rate bill, the Sioux Indian land grant and the Menomonie timber steal." A system was at work of which Sawyer was simply the agent. "Against this organized power it had been my misfortune—perhaps my fortune—to be thrown by circumstances."[30]

"*Perhaps my fortune*"? Indeed so. Twelve years earlier, a brooding young lawyer had written that the sufferings of his fatherless boyhood had hardened the steel of his nature and taught him "the value of antagonisms." Now, on the threshold of maturity, he faced an antagonist with the freedom of an entire state at stake on the outcome of the fight.

So out of this awful ordeal came understanding; and out of understanding came resolution. I determined that the power of this corrupt influence, which was undermining and destroying every semblance of representative government in Wisconsin, should be broken.

I felt that I had few friends; I knew I had no money—could command the support of no newspaper. And yet I grew strong in the conviction that in the end Wisconsin would be made free.

. . . I knew that Sawyer and those with him were allied with the railroads, the big business interests, the press, the leading politicians of every community. I knew the struggle would be a long one; that I would have to encounter defeat again and again. But my resolution never faltered.

So the Fighting Bob of legend was born. This was the self-image he cherished and would display to the world, the lone insurgent, grappling with the hosts of unrighteousness on the people's behalf. It is, of course, the view of an actor in the role of a lifetime. Some recent biographers and historians have dismissed it as self-aggrandizing, theatrical, unfair to La Follette's opponents, and untrue to the complexity of the American political system in which he operated, when necessary, as pragmatically as any other player. He has been charged with vanity and ambition, with using or even creating the bribery incident to get himself back into politics and into power. He has even been put on the couch, old Sawyer supposedly becoming the surrogate for the dreaded stepfather, John Saxton, and needing to be symbolically slain for Bob to assume his own manhood.

But those "explanations" say as much about the biographers and their times as they do about their subject. Value-neutral "scholarship" may seriously underestimate the sincerity with which an earlier generation believed in its causes. Spotlighting La Follette's quarrels with his own supporters, or his unacknowledged borrowings of ideas, or his wooing of specific constituencies is legitimate historical work but carried to excess it needlessly diminishes the man and his contemporaries. La Follette was a harsh antagonist himself because democracy for him was a passion, not a slogan. He was a loner because he was completely without fear of falling out of step with the majority when he thought the majority was temporarily wrong. And there really were — and are — corrupt alliances between money and politics, corporate crimes and injustices that only the comfortable can easily ignore. The evidence is in the record. La Follette did not confront imaginary dragons.[31]

Most important of all, however, the post-1891 Robert La Follette needed and drew upon his wife and family as never before. "Mine must be a life of warfare," he had predicted in his 1879 night musings, and so it had become, and home was needed more than ever as a center of peace and a fountain of renewal in a world that resisted truth and crucified prophets.

But nursing, supporting, and emulating a visionary could be a hard burden for loved ones. Scripture does not tell us that the prophets had contented families. What it does say is that they were extremely demanding of their followers.

So was La Follette as he began to throw Wisconsin politics into turmoil. The year 1892 was the turning point of his life, his transformation from an independent-minded but manageable young Republican into the great insurgent. It was a crossroads for the state, too, because the state was ready for the message.

"All great movements . . . are matters of growth"

La Follette never claimed to have invented progressivism. Quite the contrary, he specifically denied it. When he wrote about his irreverent insistence on running for D.A. without consulting county "Boss" Keyes, he said: "I was merely expressing a common and widespread, though largely unconscious, spirit of revolt among the people — a movement of the new generation toward more democracy in human relationships."[32] And he said that in his most public self-portrait, the 1911 autobiography.

Just a year before 1911 when a correspondent had asked him why embattled insurgent congressional Republicans did not bolt and form a new national party, he had been equally unequivocal. "New parties are brought forth from time to time and groups of men have come forward as their heralds and been called to leadership and command. But the leaders did not create the party. It was the ripe issue of events . . . [S]ome will say that the leaders made the party. But all great movements in society and government, the world over, are matters of growth."

He burned no bridges to the national party in 1892, that year of his second "graduation" into the world, twelve years after leaving Bascom's classroom. The next twelve were intensely tangled with Wisconsin politics, whose intricate details need not be mastered to understand La Follette completely, but cannot be ignored because personal, political, and family matters were inseparably welded together in his being. The first fact of political life was that he could not afford the complete loss of a footing in Republicanism. He *might* win control of the party machinery; he could not possibly replace it with something new.

La Follette's popularity as a speaker allowed him to strike a deal with the State Central Committee that summer. If they did not excommunicate him, he would campaign for the G.O.P. presidential candidate, Benjamin Harrison, and ignore all questions about the Sawyer affair. After that he began to point toward a challenge in 1894. He started to draw more heavily on an antimonopoly, anticorporation tradition in Wisconsin politics going back twenty years to the so-called Granger Laws (later struck down by the Wisconsin Supreme Court) to regulate the railroads. The state's chief justice in 1873, Edward G. Ryan, had sounded the theme in a speech to graduating seniors at the university. "There is looming up a new and dark power . . . For the first time really in our politics money is taking the field as an organized power . . . The question will arise . . . 'Which shall rule—wealth or man; which shall lead—money or intellect . . . ?'" Bob loved to quote that, and it struck a resounding note in the 1890s when the Populist party's crusade against the symbolic and actual power of banks, trusts, and "gold" was reaching a crescendo.[33]

Populism did not play well among Wisconsin citizens, but what would be called progressivism did. Changing times made the hour ripe for a change in leadership. Wheat farms, lumber camps, and railroads had been the first props of the state economy, and in the 1880s Wisconsin's two Republican senators were Sawyer, the lumber millionaire, and John C. Spooner, who was what La Follette might have been if La Follette had been a conservative. Twelve years older than Bob, he was also a University of Wisconsin graduate and a gifted lawyer who had become not only the attorney but the chief lobbyist at Madison for three major railroads. The 1890 census, however, confirmed a major shift in agriculture from wheat to dairy farming and the rise of urban industrial centers. Breweries, foundries, machine shops, and packing plants were growing in Racine, Oshkosh, and La Crosse while Milwaukee, the metropolis, had a population of over two hundred thousand. Accordingly, in 1890 the powerful secretary of the Republican state committee was Henry Clay Payne, whose business interests included Milwaukee telephone, street railway, and utilities companies. Payne was also a supporter of oleomargarine manufacturers in their intrastate warfare with the dairy farmers whom La Follette courted.

Both conservatives and reformers wooed a changing, volatile population. A good part of it—about 45 percent—consisted of foreign-born or first-generation German and Scandinavian immigrants. Compared with still-developing Great Plains states to the west, Wisconsinites were better educated, or at least had more high school diplomas and degrees from the university. As cities and factories bloomed on the landscape, there were more socialists and union members, and also more doctors, dentists, lawyers, teachers, ministers, journalists, managers, and engineers ready to lend an ear to fresh ideas.[34]

These were the waters in which La Follette and his supporters fished. It is impossible to overstate how convinced all of them were that the world was moving forward. It suffused everything they thought and did. For them, material and intellectual progress could not be separated or halted in an inexorable march toward greater democracy.

The rest is detail. In 1894 La Follette launched his revolution by getting Nils Haugen, who had a strong base among his fellow Norwegian-Americans, to be the antimachine candidate at the state convention to nominate the next Republican governor. Haugen agreed, and La Follette wrote no fewer than twelve hundred letters to potential supporters, the community leaders whom he had culled and cultivated when he was in Congress. The final organizing meeting took place in La Follette's home, the letters came from his busy desk, and while Haugen was the man on the ballot, La Follette was the focus of controversy. Haugen was beaten out by the conservative William Upham, who went on to win the general election and inaugurate a long period of Republican dominance.

Two years later La Follette was back as a candidate on his own. This time he thought he came to the convention, held in Milwaukee, with enough delegate pledges to have the nomination locked up, but it was not to be. Charles Pfister, a new Republican kingpin and the heir to a leather-tanning fortune, was working against him. According to La Follette, Pfister made a midnight visit to his hotel room just before the balloting started and announced: "La Follette, we've got you skinned. We've got enough of your delegates away from you to defeat you . . . tomorrow. Now, we don't want any trouble . . . We don't want to hurt the party. And if you will behave yourself, we will take care of you when the time comes."

La Follette declined the offer but Pfister's prediction was on the mark. Enough delegates defected to the Pfister-Payne choice, Edward Scofield, to put him over. La Follette was sure they had been bought—some of his loyalists swore to having rejected cash offers for their votes—but he had no proof on others who, he believed, had not refused. He gathered his faithful ones at headquarters afterward for one of those tableaux he loved, unimaginable today, and recited consoling poetry to them.

> Out of the night that covers me
> Black as the pit from pole to pole
> I thank whatever gods there be
> For my unconquerable soul.

Then he went forth, bloody but unbowed, to support the national ticket headed by his Washington friend Major McKinley. After the victory McKinley offered him a Washington job, comptroller of the currency, but by now La Follette was committed to battling it out in Wisconsin.[35]

Until then he had hoped to break the machine through the uphill work of winning delegates at local caucuses. Now he discovered the direct primary as a way of changing rather than capturing the nomination process. It was a perfect issue. He had as yet no economic program other than fair taxation and opposition to a small but visible and irritating corrupt practice—free railroad passes to state judges and legislators. And it would take time to educate both himself and the voters to the nuances of a new kind of economic democracy. But taking the naming of candidates out of the hands of bosses and lobbyists and giving it back to the people was straight-forward and surefire. "Go back to the first principles of democracy," he exhorted in February 1897 in a speech in Chicago called "The Menace of the Political Machine," which he was to repeat hundreds of times. He painted a utopian picture of the results. It hurts to read it ninety-five years later, with the reform accomplished and voter participation steadily shrinking all the same.

[E]very citizen will share equally in the nomination of the candidates of his party and attend primary elections as a privilege as well as a duty. It will no longer be necessary to create an artificial interest in the general election to induce voters to attend. Intelligent, well-considered judgment will be substituted for unthinking enthusiasm, the lamp of reason for the torchlight. The voter will not require to be persuaded that he has an interest in the election. He will know that he has."[36]

The direct primary put solid ground of principle under his feet and was bigger than merely statewide issues. His speech and a model direct-primary bill were widely reprinted and gave him valuable exposure. That fall of 1897 he began his campaign a year in advance, stumping the county fairs that were the high-water marks of the harvest season. Standing on wagon beds amid whickering horses and piles of prizewinning pumpkins, he set rural audiences ablaze. "His words bite like coals of fire," said a reporter. "Disgust, hope, honor, avarice, despair, love, anger, all the passions of man he paints in strong words and stronger gestures . . . He never wearies."[37]

Nevertheless, La Follette lost the nomination again in 1898, while the direct-primary bill, plus other reforms, died in the state legislature. And he did, in fact, weary. He would travel and talk for hours, day after day, toss sleeplessly in strange beds, live on sandwiches and milk wolfed down in stolen minutes once or twice a day.

Such compulsive overwork had its price in breakdowns. In the fall of 1896 he became "seriously ill" and had to take a long, recuperative trip south with his friend and family doctor, Philip Fox. In 1898, after the convention that climaxed the county-fair campaign, he was felled again. Fox again prescribed a warm climate, free of respiratory illnesses. This time Bob went to Southern California, already a health-seeker's Mecca. Without hesitation, Belle left the children with relatives and joined him. They spent several weeks in San Diego, which then had fewer than twenty thousand people, and took beach rambles in the vicinity of lonely La Jolla.

Even after returning, he spent much of the next six months in and out of bed.

Without more specific information on his symptoms it is impossible to submit Bob's medical history to modern doctors for diagnosis. The complaints in his correspondence are usually of chronic inability to sleep and of cramps, nausea, and diarrhea that he generically called "bowel trouble." There isn't any question of their psychological components as reactions to conflict and defeat and the simple, crying need to let down. The sicknesses of 1896 and 1898 had special usefulness. They gave him legitimate reasons not to campaign for the organization candidates who had beaten him. But in June of 1901, when he was already governor and had lost some bruising fights in the state legislature, he collapsed again with weight loss, generalized pain, and, this time, profound and debilitating depression. "I do not remember ever having felt so helpless," said Belle.[38]

In 1900 his hour came round at last. It was not quite the sweet and clean victory that would most have satisfied the pure of heart. Rather, it was the classic pattern of a revolution succeeding when infighting breaks out among members of the establishment. A prosperous lumberman, Isaac Stephenson, was angry at the machine for denying him a Senate nomination in 1899. He joined and bankrolled La Follette, as did a number of Milwaukee businessmen and attorneys disgusted by a bribery scandal. Sawyer was at the point of death; Spooner, Payne, and Pfister were more preoccupied with national ambitions and business problems than with the war on La Follette.

Through intermediaries, conferences were arranged. La Follette assured the conservatives that he stood for fair but not confiscatory taxation of railroads, and of his reasonableness on other matters. In fact, they all misunderstood each other. He thought his enemies had seen the light. They thought they had him tamed. But one way or the other there was a truce, a 1900 convention of sweet harmony, and a Republican nomination for Robert Marion La Follette. He turned his guns on the Democrats, delivering 208 speeches in 61 counties—ten to fifteen speeches a day, six days a week. He won by a hundred thousand votes, just eight years after the galvanizing meeting with Sawyer. It was a generally good year for the Grand Old Party, which won a second term for McKinley largely through support of keeping the island possessions recently won from Spain. (La Follette was in favor of it, too, at the time, though he was later to become a convinced anti-imperialist.) But the moment of triumph in Madison was temporary. Progressivism had not won anything like total victory.[39]

"Simply because the regulation is scientific"

"We are slow to realize," La Follette argued five years after he left the governorship, "that democracy is a life; and involves continual struggle."[40] His own education in the matter came soon enough after his inauguration. Wresting the nomination from party regulars was one thing. Getting a program enacted was another. In the legislative session of 1901 the "stalwarts," as the defenders of the old way called themselves, killed his two key campaign pledges, the direct primary and a bill to tax railroads on the actual value of their property as determined by independent experts rather than their own auditors. He stormed at the stalwarts, accused their lobbyists of buying votes with money, liquor, and "lewd women," and sank into months of sick melancholy. But he bounced back into the fight in 1902. It would take him three terms to win the next round, and in that "continual struggle" he added more polish to his weapons and tactics and began to become a national figure.

A governor battling for his program was a novelty to the Wisconsin legislature, long accustomed to go-along executives. The stalwarts—that is, conservatives—were taken aback. They charged that La Follette was self-righteous, used the club of patronage freely, talked democratically but acted like a dictator, and would not "consult," meaning primarily that they no longer had their accustomed free access to the governor's office.[41]

La Follette's counterattacks were unrelenting. When his direct primary bill was gutted and replaced by a feeble compromise, he vetoed it with a message so vitriolic that it got him censured in the state senate. Told by moderates that politics was, after all, the art of the possible and he should accept the compromise under the old principle of "half a loaf is better than no bread," he answered that "in legislation *no bread* is often better than *half a loaf.* I believe it is usually better to be beaten and come right back at the next session and make a fight for a thoroughgoing law than to have written on the books a weak and indefinite statute." Half a loaf dulled the appetite and clouded the principle that the public was being educated to accept. "I believe in going forward a step at a time, but it must be a *full step.*"[42]

By 1902 the conservatives who had come to terms with him two years earlier were in open opposition again, but this time they were the outsiders and he had no trouble winning renomination and reelection. But the stalwarts still controlled enough seats to fight off another direct-primary bill in 1903, setting up a major test of the issue in 1904.

Orator, insurgent, and husband: Governor Bob.

By that time La Follette's platform had broadened to include one or more permanent commissions to control railroad and telephone rates, and grade crops independently. (Farmers had long complained that companies buying their harvests persistently declared them inferior and paid accordingly.) The logic of reform was pushing him toward the regulatory state.

He had started by simply attacking the domination of the bosses over nominations. Then he had been forced to go after the railroads and corporations who paid off or provided the bosses, and now he had learned that even when the corporations could be beaten at an election their influence lingered on, a permanent force amid the changing waves of popular feeling registered in frequent elections.

A permanent mechanism would therefore have to be devised to make them answerable in season and out. The whole nation was making the same transition from the trust-busting philosophy of the 1880s and 1890s to the new idea of commission control—trying, so to speak, to leash the beast rather than kill it. In time, business itself would warm to the idea of independent regulators imposing safeguards against waste and crookedness, and creating a more predictable economic climate than pure *laissez-faire* allowed.

In time, but not in Wisconsin in 1904. Stalwarts continued to hammer at La Follette as an agitator and a demagogue who was ruining the state economy. And La Follette found, in fighting back, a perfect field for playing knight-errant and dragon-slayer. Taking his case to the people, he tried to nullify the demagogue label by avoiding simple appeals to emotion and dealing instead in hard numbers. Illinois and Iowa already had railroad rate commissions, and on the stump La Follette quoted freely from their rate tables to show Wisconsin shippers that they were disgorging much higher rates to carry the same products the same distances. The figures made dry reading, but he had an extraordinary talent for holding audiences with them. Perhaps it was because he genuinely did trust their intelligence.

In addition to almanacs and commission reports, his road baggage contained legislative journals, and he began a practice that he named "calling the roll." In each district he read off the voting record of its state lawmakers on reform measures and asked listeners to consider whether their representatives had voted for their interests or those of the corporations. It was effective enough, and unusual enough, to raise howls of protest. It seemed like picking on individuals who might have a variety of local or party motives for particular votes, or honest disagreement. As Belle noted, "It was a new thing to judge public men by their votes instead of by their neighborly conduct and good standing in the community." Whether it was in fact a complete novelty is debatable, but it certainly had not been the custom since the passionate days of pre–Civil War abolitionism, and it struck many as especially abrasive. But Bob's rejoinder was that taking responsibility for one's vote was part of the democratic process; otherwise,

Belle as a deceptively proper governor's lady.

why did the national government print the *Congressional Record?* Furthermore, he said, "this is no time for bouquets or soft words; *we* are getting none."[43]

When convention time came in 1904 the stalwarts organized a walkout and nominated their own ticket, which they claimed to be the legitimate

Wisconsin Republican slate. But the courts denied them the Republican line on the ballot and they pulled only a feeble twelve thousand votes in the fall general election. Meanwhile Bob undertook a grueling statewide campaign by auto—a hallmark of being up-to-date—and won his third election by a huge majority. What was more, for the first time, his progressives got majorities in both houses.

Some last-minute publicity was an important break for Bob. In June, Lincoln Steffens had shown up in Madison to interview him for an article. Steffens was then forging a national name as a muckraker. His book *The Shame of the Cities* had been a best seller, and now he was working on a series of exposures of corruption and reform in the states. He was promptly brought home to dinner where he began a lifelong friendship with Belle, Bob, and Fola. A few days earlier, Fola had been graduated Phi Beta Kappa from the university.

Steffens was then thirty-eight years old, a keen and curious figure who was the kind of journalist of ideas rare in America, which tended to produce hard-boiled reporters or book-writing academics. With his hair combed over his forehead, *pince-nez* eyeglasses, and a little goatee, Steffens actually looked professorial. The son of a rich Californian, he had done graduate study in philosophy in Germany and, undecided on his life's work, worked as a police-beat reporter in New York City. Pounding the streets, he became a friend of the young commissioner of police, Theodore Roosevelt. After a while street-life and crime stories bored him. He quit, tried a novel, then joined the staff of a national monthly, *McClure's* magazine. It was a series for *McClure's* that made his name. Assigned to do a piece on machine rule in St. Louis, Steffens found a career and a calling. He was fascinated by the search for behind-the-scenes causes and larger meanings, and though he was an idealist and reformer, he did not fit the do-gooder's mold. He enjoyed the company of some toughly realistic bosses and businessmen who were allied in the drive to get things *done,* even crookedly, and preferred it to that of the righteous. (His political goal came to be to legitimize the boss system's better parts.)

The St. Louis article became the nucleus of his first book, and in 1904 he was carrying his pursuit of the story to the next highest levels of government. In 1904 friends had steered him out to Wisconsin to check on La Follette's war against "the system."

Steffens spent many hours closeted with Bob, and then left to interview a long list of Bob's enemies. Belle said she awaited the article "with anxious heart," but when it appeared it turned out to be an almost complete endorsement and an unrelieved indictment of Sawyer, Payne, Spooner,

Madison's executive mansion, where "Bobbie" and Phil learned politics in knee pants.

Keyes, and the stalwart chieftains. "[T]he fight in Wisconsin," Steffens concluded, "is for self-government, not 'good' government; it is a fight to re-establish a government representative of all the people . . . [N]o matter how men may differ about Governor La Follette otherwise, his long hard fight has developed citizenship in Wisconsin—honest, reasonable, intelligent citizenship."[44]

Coming a few weeks before election day the piece not only helped in the victory, but it turned a benign national light on the forty-nine-year-old governor. His next term was a huge success. He got not only a final version of the primary bill but measures to regulate railroads and telephone and telegraph rates and likewise to strengthen the civil service, force lobbying activity into the open, protect labor rights, safeguard forests, and monitor waterpower franchises and electricity charges. This package, known as "the Wisconsin Idea," made the entire state an "experiment in democracy." La Follette originated neither phrase—each furnished the title of a book about the state's progressive movement—but he was that movement's most visible champion. He denied charges that it was radical and insisted that it merely embodied the enlightened intelligence of the day. In time, he argued, even investors in utilities and railroads found that fair regulation

42

brought them higher returns. Why? "Simply," he answered, "because the regulation is scientific." That was the key to the faith.[45]

L'ENVOI

But these victories came while La Follette was a lame duck governor. In January of 1905 he consented that the legislature elect him to the United States Senate, though he stayed on for a year to complete his work. His motives are still unclear. Some believed that he did it to forestall a destructive, divisive quarrel among several progressives who wanted the seat, in effect, becoming the compromise candidate himself. Others said he was itching for the national stage. He himself explained, not entirely convincingly, that greatness was thrust upon him. He said that "I never went anywhere that leading progressives did not urge me to go to Washington and carry forward the fight on the wider national platform." And, he agreed, "there is no reason now why the movement should not expand until it covers the entire nation."[46]

It was in fact beginning to cover the entire nation, and it was spreading from centers other than Wisconsin. Now he probably believed that his work was done there and it was time to leave for new scenes, new fights, and greater personal opportunities. He was prematurely optimistic. The stalwarts were not done in. They would war with the progressives throughout La Follette's lifetime (and beyond), often winning temporary control of the state. He was never free of the tug of local political battles to preserve and extend his victories, and what is more, his departure left a vacuum in Wisconsin's progressive leadership that was not filled in good measure because he discouraged other aspirants. It is even arguable that he was leaving a job where he had genuine power for one in which he could never be more than marginal.

But that is clear only in hindsight. In 1905 he was ready for a larger stage, where he expected once more to rise to top billing. A new chapter of his life began, and with his entry into the Senate, so did the real family history of the La Follettes.

2

Bob: On the Road
and on the Rise
(1906–1911)

"The dear old rotten Senate"

The Senate of the United States is distinguished as a deliberative body for the surface good manners—most of the time—with which it carries on brutal political battles. Bob La Follette's first day as a senator, January 4, 1906, was a sterling example. Custom calls for a new senator to be presented to the vice president by the senior senator from his state. In Wisconsin's case that would be John C. Spooner who, just a year earlier, had split the state's Republicans rather than accept La Follette's third nomination for governor. After a little brief sparring over who should first approach the other, protocol triumphed. As Bob described it:

Spooner greeted me cordially. I responded likewise . . . The hour of twelve o'clock being at hand, we walked into the Senate chamber together . . . Two vacant seats remained, one near the door and one in the second row from the rear. The senior [senator,] fearful that my occupancy of the front seat would subject me to a draught, suggested that I take the *back one* . . . After the prayer . . . Spooner arose, presented my credentials . . . and requested that the oath be administered. The vice president requested him to present me. He offered me his right wing, I yoked up with him. The murmur of the galleries smote the ear. We passed down the center aisle . . . the oath was then administered . . . an audible sigh swept down from the galleries as the tension relaxed . . . Spooner crooked his arm, we coupled up, filed right . . . went on around the chamber to the vacant seat . . . I extended to him my hand, and thanked him for his courtesy. The thing was done.[1]

44

The note of mockery in Bob's words was for the family's private ear, but there was no secret about the tension that crackled between him and the Senate's Republican leadership, of which Spooner was a key member. The desk assigned to La Follette was on the Democratic side of the chamber, all those on the other being taken. Burying him in a back-row seat with the minority party could be explained as a coincidence and could be carried off with great courtesy. But it also symbolized very well what the "regulars" had in mind for him. "I have been repeatedly warned," he wrote to a friend, "that I have already been disposed of; that the 'hole is prepared' for me and the cover ready."

He, for his own part, had no intention of accepting the yearlong role of modest silence expected of new senators while they learned the ropes and patiently built bridges. Insurgency had defined his life and career, at least since 1891, and he was more than ready to find and grapple with new enemies in Washington. In his autobiography he called himself "alone in the Senate" on his arrival. To him, its time-consuming, clanking machinery of legislative compromise simply helped "the interests" to divert and diffuse waves of reform sentiment until they became impotent trickles. Some colleagues might call it the greatest deliberative body in the world, but his own confidential label, in a letter home, was "the dear old rotten Senate."[2]

Bob did not intend, however, to knock his head against stone walls. He learned and took advantage of whatever procedural rules would help him push bills or amendments he favored. But he rarely compromised to avoid defeat. When beaten, his strategy was to go public with his case and build pressure on the unconverted, widening the chances for victory next time. He would both use and criticize the Senate in the interest of his own national agenda. It was a strategy of patience made possible by his conviction that time was on the side of the reformers, a faith he shared with most of his progressive contemporaries.

In the short run, confidence seemed justified. The mood of the country was for change, as he learned during almost continual travels through it. By the end of his first Senate term in 1911, a political revolution had started that broke a long spell of standpat Republican domination of Congress. In the same year the guns of party rebels were also turned on the White House, where William Howard Taft, the embodiment of judicial caution, had replaced a dynamic, future-oriented Theodore Roosevelt. Almost overnight, La Follette the loner had become La Follette the insurgent chief, even La Follette the presidential possibility for 1912.

But there were personal prices to be paid.

"The peer of any man on the floor"

La Follette made his speaking debut in April, only three months after being sworn in, plunging into debate on a subject to which he brought expertise, passion, and reputation—railroad regulation. The measure on the floor was a bill introduced by Iowa's aging Representative William Hepburn that would let the still-young Interstate Commerce Commission—for which young Representative La Follette had voted in 1887—enforce maximum freight rates and otherwise extend its original powers, weakened by recent Supreme Court decisions. The issue was red-hot both in what it aimed to do and what it implied for the future, and it was kindling fraternal war among Republicans.

La Follette was eager to get into the fight. He had asked for assignment to the powerful Committee on Interstate Commerce, which handled railroad bills, precisely because of the experience he had accumulated in Wisconsin. And precisely because of his reputation as a "radical" on the subject, the conservative leadership of the Senate denied the request and instead assigned him committees more customary for a "beginner." These included Pensions and Claims, Immigration, the Census, and Indian Affairs. He also was made chairman of the Select Committee to Investigate the Potomac Riverfront. No bill had ever been referred to it and its office was in a remote, dimly lit basement corridor of the Capitol. Belle had meanwhile found them a furnished apartment near the zoo, where the occasional roar of a lion or howl of a wolf enhanced their sense that they were not entirely welcome in Washington.[3]

La Follette most probably had Spooner to thank for the attempted entombment, but Spooner was only one member of an inner circle of four powerful Republican senators who had been dominating the Committee on Committees, and the Committee on Rules, through both of which they controlled what legislation reached the floor. Another was white-bearded William B. Allison of Iowa, who had been in the Senate continuously since Reconstruction. A third, Connecticut's equally venerable Orville Platt, had only just died. But the most important member was at the peak of his career. He was Senator Nelson W. Aldrich of Rhode Island, a onetime grocery clerk who had become a millionaire by skillful investments in rubber, sugar, gas, and electric and street railway companies. He had twenty-four years' worth of seniority and was chairman and autocrat of the Finance Committee that handled banking and tariff issues, on which he was a dazzling expert. He also oversaw the distribution of funds for Republican congressional campaigns and was a masterful parliamentarian. These credentials added up to solid clout. Cultivated and white-moustached, Aldrich rarely made speeches, raised his voice, or figured in headlines and news photos. Nevertheless, he was clearly understood to be the boss of the Senate.

He was also the embodiment of conservatism, the mirror opposite of everything that La Follette represented. His opposition to stronger federal control over railroads put him at odds not only with men like La Follette but with moderate Republican colleagues and with President Theodore Roosevelt, who backed the Hepburn bill.

It was a good political choice. Curbing the railroads had strong popular appeal. They were among the most visible signs of the growth and power of organized wealth in the early 1900s. It is hard to realize that today, except when looking at the few remaining big-city rail terminals that resemble Renaissance palaces. Americans loved what speedy steam power on rails did for the economy, but worried about fitting the railroad masters into a democratic mold. Rail corporations owned millions of acres of farm, forest, and mining land. The differing rates they charged made or broke business fortunes in entire towns and regions. Their high-volume discounts to large-scale shippers helped to speed the formation of trusts, and their own ownership was concentrated in very few hands. The country's financial health rose and fell with the changing prices of their stocks and bonds. Their lobbyists and lawyers—the best money could buy—seemed always to be at work in state legislatures, heading off critics and regulators.

Railroad defenders like Aldrich argued that there were prudent business and competitive reasons for existing rates and practices. Federal regulation, they warned soberly, was the thin edge of the wedge and would end in government takeover, although Roosevelt and La Follette, among others, specifically insisted that their support of regulation was to head off outrage that would lead to such a socialistic outcome. And in the spring of 1906 public irritation with the roads was great enough to put Aldrich under heavy reform pressure. He was, therefore, fighting a delaying action at the time La Follette spoke, trying to weaken the legislation by adding amendments calling for tough court review of ICC decisions before they could take effect.

La Follette himself did not like the bill as it stood. But where Aldrich found it too strong, he thought it was weak, and his idea was to put teeth in the ICC's rate-making oversight of the railroads' bookkeeping by empowering the ICC to make a physical valuation of rail properties, rather than accepting the owners' figures on costs and profits. It was something he had succeeded in setting up in Wisconsin. He knew that his proposed amendments to the same effect in the Senate would have no chance of passage, but this first speech was to establish his presence and get his best case before a national jury. In all of his first three sessions of Congress, 1906 through 1908, the principal targets of his speeches and votes would be the roads.

He began on Thursday, April 19, and had not spoken more than a few minutes before opening fire on fellow senators. Many of them were shuffling papers, talking audibly, and heading for the cloakrooms. Even Belle, sitting in supportive pride in the gallery, was not sure "it was *altogether intentional,*" but her husband saw it as a planned walkout—or pretended to. All his life the actor in La Follette tended to rage when cheated of an audience. On the other hand, the actor in him also knew when to strike an effect. In either case he paused, looked squarely at the offenders, and addressed the chair in a voice aimed clearly at stenographers, reporters, and spectators: "I can not be wholly indifferent to the fact that Senators by their absence at this time indicate their want of interest in what I may have to say upon this subject. The public is interested. Unless this important question is rightly settled seats now temporarily vacant may be permanently vacated by those who have the right to occupy them at this time."[4]

It was a plain threat to get the hides of reform's opponents. Belle said her heart stood still, and John Hannan, one of the two secretaries Bob had brought along from Madison, wanted him to strike it out of the version in the *Congressional Record.* But La Follette insisted on keeping it as well as all of the text, a full 148 manuscript pages. He spent three afternoons delivering it, a period that included interruptions and parry-and-thrust with opposition spokesmen. He won all those skirmishes. His desk was lost to sight under teetering piles of documents. He cited ICC reports, newspaper articles, court decisions, official records of foreign governments, almanacs, and directories. He put into the *Record* page after page of evidence on numbers, salaries, and working conditions of employees; comparative rates on carriage of identical products; total traffic volume; capitalization, earnings, and dividends; holdings of securities and interlocking of directorates. "I am inclined to be discursive," he said at one point. "I know that." But people had longer attention spans in 1906. The galleries had been steadily filling as word got around, and the crowds stayed on and now and then burst into applause that was quickly shushed by the presiding officer.[5]

The thorough preparation and mastery of fact refuted the constant charges that he was simply a ranter playing on crowd emotions without knowing the facts. But the emotional tug was there. "The organized wealth of this country is aggressive," he told his listeners. "I believe the existence of government—real representative government—is at stake." He was not an enemy of property rights, but only of evil bargains that choked off real contributions and created unjust, not honest gains for the lines. "The thief can have no vested rights in stolen property," ran his argument. "I resent the assumption that the great wealth of this country is only safe when millionaires are on guard. Property rights are not the special charge of the owners of great fortunes. Even the poor may be relied on to protect property. They have so little—the little they possess is so precious—that they are easily enlisted to defend the rights of property."

Congress had dallied too long over the problem. If public confidence in House and Senate was lacking, the villain was not "jaundiced journalism" but "years of disappointment and defeat." Yet the course could be reversed. "Our duty is plain," he ended. "If a true spirit of independent, patriotic service controls Congress, this bill will be reconstructed on the broad basis of public interest." He sat down to more applause, the most enthusiastic coming from Belle. "Whatever comes," she advised Fola (now twenty-three years old and a touring actress), "he has established himself right in the beginning, as the peer of any man on the floor of the Senate, and a *new kind* of leader."[6]

It was in fact a trial lawyer's great closing argument, but the verdict in the Senate was a split one. After another two months of battle that saw La Follette's amendments fail, Roosevelt accepted that he could not prevail completely over Aldrich. He authorized administration followers to settle for a compromise Hepburn bill that included court review of ICC decisions, though it put the burden of proof of "unfairness" on the railroads.

It also enlarged the ICC's reach in other important ways, and Roosevelt hailed it—and was praised for it then and later—as a victory. In a sense it was, but not in La Follette's eyes. His views on compromise were far from those of the president, as he found out when they tried to work together.

"He will always say a lot of good things"

The two men held one early and prophetic meeting on the Hepburn bill. At the suggestion of Lincoln Steffens, Roosevelt invited La Follette for a Sunday night talk at the White House. La Follette described the tough controls that he thought were needed. "But you can't get any such bill as that through this Congress," the president protested. "I want to get something through." In spite of the demurrer, the mood of both men was cordial.

49

Bob described Roosevelt as "a very good listener" in a letter to Belle. Steffens, who met with TR just after La Follette's departure, called him enthusiastically at 2 A.M. with the news: "I have just left the President and he said you did a bully job."[7]

Then a matter arose that seemed to offer good prospects of collaboration. It combined conservation, a favorite subject of Roosevelt's, with curbing the railroads as La Follette wished. In the Indian Affairs Committee the senator was asked to vote on a measure for the outright sale of some thousands of acres of coal-bearing lands on Choctaw and Chickasaw reservations, which were currently under lease to private holders. Characteristically plunging into research, he found that a number of mining companies working the lands were in fact railroad owned or controlled, a situation that allowed the roads to set noncompetitive prices in buying, selling, and hauling the coal. As La Follette saw it, they were, as usual, milking the public domain.

The government's leases did provide a few restraints. These would disappear if the lands were sold, so La Follette voted against the idea in committee and was promptly and foreseeably defeated. When the bill came to the floor he tried to amend it by barring railroad lines as purchasers and limiting the size of holdings. The amendments lost, but after a two-day debate drew public attention to the matter the plan to sell the lands was dropped.

Roosevelt was pleased. "By Jove!" he told La Follette at a routine encounter later. "You struck a mighty good lead on that coal matter in Indian Territory." La Follette tried to push the door open a little wider and got a meeting at which he asked the president to bar all sales of coal land in the enormous tracts still under federal jurisdiction. Roosevelt wanted congressional backing for so sweeping a step and asked La Follette to prepare a comprehensive coal conservation bill for the next session. During the summer of 1906 he withdrew millions of acres from sale on his own. The next January he looked over the measure that La Follette had prepared with help from the attorney general and after study of comparable laws abroad. He called it "admirable" and sent La Follette back to the Senate with permission to say that the administration was behind him.[8]

Then he took back his blessing.

After conferring with the Republican leadership Roosevelt became convinced that La Follette's bill could not make it through. He sent him a note to that effect, asking that La Follette get on board instead behind a weaker administration-drafted bill or one introduced by Minnesota's Senator Knute Nelson. La Follette refused, believing the Nelson bill to be a "weak, sloppy thing"[9] and the other not much better. Roosevelt's response was that if conservationists could not unite behind "'something which could be passed'" he would wash his hands of the matter, which in effect he did. La Follette's bill died in committee.

Nothing could highlight basic differences between the two progressives better than the correspondence they exchanged on the subject. Roosevelt argued that "to struggle for one particular bill as against all other bills is to play into the hands of the men who wish to do nothing." La Follette's response was: "The interests of the public will be better served by temporary defeat of an effective measure . . . than by compromising on a bill which . . . is weak or silent on vital points."[10]

It was the half-loaf argument that he had used in Wisconsin when he threw a compromise direct-primary bill back to the legislature with a veto message. He restated it in his *Autobiography* a few years later in describing the run-in with Roosevelt. "Half a loaf, as a rule, dulls the appetite and destroys the keenness of interest in attaining the full loaf . . . It is certain to weaken, disappoint, and dissipate public interest. Concession and compromise are almost always necessary in legislation, but they call for the most thorough and complete mastery of the principles involved, in order to fix the limit beyond which not one hair's breadth can be yielded."[11]

The principle in the coal-land dispute was not conservation, in La Follette's mind, but curbing the railroad barons. He thought that twenty years of agitation had readied public opinion for a major breakthrough toward real control. Concessions in 1907 would freeze further progress by giving an illusion that the problem was solved, and allowing popular attention to be diverted elsewhere. But Roosevelt's view as expressed at the time to his friend William Allen White was that La Follette "throws away the possible by demanding the impossible."[12]

American political life is so organized that reform has almost always moved at Roosevelt's piecemeal pace rather than in cleansing tidal waves. And historians in general endorse pragmatic compromise as the only realistic avenue to change in this diverse republic of many interests. There is no way of telling, however, where roads untaken—like La Follette's unswerving insistence on principle—would have led us as a people by now, and with what costs and setbacks.

Not that Theodore Roosevelt is to be confused with a moral relativist or what would today be called a "hard-nosed" deal maker. No one exceeded him at denunciation of opponents as "noxious demagogues" or workers of "iniquity" or practitioners of "greedy lawlessness"—not even La Follette, who was, and still is, accused by critics of chronic ungener-

51

osity and suspicion of the motives of those who disagreed with him. But TR would accept the half loaf. And, with equal self-righteousness, he would attack fellow progressives as well as conservatives when it suited him, leaving around his record a cloud of contradictory impressions as to how much of his reform talk was in the grain and how much was mere veneer.

There wasn't much doubt for La Follette, whose private opinions became increasingly critical after the cordiality of their early meetings. "He was very effusive again in his greeting," he reported to Belle at the opening of the 1906–1907 session, "but I never know how much he is really *dee-*lighted." He asked her opinion of the annual presidential message to Congress, but was unconvinced by her temperate, condescending response, which was: "In spite of his failings I can not but feel that he belongs *more* to *us* than to *them*."[13]

Roosevelt's "kerflop," as Bob called it, on the coal lands issue pushed him in the direction of bitterness. "You know, Bev," he confided to Indiana's Senator Albert Beveridge, "I shall always remember how the Pres. threw me down and govern myself accordingly." When TR also appeared to waffle on a promise to recommend physical valuation of railroad properties to Congress, La Follette gave up the idea of collaboration. He repeated his intention of denying support to compromises favored by the White House. "This I suppose will make the Pres. mad . . . but he'll get over it or if he don't it won't matter . . . [H]e is such a mixture . . . He will always say a lot of good things and half do a good many things. But it all ends rather disappointingly . . . I don't propose to go and jump in the Potomac because he throws me down every day or so — although it is somewhat depressing."[14]

La Follette disdained what he saw as Roosevelt's almost boyish superficiality. "If he gets *a* bill it fills him with glee,"[15] he complained. His growing contempt was matched by the president's own anger. He was especially furious at La Follette for voting against the compromise version of the Hepburn measure "on the idiotic ground," as he put it to White, "that no matter how proper an amendment was, if Aldrich supported it nobody else could afford to do so. La Follette impressed me as a shifty self-seeker. He is in favor of some excellent things, but his usefulness last winter was very much limited because his real motives seemed to be not to get something good and efficient done, but to make a personal reputation for himself by screaming for something he knew perfectly well could not be had." Two years later he described La Follette to his son Kermit as "an entirely worthless Senator."[16]

White, the small-town Kansas editor whose battles in the front line of progressive journalism rarely reduced the undammed exuberance of his letters, editorials, essays, and novels, understood why the two men disliked each other. They were too much alike. Each was dedicated, idealistic after his own fashion, literate, and energetic. And each was opinionated and theatrical, craved center stage, and was devoted to a conventional family whose return worship they took for granted. White's analysis was that "La Follette was a 'lean and hungry' Cassius to Theodore Roosevelt's Caesar. It was inevitable that they should clash; and, clashing, it was written in the stars that they should never respect one another. And I think, as a friend of both, I am fairly safe and charitable in saying that they were jealous of one another, constitutionally, temperamentally, inevitably."[17]

Roosevelt in the role of Caesar was not without accomplishments. His first term saw the passage of the Elkins Act (forbidding railroad rebates) and the Newlands Act (a conservation measure) and the launching of a major antitrust case against the Northern Securities Company, which controlled several major rail lines. In his second term, Congress passed the Pure Food and Drug Act and the Hepburn bill itself (though in a form thought too weak by La Follette) and initiated further regulatory steps and began at least to consider currency and banking reform. The public mood, energized by TRs popularity, sustained these changes, and La Follette profited by the momentum in the promotion of his own agenda. Roosevelt, in turn, got a political boost through being able to present himself as the reasonable alternative to "radicals" like La Follette, who would take over if conservatives did not adopt Rooseveltian moderate reforms. Both men used each other, in a sense, in the ongoing dialogue of reform from 1900 to 1912, but neither would have willingly acknowledged it.

"The dreary grind of makeshift and sham"

Having the president as an enemy rather than an ally simply confirmed La Follette's commitment to the role of Washington outsider. He did not altogether spurn the possibility of getting his name on constructive legislation. In the spring of 1906 he introduced a bill to limit the hours of consecutive service that could be demanded of railroad employees to sixteen. (Unbelievably, they sometimes worked thirty-six straight hours and were terrifyingly accident-prone.) It was during the honeymoon period with Roosevelt, and La Follette had White House backing as well as strong support from the rail unions. What he had to do—besides providing chilling statistical arguments on deaths and injuries—was to make sure that it was not pushed off the calendar by the leadership. He explained it to seven-year-old Mary in an irreverent note: "I have got one bill that I just have to watch so I won't lose my place. Did you ever play pussy wants a corner? You know if you have a corner & get away from it some one (who is playing pussy) dives in? . . . If I get away from my corner some one else will slip in and get the good corner for his bill. So I just have to keep right in my corner every day and watch."[18]

His vigilance paid off; he got the bill to the floor on January 10, 1907, and it passed on a roll-call vote of 70 to 1.[19] He had been obliged to accept amendments, like any other floor manager of a piece of legislation, and in this case they left his conscience untroubled. But a long, slow succession of such victories, the reward of the born legislator, arranger, and "inside" dealmaker—a Nelson Aldrich or a Lyndon Johnson—was not what appealed to him. He had tasted executive power and leadership and he missed it. Even more, the Senate floor was not the theater of his greatest strength, crowd-pleasing. His life was cramped by walls. He had found fulfillment as the open-air evangelist of democracy—like William Jennings Bryan but without Bryan's scriptural portfolio—in those dusty Wisconsin campaigns when, day after day, he denounced the "interests" and those who served them to cheering crowds. Both men were creations of the moment in the 1890s when political oratory and improved transportation met and fertilized each other and created the golden age of the speaking campaign.

So instead of outmaneuvering his Senate adversaries, La Follette took to the campaign trail to bait them. In the congressional campaigns of fall 1906 he revived his Wisconsin practice of "reading the roll call." He went into states where conservatives were up for reelection and laid out the records of their votes against the public interest, forcing them onto the defensive. "The 'Roll Call' *is going to go down in history,*" Bob enthused in a letter home. "It *goes* and some Senators will find a back fire to look after."[20] He boasted of the success of these efforts in gradually retiring standpat senators—twenty-four up to 1912 was his claim.[21] It was actually impossible to know what part the roll call played in the rising progressive tide, but nothing shook his conviction (shared by the muckraking journalists who were flourishing just then) that people cared about their senators' votes and would, given the "facts," throw out those who "betrayed" their trust.

The roll call multiplied the number of his necessary enemies—Roosevelt, Aldrich, and an indeterminate number of senators. According to one Washington correspondent, after surviving freshman hazing La Follette was "spreading havoc and destruction in the ranks of the hazers and giving several of them the job of their lives to get re-elected . . . The Senators still snub him in the cloakrooms, but not on the floor. He is bitterly hated, but also feared."[22]

There was some exaggeration there; he could not function in complete isolation. But he did deliberately force yea and nay votes on doomed, symbolic amendments with the clear purpose of getting ammunition for the next season's roll call. In 1906 he got a record vote on an amendment to the Hepburn bill providing that no federal judge should sit on a case involving the rates charged by a railroad whose stock or bonds he held. It went down 40-27, with only three Republicans joining him in the affirmative. Three years later he tackled one of the most sacred of cows with a futile proposal that members of the Committee on Naval Affairs should not come from states where naval appropriations would be spent, so that they would award contracts to the cheapest facilities instead of favoring their own states and districts. To a pragmatist, such windmill-tilting simply threw away opportunities for constructive battles, in favor of poses. But La Follette believed that no fight was lost if it educated voters in how their government really worked.[23]

The most dramatic moment of his first term was another milestone speech. This one was an all-night filibuster that pitted him directly against Aldrich and almost the whole Senate on May 29 and 30, 1908. The ostensible subject was money, but the target was once more the power of railroads and banking syndicates over Congress. At stake was a bill that would allow banks, in times of a credit crunch like the financial panic of 1907, to issue "emergency currency" on the basis of securities that they held. It had already passed both houses in differing forms that were reconciled in conference, and the conference committee's final version, in a form that did not permit amendments, was supposed to be gaveled through before the slated adjournment of Congress for the summer and fall.

La Follette had already denounced the bill on its first passage through the Senate as a scheme to inflate the speculative value of the stocks and bonds of firms held or controlled by Wall Street banks through interlocking directorates and dummy corporations. He wanted instead a more decentralized system, friendlier to smaller bankers. "I do not direct my attack against a Rockefeller, a Morgan, a Harriman," he claimed. "They are but types . . . Men are as nothing; the System which we have built up by privileges, which we have allowed to take possession of Government and control legislation, is the real object of my unceasing warfare."[24]

Now he made a last stand, particularly questioning Aldrich about a provision to include railroad paper in the currency base. Dropped from the original bill, it had mysteriously reappeared, in ambiguous form, in the conference version. Again and again La Follette tried to pin the imperturbable boss to a specific yes or no on whether rail securities—widely thought to be overvalued and unstable—could be included by banks as backing for notes they would issue. When Aldrich ignored him, La Follette would genially insist that the senator from Rhode Island pay attention, or come closer so that La Follette's voice, weakened by a recent bout of influenza, should be audible. When Aldrich replied at all it was to insist that the time for discussion was past and the only business pending before the chamber was an up-or-down vote on the conference report. That would, he said with a rare suggestion of irritation, remain the business of the Senate until March 4, 1909, if necessary. With heavy courtesy La Follette replied that his voice would hold out that long.

La Follette began at some time after noon on a Friday and continued hour after hour, his short, determined figure leaning now and then against a corner of his desk piled with papers, a glass of eggnog, and a turkey sandwich. He managed to wolf down several of each during the roll calls that he repeatedly demanded to establish the presence of a quorum. Though he had some allies on the Democratic side, it was essentially a one-man show, and it was becoming vexatious to other senators who had already made reservations to leave Washington on evening trains. "As the afternoon wore on," a congressional correspondent told his readers, "the spectacle was presented of Senator La Follette standing alone like Ajax defying the lightning, the lightning in this case being the withering glances of reprobation cast on him by colleagues from both sides of the chamber. At last accounts Senator La Follette was still refusing to be withered."

So he was. When other senators pointedly left the chamber or wandered around the floor carrying on loud conversations, La Follette would stop, remind the presiding officer that he was entitled to a quorum and to order, and straight-facedly wait until both were reestablished. At one point in the small hours of Saturday, that meant routing sleepy senators out of the cloakrooms where they were napping or having the sergeant-at-arms track them down at home and bring them, half-dressed and unshaven, to the floor.

On Friday night a large crowd, alerted by the late afternoon editions, crammed the galleries to watch the fine theater of parliamentary parry-and-thrust. Points of order, rulings, appeals, and votes on appeals went on amid the swaying of palm leaf fans in a chamber suffocating under Washington's ninety-degree heat. At one point La Follette swigged part of an eggnog, made a face, and handed it to a clerk, shouting, "Take it away! It's drugged." Soon after, he was wracked by spasms of diarrhea, which he managed to relieve during more roll calls. He never seems to have relinquished the idea that someone tried to poison him, though a reasonable explanation is that the combination of raw eggs and milk spoiled quickly in that steambath while waiting to be drunk. His obvious pain, perspiration, and fatigue only enhanced the spectators' impression that the pompadoured little senator was as gritty as they came.[25]

It was a fine ending, from his point of view, for a third spring in the Senate: the perfect enactment of the man against the institution. Of course, the institution won. Aldrich finally managed to get rulings that cut off the frequent quorum calls, and at 7 A.M. Saturday Bob finally yielded the floor to one of two Democratic allies who were supposed to hold it until he returned from a rest at home at 4:30 P.M. But through a misunderstanding one of them, Oklahoma's blind Senator Thomas P. Gore, sat down moments too soon. Aldrich leaped to call the question and La Follette rushed in too late to head off the vote that put over the Aldrich-Vreeland bill at last.

Its passage was not as profoundly dismaying as La Follette believed. It was a first step in the march toward government intervention to provide a flexible currency that would end in the creation of the Federal Reserve system five years later. Moreover, it turned out to be almost a last stand for Aldrich, who would leave the Senate in 1911. For La Follette, however, as he packed his bags for a lecture tour, the episode was further confirmation of his generally distrustful view of how what has been called the greatest deliberative body in the world really operated. There is nice irony in the fact that since 1959 his portrait has hung in the Senate reception room as one of the five great senators of all time. The committee that conferred the honor, long after he was safely dead, either was unaware of or overlooked his comment to Belle on Senate life: "It is sometimes very depressing here . . . I can see how the dreary grind of makeshift and sham would in time sear over and harden the average conscience . . . One has to struggle *so much* of the time here against the feeling that the thing which is uppermost and controlling is to *keep up the performance* — not to do some *real thing* . . . [I]t certainly teaches the virtue of patience, but is deadening at the same time."[26]

Out on the stump, however, he could forget worries about calluses on his conscience and throw patience to the winds. There he was not deadened, but at his most alive.

"Had triumph here and did something for the cause"

The itinerant's platform, especially in the West, was his element, the sea he swam in. It gave him exposure, income, broad contacts, the thrill of crusading, a taste of America awakening to regeneration. He was out in

Bob in full throat on the West Coast, 1907.

Colorado and the Dakotas in 1903. Between June and October of 1905 he swung through Illinois, Indiana, Iowa, Missouri, Kansas, Nebraska, and Minnesota. In 1906 he was on an extended speaking tour of the West Coast. Following the adjournment of Congress in March of 1907 he rushed westward without pausing to visit Madison and lifted his voice in a dozen states of the Pacific Coast, the Great Plains, and the Rockies. In 1908 he stayed close to Wisconsin, campaigning for the state and national tickets, but in 1909 he embarked on another long tour full of day-after-day engagements in Missouri, Montana, Wyoming, and California.

Not all his speaking dates were strictly political. Some, if not most, were part of the "Chautauqua circuit" that covered rural America with speakers and performers who offered a particularly American combination of adult education and entertainment. Doomed eventually by the automobile, radio, movies, and finally television, the lecture trail was a key part of progressive culture, too easily forgotten. Bob was booked for frequent repeitions of such canned orations as his own "Hamlet," or "The Menace of the Machine" (just as Bryan reiterated the "Cross of Gold" speech hundreds of times after its initial delivery in 1896). The announced topic did not prevent him from ad libbing afterward about politics. Often lingering to absorb the applause with utter disregard of clocks and timetables, he wrote home, in mock despair, "It took me half or three quarters of an hour to get away from them," yet his real exultation was palpable. He was taking soundings into the depths of popular democracy. "Had triumph here and did something for the cause," he wired one summery day from Red Oak, Iowa. Two days later he wrote from Elkader that it was "a fine, progressive little city with a good up-to-date lot of people." Onward to Waterloo, which had recently played host to Bryan, Missouri's progressive governor Levi Folk, and evangelist Sam Jones — and there he glowed when a listener to his two-hour speech told him "he must not go *near* the U.S. Senate . . . but spend every day on the platform where the people of the country could be reached and . . . *they* would then take care of the Senate."[27]

Bob and his audiences shared a faith in old personal values and an enthusiastic respect for the material wonders of modern life. The trick was to have both if possible, but La Follette saw the pitfalls. Local loyalty could become boosterism, or self-rule could take a back seat to self-enrichment. Of the people in the Far West he said:

I like them very much and the country and people are full of great promise. They are too eager for wealth and rate it too high. They want justice, not from *patriotic* motives yet — but to help the town and *boom* the country. They insist on taking you out in autos and carriages to show you the holes in the ground where they have taken out so many million and are sure to get so many more. They say little about their schools which are good, except to tell you what it cost to put up the buildings. Their money standards are high but they have only just begun to think of graft as a thing to be stamped out rather than openly accepted and practiced. But they are awakening . . . I told them they had interested and amazed me with their marvellous production of copper but I'd like to know what kind of men they were producing — what kind of citizenship they were building into their new commonwealth.[28]

Progress in citizenship wasn't automatic. In Wisconsin in 1906, in the first trial of La Follette's open primary law, his own choice for the next governor, Irvine Lenroot, was beaten in the Republican primary. The problem was one of those fractures in the state progressive coalition that were to dog La Follette throughout his life. Lenroot was opposed by James Davidson, who had been lieutenant governor under La Follette and succeeded him, and while Lenroot's credentials as onetime speaker of the state assembly and manager of the 1904 state Republican convention were impressive, Davidson drew enough support—aided by incumbency—to win.

Lincoln Steffens consoled him by mail. La Follette's man had lost, but after all, his principles had won. Bob himself was not crushed because "the people" voted the wrong way. "They may be misled," he reasoned. "They may seem to forget or even be ungrateful—but if we get at the psychology of it we will not so much blame them as the conditions, the environment." Short-term reversals hurt only for a while. He looked into the faces of his audiences and concluded: "They are helpful. They inspire me and renew my faith and restore my courage." He needed them, and he was convinced they needed him. "My work is counting for the country," he told Belle. "I know I can not be mistaken about that, and that covers everything— that is the lasting thing—the all-needful thing."[29]

He needed them in more than the mere psychological sense, too. The lectures were paid performances that made it possible for him to live the middle-class life that reformers and reactionaries alike would not separate from respectability. He was not greedy, but he enjoyed a pleasant home, good books, and "proper" clothes for himself and his family. These were part of the American way, and so was going into debt to have them. In the autumn of 1905 he and Belle finally bought the "farm" they had talked about at graduation. It was called Maple Bluff and was hardly a rural retreat. Its sixty acres had a quarter-mile frontage on Lake Mendota from which Madison, only about four miles away, could be clearly seen. It already adjoined a golf links and belonged to a banker's son and gentleman farmer who sold it to the La Follettes for a stiff five hundred dollars an acre. They never regretted it. The solid brick farmhouse with its vine-shaded porch and the sheltering orchards became, as expected, an anchor of family solidarity as it slowly filled with books and papers and furniture and memories (for the children especially) of fragrant summers, warm winter kitchens, parties and chores, holiday reunions, crises, conferences, buzzing life.[30]

But it was grossly expensive, as any amateur "farmer" knows. The La Follettes—absentee owners much of the time—tried to raise ponies, establish a dairy herd, and market fruit and eggs and vegetables. The efforts provided wholesome chores for Bobbie, Phil, and Mary, but only

The Maple Bluff home. Solid comfort was not inconsistent with political insurgency.

added to the constant stream of bills for equipment, repairs, and hired help.

Meanwhile there was the Washington home that they rented and furnished from 1909 through 1913 after a couple of nomadic winters. "Belle," said Bob, "I want you to furnish this house completely and comfortably and in good taste. You don't need to skimp and economize." Belle did faithfully as bidden, conscientiously haunting antique shops and auction sales to fill the four-story building at 1864 Wyoming Avenue.[31]

And as if the home and farm bills were not enough of a drain on the $7500-a-year salary of a senator (raised to that level in 1907), Bob also gave freely to his favored political causes. In 1909, in a decision that had a major impact on the whole family's life story, he founded *La Follette's Weekly Magazine* as his house organ. It was soon eating up as much as $15,000 a year. "I have *not one dollar* to begin a campaign," La Follette told his friend and former law partner Gilbert Roe (who had moved to New York City) in the senatorial reelection year of 1910. "The farm is mortgaged for $12,500. I have had to borrow $2,000 at the Cap C. bank to meet expenses *here*."[32]

Lecture money, therefore, was indispensable. At one or two hundred dollars a night it added up, over a tour of several months, to as much as an additional salary and a half. His correspondence with Belle contained intermittent streams of reassurance that he would literally talk their way out of debt. She, who handled the finances, once sent him a doleful list of bills due. No matter, was the response. "I will hit the high places a clip here and there as fast as I can and string them along till my work starts in regularly, then I will clean them all up hand over fist." Only a little while later he was buoyed by assurances from a booker that a good lecture season was in prospect. "I will clean up every debt," he crowed, "and you will be *free, free* . . . I shall feel a great load off for the first time in forty years."[33]

They never did achieve that total freedom and were often driven to curious makeshifts—like Belle's bringing along two local farm girls to Washington as household help in December of 1907, plus a retired teacher as a "nanny"—and brown-bagging meals on the train to save dining car costs. Yet nowhere in the letters did either of them whine, nor is there evidence that La Follette ever accepted a questionable dollar. In fact, he voted against the salary raise of 1907, explaining to Belle: "I cannot make it seem right for a member to vote to increase his own salary during the term for which he was elected." She did not approve of his decision. It was one of the few times they disagreed on a matter of principle.[34]

"Bowel trouble again"

Bob's travels might be vital to him, but their physical cost was appalling. Lecture managers arranged overnight "jumps" with minimal attention to actual railroad schedules. One example is indicative. At 1:30 A.M. on a July morning he scrawled a note to "My Dear Ones All" on his lap as he sat in the empty depot at Indianapolis. He had talked the preceding afternoon at Celina, Ohio, and taken a 7:45 P.M. train to Muncie. There he waited three and a half hours for the ninety-minute ride to Indianapolis. At 2:20 A.M. he was due to catch a train for Lafayette, where he would arrive at 4:20, to await a 6 A.M. train to Peoria. With luck he would be in Peoria at 11:15, wait until 12:30 for a train to his next engagement in Little Havana, Illinois, and arrive with forty-two minutes to spare.[35]

On such nights he would not sleep in a bed at all. Sometimes he would stay overnight with local hosts who, with the best of intentions, kept him up half the night talking. Sometimes he put up at small-town hotels with special hazards. On a June night in Excelsior Springs, Missouri, he recorded an epic combat:

Constant travel was a part of La Follette's mission as he spread the Progressive gospel.

Went to bed at 8:30 and fought bed bugs steadily till out in the morning. Made a great killing but as they kept gaining on me I got up and searched my person and clothing and dressed, then taking my rubber pillow lay down on the floor at exactly equal distances from the four walls of the room as being the furtherest I could retreat from the enemy. I strongly thought of filling the bath tub and getting in, but being very tired and somewhat weakened feared I might fall asleep and drown. I left a bed which looked like the killing ground of a slaughterhouse.[36]

There were bedbugs in other places, too, and "cockroaches as big as quails" scurrying over the floor of the St. Louis railroad depot. Meals were random and swift—occasionally dinner with a local host, but more often a slice of cake, a hard-boiled egg, or an orange snatched at a railroad counter. One reporter had described Bob as having "the face of a Savonarola and the physique of a Daniel Boone," but no physique could last long under the punishment he gave it. His letters ring with tales of colds, cramps, nausea, and diarrhea. He lectured in tents turned into ovens by August suns, coming off the platform dripping wet and beset by dizzy spells. "Bowel trouble again and was not fit to go on last night," he reported and described a horrifying session at Miller, Iowa: "Had been talking half an hour when I began to grow sick and to gripe. The house was full of people. I was determined to go on and did so to the end but I had to excuse myself *often* and go into a little boarded up room off the stage and vomit into a pail, and then use the pail immediately for diarrhea. I don't know how many times I had to excuse myself. The audience was kind—but I was weak when I finished."[37]

With few chances to bathe he spent days feeling "dirty and sweaty . . . just as gritty inside as out." Though he was a formal dresser when lecturing, he finally conceded to reality in 1909 and bought white duck pants and shoes. After warming up, he would shed his senatorial black alpaca coat and stand forth, "the swellest looking fellow that ever came down the pike" in the purity of white collar, tie, shirt, pants, and shoes.[38]

But the bowel trouble and other ailments continued relentlessly, while Belle anxiously begged Bob by mail to stop violating "the laws of health."[39] His frequent illnesses had a psychological component, but as time went on they were also rooted in exhaustion. He thought of his aches and pains as combat wounds and allowed himself virtually no vacation time to recover from them. His only rests were spent in bed under doctors' orders, or in convalescence. La Follette died at the age of seventy of cardiac exhaustion. It is not too farfetched a judgment to say that the relentless travels, which were so sustaining to his life, also helped to kill him.

His ever-moving tent show of reform was also absolutely central to his unique relationshp with his beloved and much-used family.

"We *will* have more time together after a while"

His had been the conventional dream of the men of his generation: a home that was a sheltering anchorage after each day's storms. But the reality of his middle age, when three of the four children were growing up, was one

64

of long absences, homesickness, and the unsettling awareness that during his road trips it was Belle who had to weather the tempests alone. She wrestled with the bills, the children's education and illnesses, the management of the "farm," and the constant travel between two homes. At the same time she continued to be Bob's editor, private secretary, counsellor, political hostess, and intelligence bureau, especially when she was in Wisconsin without him. It was particularly hard on her own somewhat shaky self-confidence. He knew that. At least some of his self-punishing overwork and occasional depression could be traced to the uneasiness about it that showed up in his frequent reassurances to all that his love held true even on the wing and that things would eventually go better. As early as 1896 he wrote his "Dear Little Daughter" Fola, then going on fourteen, "*I will make things jump* when I get home . . . I shall surely be in good shape to work and things will come our way in whole troops." A full eight years later he was still promising all the "Dear Ones" that "we will have more time together after a while."[40]

His love song was an endless hymn of faithfulness and encouragement, with stanzas added from time to time as they came to him in mid-journey. "I love you all dear hearts," he wrote from Mattoon, Illinois, on an August night in 1905. "I love you all with all there is in me," from Mankato, Minnesota, a month later. "Now dear heart [Belle], I know you are worrying . . . Don't do it. It is coming out all right some way," two days afterward. "But if you get down over it," he promises, "and feeling as you do, you will — then I will come home *at once*." She believes him but will not exact fulfillment from him. He knows it and she knows that he knows. It is one of their bonds. "Dear heart," she reads as she tears open his next envelope, "I hope you are feeling better. I know how it depresses you when you are having one of those taxing times. I love you always."[41]

The summer of 1905 draws to an end, and despite everything he extends the tour by an extra lecture in Michigan. "Don't scold me for it, will you now?" he begs Belle, explaining that it allowed him to duck a political invitation he didn't want to accept. "Besides it had $400 to recommend it." Finally he is home and he and Belle go off to Washington, leaving the small children behind, for his first term. No sooner is it over in June of 1906 than he is on the move again, dashing off a brace-up line enclosing a fifty-dollar check to Fola, the aspiring actress who is in a downhearted mood. "Dear one, if you only won't worry there is no trouble. I'll gamble on you as long as you live if you won't let it get on your nerves. Don't do that." He spends just a few days at Maple Bluff, where Belle is trying to get the family settled in, and is sobered as he heads off westward: "Life is driving you, too, I know how hard with the farm and politics to worry you. You are right at the center of it and get the pulsation every hour of the day. Dear ones all, if we can hold on for another year and I can make the full season next summer then we will be out of debt and take things easy and have life together. I will work after that only when the cause demands it. What a joy it will be in our hours of rest. Kiss each other all round for daddy whose heart is hungry for you all."[42]

But the demands of "the cause" never cease. When he gets back to Wisconsin there is a busy time campaigning unsuccessfully for Lenroot. Then in December he goes back to Washington for the "short" session lasting until March of 1907, and it makes no economic sense for Belle to join him there for so short a time. She stays in Wisconsin and, from the capital, he implores: "Oh, you dear, rare woman, save yourself for the family and all the world." In the next breath he answers her concern that the local school is inadequate by suggesting that she simply keep them at home all winter. "No school," he says, "is better than an unsatisfactory one," not thinking much of what it will mean for her to have three children under twelve to watch all day. She compromises by sending Bobbie to school in Madison and teaching Phil and Mary herself.[43]

It is not an easy winter for him, either. The strain tells. He complains of lumps in calves and forearms, cracking and bleeding fingers. He runs up to New York on business by train, is wracked by headaches and nausea on the return trip, and is put to bed with a severe case of influenza by the old college friends with whom he is staying. Shadows surround him that need to be fought off. In January he goes to see Ibsen's *Peer Gynt* and complains: "[T]he play is depressing—weird and wanting in dramatic interest or spirit. It sounds the sad note in life—the despairing note I . . . almost said . . . [E]xcept to 'see it' once I should not care for it."[44]

The sad note will not leave him. At the end of the session, despite the triumph of the hours-of-service bill, he laments of "so many things crying out on every hand. I wish I could accomplish more." Hardly has he drawn breath at Maple Bluff when he is on the coaches again, bound for the West Coast, facing weeks of "not more than three hours in bed a night and sometimes not more than an hour and a half," and it shakes even his own sense of mission. He looks on Mount Shasta pale in the moonlight, "white and majestic and awesome," and thinks, "How small it makes man; how brief his little flutter of life." Two weeks after that, in California, he wrestles with himself, one moment reassuring himself that his work for the country is worth "everything" and the next writing, "Oh, if life did not go so fast and the children did not grow away so fast." On a sleepless May night in California he watches the eternal breakers crash repeatedly on the rocks: "It made me very homesick to be here without you. It made life seem so short. It made it seem so wrong to be gone all the time. What is left will go so soon. Belle—this is not the way to write and not the way to feel I suppose."[45]

"Dear ones, be sweet and tender with each other"

But the very next letter spoke of Bob's excitement at the thought that he would be home in June and soon after would get some rest on a hunting trip in Colorado with his law partners and Lenroot and Bobbie, whom he would take along. He lived on a seesaw, tugged between his sense of public duty and love of the children; between his enjoyment of political grail-seeking and knowledge of Belle's burdens; between a fundamentally optimistic nature and a growing sense, after turning fifty in 1905, of the ticking clock.

The divisions of his nature spilled over into his fatherhood. He clearly wished to be the loving father he had imagined in childhood, as far away as humanly possible from stiff and unhearing John Saxton. But even the kindest father in the hardworking world of La Follette's boyhood was inescapably a taskmaster and a rock of authority. It was natural to imitate that style, especially when fatherhood had to be exerted so often from a distance.

La Follette was therefore a special mixture of Victorian and casual parent, following practices that were dictated by the commonly held beliefs of his time, yet seasoned with his own temperament and special commitments. On the one hand, the La Follette children, from the very start, were admitted to the adult circle without hesitation. It seems to have been true of Fola, growing up alone for her first thirteen years. And visitors to the Wisconsin executive residence between 1900 and 1905 noted that the younger children likewise were never sent away from the table or the parlor except during highly formal occasions. "During my father's governorship," Phil remembered, "he often brought his political friends and associates home to dinner. Current political problems and issues were daily fare for Bob and me all through our childhood and youth." The practice continued in Washington, when the dinner guests were likely to be senators, Supreme Court justices, diplomats, and star reporters. Strategy huddles were held and letters were discussed and answered in the children's presence and with confidence in their discretion. They played comfortably amid the noises of their parents' workshop and learned by imitation. When Phil

Phil "rescues" Mary from Bobbie, 1906. Role playing was La Follette family fun for all ages.

was seven, the state's conservative Republican chief justice, a neighbor, would amuse his houseguests by getting the boy to stand on a front porch railing and orate on the direct primary.[46]

Belle and Bob were playful, loving parents with no qualms about expressing physical affection. When he was home there were games, readings, "stunts," hugs, and laughter. When traveling he wrote to them often and engagingly:

It is late but I must write you a word to say that all is well with me here. You have kissed good night and gone to bed long ago and peace reigns over our snug home at Maple Bluff . . . You did not know it . . . but—I just tiptoed over the grape vine porch, slipped through the keyhole, up the stairs, into your rooms, kissed each one of you six times and off again and am back here at my desk and never even got cold the tiniest bit. What's more I shall come every single night. Why, it's only a flash and I am over the mountains and streams and cities, up the driveway and home. Who wouldn't come? No time lost, no railroad fare, and oh, such a joyful, heartwarming time. You need not sit up for me but you can go to bed every night, conscious, eternally sure that I shall be with you.[47]

The two of them freely opened windows on their souls to their children not simply as a matter of love but because they respected their intelligence, just as they respected the intelligences of their political audiences. It was an understanding among people bound by the same code. But there was no thought of rearing sons and daughters freely to choose "new" values of their own, or of abandoning the traditional parental role of guides through a fixed moral landscape.

Expectations were normal, and with the La Follettes great love begot great expectations that were special and difficult. On the one hand, the little La Follettes were consciously drilled to carry on a never-ending fight for reform. Such ordinary things as a homework assignment for twelve- and fourteen-year-old sons were full of solemn significance: "The work in school is preparation for the battle of life, boys. Day by day you are forging the armour for the great fight . . . A bad lesson is a weak plate— a false rivet . . . So sweat and tug, no matter how hard it is, just remember you are at work on the armour and weapons with which to wage a great fight against the wrongs which oppress and the evils and ills which afflict the world in which you live."

The boys' ten-year-old sister was not left out either. "I expect little Mary will have to be locked out of the lesson shop or she will be working on her armour and sword and shield all the while. She will be like her mamma was as a little girl and a big girl too." His was not simply a pep talk contrived for the occasion; this father meant every word. "I was rejoiced," he told Belle in the fall of 1909, "to hear that Bobbie, Phil and Mary were all doing so well in school. It will put them in fine shape for entering the fight at Washington."[48]

But though the children were urged to be tough slayers of dragons, they had to preserve a tender side with each other. Bob passed on to them his own youthful fear that the rough-and-tumble of law and politics would harden his conscience, which made it all the more important to have a haven of love under his own roof. When Belle reported a squabble between the two brothers, he wrote: "Dear ones, be sweet and tender with each other . . . When you are all grown and each has taken up the work you are to do it will always be a joyful thought to recall the little kindnesses which you do for each other now . . . Every good deed is a peace and comfort for all your lives. Every naughty deed leaves its scar."

"You must make up in loving kindness to one another for my being away," he told Phil. "I want to think of my little family as a happy and joyous little group sticking close together. You are old enough," he added, "to understand how much it hurts us to have you unkind toward each other."[49]

Just before young Bobbie's twelfth birthday, his father arose at 5 A.M. on a snowy morning in Chevy Chase to write him a typical letter, uncondescending and companionable when seen in one light, preachy and demanding in another. It began: "I have some work to do but thought I would chat with you a little before taking that up." It was snowing heavily, but he had heard a streetcar go by, so he knew he could get to the Capitol without having to get out his "flying machine." (He had not yet allowed himself an automobile.) He continued:

My dear little boy you will have another birthday by the time this reaches you. I wish I might be there with you all to enjoy it. It is hard to let a birthday go by for any of my little ones. It simply emphasizes the broken life we are leading and makes me repeat over and over again that we shall all be under one roof and around one table very soon I hope. I hope you will have a most joyful time and that the new year upon which you are starting will be one [of] great happiness and great good to you. You are coming now to the time when each year means a year of important growth in character as well as body.

Look well to it that you grow in gentleness and tenderness as well as in strength . . .

The boy, Bobbie, is a mighty important part of the man . . . Every day and hour of life is precious. Every act lays the foundation for another. I love you dear lad — and count on you for many things in the future. Ever and always your loving Papa.

Don't nag and don't dispute, he lectured to them both. "Kiss each other good night; greet each other in the same way in the morning . . . There is nothing in the world that Mamma and Daddy would not do for you — won't you two do this for us?"[50]

Each child reacted individually to these doting and burdensome messages, but as they reached adulthood they were united in a sense of separation from the world. There was a special La Follette quality that could only be understood within the immediate family circle. It expressed itself in those thousands of affectionate letters that the parents and children wrote to each other before the triumph of the telephone age. It was full of tensions between public rectitude and private warmth, public certainty and private anxiety. For Fola, Bob, Jr., Mary, and Phil there was an extra tug between seeing their parents both as idols and as intimates, demanding and familiar at the same time.

Their own confusions are pardonable, for Bob and Belle were not always easy to read. He was not the man of ice or iron that we expect reformers to be. His feuds were rarely personal; his suspicions and tempers did not prevent him from having warm friends; his offstage presence prompted one reporter to call him "the smilingest reformer who ever fought iniquity" (though that was not a universal opinion). To Josie and Will he was a warm and generous brother, and once when Josie complained that

The Robert La Follettes, father and son, in one of the senator's infrequent stays at Maple Bluff Farm, 1906.

her son Karl had made an unwise marriage, Bob told her: "He was silly about it but God in Heaven, if all of us who have done *foolish* things are to have them treated as great-and-wicked wrongs, the world will wear mourning all the time."[51] He could even tease himself on occasion.

But he believed that life and politics were, at root, serious business. That makes him hard to understand in our culture of amusement, of smiling politicians, of snoopy cameras that erase the line between public and private life and falsify each one to match the other.

"I stand ready to go to the front"

La Follette's repeated promises that the family would "one day" have more time together never seemed further from fulfillment than in 1909 and 1910. In those years the Progressive movement throughout the country came to a boil, and for a brief, heady hour, it appeared that Robert La Follette might become the architect of a takeover of the national Republican party that would recapitulate his capture of Wisconsin Republicanism and its governor's chair. That image of coming from political limbo to leadership mastered Bob's imagination. But in Wisconsin he had easily become a dominating figure, whereas in the national arena he faced the constant shadow of Theodore Roosevelt, who was, incidentally, enthralled by a similar metaphor, his own self-advertised conquest of boyhood weakness.

Roosevelt, however, deliberately took himself out of the running when his term ended on March 4, 1909. He went off to Africa on an extended hunting trip, turning the White House over to William Howard Taft, whom he had designated as his successor to an obedient Republican convention the preceding summer. Taft was well regarded by progressives, including La Follette, who supported him in the 1908 campaign, the last time in his life he would back a Republican presidential candidate. (Bob had been a favorite-son candidate at the convention, but there is no reason to doubt Belle's word that his realistic goal was merely to get a stronger voice in the making of the platform, if possible.)[52]

On Roosevelt's return in June of 1910 he stated that he would devote himself to writing on public affairs and play no active part in national politics. He would remain technically true to this pledge until the end of 1911. During that withdrawal period of nearly three years, progressive men and measures surged ahead in both parties, and among the once-dominating Republicans, hell broke loose.

Within a year of taking office, Taft split the party and guaranteed the collapse of his presidency. There was, first, the question of the tariff, which had symbolic importance that politically outweighed its economic impact. Many of the country's largest industries could easily undersell world rivals, and so tariff "protection" was widely perceived as simply a subsidy to big business that kept the cost of living high and competitors at home choking in the grip of the trusts. It was a view that oversimplified the economic expertise required to write tariff "schedules" and the bipartisan, sectional logrolling and horse trading that it took to get them enacted. But it had basic substance and strong voter appeal in 1909. So when Taft signed into law that year's Payne-Aldrich Tariff, which started as a tariff-reducing measure but ended up with little change in overall levels, he enraged those of his own party who were trying to curb the power of major corporations.

Taft next alienated them further by the part he played in a bitter conservation controversy. Richard Ballinger, his secretary of the interior and an expert in mining law from the state of Washington, was accused by two officials of his department—one of them, Gifford Pinchot, a leading conservationist and close ally of Roosevelt—of covering up a land-grab by Alaskan coal-mining companies. Taft took the side of Ballinger and the developers and eventually fired Pinchot. The situation was actually somewhat complicated, but the firing made Taft appear to be supporting exploiters of the public domain. By the spring of 1910 the big and slow-moving president had, by choice, temperament, or ineptitude, solidly lined himself up with conservative Republicans. Defenders have since pointed out that in implementing trust-busting and other reformist policies, he was as vigorous or more so than Roosevelt, if the Rooseveltian rhetoric were subtracted. But the rhetoric mattered. And what mattered even more was the clear sign that Taft would not be renominated in 1912 without an intraparty fight.

Meanwhile, in Congress itself, "bossism" was on the run. Senator Spooner had resigned in 1907; Senator Allison had died in 1908; and in 1910 Senator Aldrich decided that he, too, would leave the Senate the following year. Over in the House a bipartisan revolt in March broke the autocratic power of Republican Speaker Joseph G. Cannon, the antireform Illinois representative who was as aggressively unpolished as Aldrich was suave. In November, the disarray of the Republicans had its logical consequence: the Democrats won a majority in the House for the first time in sixteen years and picked up nine Senate seats. But La Follette's was not one of them. He won a second term without much trouble.

And out in the country at large, the progressive tide kept rising. Mayors and governors from both parties were chosen on broadening platforms for change. There was pressure for the initiative, referendum, and recall of officials and judges; for direct presidential and other primaries; for city administration by nonpartisan commissions and appointed managers; for corrupt practices acts and the publicizing of corporate contributions; for the direct election of senators, which was finally added to the Constitution in 1913.

Progressives also began to advance beyond simply cleaning up government and making it machine-free, beyond La Follette's initial objectives. In cities and states where they won, they pushed through laws that regulated the hours of labor of women and children; provided compensation for injured workmen; authorized farm marketing cooperatives and enlarged agricultural education and extension programs; created expert panels to regulate and control transportation, utilities, insurance, banking, mining, forestry; set up departments of highways and public health; broadened the tax base to authorize income taxes—also added to the U.S. Constitution in 1913. All of these steps were short of outright socialism, but American socialists also expanded their small voting base in many industrial cities.

These state responsibilities are so taken for granted eighty years afterward that it is hard to see them for the breakthroughs that they were. They came hand in hand with the modernization of the economy. "We who were the leaders of that day," William Allen White wrote, "rejoicing as a bride-

73

groom coming forth from his chamber, we were strong men running a race . . . How little did we realize that we were merely reflexes of deeper change."

But White also realized that the changes were not automatic, but conscience driven and broad based.

[I]t was a people's movement . . . What the people felt about the vast injustice that had come with the settlement of a continent, we, their servants—teachers, city councilors, legislators, governors, publishers, editors, writers, representatives in Congress and Senators—all made a part of our creed. Some way, into the hearts of the dominant middle class of this country, had come a sense that their civilization needed recasting, that their government had fallen into the hands of self-seekers, that a new relationship should be established between the haves and the have-nots . . . We were joyous, eager, happily determined to make life more fair and lovely for ourselves by doing such approximate justice as we could to those who obviously were living in the swamps, morasses, deserts, and wildernesses of this world.[53]

White's editorial "we" was generous. Not every progressive was a happy warrior; La Follette himself, who deliberately avoided levity in public, sometimes struck even friends like White as "grim." Not everyone was without self or group interest, either. Not everyone was a rebel against orthodox party loyalty or business as a system. But never before had there been such a serious, far-reaching and broad-based drive for a fair overhaul of the American political and economic system. It deserves more respect than it has recently gotten from some professional historians.[54]

Those who were involved in it as it moved, in 1910, toward the peak it would reach in the next six years were looking for a national leader. And for Republicans, at least, especially with Roosevelt theoretically a non-contender, Robert M. La Follette was looking more and more like the available man for the next presidential nomination.

La Follette, in the meanwhile, did nothing to discourage the idea. The inevitable question is whether his ambition had pointed this way all along. The same can be asked about any man who ever formally declared his candidacy, and with the same uncertainty as to the exact moment when the taste entered the would-be king's mouth. La Follette's letters home never express a desire for the prize, and in his political correspondence he made the conventional (but not necessarily false) disclaimer that if he ran it would be for the cause, not for himself. When he began to solicit campaign funds he wrote to one potential donor, "It is decided that the future of the progressive movement demands opposition to Taft's candidacy now . . . It falls to me to lead the fight." To another supporter he said around the same time, "I stand ready to go to the front and take all the chances on beating

74

the administration . . . But I am not willing to undertake the job, nor is it for the future good of the progressive cause that any one should stand *until* and *after* a campaign fund is—not promised, but in the hand." Of his war on "the System" and "the Money Power," he declared to a California friend and editor, "It pursues me. It is vital to make the country see."[55]

Whatever his personal feelings, he was reaching out for nationwide backing. At the start of 1909 he launched *La Follette's Weekly Magazine,* whose front page showed a hand holding a pen inscribing "The Truth," and the scriptural motto: "You shall know the truth and the truth shall make you free." It was an ambitious effort to match the impact of national muckraking journals like *Collier's, McClure's, Munsey's,* and *Everybody's.* Unfortunately it was precisely at the time when those publications were themselves having trouble sustaining long-term popular interest in the exposure of wickedness in high places. Two years after the first number appeared, featuring articles by Steffens and White, the circulation had stabilized at a sluggish forty thousand and the journal was draining money from the senator's pocket.

Whatever else it did, *La Follette's* offered him a pulpit, as did comparable journals begun by two veterans of Populist days, William Jennings Bryan's *The Commoner* and Thomas E. Watson's *Tom Watson's Magazine.* It did more, too, since La Follette also regularly read and excerpted for its pages other progressive journals and speeches. Much as he spoke of fighting alone, La Follette never actually suggested that he invented progressive ideals. They were not the work of any one figure, of course. He himself was familiar with the publications of the whole array of progressive thinkers—theorists like Frederic Howe and Lincoln Steffens, politicians like Cleveland's Tom Johnson and Toledo's Brand Whitlock, journalists like Ida Tarbell, Ray Stannard Baker, and William Allen White. Many were his personal friends. If he was beginning to stand out in the crowd it was because few other progressive politicians matched him in the passion and power with which he delivered the message—or in his knack (like Roosevelt's) of appearing to make generalized reform arguments into personal statements.

In Congress during the 1909 and 1910 sessions, La Follette supported regulatory and conservation measures opposed by Taft and became the acknowledged leader of a group of independent-minded senators that included Jonathan Dolliver and Albert Cummins of Iowa, Albert Beveridge of Indiana, Oregon's Jonathan Bourne, Minnesota's Moses Clapp, Idaho's William E. Borah, and Benjamin Bristow of Kansas. In January of 1911, at a meeting held in his Washington home, these and other insurgent Republican House members, businessmen, governors, and journalists organized the National Progressive Republican League. Its official reason for being was to coordinate the party rebellion. It made no initial statements about the presidency, and La Follette held no office, but it was obviously a potential nucleus for a La Follette campaign.

On the stump he continued to be a winner; "watching him speak is unforgettable," a reporter said, "the hand clenched, the delivery rapid and impassioned, the clarion voice and the intense and sincere earnestness claim more than unrivalled interest." And during his road trips Bob constantly widened his contacts with leaders and followers in the revolt. It was a setback for him both financially and politically that in 1910 his travels were limited, first by the need to attend to his reelection in Wisconsin and next by illness. In October, surgeons at the Mayo Clinic operated on him for gallstones, and he spent the last part of the year in slow recovery. But in the interim he got good press attention. Articles began to appear in major journals like *Harper's Weekly* and the *Saturday Evening Post,* talking of how the "lonely man in the Senate" was turning into a recognized voice for a whole bloc of administration enemies.[56]

The attention, the constant meetings, the article writing, the grind of travel as a "hopeful" had a heavy impact on all of the members of the La Follette clan in 1911—on Fola, reaching a plateau in her career search; on Belle, reaching a midlife turning point of her own; on the two sons on the doorstep of young manhood. What happened to them needs to be understood to tell La Follette's story in full dimension.

It was still a happy family. Such was the testimony of Ray Stannard Baker, muckraker and editor, who showed up (along with many new progressive friends) at 1864 Wyoming Avenue in Washington, early in 1911. La Follette had taken one more step that smelled of candidacy. He had contracted with *American* magazine to do a series of articles on his thirty-year career in politics—in effect, a campaign autobiography. Desperately pressed for time, he arranged to have the help of Baker, one of the magazine's insurgent writer-founders. Baker spent days in the office sifting documents and interviewing La Follette and would often be invited to drop in for dinner afterward. He remembered the place as "one of those hospitable, oldfashioned homes which reminds me of my own house in Wisconsin . . . the long table filled with family, young and old, and often guests dropping in, and much good talk and laughter." After dinner, there was more good talk of a different kind. La Follette or a guest would read aloud—usually fiction or poetry as far removed from politics as possible.[57]

Baker noted that "Mrs. La Follette, whom I came to admire greatly, was the heart and soul of it." So she was, but it was not easy for her.

3

Belle: A "New Woman" and Her Family (1891–1911)

"It is not recorded who won"

One day when twenty-year-old Belle was teaching school in little Spring Green, Wisconsin, Bob came up from Madison for the happy visit of an engaged lover to his lass. "I do not remember it," she wrote long after, "but was told not long ago there is a tradition that Bob La Follette and Belle Case ran a race 'right in the village street.' It is not recorded who won, but I was a good runner for a girl. When I was nine years old, there was only one boy in school who could run faster than I could."[1]

There is a great deal of Belle in that tantalizing glimpse, one of many that flicker through the biography of Bob that she had been working on for five years when she died in 1931. Its twenty-six chapters, which cover the period from his birth to 1910, are as close as she came to a memoir of her own, and her appearances in them independently of Bob are rare and controlled. They take a certain amount of interpretation.

Why would Belle include the story if she could neither remember nor verify it? The odds are long that the race was run and that Belle, in heavy skirts, lost. But win or lose, it was a defiantly unladylike thing for a young schoolmistress and assistant principal to do on a public thoroughfare. That rebellious posture was not one that Belle enjoyed. Nor would she happily admit either beating her fiancé or losing to him. So telling the tale as a town legend, without recorded results, became a neat solution that let her

77

do what she could not resist, namely, to tell the reader that she had been a good runner and did not care who knew it. That is how Belle's retiring but insistent ego worked.

She really did not like to talk about herself in public, despite the hundreds of first-person magazine columns and articles she wrote on political and domestic subjects. The woman who spoke in these, however, was almost always a dispassionate advocate or an unruffled adviser offering the insights of "current thinking" to her readers. The world did not suspect that behind the pedagogical demeanor was a woman rent, until at least midlife, by conflict and anxiety.

Belle never divorced herself from the traditional domestic expectations imposed on women of her background. She never completely surrendered her individuality or social conscience to them, either. Caught in a tug of war, she struggled long and hard with a gnawing sense of inadequacy. But it was that private vulnerability, leavened by warmth and the ability to drop her normal seriousness and share in family fun, that made her not just a respected but a cherished figure in her intimate circle.

Those outside it were never aware of how hard she worked to be simultaneously a model citizen and homemaker, or of how much she gave to—and took from—her children in the process.

"Thus are the precious human ties interwoven"

Belle's unconventional enterprises were neither concealed nor flaunted. Her attendance at law school was on record, and so was the fact that she did not practice law, though when Bob was in the House a Washington reporter for the Boston *Transcript,* doing a color piece on the young congressional couple, mistakenly assumed that they shared a law office back home. He described the two of them as "a youthful pair, and of small stature," and added that "Mrs. La Follette would be taken anywhere for a pretty girl, rosy and blonde, . . . a happy light-hearted character, but as little of the woman lawyer as it is possible to imagine." He also said that she was taking a course of law at "the Columbia college," in the capital district.[2] In fact, there is only one recorded instance of Belle's direct involvement with her husband's law practice. Sometime during the nineties, when Bob was overwhelmed with work, he did ask her to prepare a brief in an important case of his that was coming up before the state supreme court. She did so, and when the chief justice complimented him, he beamingly revealed its authorship by "altogether the brainiest member of my family. Mrs. La Follette wrote that brief, from start to finish."[3] There is no specific evidence that it happened more than once, but no particular reason to think that it did not.

She consciously chose to have "the family we had always planned" after 1891 and bore three children in quick succession: Robert, Jr., in 1895, Philip in 1897, and finally Mary in 1899, who arrived some four months after Belle's own fortieth birthday. She was a mature and healthy mother, undoubtedly supported in the rigors of having borne three infants in four years by hired help and by the traditional women's network. Her mother lived in nearby Baraboo; sister-in-law Josie Siebecker was there in Madison; and closest to home was Fola, whose teens coincided almost precisely with the babyhood of her siblings and her father's battle to win the state. Belle was able to help Bob in his work because of Fola's helpful presence. "My conscience always troubles me," she admitted, "when I recall how much responsibility I let her carry." But far from resenting it, Fola seems to have slipped easily into an independent role between the generations, extending a furious protectiveness both to her parents and to her baby brothers and sister that lasted through all their lifetimes and completely infused her own. She was, Belle remembered, "their comrade and at the same time their oracle," and while they had "the best time in the world with 'Sister' . . . they never questioned her authority."[4]

The enlarged family took shape during the emotional upheavals of the intraparty wars and also during a time of financial stress for the La Follettes. Looking for the golden dream like so many other middle-class Americans, Bob invested some of his trial-work income in a thousand acres of Dakota land that was supposed to become a Percheron horse ranch, run by his nephew Orville Eastman, the son of half-sister Ellen. Droughts, accidents, and especially the Panic of 1893 wiped out the enterprise and drained Bob's bank account without mercy until, after some years, he finally unloaded the property.[5]

In the midst of these tribulations Belle launched into her first independent cause, the physical education of women. In 1893 she became the president of the Emily Bishop League in Madison, Bishop being the principal of a "school of expression" at the Chautauqua Institute in New York. Having met Bishop in Washington, Belle got the "preceptress" of the Ladies' Hall at the university—in effect the dean of women students—to invite her to Madison one year to lecture the coeds on dress and health. She was so well received by the entire capital community that she came back a second year and organized a regular program of continuing exercise classes. The "league" was basically a club to carry them on.[6] Belle took over its administration and leadership and participated in regular calisthenics with other Madison matrons. The local press reported on the program derisively.

But Bishop was far more than a glorified gymnastics instructor. What drew Belle to her and formed the basis of lifelong friendship and respect was the intellectual context of Bishop's prescribed stretches and bends. She based her teachings partly on the methods of François Delsarte, a French acting and singing coach who was interested in the expression of emotions through bodily changes and movements. Bishop's theory, according to an assistant, was based on "the principle of relaxation and release from nervous tension not as an end in itself but as a means of finding the basic centers of feeling and being." If it sounds vaguely Californian to the modern ear, it had a more political resonance a century ago. Getting genteel young women out of tight corsets and encumbering yards of skirt and petticoat—teaching them to breathe deeply, to perspire without apology, to stretch their muscles and discover their physical selves—was a major step in liberating them. They had long been discouraged from any kind of hard work or higher education on the ground that too much mental or physical effort would harm their fragile constitutions and nerves and endanger the health of their children to come. The proper Victorian model was the pale and unexercised mistress of the parlor who ate like a bird. Bishop's forthright endorsement of calisthenics, nature walks, fresh air, sunshine, and sturdy diet was, therefore, moderately revolutionary.

What was more, Bishop argued, the role of good health in women was to improve their mental functioning. The age-old doctrine of "a sound mind in a sound body" was just beginning to apply to women in nineteenth-century America. Catherine Beecher, for example, a pioneer feminist, had written *Physiology and Calisthenics for Schools and Families* in 1856, and as the century neared its end the idea gathered behind it the authority of current science. Modern psychology, in its birth process, was curiously poking into how mental and emotional activity actually took place in human brains and nerves. Bishop had studied with one of its founders, G. Stanley Hall, who had been a disciple of Belle and Bob's idol John Bascom at Williams College. Like Bascom he had begun as a ministerial candidate, branched out into general philosophy, and then become a professor and college president with a special interest in scientific pedagogy. The title of the book he published in 1904 told the tale: *Adolescence, Its Psychology and Its Relation to Physiology, Anthropology, Sex, Crime, Religion and Education.* But Hall's researches in no way reduced his desire for human betterment or his conviction that Christian ethics were perfectly compatible with the laboratory method of examining experience.

There was a web of connection among science, good health, mental functioning, and moral and political improvement. It drew together progressive-minded educators like Bascom and Hall and William James and John Dewey, and it linked them in turn with enthusiastic democratic reformers like the La Follettes. It drew in women, too, and gave them a special niche that did not divorce them from the sacred home. They must follow the laws of health and of "mind," because they were the mothers of the race, the children's earliest teachers, the authorities and models in the first "community," the family. Their influence for good flowed from the nursery outward to the entire human race. More than anyone, they needed to share in the finest of the new learning and the debate on how best to apply it in society.

When, therefore, Emily Bishop taught Wisconsin girls to express themselves in motion she was not concerned merely with good looks, self-esteem, or longevity. Neither was Belle, who continued to run intermittently throughout middle age without noticeable effect in slimming down her somewhat rounded five-foot-four figure. They were laying foundations of female enfranchisement for noble purposes. Fully alive women would have hygienic homes and soundly educated sons and daughters. On the next higher level they would help their husbands to establish clean governments and a humane economy. From there the ladder stretched heavenward to goals like peace and disarmament. To be a fit woman was to be conditioned for the work of building a better world.

Progressive impulses also hummed along various historical and personal webs. Through her own Yankee ancestors and through Bascom's teaching, Belle was linked to New England's reforming past of Puritanism, transcendentalism, abolitionism, and a variety of other do-good-isms. And then the work of the Emily Bishop League brought Gwyneth King, another bold female spirit, into her life.

Nine years Belle's junior, King came to Madison as Bishop's assistant. Raised in South Dakota and in Washington, the daughter of a western lawyer who untypically handled land cases for Indians, she was an outspoken suffragist who urged her swaddled sisters to join her in wearing simple, one-piece shifts. Through the La Follettes, she met Gilbert Roe, Bob's young law partner. They fell in love, contracted a marriage of rebellious minds, and moved to New York where Roe, who stayed associated with Bob, spent a long lifetime in the courts battling for unpopular left-wing causes.

To the La Follette children the Roes became "Uncle Gil" and "Aunt Netha." (Bishop herself was "Aunt Emily.") They were among the earliest of a select, supportive circle of like-minded La Follette intimates who evoked Bob and Belle's warm loyalties. Fola lived with them at intervals when she was a struggling actress in New York, and Belle was happy to see her daughter looked after by the "Beloved Netha" to whom she addressed long, confiding letters. The Roes' oldest child, John, born in 1906, grew up to become Fola's own lawyer. "Thus," in Belle's words, "are the precious human ties interwoven and the currents of life separated and united again."[7]

Belle had little time for public role-playing on her own during the six years as Wisconsin's first lady. Taking care of three high-spirited children and managing official entertainments in the comfortable old executive residence were occupation enough, particularly when meals and receptions were often contrived to bring together progressives and possible converts to progressivism from the legislature, the press, the university, and the professions. Phil recalled how, as a child, he innocently tipped off the secret of Belle's seating arrangements to a curious neighbor: "She seats first a dull one and then a bright one, and so on around the table." Her tenure as an official wife was dedicated to helping Bob battle his enemies, and in addition she was deeply absorbed in caring for him during his lengthy physical breakdowns. His needs, by her conscious choice, came first. Even the children were a close second. Whatever talents of her own Belle Case had to cultivate were placed last. The first few years of Bob's senatorship did little to change the order of priority.

"It is sweet to have you say you love me"

In the winter and spring of 1906 she went to Washington with Bob to help him get settled, leaving the children at a boarding school in Spring Green run by two maiden ladies, aunts of Frank Lloyd Wright. Although it was anything but a Dickensian nightmare, eleven-year-old Bobbie was wretchedly homesick the whole time and thereafter Belle did not break up the family again. Whenever she spent a congressional session at Bob's side, Bobbie, Phil, and Mary went along to the capital at whatever cost in changes of school, friends, and routine. They did pass 1907 uninterrupted at Maple Bluff, when both parents agreed that Bob should spend the short session that occupied the first nine weeks of the year on his own, staying with old university friends in Washington.

But even then, Bob's needs rang alarms she could not ignore. At the session's end he was bedridden with a respiratory infection. A few days after its inception, a late-night telegram told Belle that he was fighting a serious case of influenza. Leaving a note for the children, she packed a bag, walked three and a half miles to Madison in freezing darkness, and was off to her husband's side on the morning train. "How it did surprise

Robert to find that mama had gone," nine-year-old Phil wrote soon after. "He pretty near fainted."[8]

La Follette's extensive lecture tours meant long months of separation, and during them Belle's letters showed how much, in her mid-forties, she was still uncritically in love, lonely for him, and terrified of losing him to illness. "Most beloved," she wrote when he had just begun the last speaking tour during his governorship and she was left in a house empty of his presence, "my heart and most of my thought has been with you since you left us. It seemed hard to have you go without a moment in which to gather yourself together after the months of uninterrupted strain . . . I long to hear from you." But longing to hear or not, she urged him to write only a daily postal card, not letters. "It is a tax on your strength and time. And we do not need to have you tell us that you love us. Just tell us how you are."[9]

Happily, he ignored that advice, yet even his regular flow of letters did not soothe the ache. "It has been a hard summer for me," she wrote after a time, "no chance to let down and really be by ourselves." His schedule permitted a brief home stopover, and she proposed to go down to Chicago and meet him to share the 150-mile ride to Madison. "It would be quite a while together without any great additional expense," she reasoned, "and I am getting to value more and more the precious hours we can spend together as I see our truly beautiful family growing up and realize how short the time at best we can call them *ours* . . . I long for more days together."[10] What she wanted more than anything was precisely what the dutiful pattern of life to which they were both sworn denied her—privacy in their companionship. Once after writing him a catalog of domestic happenings, she said that she hoped that it would give him some rest to focus on such trivia, as it did her. At least she wanted to think so. "I often smile at myself," she confided, "and wonder if I really am forgetting the outside world or only making myself believe that I am. I know I am very tired of the outside and fond of the inside. If only you were here to share." It takes a full knowledge of her yearning for the "inside" to appreciate the effort it took her to break into the world with an independent voice.

But her unconditional devotion sometimes seemed to deny any aspirations of her own. "My dearest one," she writes while he is chugging through a Chautauqua schedule, "I just read your letter and it is sweet to have you say you love me. Whenever I get discouraged I always think there is nothing I would rather be than your wife and the mother of your children and I have no ambition except to contribute to your happiness and theirs and to your success and theirs."[11] One wintry Wisconsin evening, she concludes, "Good night, dearest, I can never imagine how any man can be as interesting, fascinating, loveable to any woman as you are to me."[12] And she accepted—perhaps even helped to create—her husband's proclaimed public image as the lonely hero. When Steffens wrote the favorable article in *McClure's* that helped La Follette win the bitter gubernatorial contest of 1904, her gratitude erupted:

God bless you and Mrs. Steffens for "taking sides." It may be I see only one side, but I have seen that side from the *inside*. I know the stuff Mr. La Follette is made of, and what the struggle has been. I saw him—who could have been the idol of his party—choose his course . . . in that Sawyer affair. I saw him . . . accept the consequences . . . although it left him almost friendless personally—and quite friendless politically . . . I saw him rise from this position of political friendlessness without money or any influence to help, except his own personality, and overcoming all obstacles, in spite of defeat after defeat, keep fighting for certain ideas.[13]

And when La Follette made his first Senate speech Belle, supposedly the less temperamental member of the pair, wrote to Fola: "My judicial and logical faculty compel me to see both sides. But there is no *other side* to this event, so far as its being a triumph—an unalloyed triumph for Papa."[14]

It was far from a relationship of dominance and submission. Belle remembered that they had their differences, and that one or the other was occasionally hurt, but treated it like a cut or bruise that would soon be forgotten. Essentially they were, in her words, "good comrades," but the actual circumstances of the comradeship between 1905 and 1909, when he was establishing his national reputation, plus the general marital conventions of the time, which she did not entirely reject, demanded a great deal more from her side of the comradeship. She gave it willingly, not merely because she loved him but because she had genuine faith in what he was doing. Thus the lonely nights and busy days without him became her contribution to a higher end. "I want to get thoroughly rejuvenated," she told him the day after New Year's Day of 1907, "so I can enter your work in the right spirit." Later that year she added, "Your ideals have been right and we have lived to see your work recognized on the basis of your ideals." Rarely did she take note of a progressive defeat without lamentation, or a victory without applause, and to those victories she was willing to contribute Bob, for after all, "*good* politics need men actively at work."[15]

And so, while she was not beyond criticizing him gently, the only persistent and genuine complaint at the height of his lecturing career was that he did not take care of himself. "I do not see how you can keep up strength to speak without being able to eat," she lectured him. "There is so much more danger than as though you had not violated all the laws of health for so long as regards rest and recreation." Chronically unable to stop talking while he had a receptive audience, Bob compounded the difficulties of his schedules by missing both meals and trains. Trying to change his ways was a lifelong, losing battle. And sometimes loneliness led to something remotely approaching a reproof. "I hardly know why the time seems so precious that we spend together and so vacant when separated. I realize the great value of your work and would not keep you at home, but I always have the sense of waiting for your coming."[16]

The waiting was endurable because she did not sit moping by the hearth. She was constantly busy, which was therapeutic in its way. But she was likewise dogged by an unrelenting fear of failure. The courage that led her into unconventional settings like law classrooms and jogging paths was the more remarkable because its reverse side was uncertainty about herself. She drew heavily on Bob's buoyancy in his positive moods, but even though his words were reassuring his actual behavior multiplied her burdens and left her to long intervals of solitary wrestling with the demons of self-blame.

"I am not well adapted to home making"

"[S]ometimes I feel," Belle lamented in the twenty-third year of their marriage, "that I am not well adapted to home making, and the constant effort to hold myself and keep my balance in the midst of so many distractions wears me out." She refused to justify herself by dwelling on their marital arrangements as a major source of the distractions.[17]

She took on her own shoulders a good deal of worry over the limping family finances. "I have always felt I could live within our means," she apologized to Bob, "by adopting a simpler style of living but I can not watch details and make a good showing on the money expended. A sense of helplessness always haunts me in regard to our finances." His comforting and perfectly correct refusal to blame her made no difference. "[T]here is a painful sense of responsibility that I can not reason myself out of or away from. Your generosity makes me feel all the more sensitive to my obligation."[18]

At best they would never have reacted to debt in the same way. His inherent, typically American confidence in the future let him see unpaid bills as temporary inconveniences, where her hyperactive conscience counted them as moral lapses. But it was easier for him to whistle his way through a hard month because, at least when he was traveling, it was she who actually handled the "awful list of bills" that poured in (though she dutifully reported them to him). They "sort of take my breath away" was her assessment in October of 1906 when their bank balance was $572.20 and, after writing checks for insurance premiums, bank loan installments, horse feed, and a new dress for Fola, she still confronted five unpaid statements totaling $306. She hoped there would be "clearer sailing ahead," but there was not. They borrowed money to stock a pony ranch that they hoped to run at Maple Bluff, agreeing that it would be pleasing and a useful experience for the children. The result, as recorded by Belle in a letter of the following year, was predictable. "With . . . what we owe on the ponies it will almost seem that we have made no headway."[19]

The La Follette style was not opulent, merely expected. It was especially important for political insurgents to dress and furnish themselves "properly." Belle and Bob, like all their generation's reformers—and quite unlike "progressives" of the 1960s—did not dream of attacking the cultural conventions that were the strong skeleton of the social structure. If anything, economic inequality angered them because it put respectability beyond the reach of growing numbers of Americans. Nevertheless, keeping up appearances on limited means was especially hard for Belle, who told Phil as a grown man that her "horror of debt" kept her in a constant state of agitation. But all she said to Bob in 1906 was: "It is not pleasant to leave the bills to run."[20]

Motherhood was still "the supreme experience" for her, but rearing the children had special trials for someone juggling instinctive warmth, traditional rules, and a set of modern "authorized" expectations. Small decisions became the occasion of soul-searching. One day when Bobbie was ten, the acting company with which sister Fola was on tour played Janesville and he was allowed to go with an adult supervisor and stay overnight. Phil and Mary's protests were consoled with a treat. It seems natural enough, but it was not to Belle. "I know this will have your approval," she wrote Bob, "as it had Fola's, but I still cannot feel it is right education from several standpoints. Philip and Mary were bribed; bad education again." And she sighed, "I wish I were not troubled with ideals, or if I must have them I wish I had not a conscience to trouble me when I violated my principles."[21]

Still, she would not readily turn the responsibility over to old-fashioned schools that she distrusted. In the first December at Maple Bluff she went to look at the local school and told Bob, in Washington, it was impossible. "I suppose it is a good average school. And yet [i]t was so *deadening.*" His suggestion was to keep them out, and her response was to send Bobbie to school in Madison and tutor Phil and Mary at home. It added to the "distractions" of which she complained and was one more source of anxiety. But flashes of humor, usually shown only in private, helped her through the turmoil. Once, in mock helplessness, she abandoned a letter to Bob because the children, having just read a novel called *Behind Closed Doors,* were playing detective. Mary was the robber, Phil the detective, and Robert the high official patsy. "Well, dear," ran her concluding paragraph, "there is so much shooting and dying about me that I think I shall have to stop writing a while and give the house over to the distinguished assassins and their victims."[22]

And as if she did not have enough to fret about, she also cudgeled herself for mismanagement of her time. "*I must begin work tonight,*" is her vow one November day. "I never in my life had such constant interruptions." In another letter she tells Bob, "I think I must manage badly, for I seem to be so driven all the while that there is no time to think and consider. I keep looking forward to a time when I can systematize and regulate things but the time does not arrive and I am concerned I must have fallen into bad habits."[23] It is the more touching because it came from a woman who would preach to others the gospel of relaxation and recreation but who was herself a very ant for diligence.

Belle paid the bills, ran the household, tutored the children, and helped Bob with speech and article drafts. She was also his representative and chief of intelligence on the Wisconsin political front, which remained critical to him not only at reelection time, but between elections as well, since stalwart revolts and progressive defections constantly threatened his work. Her letters suggest a more-than-casual level of involvement in appointments and maneuvers. "Alf and I had a conference," she writes (Alfred Rogers, La Follette's law partner in Madison), "and decided if we could arrange the Board of Control and other political matters over the telephone we would not try to push on as we had planned . . . Alf has been very much concerned about the game warden and I . . . over the Board of Control . . . The State Institutions seem to me especially above political consideration and to call for disinterested care and protection." She submits three marked volumes of unidentified documents for the consideration of Haugen and John R. Commons, the economics professor who was part of La Follette's team of expert consultants. She invites Irvine Lenroot to dinner to find out how his mind stands on running in the next gubernatorial primary and reports that he is reluctant. "I think the real cause of Mr. Lenroot's hesitation is his feeling that he would rather be Congressman than governor. That is his true *liking* . . . but he will come to it, I think, and is going to think it over." (In the event, he loses the primary and eventually does serve in both houses of Congress.) She nudges someone referred

to only as "Victor" to get to work on a pamphlet on railway rate regulation and holds off an applicant for a job on the Dairy and Food Commission until Bob can return from the road. Nils Haugen and another member of the La Follette alliance meet at the mansion and she relays the news
that they will defer "levying a tax" until they have met Bob in Chicago
and made other arrangements to launch it with proper support.[24]

Those events occurred in 1905. In the spring of 1907 the running
testimony of her letters is of crowded days and nights. At the beginning
of the year she welcomed the "good hard physical work" that would rest
her nerves, "taut too long," as she went about taking down the Christmas
tree, washing all the woodwork, cleaning lamps, and feeding chickens. Next
she was enmeshed in agricultural chores. A professor from the university
came to advise on spraying and pruning the orchard; a cedar tree in the
yard was cut down; she hunted frantically for two men to do plowing and
planting and a maid to share the consuming routines of housewifery. She
worked indoors and out relentlessly. Phil recalled that when strategy meetings took place at Maple Bluff, it was Belle herself who made the doughnuts for everyone, and he once greatly irritated his own wife by pointing
out the shaggy condition of the lawn in front of their house and saying
that "Mother" would have scythed it by hand long before.[25]

Belle also continued to send Bob ideas and material. "It is midnight,"
one letter begins, "and I want to be brief." She then enclosed a former speech
with certain portions marked in red pencil that "you could use to advantage." "It seems to me there would be more political capital in the circulation of your Milton Junction speech than in a campaign textbook," she
advises in another letter. And in yet another, "I am having Mrs. Nelson
write out hurriedly an outline that I have roughly culled from your [speech
on] representative government. I have really done no work on it . . . [but]
thought you would be able to . . . determine whether you thought it could
be worked into an editorial . . . If I could only get a few consecutive hours
to formulate some line of thought." Between them there is the familiarity
not only of husband and wife but of co-workers who understand their
common assignments thoroughly: "I do not know whether I have written
intelligibly or not but you are good at reading between the lines."[26] The
constant grind was wearing, but the results justified it in her mind, and
when she sat at the kitchen table by lamplight to write him five or six
longhand pages she consoled them both with the reflection that, for all
the pangs of separation, "our lives have been rich and complete."[27]

Yet her consciousness of effort and contribution was still not enough
to bridge her way completely over an abyss of self-doubt. "I fall so far short

of my own ideals of helpfulness to you and the children that I should get very much discouraged," she lamented, "if you did not all brace me up as you do now and then." Fortunately Bob and Fola, and the other children as they grew old enough, understood her need and were generous with reassurances when she became discouraged over her "bad habit of being driven."[28]

But eventually a line was crossed. Sometime in 1909, Belle began to emerge more clearly as a separate but equal partner in the marriage. The reasons are not entirely clear from her letters. In part it may have been the arrival of her fiftieth birthday, a milestone to spur reflection and new resolves. Transitions were going on in her life. Mothering required less of her time as the two boys reached adolescence and were able to help her with the farm chores. As the Progressive movement scored political victories, Bob himself no longer appeared quite so much the loner in need of her total dedication. Her father's serious illness may have reminded her that there had been a time before Bob came on the scene when she was Belle Case, with plans and a life of her own. That much is speculative. But there is much firmer evidence that Belle finally arrived at a realistic assessment of the financial future before her. During the first few years of Bob's national knight-errantry she may have dreamed that a time of tranquility would someday arrive when they would be a debt-free and happy family. That would be the culmination of her complementary tasks as homemaker and political woman.

But in 1909 it became clear that there would never be clear sailing and stormy financial weather was a permanent forecast. What made it so evident was Bob's plunge into publishing *La Follette's Weekly Magazine,* which took all of their existing savings and more or less mortgaged all those for the foreseeable future. It was then that Belle finally began to move toward a more clearly defined, independent role for herself. It was also then that, for the only time, she let outright anger at Bob overflow onto paper.

"All the riches I ever hoped or cared for"

The founding of the *Weekly* was a clear announcement of La Follette's wish to take the leadership of the swelling armies of progressive voters and officeholders. Its opening editorial was as clear a statement as can be found of their spirit and credo. "It is a glorious privilege to live in this time, and have a free hand in this fight for government by the people . . . This magazine recognizes as its chief task that of aiding in winning back for the people the complete power over government — national, state and mu-

La Follette's Weekly, begun in 1909, became Belle's first regular published outlet, though she hated its drain on the family finances.

nicipal—which has been lost to them by the encroachments of party machines, corporate and unincorporated monopolies, and by the rapid growth of immense populations."[29]

There was also personal satisfaction in it for the senator. "Ever since he had owned and edited the *University Press,*" Belle recalled, "he had felt the lure of such an enterprise." Yet she was aware from the start, as he was not, of the enormous drawbacks. One would be the further drain on his overtaxed system. One summer day at Maple Bluff, during a planning meeting, Steffens—one of a blue-ribbon group of writers and experts who had promised articles—pulled Belle to one side and whispered, "You mustn't let Bob take on this terrible load. It will kill him." Belle's answer was a resigned laugh. Steffens knew as well as she did that nobody could stop Bob when his mind was made up.[30] And nobody did. He rushed into the project at the precise time when he was waist-deep in organizing the anti-Taft bloc in the Senate, which he followed up after the 1909 session with a punishing four-month lecture tour ending in November, shortly before the *Weekly*'s first birthday. Yet it is exactly in the infancy of a publication, when all policies and decisions are not yet routinized, that it most needs the attention of its chief editor and publisher. Though he trusted his associate and managing editors, Herbert Quick and Fred MacKenzie, La Follette's timing was terrible.

The other near-certainty about new magazines is that they are money-eating machines for months or even years until, if ever, they get established. Despite some help with start-up costs from a few financial backers, including the wealthy liberal Charles R. Crane, a plumbing-supply manufacturer in Chicago, La Follette himself had to make up the inevitable regular operating deficits. They devoured his lecturing income just when he was furnishing the new home and headquarters they had rented in Washington and facing the costs of a 1910 reelection campaign. So it was that Belle's hope of freedom from unpaid bills faded with each issue.

She saw still another problem, which Bob brushed aside. As editor he would be held responsible for every word in the publication and expected to comment on issues as the news broke, even when, as a politician, delay or silence might be wise. But he insisted that his life was "an open book" and that he could play both roles. "In spite of the long years . . . together," she remembered, "I had never before quite understood how inherently frank and unafraid he was." Even in her doubts, she could not help admiring his spirit.

Moreover, there was an assignment for Belle herself in *La Follette's Weekly* that encouraged her to begin speaking in her own right. She was to edit, along with Professor Caroline Hunt of the university's home economics department, the Home and Education Department. Whose idea this was is unclear, but Belle took the job with characteristic seriousness that showed she welcomed it. She reserved one of the two third-floor bedrooms at 1864 Wyoming Avenue as her study, and in June of 1909, much as she yearned for the scented orchards and buzzing vines of Maple Bluff, she sent the children ahead to the care of Josie Siebecker and lingered in Washington's humidity to write her articles.

Given her own dedication and sacrifice, it is no surprise that Belle fell into panic and then something close to rage when she learned from MacKenzie and others that Bob himself, stretched to the limit on the road, was not furnishing expected copy.

In mid-September, Anson Case suffered a mild stroke, the preliminary to one that would kill him the next year. Belle rushed to Baraboo to help take care of him—her mother had died five years previously—and spent a taxing few days at the bedside. On September 27, back in Maple Bluff, still distraught and burdened, she began a letter to her husband. It saluted him in her usual way as "Best Beloved," but then rapidly turned into a soul-cry of criticism which, on reading over, she may well have decided not to send. Fola found the letter in Belle's personal belongings after her death and was unable to determine whether Bob got it and returned it or Belle simply left it unmailed.

Belle said that the staff had been especially glad to get his latest itinerary because they had not known how to reach him. The working group now included Bob's friend and law partner, Alf Rogers, who was troubled by the senator's apparent decision to have someone else act as a chief deputy. Belle reported:

He is just sick because you do not write something for it every week. He thinks it a crime that you should leave to Drew or any one the writing of editorials that should [be] and are taken all over the country to be *yours*. He thinks you can not realize how important it is that the paper started by you for the express purpose of expressing your policies should have some of your own work in it. The name is not enough. He says it is awfully disheartening to him, to MacKenzie and every one. His conclusions were so exactly along the line of those I had reached when I was at Baraboo that I can not but feel that they are vital and that I ought to tell you how I feel about it even though it is hard to do so and though I fear you may misunderstand me.

Her scolding continued, "You think you are doing your part by furnishing the money, but you don't realize the *necessity*—the absolute *necessity* that the paper should have something from you . . . It lacks your personality."

She went on unrelentingly to confront, for both of them, the cost of his combination of overconfidence and perfectionism that plunged him into obligations and then paralyzed him until the imminence of disaster.

You do not know how much it costs me to say it—but I have thought it all over and some way I feel bound to. We have lived together almost thirty years. You do not know how deeply I love you, how precious your personality, your charm, your wonderful versatility, your strength and boldness and persistence. Others may love and admire you but I question if any one *appreciates* you as I do . . . But it has always seemed to me that all the work which had to be *planned* for—that which was not an *immediate* call to action—cost twice the effort it should because of a dread to get at [it], a desire to put it off . . . I have often tried to analyze what it was that kept the preparation of a speech that did not have to be made hanging over the household like a nightmare for months, seeming to wear out your nervous vitality with dread and anxiety, and yet when you were forced to get into the arena and do the thing it comes easy and you are ready and happy and all the long siege of strain and waiting seems so unnecessary and foolish.

There were unfair contradictions in her indictment. She, who begged Bob to spare himself, was now complaining that he did not do more. And she, who was always oppressed by a sense of the great undone, was railing at him for overcrowded schedules. But momentarily at least she had gotten beyond reasonableness and deference. For the only time in her thousands of letters to Bob, she was freely admitting her own needs and resentments.

When you started the paper I tried to be glad. I know I am foolishly apprehensive but I tried to be passively courageous about it. It cost me more than you can think. The peace of mind that had come to me when the farm was paid for—it was all the riches I had ever hoped or cared for—slipped away . . . Last winter when you let week after week go by without ever writing for the paper, sometimes hardly reading it, putting aside all the opportunity and obligation that went with [it] other than to meet the expenses . . . it seemed to me I should go frantic and it seems to me I can not live through another such winter. I know you can write a page for that paper every week easier than I can. Not only because you can write easier but because you have as much time as I have. My time is not as valuable. It is not taken up with as important matters. But it is as surely and inevitably occupied and demanded. What I do is not worth mentioning and I do not trouble any one with it. *But the little leisure is as needful and precious for all that.* [Emphasis added.] . . . [I]f you felt as I do that you *must* write your page each week you could do it and . . . it seems to me that unless you can do that much the paper is not fulfilling its promises.

The essence of Belle was there. She wanted perfection from him—she had said as much once, when reproaching him for dosing his ruined digestion and nerves with patent medicines: "I want you to be perfect in all things. I want you to be a model in physical health as well as in moral character."[31]

She also yearned for perfection from her country and her children—and from herself, though she put herself last of all in importance.

It was no wonder that she was tripped up again and again in choosing among love, duty, and hope. She wanted to keep the children happy but unbribed; to keep Bob healthy but active in the cause; to be herself without stinting obligations to others. It was a great deal for one small woman to handle.

Lincoln Steffens, Belle's devoted admirer, had an instinctive sense of her dividedness. He thought of her as a prudent counterweight to airy spirits in the progressive circle, and he even teased her about her "intelligent toryism." But he believed that there was a gypsy within. At her funeral in 1931 he told of a moment during one of his early visits to Maple Bluff. She invited him to join her in a ride. When two saddled horses appeared at the door she leaped onto one and without a backward look raced off at a full gallop "as fast and as far as her horse could run," leaving him to catch up. When dismounted she gestured ahead and said, "That's what I would like to do, only faster and farther, much faster, much farther." But they returned at a walk, with Belle talking to Steffens the whole time about himself and about Bob. "She wanted to fly," was his judgment; "she inspired flight and she bore fliers, but she herself—Belle La Follette—walked all her life on the ground to keep the course for her fliers. That was her woman's victory; that was a woman's tragedy, too."[32]

"These few intimate friends whom we know understand"

For all the grief the new magazine caused her, it helped Belle through a transition of her own. She appears to have reached a culminating moment of insight into Bob's and her own natures. Her column in the *Weekly* allowed her to get her feet wet and develop style, confidence, and connection with an audience. She began with simple pep talks on behalf of physical education but very soon emerged as the Belle La Follette that people would know in the 1910s and 1920s, the speaker and writer on subjects that were broader than clean politics and votes for women—humane treatment of children, the reclaiming of slums, justice for blacks, protection and fair play for workers, international conciliation, and disarmament. The array of interests would later be preserved under the label of "liberalism," once the idea of "progress" fell into disuse. She became a woman who was first known through her husband and subsequently shone in her own light, something like Eleanor Roosevelt, who was a quarter century younger than Belle and outlived her by thirty years. Both were women marked by a combination of gentility, conscience, toughness, and reserve not easily duplicated in other times.

The development of Belle as social critic was quickly evident in her columns. She began tentatively enough. Her first column dealt with as innocuous a subject as could be imagined—yawning. "Stretch and yawn," she advised her women readers, "not a suppressed yawn but a great big natural yawn. Stretch as a cat stretches . . . We can stretch and yawn away more small troubles in a minute than we can argue out of mind in a week." In another column, she sang the praises of running or brisk walking as an antidote to depression. But before long she was calling attention to a book by Charles Weller, *Neglected Neighbors in the National Capital*. It dealt with the alleys of Washington, "where nineteen thousand people, or one-twelfth of the city's population—by no means all colored—live in squalor and degradation, bringing up children who will fill the hospitals, asylums and prisons of the future." Another week's "Home and Education" page likewise began with a discussion of improving the manners and physical poise of children, then shifted to a report on the Women's Twentieth Century Club of Washington, which allowed Belle to complain of Washington's crowded streetcars, dirty water, and gas "high in price and notoriously bad in quality. The Washington Gas Company . . . has watered its stock to the amount of $5,800,000 . . . Not satisfied with this it has resorted to the practice of watering its gas in order to make greater profit on its watered stock. Water is cheap but water-gas is poison . . . But all legislation regulating the price and quality of Washington gas, died in this last session of Congress."[33]

The serenest messages could carry a sting in the tail. A mealtime grace attributed to Belle by her granddaughter ran: "We would learn to use effectively the strength of mind and body obtained from this food, in the effort to secure a fairer distribution of life's blessings."[34] She knew what she was doing and gradually became more forthrightly proud of the results. Two years after starting the department, she proposed a sales pitch to the *Weekly*'s circulation manager. Agents could say, suggested Belle, that "the Home and Education Department is conducted on broader and more progressive lines than any other magazine in this country. The editors started out with the express purpose of making it meet the demands of intelligent and progressive women. In spite of the protests of experienced newspaper men who said that no woman's department could be made a success that did not have paper patterns, beauty recipes, etc., the department has met with striking success."[35] She was announcing her own credo—homemaking was not for featherheads.

Other editors began to make offers to her, and she was not retiring in her responses. She told the North American Press Syndicate that she could do a column as they suggested, but she would want a weekly list of the subscribing papers and a minimum guarantee of twenty-five dollars a week. She would discuss her childrearing philosophy, talk about health, or urge women to read newspapers and magazines broadly and "not . . . confine themselves to the stuff dished up for them on women's pages." She would make straight-out statements on women's suffrage and politics or "continue to make them varied and apparently disassociated, while really covering a line of thought on each of them." (The "apparently" is a neat touch.) Eventually she did run a syndicated column on the lines suggested. In 1911 she was also contributing articles to *American* magazine (which would also serially run Bob's autobiography that year, no surprise since it had been founded in 1906 by a group of progressive journalists). "It keeps me jumping," she told Fola.[36] Not too long thereafter she would begin to hit the trail for women's suffrage.

Belle was finally fulfilling the promise seen by the college professors who had praised her writing, but she still tended to keep her feet planted in the "appropriate" soil of domesticity when she wrote. One of her *American* articles praised the work of Clifton Hodge, a biologist on the staff of Clark University who was waging a vigorous war on the flies of Worcester by involving local children in competitive campaigns, with prizes, to set fly traps near garbage cans and livery stables and put up screens wherever possible. That put Hodge's work under the heading of education and allowed Belle to put in a claim on behalf of nature study and education in conservation. Hodge wanted his brand of "social hygiene" taught in the public schools, to "save" the young—especially those of parents who were "heterogeneous, busy, untaught, scattered, often foreign, immoral sometimes themselves"—from becoming "contaminated through ignorance."

Belle reported these xenophobic Yankee judgments dispassionately and picked out an element on which to build a gentler, less militant, and more wifely conclusion. Education was certainly important. If children could learn about insect and plant life through lessons in gardening and the planting and culture of fruit trees—"everything that will bring the home up to its possibilities of comfort and beauty"—it would be easy to pass on to bacteria control and "intelligent cleanliness." That would hit the problem at the root, where it affected the individual home. And, she concluded, "if every home is made ideal, the whole country will be, and the only way to bring this about is to start the children right."[37]

Independent advocacy was one force changing Belle's life as the excite-

The suffrage issue brought Belle to a new role as a public speaker in her fifties.

ments of 1910 and 1911 washed around the family. With her own type-writer, her own study, sometimes her own stenographer, her ego was less of a hostage to Bob's standing. She also drew comfort from a widening circle of kindred spirits fighting on progressive fronts who filled both La Follette homes with warmth and laughter on their visits. In addition to

Steffens, there was Frederic C. Howe, who had a degree in sociology from Johns Hopkins and had gone from the classroom to the trenches of urban reform. Though La Follette was a governor and not a mayor, Howe was smitten with his encouragement of applied expertise to social problems and wrote a well-received book that applauded Wisconsin as a laboratory of democracy. Howe and his wife, Marie Jenney, a Unitarian minister in her own right, moved comfortably in the La Follette circle.

So did other midwesterners, like Iowa Senator Jonathan Dolliver, the son of an abolitionist and Methodist circuit rider in West Virginia. Dolliver came late but enthusiastically to progressivism. Tom Johnson was also a convert, from a hard-shell steel and traction magnate to a believer in social justice. The transforming influence for him was reading Henry George's *Social Problems*. Johnson switched sides, became the four-term reform mayor of Cleveland, ran town meetings in a circus tent, battled streetcar fares down to three cents, and unsparingly cried for wresting utilities away from private monopolies and putting them under municipal ownership. Howe had worked in Johnson's circle of advisers and brought him into contact with the La Follettes. Belle, Bob, and Fola were deeply shaken when both Dolliver and Johnson died unexpectedly in middle age, in 1910 and 1911.

Other new friends were from New England. One was Elizabeth Evans, the widow of Glendower Evans, another gifted man snatched away by death well before his time. He was a Harvard Law graduate, a friend and disciple of William James, and a shining example of liberal Boston at its most idealistic. Among his reformist friends in the Boston bar was young Louis Brandeis, already carving out a reputation as a keen-witted and thorough-going advocate of "the people," especially workers, against monopolies and exploitive employers.

Evans carried on her husband's crusades, one of which—the Women's Trade Union League—brought her into contact with Belle and Bob. Their meeting in Madison was followed by a happy visit, first of many to Maple Bluff. Evans recalled it with enormous pleasure—the house with its vine-clad piazza, the view of the capitol dome across the sweep of the lake, the gardens and orchards, and especially the three younger children: Bobby at fifteen, serious and solid; thirteen-year-old Phil, "volatile like quicksilver"; and blue-eyed Mary, then eleven. They were always "treated as persons" and shared in all discussions. "There was a solidarity about the La Follette family," Evans testified, "beyond that of any other I ever encountered . . . The right government of the country was the very life of the household." Belle, in turn, was charmed by Evans's delight in the clan that she had mothered. A year and a half later she was writing to her, saying, "Beloved Elizabeth. I do love you and long to keep in touch with you. This does not mean that we shall write long, school girl letters to each other, but just a word now and then to be sure that each knows what the other is doing."

In the winter of 1909–1910 Brandeis went down to Washington to do some legal work in connection with the Ballinger-Pinchot controversy. On Evans's advice, he looked up the La Follettes, calling up the stairs of their home as he arrived, "Have you got a cold potato to give a wayfarer?"[38] Brandeis and La Follette had a special affinity for each other despite their widely different backgrounds (Brandeis was the son of a well-off Jewish family in Louisville). Each was devastatingly complete in assembling a case, for each had a profound faith in the power of the facts to move mountains.

Brandeis and his wife became new members of the children's unofficial extended family. They were "Uncle Louis" and "Aunt Alice," just as Bishop was Aunt Emily and the Roes, Uncle Gil and Aunt Netha. Evans became "Aunt Bunkie." What united them all with other progressives—whether in politics, law, business, journalism, or the academy—was their assumption that society could be made better and fairer by the conscious, willed efforts of citizens of strong individual character and family loyalty, who took responsibility for their community and country. They were neither utopians nor innocents, but they shared the conviction that the new century was bound to warm the germinating seeds of an improved humanity.

Belle and Bob both took extra comfort in these relationships, and they were especially important to Belle. They extended her circle beyond the immediate family, which still had absolute priority for her but no longer constituted almost her entire emotional universe. She became slightly more relaxed and confessed to Fola in 1913 that she was sometimes "lazy" about getting her work done after an afternoon's auto ride or about walking to help control her weight at 135 pounds where it stubbornly stayed. (Her definition of laziness, however, discounted the diligence that kept her sitting up much of one night making out eighty household checks.) She enjoyed the chance to make money on her own and was flattered by requests for articles and lectures.

But she was still Belle, still the harshest critic of "my own poor scattered efforts," and therefore all the more grateful for the commitment and love of such friends as Evans. "You have given me new life and spirit to live," she wrote her. "You have given me [a] new point of view, new enthusiasm, faith that the struggle is worth while. Will you not accept something from me? Just a small share of my great love and admiration for one

In her last decade, Belle's face showed the serenity gained in a life of disappointment without surrender.

Elizabeth Evans?"[39] And to "Beloved Netha," her intimate of so many years, she wrote with the forthright emotion that was a family characteristic one summer day in 1913, "I wish you were here today, dear. It is a delightfully cool morning, and we would go into the Park and talk it out. That is such a comfort. And oh, how grateful we should be for each other—for these few intimate friends whom we know understand us as we do them. Always in my thoughts with Fola and Alf [Rogers] are you and Gilbert. If only we could be nearer together in fact as well as in spirit."[40]

The comradeship of progressivism—or of families close to each other within the progressive movement—still tingles in the letters that the La Follettes exchanged with their intimates. It found special expression in the life of Fola, who inherited Belle and Bob's dreams and made an initial stab at applying them in the theater, where other young spirits were also hoping to light torches for their audiences.

4

Fola: From Art to Activism (1904–1911)

"I have the possibilities of growth along this line"

On Christmas Day of 1900 Fola La Follette dreamed in her eighteen-year-old way of a brilliant and rewarding stage career that would allow her to spoil her adored Daddy. To Bob, the governor-elect, she gave the token gift of "a pad of shaving paper" and a promise. "When I'm famous and earning five hundred a week it'll be the same girl, same father, but you won't be guessing at the time of day any more, you dearly beloved, bestest father that any girl ever had."[1]

She never did win independent fame as an actress, nor does the record show that she bought her father a watch, perhaps because she came to realize that if he did not carry one it was by the choice of a man who did not want to be reminded of hours flying by when there were fights still unfinished. Money was not the issue. He had enough to send her on a chaperoned educational trip to Europe the next summer to polish her German. From Munich, Bonn, Venice, Capri, Gibraltar, Paris, and London she mailed long, chatty travelogues, by turns homesick, enthusiastic, and disdainful, filled with the typical impressions of any proper young American picking her tourist way among beggars and monuments in an era when the United States supposedly had neither. But these were deceiving. Fola was anything but typical.

She was the firstborn of Belle and Bob, and so the first to face the problem of becoming her own person while remaining their child, a La Follette and a warrior for justice. She managed a reasonable balance among her endowments: his love of public performance, Belle's earnestness, and the passion of both parents for words at work. Had Fola been born male, the pull of politics as the family business would likely have drawn her career choices toward law or journalism. As it was, she did not escape the tugs of reform and clan solidarity. Her most memorable appearances turned out to be in a one-woman traveling show on behalf of suffrage. And while marriage took her eventually to Greenwich Village, Paris, and Hollywood, she dedicated almost the entire last half of her childless life to the culminating role of La Follette biographer and archivist.

Throughout it all she kept a discernible identity, though not without some inner struggle. The four children, though commonly imprinted by their heritage, were anything but cookie-cutter duplicates. Unlike either her father or mother, Fola could relax and play. And although, like Belle, she did not openly push for equal access to the jobs and privileges of a man's world, she wore small, clear labels of equality, such as the uncommon insistence on keeping her maiden name. She was likewise free of Belle's perfectionist anxieties. "I handed in my long theme today," runs her first letter in the family collection. "Don't think it was much good but then I did the best I could and I can't do any more than that."[2]

Her best (as she perhaps knew) was very good. Despite—or perhaps because of—having been tutored at home by Belle until she was of high school age, she loped through the University of Wisconsin at a Phi Beta Kappa stride, finishing the Letters and Science course with a senior thesis on "Social and Economic Life in the Fox River Valley from 1800 to 1840." But acting had been her aim all along. Edwin Booth was the subject of her commencement address at the precollegiate Wisconsin Academy; on the Madison campus she had been the "leading spirit" of the dramatic club, starring in both English and German plays. The *Badger,* the university's yearbook, speculated that the success or failure on the stage of "this young, strong, well-balanced, modern college girl" would be "significant and interesting."[3]

For a governor's daughter her choice of apprenticeship was democratic and spunky. It was a knockabout summer tour of Michigan and Wisconsin with a traveling stock company. Fola chose to make it an adventure in personal development that would lead to some undefined form of wider service. If she was literally acting out Bob's boyish theatrical ambitions, she nevertheless did not intend to lower the adult horizons he had set. Something beyond fame and five hundred dollars a week was the spur, and trouping served for her the same improving ends as self-imposed schedules

Fola: star student, governor's daughter, and future actress, in her junior year at the University of Wisconsin.

of conscientious exercise or readings in classical and modern drama and poetry.

It was a hard life, but she thoroughly enjoyed it, to judge by the letters she wrote during June and July of 1904 as the Walton Pyre Stock Company made its way through places like Janesville, Fort Atkinson, Ishpeming, Stevens Point, Sheboygan, Manitowoc, and Houghton. They did three plays, now long-forgotten—*Prince Karl, Esmeralda,* and *The Russian Honeymoon*—and they were at the bottom of what might be called the minor leagues of theater. All the same, the company carried into the "opera houses" of those little Main Streets some of the magic aura that clung to live drama when it still monopolized the business of illusion. (Hardly anyone realized how swiftly the infant upstart movies would capture the market.) For the actors, that small touch of glamor had to make up for a great deal of hard, low-paid work. The usual schedule called for afternoon rehearsals and evening performances six or seven days a week, sooty travel by milk train, dismal meals and accommodations, and an almost total lack of dressing-room amenities and personal leisure time. But Fola's reports home made light of these inconveniences, all the more so because she was eager to show that she craved no special favors.

"These one-night stands are rather strenuous and I go jumping from pillar to post," she admitted. College dramatics had not prepared her for such eventualities as a drunken partner in a scene one night. Iron Mountain was described as "this hole"; a noisy convention of Eagles and a band rehearsal at Chippewa Falls wrecked possibilities of rest; and she ate only two meals a day, skipping breakfast to catch up on sleep and save money. She hated Sunday performances, and she frequently asked Belle to mail her various skirts, shirtwaists, and baubles from her personal wardrobe, for then the women in the cast were expected to provide their own costumes.

Despite it all, the applause of the crowds had its perennial intoxication for players, which even a high-minded girl trained to resist egoism could not resist. A good house in Marquette demanded a curtain call that "even I—much as I hate curtain calls on the whole—didn't mind answering the least little bit." She took careful note of the house at each performance. "Wish you could have been at Oshkosh last night! We had a splendid house—the best since our first at Madison and oh so enthusiastic." These cheered her, as did moments of pure diversion like a quick visit to a circus in Ishpeming where she was still child enough to enjoy pink lemonade and want to feed the elephant.[4]

She was the blonde and blue-eyed picture of a happy innocent, but underneath was the La Follette seriousness, constantly monitoring and criticizing her own performance. "I write you of little else than my work," she apologized to Belle, "but I'm so interested in it that I can't help thinking of it." In actuality she was taking a lively interest in her father's third campaign for governor in that crucial summer when he drove the stalwarts onto a separate ticket. She closely followed the battle for the Republican line in the papers bought along the route, and enjoyed eavesdropping on the salvos of political argument that rattled and popped in hotel lobbies and restaurants. Her gratified sense of things was that La Follette was well ahead in popularity; even in Michigan people were "much interested in Wisconsin politics and . . . father's good fighting spirit appeals to them." Bob himself, according to Belle, was delighted with his little girl's interest in political matters.

In truth they could hardly be avoided. In town after Wisconsin town, friends and supporters of the governor came to greet and entertain her and to watch the show, for this was his well-cultivated heartland. It was both a comfort and a problem to her. Fola was smart enough to know that Walton Pyre realized as much, and that she possibly owed her job to the fact — the classic dilemma of a celebrity's child. "I'm glad of these weeks in Michigan," she observed in the town of Hancock, "for it has given me confidence getting away from Madison and made me feel that what little success I've had was not *all* because my name is the same as my father's."[5]

On the other hand, no one could have cherished the name more, as she explained to "dearest Papa" at the campaign's height. "I'm more than proud of you, father mine. They couldn't hire me to take a different stage name now even if I had contemplated it before — which I hadn't. I'm glad I belong. No matter whether you get the support of the men of the state, you've got one small girl with you clear through to the end and beyond. You're a great man 'Little Bob,' but you're more than that, you're a good and noble honest man 'thru and thru' and about the dearest father that ever lived."

Fola worshipped them both, but where Bob was an idol, her love for Belle had a strongly protective, almost patronizing flavor. "I suppose the political strain has been too severe to permit you to relax much," ran one letter from Wausau. "Dearest little heart, you certainly do have your share. But you're always such a beautifully poised, unselfish, noble little woman, smiling as if you had no more than most people to worry you. I only hope I can always live up to your example." But however much she insisted that "the knowledge that . . . I'm *your daughter* is always an inspiration to me," Fola did not elect to pursue Belle's course of becoming some man's wisest and best political counselor. Once, she expressed the wish that she were a man and could help her father, and what she said to him directly was: "[Y]ou have my heart and would have head and hand if I were a man." But active politicking was man's work, and Fola was determined to be an independent woman and—in 1904—an actress.[6]

Her father's frankly emotional and artistic temperament, the very qualities that Belle tried to diminish within herself, kindled Fola's art. She felt possessed by inherited qualities that she labeled French and Irish (though her actual "Irish" ancestry was Protestant and northern). Her problem was to translate them, in a calling generally esteemed light-minded, into actions worthy and suitable. As the tour with Pyre drew toward its end, she was not sure how she would achieve that; she only knew that there was serious learning to be done and that in some still undefined way she could harness her dramatic talents to her father's ideals.

Fola tried to clarify the still-unfocused picture when she sat down, like thousands of stagestruck Middle American sons and daughters, to write both parents for permission to take the momentous step of moving to a big city—it turned out to be New York—for further work and study. To "my dearest Mother," she explained: "I can't tell you how I have enjoyed the working and most of all the feeling that I have the possibilities of growth along this line. I never have felt sure of it before as I do now. I don't think it's conceit or any thing of that sort but just a realization that somewhere within me there is something I can work out—that perhaps it may take a long time and many hard experiences to do it but that it's there to develop . . . I wouldn't take a great deal for what this summer has given me." To "dearest Papa" she wrote a slightly more practical prospectus. She wanted to get a job with a resident stock company, take singing lessons, and earn by "outside work" her living expenses in a rented room in some private home. What the end would be she couldn't quite put into words. "I realize how utterly futile it is to try to express the thoughts which lie nearest our hearts," but "because you are you and I am I you'll understand all this without being told." Half a year later she could put it a little better after watching the great British actor Johnston Forbes-Robertson do Bob's beloved *Hamlet*. "[S]omewhere in me crying for expression is just what you express and that you would have expressed had you chosen to make that your work." But she could not verbalize what it was.[7]

Without any outward sign of hesitation, Belle and Bob gave their assent. Fola had brought them nothing but pleasure, and neither of them appeared to share the fast-fading puritan attitude that there was something inherently disreputable in stage work. They were also happy with where Fola landed, in New York. Emily Bishop was now there, still teaching the theory and practice of expressive movement, and so were Gilbert and Netha Roe to exercise whatever chaperonage might still be considered necessary.

On her twenty-second birthday then, September 10, 1904, Fola signed a one-year contract that made her an employee of the growing Shubert theatrical organization. She had put her foot on the next upward rung of the ladder of theatrical training, blissfully unaware of how widely spaced and slippery they became higher up.

"Real plays for real people"

Fola still faced the problem of her famous name. Lee Shubert and his brothers, Sam and Jake, were sharp entrepreneurs, and undoubtedly they had the box office in mind in signing up the daughter of a nationally known politician. Fola accepted the inevitable. When the first contract expired, rather than knocking on other producers' doors she tried for and got a renewal. "Evidently the Shuberts think," she reported, that "the La Follette bonanza may bear fruit yet and that they'll keep a weather eye on the youthful daughter."[8]

She was entering the world of American theater at a specially yeasty moment. It had been mostly derivative and provincial, rarely looking beyond the simplest level of entertainment and borrowing ideas, scripts, and stars from Europe when it did. But around 1914, a few years after Fola went to New York, an outburst of creativity from playwrights, actors, designers, composers, librettists, choreographers, and producers born or raised in the United States would launch a golden age of some thirty to forty years' duration, with New York—or more specifically, a few midtown blocks of Broadway—as its universally recognized Athens. The electricity was building, and the "youthful daughter" of Bob and Belle was especially sensitive to the crackle in the air.

But the reverse side of "the theater" was "show business," and it was a business that also followed the pattern of the times in becoming ever more concentrated at the top level, and sweating its "workers" at the bottom, where Fola was starting. Her first assignment was with a touring repertory group in which she had a one-line part in *The Taming of the Shrew* and another walk-on in *The School for Scandal*. The practice was to send such a cast out with an established star as a drawing card; in this case it was the Irish-born and American-raised Ada Rehan, a renowned and veteran performer of Shakespeare. The tour began in Boston in November, and in the course of the winter Rehan's company meandered through the cities of the Great Lakes and the Ohio Valley, getting as far west as

Missouri and as far south as West Virginia. For Fola, one-night stands or longer in Buffalo, Syracuse, Detroit, Columbus, Toledo, Wheeling, Pittsburgh, Chicago, and St. Louis were an undeniable upgrade from appearances in Ishpeming and Manitowoc.

But the conditions were still harsh. The salary might be enough to cover lodging in dollar-a-day hotels and meals in cheap lunchrooms, but it could not provide extra clothes for bitter weather. The family came to the rescue with money for a squirrel muff and collar after Fola's stories of freezing her fingers and shivering in "long pant union suits." The holiday season featured extra matinees—her Thanksgiving dinner in Boston was a hasty ham sandwich between curtains—but it was not customary for the troupe to get additional pay for such performances, which some managers added at the last minute. On the other hand, actors could be and were docked when performances were canceled on short notice, and it was not unheard of for a whole tour to be broken off when not drawing well, leaving the cast penniless and stranded. Fola escaped such calamities on this first swing, but endured some of them in later years and was indignant at their continued threat. She would, without hesitation, become a member of the players' union, Actors Equity, when it was founded in 1913.[9]

The Shuberts were not necessarily more exploitive than average for their trade. They themselves were locked in competition with a monopolistic booking syndicate in a struggle that would have few survivors. One way or another, independent and locally controlled troupes like Walton Pyre's were disappearing or being consolidated as inexorably as small business establishments of every kind. Whatever the process did to improve the quality of the "product" and the long-run stability of working conditions, it was destroying a folklike spontaneity in American communities that also nourished the roots of political democracy. Fola's progressivism-by-inheritance was sharpened by the experience of being caught up in the process.

She followed Bob's 1904 triumphs with mounting elation. Election day found her in Washington, calling on "Aunt Lu" Thompson, Belle and Bob's college classmate whose husband was in government, and wishing nostalgically for her short skirts and roller skates. When she returned from the theater to find that Bob had carried the state, she wrote in immediate exhilaration: "I'm so happy for you dear hearts. I was almost tempted to go get drunk but confined my dissipation to an ice in the cafe of this very delightful and eminently respectable hotel. This town is going wild and I wish I had a man to go out and watch it with. Being a woman isn't half bad if you can have such a father and mother but there are times when

I should like to don trousers and wander forth. But since I can't I'm going sedately to bed and dream of a grand spree."[10]

She was divided between her own intense loyalty to the family name and what it stood for, and a wish to prove that she could earn recognition without it. "Mother, I've written a lot of 'ego' here," she apologized to Belle, "and fear you may think I'm attributing all this to 'my own beautiful face and figger and charming personality.' But set your fears at rest. I appreciate that mighty little of this attention would I get if my father didn't happen to be a splendid fighting governor in the West." She promised "Papa" that she would never "intentionally do anything to bring down the name you've always kept so honest and clean and strong." Sometimes she seemed almost apologetic for the self-absorption characteristic of her chosen calling. Actors are not, by nature, modest and retiring souls. But Fola worried about her perfectly understandable tendency to dwell on the ups and downs of her infant career, to repeat each cherished compliment and smile through the tears at each rejection or bad review. "I seem to fill my letters up with *Ego,*" she chided herself, "and then there's no time for anything or any one else — perhaps I'm getting 'spoiled' and this attention is making me 'self-centered.' I'll try and reform next time."

She never could quite close the gap between her two strong drives of self-realization and loyalty to the family. Her style was molded by the resulting compromises, starting with the decision *not* to adopt a stage name other than her own, a simple step that would have avoided a good deal of soul-searching. Other signs of her special brand of double life were unmistakable in the early years in New York.[11]

At the basic level she was just another young woman scrambling for opportunities and notices available only in "pop" shows that were the equivalent of B movies and television offerings. After the Rehan tour, she got work in a Newark-based stock company run by Gabriel Kolker playing Polly in *The Lost Paradise;* in the course of 1905 she also appeared in New York in shows destined for quick oblivion, like *The Christian* and *The Music Hall Girl.* There were also small appearances in second and third companies of sentimental favorites like *Charley's Aunt, Camille,* and *Captain Jinks of the Horse Marines.* In 1906 she had a brief role in *The Second Mrs. Tanqueray,* but from that plateau of cautious realism (it was a melodrama whose heroine was fighting for acceptance in "society") Fola stepped down to a twenty-minute sketch in a vaudeville tour with Edwin Arden's company. The year 1908 brought parts in *Button, Button, Who's Got the Button* with Leo Ditrichstein, as well as *Harriet's Honeymoon, The Ambitious Mrs. Alcott,* and *A Superfluous Husband.* Fola's role was almost always that of the ingenue, "a sweet young girl of eighteen . . . simple and dear and silly," as she put it, or "a catty little Fluffy Ruffles bride."[12]

And there she seemed to be stalled. The 1909 season, her fifth as a professional, brought no improvement in bookings, billings, or income. She earned twenty-five to fifty dollars a week when employed, but in the long dry spells the money for special lessons, clothes, and doctors' bills could only be gotten by apologetic appeals to Mother and Father. "Oh, how I wish I could be *earning* instead of always *spending*" was her lament after one appeal. "I've tried to find something in some other lines but have not been brilliantly successful so far." Her scarce odd jobs included one stint as a live-in baby-sitter. Her anonymity was broken when the child's parents received a telephone call asking their nursemaid to return Senator La Follette's call. Fola met setbacks with a stubborn optimism worthy of her breeding. "My sublime confidence in the ultimate *rightness* of things," she assured the family, "is wondrous and some way in the end always triumphs over my temporary fits of ultra impatient ambition . . . I think that if I'm patient and work hard and steadfastly, even though I may fall down a goodly number of times, that in the end I'll win out." Even when she broke down in despair as she admitted in one letter to Belle, she bravely swallowed her sobs. "Adios for a while," her letter ended, "and forgive this childish outcry. I'll try to grow up now and be a woman for a week or two."[13]

Yet whatever hard thumps she was taking, she was not faceless and alone in the city, and whatever trivial entertainments she took part in to learn her craft, she was inescapably serious. A series of mentors gladly took Miss La Follette under their wings, starting with Ada Rehan herself. By Rehan's order, Fola was allowed to sit in the wings when her own on-stage presence wasn't required and watch the leads at work. "How else," explained the star to the stage manager, "are the young people to grow?" An even more important token of favor was the loan of her promptbooks for various parts. These were scripts containing an actor's notes on business, timing, inflection, and interpretation, based on long experience of what worked with what audiences. They were an inimitable tutorial, a personal treasure that a luminary shared only with especially promising novices. Fola spent long but grateful hours in copying them in longhand.

Fola got support from other sources, too, in addition to the ever-available Aunt Emily and the Roe family. Veteran actor-producers for whom she worked, like Kolker, Arden, and Ditrichstein, encouraged her. She was introduced to Bertha Kunz Baker, a drama coach, "a wonderful woman, a *great inspiration*." When she was in Baker's presence, Fola felt that "a new and undreamed of self awakens—a something within comes out, of which I have only been conscious at intervals before and then only dimly." Another teacher to whom she was recommended, an aging German named Reiman, sent her into raptures. "At last I've found the thing or rather the being with a capital B for whom I've been searching and longing for time without end—Mr. Reiman . . . He is to me in a way what father always is, a great inspiration." She felt lucky in "the dear, beautiful people who have come into my life."[14]

Baker, Reiman, Bishop, and other parent-surrogates pushed Fola in the direction that her natural instincts already pointed, that is, to thoughtful study of the realistic dramatic literature that was emerging in Europe and would presently challenge the romantic artifices and conventions that still dominated the American stage. On tour with the Rehan company in Syracuse she spent an afternoon burrowing into George Bernard Shaw's *Love among the Artists,* pleased, like any recent graduate, that she was no longer bound by required assignments but could read whatever took her fancy. Still, she mused, "I suppose that might get me into bad habits if I let it run wild." So she set herself to reading plays and novels in German and French, vowing "I'm *not* going to let myself *slump.*" Nor did she. She took out a library card and promised herself, at least, to begin systematic reading in such eighteenth- and nineteenth-century critics as Lessing, Goethe, and Ruskin. Her letters showed familiarity with Ibsen, Strindberg, and Chekhov. Between tours she was able to visit Russian and Yiddish theaters in New York's immigrant neighborhoods and to see some of the world's best actors interpret meaty works old and new on Broadway. Alla Nazimova in *Hedda Gabler* (to which Fola "responded with every nerve, every sensibility in my being"); young Ethel Barrymore in *A Doll's House;* Sarah Bernhardt in Sardou's tragedy *Fédora;* Edward Sothern and Julia Marlowe in *Twelfth Night.* And there were operas, lectures, all of the bounty that made the city itself, with the proper guidance, one great postgraduate campus for a young woman from Madison.[15]

These experiences were part of the duality that marked Fola's stage apprenticeship. She was learning the entertainment business at the bottom. But she was also becoming aware of a new kind of theater that could not only amuse and hold the mirror up to society but possibly even revitalize it when it had become stale, artificial, and unjust. As she put it to her father:

Just at present I feel as if I'd like to start a stock company down on the East Side— good plays—plays that deal with life—with the problems men and women have to meet in their struggle for existence. Those plays and the classics at popular prices—for real genuine people—that's what the East Siders are. Not lovely but

Fola in the full regalia of life on stage.

real—no painted Fifth Avenue pet puppets and social parasites. No, I haven't been talking to Anna [she meant Emma] Goldman. I just walked up Fifth Avenue today and looked into the faces of the men and women strolling and riding up and down to see and be seen.[16]

Not every moment was earnest. She saw Maude Adams in *Peter Pan* and insisted that "[a]nyone who doesn't believe in fairies after seeing it is a brute." She admired the "dainty, bright and clean" charm of Fritzi Sheff in *Mademoiselle Modiste*. Her letters to "the chilluns" at home bubbled with affection. Her zest for country excursions to the Catskills with the

Roes showed a capacity for fun in idleness that only her brother Bobbie, among the six La Follettes, would quite equal. And though she spoke of it little, she did not lack for courtship.[17]

But in those years from 1905 to 1910 there was no way that she could or would forsake a solid commitment to the solemn purpose of advancing the La Follette brand of politics. When she was not ingenue-in-training, or studying for membership in a new, socially useful theater, she was part of her father's circle and welcome at the dinner tables of the reform elite. In New York Steffens kept her in close contact with such fellow progressive and muckraking journalists as Finley Peter Dunne, Norman Hapgood, Samuel Hopkins Adams, and others. The Roes were her avenue to meeting Lillian Wald and visiting the Henry Street settlement house. Gilbert Roe took her to night court once, and her generous response recalls a time when solutions to the problem of crime seemed easily reachable. "It makes the heart ache," she wrote home. "If I were a lawyer I should have to . . . de-vote myself to getting all the poor devils off—for we're to blame, not they. Some day, perhaps, it will come."[18]

During a run in Cleveland she was entertained by Fred Howe and Tom Johnson, whom she found touched with a Lincolnesque melancholy, "one of the saddest men I've ever met." And yet she could not recall "having seen him without a smile either in his eyes or lurking in the corner of his mouth . . . I love him. Tonight he was talking of his religion—of why he was in politics." La Follette, too, called democracy his religion. Fola had no doctrinally defined God, but she echoed broadly spiritual impulses. Charmed by a Presbyterian sermon in Alexandria, she decided that he was "preaching more socialism than Presbyterianism." But "after all, it doesn't matter much what we call it—the religion of humanity."[19]

In the midst of such company Fola may have begun to feel twinges of guilt at being what she playfully called a "mere mummer." Standing out-side the arena was not the way to pursue the La Follette destiny. Theater work might have socially redeeming possibilities, but she was not realizing them in her sweet-young-thing roles even though the résumés she dropped off at producers' offices were getting longer. As early as 1907 she was think-ing of an educational lecture for women's clubs, based on her wide reading of the works of George Meredith, whose novels, especially *Diana of the Crossways,* had some inspiring things to say about the spiritual equality of women.[20]

Nothing came of it at the time. Two years later, as Fola celebrated her twenty-seventh birthday, Belle expressed some reservations about Fola's course, though Bob gallantly insisted that the sturdy little daughter to whom he was bonded in the fellowship of traveling performance be given still more time. "I think it would be a mistake," he wrote to Belle from Montana, "for her plans to be interfered with . . . [W]e must encourage her to keep right on."[21]

And then, at the start of 1910, like the most contrived device of a hack stage writer, a solution to the dilemma dropped into Fola's lap in the form of a one-act play called *How the Vote Was Won*. It allowed her to become a recognized star of sorts while carrying on one of the most exciting battles for democracy of the decade that was just starting—the crusade for votes for women.

"Men Quiet When Suffraget Scores"

The play, by Cicely Hamilton and Christopher St. John, was an import from England, where it had done service in the suffrage campaign. Its special virtue, in a movement that sometimes wobbled under the weight of its own moral zeal, was that its weapon was comedy. It is the story of a stuffy bachelor who insists that women should not have the vote because it will dilute the sacred obligation of the male sex to take care of them. Thereupon, six of his independent female working relatives quit their jobs and move into his home, arguing gaily that if they are indeed such helpless creatures that they cannot qualify as citizens, then he will undoubtedly be happy to assume full responsibility for their support on his small salary. Needless to say, his conversion to suffragism is prompt, thorough, and still funny.[22]

Fola knew the work by title only, and had already passed up a chance to read it at a women's prison outside Boston when Beatrice Forbes-Robertson asked her to perform it in January at a New York benefit. By this time she was seriously exploring the possibilities of "educational" dramatic presentations, getting advice and possibly some prompting from her older women mentors. When she examined the script for the first time she found it was "the very play" that Aunt Lu Thompson had spoken of somewhat earlier. Meanwhile, Emily Bishop was already established on the reform lecture platform, sometimes reading telling excerpts from the *Congressional Record* and sometimes giving straightforward talks on such topics as "The Tariff and the High Cost of Living," as Fola heard her do in that same January of 1910, which was a heavily political month in all respects.

It started with a meeting of New York's Liberal Club, which she attended with Marie Jenney Howe shortly after New Year's Day to hear Joseph Fels talk on the single tax. Soon afterward she saw Tom Johnson, who was in the city taking a "starvation cure" for his weight problem. Then Lincoln Steffens spoke of writing a one-act play for her, and she countered by asking if in the meanwhile she could do a public reading of one of his short stories, "The Least of These." She also heard Bertha Baker read a "tremendous" play called *The Shepherd,* about "Russian Revolutionary conditions," which Fola thought would have universal appeal. That was a strong consideration in its favor, because one of the problems for builders of an American "civic theater" was still a lack of challenging plays with American authors or subject matter.[23]

All of this stirring and simmering prompted Fola to take on *How the Vote Was Won.* She may also have been pushed by growing discouragement about her career, and by the knowledge that money had never been tighter for her father, who had just confessed himself unable to send more than twenty-five dollars toward a bill she owed. (But he cheerily assured her he was behind her "until the stars melt and the universe rolls up.")[24] In addition, her friends and surroundings were sweeping her into the accelerating current of the suffrage movement itself. It was one of those political crusades whose hour (like voting rights for black Americans in the 1960s) had clearly come. It united feminists of every variety—those who believed in the traditional family and those who did not; those who were professional and single, and those who were married clubwomen; those interested in the economic conditions of female workers and the poor, and those who looked no further than clean politics and generalized uplift. The arguments against it were (as *How the Vote Was Won* showed) patently ridiculous in the face of changing conditions in society. Even conservative males, in growing numbers, were coming to recognize that. The cause was clearly on a winning roll, and one to which a La Follette woman could be freely and undividedly committed.

By March of 1910 Fola had plunged in completely. Marie Howe's energetic leadership was responsible for a series of bookings in Cleveland in March, which the *Plain Dealer* reviewed (on the sixth page of the second section) under the heading "Men Quiet When Suffraget Scores." The sarcastic reporter noted that the handful of men (including Tom Johnson) scattered through an audience of several hundred "society women" were very quiet when "Miss La Follette's characters intimated that men are inconsiderate beings, selfish tyrants and tramplers on human rights." At the conclusion they "tried to look pleased, as if virtue at last had triumphed." Fola read all nine parts in voices ranging from the deep bass of the male protagonist to the soft tones of a woman character afraid to vote because of the novelty. She found the listeners of both sexes unusually unresponsive at that particular reading. Perhaps they were unaware that laughter was permissible, much less expected.[25]

For much of the first half of 1910 Fola worked the "good cause" lecture circuit and learned its peculiar expectations and hazards. In Boston she had to stop four times for latecomers to seat themselves, and to step outside at least once to find chairs for them. At Brown University, in Providence, she got a possibly ironic "Miss La Follette, rah, rah, rah!" from the boys. In Alexandria she shared a church pulpit with a speaker denouncing child labor. At one scheduled performance in Canton, Ohio, nobody showed up, and at another in Sioux Falls, South Dakota, she observed that most of the forty to fifty listeners were friends or relatives of Old Bob. She came to dread well-meaning committees of welcome who left her no time for baths or naps. "It's very nice of people to be so cordial," was her lament, "but it's worse than playing two performances a day. I not only have to play . . . but talk to all the audience."[26]

Nevertheless, by the summer's end Fola had found her niche. In the ensuing half dozen years she did a great deal of speaking and performing for suffrage, and she also worked up at least one set of readings called "Social Forces in Modern Drama," which she took on the Chautauqua platform nationally.[27] These became the sum of her "stage" appearances. Whatever her original goals had been, her artistry would thenceforward have a specific progressive-educational focus, like the "declamations" that her mother and father had been taught a generation earlier. Her days of being a novelty, a feature story—the senator's daughter as struggling young artist —were behind her. She was a through-and-through La Follette.

Early in the autumn she came home to Maple Bluff to rest and to be helpful in a family health crisis. Doctors at the Mayo Clinic in Rochester, Minnesota, had tracked some of Bob's continual digestive trouble to gallstones and scheduled an operation for the first week in October. Belle accompanied him there soon after his primary election victory and after the surgery took him out to California for a brief convalescence.

Once the immediate danger was over, Fola could relax and enjoy the natural beauty around her. She wrote to a young dramatist and friend in New York, George Middleton: "These are wonder days. Such a mad cap riot of color I've never seen. Indian summer in this Wisconsin country is an experience. It can't be told about, only shared, and I should like to share it with you." If Middleton should find himself with a few free days to spend at the farm (which he did not) she would be happy to see him. In any case, she concluded, "I do hope that these days are dealing generously with you, and that all goes happily."

Fola spent the early part of November in Chicago doing more readings and taking lessons from Mrs. Baker. She was due back in New York on November 19 for a few weeks, before joining the family in Washington for Christmas. She informed Middleton of these plans and again suggested a hope that "you may find a loose hour when you can and will feel inclined to play with me."[28]

At that moment, ironically, she was presented with her big Broadway chance, a major role in Percy MacKaye's *The Scarecrow,* slated to open on January 18. MacKaye was Fola's kind of dramatist. His father, Steele MacKaye, had been a theatrical renaissance man—designer and builder of playhouses and stage machinery, teacher, actor, writer, and publicist. The son himself was a staunch advocate of serious stage work for popular audiences. His play, based on a Hawthorne short story, was a Pygmalion-like meditation on love and artifice. The devil and a witch endow a scarecrow with life and successfully pass off their cornhusk creation as the son of a respectable judge. In Hawthorne's version the emphasis is on the gullibility of society for trappings. MacKaye shifted the focus when he had his scarecrow fall in love with a young woman named Rachel (played by Fola) and so learn to be vulnerable, hurt, and human. While it is still to be found in anthologies, *The Scarecrow* had only a brief run, and the critical judgment on Fola was the inevitable fatal pat on the head: "Miss La Follette was a pretty and attractive little heroine." So she was delivered finally to the lecture platform.[29]

By that time, however, this setback to her footlight dreams had considerably lost its power to hurt Fola, for she was seriously in love with, and planning to marry, George Middleton. Their courtship would open still another perspective for her on what her family meant in her life.

FOLA IN LOVE

"I was all choked and trembly"

Middleton was thirty, an altogether pleasant and multifaceted man. He came of a "good" New Jersey family, which fostered the literary interests of himself and his brother Scudder, who became a published poet. But there was a fascinating dark side. Their father was, in George's recollection, what the 1880s called a sport. At least some of his income came from bookmaking at horse races and perhaps other gambling events. His philosophy of life was that "the world is only interested in the winners." George himself could not have missed the irony in having such a father and then, later in life, a father-in-law who was the prototypical principled loser.

His mother must have had a strong sense of theater, though her casting was open to question. One day she found a letter setting up a rendezvous between her philandering husband and another woman. She kept the discovery to herself. Then she sent little George to the appointed spot. When his father arrived, the boy innocently handed him the incriminating letter, as instructed, with a note attached from Mrs. Middleton: "This is proof of your infidelity." George Middleton did not describe the sequel in his autobiography, but the incident neither traumatized him nor, when he came to understand it, set him against his father. If anything, the whispered gossip and disapproving looks that he observed gave him a basic sympathy for "moral outcasts" that was useful to a budding dramatist.

He loved the many "shows" available in the New York of his boyhood, in playhouses and music halls, in the streets themselves, in places like the Polo Grounds where hard-fought baseball games between the Giants and their rivals taught him about climaxes and tensions better than whole volumes of criticism. He got his book learning at Columbia, where he was a star student of Brander Matthews, the first professor of dramatic literature to be named as such in an American university. Three months after commencement in 1902 George was helping a journeyman playwright named George Kester to adapt a short story by George Washington Cable for stage presentation.

It was the start of a nonsinful double life. Fluent in French, he read and translated continental classics (his special passion was Balzac) and kept up with the intellectual ferment in the European and English theatrical worlds. And with the other hand, more or less, he earned his living by hackwork collaboration on commercial scripts. Soon he was a successful yong member of the Players Club. With his club manners, his eastern clothes, and his eyeglasses, he naturally seemed to Senator La Follette, when first they met, to be an airy literary dude.

Fola and her family came into his life when he met her at a tea around the time of Lincoln Steffens's articles on the senator. "Are you the daughter of?" he asked, and she admitted it "a bit wearily." They became friends but no more. In the spring of 1908 George made his first trip abroad. He went to London where he met Shaw and Pinero, and then on to Paris where he had arranged a meeting with an unnamed American woman with whom he was in love. The setting was perfect—youth, infatuation, Paris in the spring—but life refused to follow the script. The affair did not work out, and a steamer brought him back home, frustrated and unhappy, on a June morning in 1908 just in time to read of Old Bob's filibuster against the Aldrich-Vreeland bill. The reporter noted that Fola was in the gallery. That brought her back into Middleton's life. Three years later they were married. "So much," he wrote after they had lived happily together for almost three decades, "for the mutations of emotion."[30]

The relationship erupted into love in the four weeks from late November to early December of 1910 that Fola spent in New York. She had to go back to the Midwest on December 19 for a week-long reading tour of Chicago and its hinterland, and by then letters were streaming in both directions. She received three of his when she checked into her Chicago hotel. "Dear, dear heart," she told him, "you don't know how hungrily, how shamelessly I [clamored?] for the clerk at the desk to find them . . . I don't understand the thing that is happening within me," she continued. "Occasionally I steal from out myself and watch Fola and I don't know her. The madcap tempestuous Fola who has surprised me so often now completely overwhelms me. I wouldn't have thought it possible that I should have waited so eagerly for those letters. I was all choked and trembly with the thought of them . . . I lingered before opening each one and then stole within your arms to read it—you didn't know it but I was there."

Middleton had awakened Fola to a first torrent of yearning to embrace someone outside the family, and in so doing had confronted her with inner doubts that never made it into her letters home. "Do you understand," she asked, "when I say at times there is a great terror on me and yet I fear nothing with you? The last little ragged shreds of fear you have taken from me. I'll walk all day with you through woods that are not dark but quiet, and over the highways that with all their dust only speak of thirst for tears . . . and be unafraid if it is you who look down at me."

It is impudent, unfair, and a little voyeuristic to read too much into the private love letters of a young woman with a theatrical bent. All the same, it is surprising to hear a usually ebullient Fola speak of terrors, dark woods, and dusty roads. Like her father's youthful night thoughts and despairs, or Belle's moments of panic, they were the other side of the family's courage and optimism. Father, Mother, and children all had what Fola elsewhere called "intense natures," and they all paid a price for disciplining their demons.

Perhaps they were fears of admitting any man to intimacy. If so, Middleton had decisively unlocked a gate that at least one before him had tried without success. On that very night in Chicago, Fola told him, she was going to *Tales of Hoffmann* with "a man who has followed my path for some seven years . . . and every few months he comes back for another refusal. This I think I can make the last and still be honest to him." She did, and wrote Middleton so when she got back from the theater after midnight. She was now all his. "I can't explain it . . . I'm accepting it with an open and mystified heart . . . Take me close in your dream and tell me good night as I do you."

His letters to her, in a virtually indecipherable handwriting, matched her own frankness in confessing his worries about writer's block and other hazards of the dramatist's trade. But they also reassured her of his strength in a way that let her relax into the conventional pose of the yielding maiden. "Dear, you make it so easy for me to turn to you with freedom, simply and without self-consciousness," she scribbled by the light of a feeble bulb in one rural hotel. "My memory of each close moment we've had is clear and vibrant, touched with fresh life and light and beauty . . . [W]here life leaps together so, there can be no self consciousness. Delicacy, yes, and that you have so inherently with all your masterful man[li]ness—your six feet and your broad breast—that I turn to you simply—unafraid and alive. Take me so and let me go on caring and drawing closer . . . Hold me tenderly and fiercely. Goodnight. I live my life on yours."[31]

"Be patient with me," she asked a few days later. "I want my giving to be strong and beautiful and joyful, but in part I must be the pupil." She might have meant any number of things, including initiation into physical love, but George's patience was actually to be tested long before the door of the bedroom was reached. For Fola's surrender had special limitations, as he learned almost immediately after receiving his first batch of her passionate confessions of love. He expected naturally that she would rush back to him in New York. It was not to be so; she was going to Washington for Christmas with the family. Of course, he reasoned, but love could find a way. He would go there. And this proposal, too, was firmly rejected.

He should have been warned earlier that wooing a La Follette would pose unusual requirements. Fola told him that anything he sent to her at home had best be marked "Personal" if he didn't care to have it become clan property.

My family sometimes opens letters which they think may be business letters when I'm away and I'd take no chances. A curious difference we have in our household. I have a perfect horror of opening other people's letters, always feeling it may intrude on the writer even though I know the recipient would be willing. But it's a "feel" that we've always differed about and that I've labored in vain to make clear to them. Not that they would ever read a letter they knew I didn't want them to, you understand—but it's just that it seems unimportant and they don't want me to miss engagements. I am always more or less the little girl to them.[32]

Middleton must have protested that he did not want to invade the La Follette hearthside, but merely be in Washington to squire his girl socially.

121

But Fola would not allow it. "[Y]our being there in the way I would want it—going and coming freely and our doing things together, which would interrupt the family's scheme of things—that might implant a subtle element of friction and we don't want that when another time it could be so different." So he had to be contented with her long, mailed description of the revels around the tree that "little Mary" had decorated. The custom was for a strictly private Christmas Eve celebration at which each member received some "foolish little gift." "Being a blonde actress," Fola got a horn shaped like a champagne bottle that made a "wild and ribald noise." Old Bob was given a pop gun. And, with the children leading, they held a parade through the house with Fola tooting, Father solemnly shooting his gun, and Mother "dancing along like a rollicking girl." That was followed by the theatrics always essential to the collective La Follette *persona;* the two boys did imitations of celebrated virtuosos. Finally, the children retired, and the three adults put their "serious" presents under the tree for next morning.

"Some day I want you to have a Christmas like this with me," Fola promised Mid, to console him as he was held at arm's length. "I think the *kinder's* joy would delight the playfellow in you."[33]

But not yet. She was wise enough to know that announcing her plans at home would be difficult. But she was not prepared for the explosion she provoked.

"Don't feel I'm leaving you"

Silence has its own importance. Fola had always been quick to share her enthusiasm over such inspiring figures as "Mrs. Baker" or "Mr. Reiman" with the family, but her new feelings clearly went unmentioned at the Christmas rendezvous, and there was no hint at its end that anyone was sharing her love for Bob and especially Belle. She wrote to Belle of "what a tug it was" to leave her after that visit, and in terms more reverent than the usual "bestest-little-mother" effusions. "Every day as I grow in understanding I learn how much more wonderful you are . . . Sometimes you seem to transcend the reach of mere mortals to me and to stand somewhere in the Beyond—a promise of the Superwoman that is to be." Possibly telegraphing what was on her mind, she went on to a declaration whose final phrase was somewhat cryptic. "I love you mother darling in a way there isn't any telling or writing of, with a love that is so of and in me that there isn't any loosening it even for a moment of expression to come."[34]

But not until March 10 did she break the news of what was "to come" with studied casualness. "For some time I've been wanting to tell you, but I haven't wished to harrow you with any possibilities until they became certainties. I'm in love, which might not be at all serious as it has happened before, but I'm going to marry George Middleton which is serious and hasn't happened before."

There were "some facts," she continued, that meant nothing to her but "I fear may be very hard for you" which "makes my joy three parts pain." She was referring to his father's occupation, about which Mid would write directly. She hoped that Belle and Bob would respond with "the same generous love you've always given me." She tried to anticipate any further objections by explaining that it was not a "sudden romantic spasm," but that they had "been together" for a long time off and on in the past. They would be as poor as the "proverbial church mice" unless and until one or the other was successful, but there was no point in waiting as "we'd both rather be unwise together than prophets apart." They were old enough to know their own minds. Fola wanted neither a trousseau nor a formal wedding, merely a simple ceremony with immediate family in attendance. "Until then, dearest ones," she ended, "hold me in your love and don't feel I'm leaving you but that I am bringing someone to you and hoping with all my heart that one day you'll both be glad."

Belle read this letter at the dinner table next day and rushed immediately to her desk, showing it to no one. She did not even want to hear the discomfiting "facts" mentioned by Fola. Her pen raced feverishly to keep up with the tumult of her emotions. "I have just read your letter and a great fear is on me. It is not for myself. It is for you. You can not know how I dread to say it. Yet I feel I must *now at once*—before anything comes from him that you might think had influenced my judgment. I have never *trusted* him—there is a *false* note that I have always been conscious of. He is brilliant. He probably loves you. But oh my beloved first born all I can say, all I can ask is *wait*. Do not deny me this."

She and Bob had already spoken of Middleton. "I know his distrust is deeper seated than mine," she warned (though in fact Bob's own family letters nowhere mention the marriage). And after tossing through the night she began another letter with the same fear-ridden outburst. "My head is hot and my throat is dry. I can not think. I can only *feel* and it is to me as though I saw you in some great peril from which I am powerless to rescue you." And she revealed the distrust of the actor's life, the sense of Fola's failure, that she had convinced herself rationally to swallow until then.

Oh Fola my beloved child, it has been wrong for you to be cut off from the real world. The disappointments you have had professionally have made you long for sympathy and Middleton has been the one to give it to you. I have always trusted your judgment. It has seemed hard to me that you should never have, in any of your attachments, had one *worthy* but I have said Fola will not be misled—she has the right standards. She will not marry one who does not measure up with *men.*

Like the most conventional of small-town mothers, Belle was reproaching her daughter, between the lines, for not yet marrying the right kind of man and for living a tinsel existence. In a third letter, sent within another few hours, she added an even more old-fashioned objection—that Fola had told them, not asked them. The issue wasn't whether Fola was old enough to know her mind, Belle insisted. "[I]f I had been as old as I am now and my mother were living . . . I do not think I could have written her that I had *decided.* I should have talked it over with her first . . . In your determined attitude, Fola, you shut your father and me out." Then she returned to the high ground of principle. Fola had never said that Middleton was "good or noble or strong" or endowed with "these essential things of manhood and womanhood according to all that you and I and your father and I hope the children may hold to though every thing else fall." She ended groping for hypothetical horrors. Suppose, in order to escape poverty, Middleton were forced to write trash; how could Fola face her own children? "I do not see how an experienced man who *really* loves you . . . could ask it."[35]

Fola had clearly anticipated some of this reaction but couldn't help answering with a cry of pain of her own. She hadn't answered Belle's letters at first because "they hurt me so I couldn't think, I could only feel." These were almost Belle's exact words, and the nearly identical outbursts show how much both mother and daughter struggled to control their emotions. The strongest admission of distress was to admit that one could "only *feel.*" But from then on, Fola worked valiantly and well at being reasonable herself while appealing to Belle's sense of fairness. "I did hope and believe so surely that you would be willing—no, that you would *want* to know or try to know Mid before you condemned him," she argued, "even when you knew the facts . . . [but] now I find you feel certain of his unworthiness without knowing them and with only having met him a few times." As for the possibility that the player's life had warped her ability to judge men, Fola's response expressed once again her conviction that there was a connection between her goals and Bob's: "You say it is wrong for me to have been cut off from the 'real world.' Dear one this is my 'real world.'

. . . All my dreams are there dear and my hope of usefulness or of happy service in work are in the theater. And dreams like that are very real. Else how could father have built the fine things he has in a world which seems so full of ugliness to most people outside." She explained in illustration that at that very moment she was rehearsing in a one-act play, *Three Women,* by the feminist writer and lecturer Charlotte P. Gilman, to be given at a suffrage benefit, the kind of "theater" to which Fola's world was swiftly narrowing.

The overall tone was conciliatory. "Dear ones, I love him," Fola pleaded. "[Y]ou seem almost to have forgotten that—and oh, how I love you—can't all that, put together, bring a feeling that you are willing to withhold this awful certainty?" She wanted to run down to Washington immediately, between rehearsals, to talk it out. Belle, slightly mollified, suggested that they wait a couple of days until there was more time, and "perhaps we shall all be able to understand each other better than now." But she repeated that she wanted Fola to slow down and be certain, and failure to do that much "would break my heart." Fola did show up soon after, but Belle could not yet bring herself to discuss the matter, so the visit was empty and inconclusive.[36]

There were short-term reasons for the vehemence of Belle's reaction. The year 1910 had been hard for her, what with the financial and other strains of getting the *Weekly* under way, Bob's surgery, her father's illness, the Wisconsin campaign, and the inevitable strains of mothering, at the age of fifty-one, two "little boys" who had suddenly become adolescent males with minds of their own. The national campaign taking shape promised only more stress and solitary responsibility. Beyond that were the underground anxieties that shifted and rumbled and shook her best resolves to be a progressive woman. She was frightened for Fola in curiously traditional ways. Despite four healthy pregnancies and deliveries, she thought of childbirth as an "ordeal" through which nature carried the mother "without any apparent permanent injury." She was revolted by the thought that the hidden "facts" about Middleton concerned another woman or women. And however much in theory she endorsed Fola's work, she thought it should not be counted on to sustain the couple. A modern woman, she explained, "must live, as it were, poised ready to take flight but also ready to accept what comes . . . [U]nless she can see happiness in life without a career for herself it seems to me she is not ready."[37]

Belle, in the end, had been jolted into Victorian fears of her daughter endangered in childbed, or stuck with a philandering or nonsupportive husband. The shock had churned up the strong emotions with which she was ill at ease. "Oh, Fola," she wrote when the crisis was in its second week, "words are so poor at best and you know your mother is least able to express herself when she feels most." Within Belle, the believer in independent womanhood and progressive childrearing, a raging voice was demanding that she not let go of her twenty-eight-year-old little girl.

Fola understood. She made a point of being rational, of getting the discussion off the emotional plane where the La Follettes were most truly themselves and yet most in danger of making bad judgments. In answering Belle she said that she had been "heartbroken" by their failure to trust her. Instead of welcoming her love in the hope that she had found the right man, they had shown "a *certainty* that he was the wrong man." And yet, all the same, "I came home to see you so you would *feel* my lack of anger. I longed to talk it over with you both, but I know, with intense natures like ours, that no understanding is gained unless all hearts and minds are open."[38]

In the end, Belle came back to earth, helped by the intervention of friends. She made a trip to Wisconsin to hire a caretaking family for Maple Bluff, and somewhere en route met Lincoln Steffens. Both of them shared their grief over the recent death of Tom Johnson. Then, when she unburdened herself to the kindly "Steff" about the hated engagement, he could not believe that she had rebuffed Fola's efforts to talk matters through face to face. "He seemed to feel," Belle admitted contritely to Fola, "I did not love you or sympathize with you as I should . . . He said you were suffering and needed our help. Well, it cuts deep to think I may not seem to meet this great crisis in your life with largest possible helpfulness."

In Madison old friend Alf Rogers also spoke up on Fola's behalf. Aunt Lu, too, reassured Belle of her daughter's basic good sense, and Aunt Emily took it on herself to relay the information that the evil secret about Middleton's father was simply that he was a gambler. She, Bishop, who was on the scene, also reported that Middleton was "clean," his love sincere, his associations blameless, and his interest in good literature serious and well informed. Belle finally told Fola that the information about the elder Middleton was "a great relief," and that if George, "in spite of the handicap of his father's occupation himself led an honorable life . . . that is all we can ask. The rest is for you and him to determine." Thereafter her reservations began to dwindle, though Belle's uneasiness over Middleton's style took time to conquer. As late as September she was writing to Bunkie Evans: "He has a superficial manner that has always made him seem remote from our kind."[39]

The chapter was not quite closed at the end of April 1911. Fola had held the line against the family in refusing to give up Middleton. Now she would show her lover that a La Follette spouse required special qualities of self-abnegation. Her promise to her parents "that I am bringing someone to you" had not been an idle one.

"Curious dominances and contradictory freedoms"

She did not rush into his arms. She returned to New York in May, after a trip to Wisconsin and Illinois to testify in their state legislatures against proposed laws to prevent children from working on stage. (She didn't consider it to be child labor, against which all good progressives set their faces.) While back in the city there were at least two occasions when George came calling unexpectedly and she did not feel dressed enough to receive him. At the close of the month she hit him with a double bombshell. She was going to spend part of June visiting friends on Cape Cod, go to Washington where "Daddy" was preparing a major speech and Mother needed her, and on June 28 sail to Europe for two months with Bertha Kunz Baker. Baker had suggested that Fola accompany her, and Bob and Belle had very willingly agreed to finance the trip which would, naturally, postpone any wedding plans.[40]

She would sandwich in a few days in New York, but George could not count on much time with her as there were many things to do. To his objections she answered: "You see the whole meaning of my life has been adjustment to the unexpected and inevitable plans of other people and so it's come to be almost second nature to me that when things have to be done they have to be done. More and more I realize what a strange household I have lived in with its curious dominances and contradictory freedoms."[41]

"Curious dominances and contradictory freedoms" perfectly describes her experiences within the bosom of the family, but George was understandably disturbed at being excluded from the "other people" whose unexpected plans could move Fola on the chessboard. She was about to vanish without him for nearly an entire summer, and what was more, she would not even consent to an engagement. The discussion between the lovers over the ensuing weeks has to be reconstructed from the sole evidence of her letters, and they make it clear that she managed him masterfully. Against his greater worldly experience and writer's persuasiveness, she pitted a beloved woman's skill in putting him in the wrong while eagerly professing that she was entirely his.

If her love was genuine, he asked her, how could she stand the fierce physical frustration of such a long postponement of their union? (Premarital sex was plainly not an option.) "Dearest one," she responded, "no matter what I suffered from passion I would not marry just to soothe that ache . . . Dear, of course I feel it and suffer from it—you are not alone there, but I can't feel that it is a true answer." After which came the pouting little reproach. "For some days my heart was quiet, but you have called it in beside the hearth of questionings again and it aches."

Then at least, he demanded, let their plans be made public. He wanted to share his happiness; the concealment was driving him into depression. Her response was all radiant innocence and moral one-upmanship: "Dearest . . . My heart aches for all your suffering . . . I try . . . to understand your feeling—the wishing the world to know that you may have the joy of being envied, and all that—that it isn't to bind me in any way but only to have it in the open—but dear it is all a language I don't understand, the joy in the envy of others." She was the constant image of serenity and cheer, though she did confess surprisingly, one night in May, to "an ugly mood" that "six lusty drinks" did nothing to dispel.

He protested that Fola was permitting her parents to buy a few months of delay with a European trip, and she responded in a "how could you?" vein. Her taking their money to go abroad no more implied a deal than if they had given her some new clothes; her only obligation to them was "one of love . . . of a feeling I have for them that makes me wish them to understand." She promised that understanding was on the way; in June, after she got back from the Cape, she and Daddy had talked it over. She told him that George was in her life to stay, and after her return she wanted him to come down to Washington "and be in and out of the house and grow into a more natural relation." Daddy had drawn her head down on his shoulder and said: "'Why of course, daughter, that's the way it must be. If this is to be a part of your life it must be of all our lives.'" Wasn't it wonderful, Fola asked George, that "it had come at last to him of himself rather than through our forcing an issue?"

George was understandably less enthused. What about his coming to Washington, he asked, and making his case for an engagement now to the senator, man to man. Ah, no, Fola countered, "it would be most unwise . . . The whole household is tense with nervous preparation for Dad's speaking Friday night. It would lose everything which our quiet waiting has done up to now."[42]

And off she went to Europe for a wonderfully progressive tour. She attended suffrage meetings in London, had a reunion with Steffens there, and got to meet English labor leaders and socialists John Burns and James Keir Hardie. "I wished so that Dad could be meeting these men," she wrote to Belle. "I think it would refresh and inspirit him." A dock strike was looming that would force a change in plans for herself and Mrs. Baker but that was all right as "[t]hey certainly must be realizing the power of united labor in the British kingdom just now."

And there was theater, of course—Shaw's *Fanny's First Play* in London, and over in Munich a revival of Aeschylus's *Orestes* cycle staged by Max Reinhardt with huge choruses of nonprofessionals—"a perfectly thrilling movement," according to Fola, "this effort to bring the drama back into the life of the whole people." Because of the strike she did not get to Dublin to see some of the brilliant work of the Abbey Theater in performing nationalistic works by William Butler Yeats and John Millington Synge. The trip confirmed her sense of linkage between socially conscious theater and political awakening, both parts of a new age fizzing around her.

There was a standard visit to Stratford where, at vespers in Shakespeare's church, she was repelled by the Anglican service, the "doleful, droning music" and the "solemn admonition of the worthy vicar to be humble and content with the universe as it is." She wrote to George that during the same sermon she had whiled away boredom by looking at the marriage service and found it "a sanction to lust."[43]

Fola also reassured George over and over of her unswerving love. "I can't tell you . . . the longing to reach out and touch you" she said on the outgoing vessel. On the banks of the Avon, watching the gliding swans, she felt "peace all about except in my heart and that was crying out for you all the while." She made shy promises to thrill and torment a man in waiting: "My heart is yours in trust and so my body shall grow to be . . . Dear, dear heart I miss you so. I want you and I want to be with you and for the privilege I can almost face the institution of marriage with all its steam whistles . . . I'll always flinch at some of them—those society blows off—but I'll walk past, dear, with you." She expected to return on September 10—her twenty-ninth birthday—"and then, if the gods are kind I shall be in your arms again and feel you close to me."

And she did so feel him—for a day or two after getting back to New York. Then she went straight and unerringly to Washington, commanding him very specifically to stay where he was. Belle and Bob were moving back into Washington quarters for the fall. Things would be far too upset for even an affianced guest. Middleton's feelings can only be surmised, particularly when Fola rebuffed even his simple request to come and stay at a hotel. She said she couldn't give him a minute of her time; Mother would be working at housecleaning like a slave, and Fola would find it impossible not to help. "I'll tell you a specific time just the minute I can, dearest," was her final promise. "If it hadn't been for the damned cleaning it would have been simple and easy; you could have been here a week ago." And for the balance of September the letters of Fola, the independent, petted and pleaded with her great big man. "Be tender with me in the transplanting until I grow accustomed to life in the new garden."[44]

And yet for all of the delay, the final curtain fell on a wedding scene, and they did live happily (and childlessly) ever after. Or at least until Middleton's death in his eighties. He deserves a good deal of credit for reconciling himself to Fola's leadership in 1911, and for the way in which he finally stepped into the demanding role of husband to "Miss La Follette"— the name she always kept. He was a genuinely mature and sophisticated man who loved her and was gallantly committed to the goals of his highly political in-laws. At the same time he had a broad streak of tolerance that allowed for the human attractiveness and sincerity of people on the other side of a question—something that came hard to born La Follettes. He was a good and willing recruit to their causes. One of Fola's letters had contained an insightful enclosure, a copy of *La Follette's Weekly Magazine* with his attention directed particularly to Belle's page and a suggestion that he think of ways in which he might "help out." He took the suggestion and swiftly became the magazine's book and drama critic, which gave him a chance to demonstrate the requisite seriousness to Belle and to correspond with her directly. "The spirit of your letter was very dear," ran her reply to his first contact, "and I appreciate it. You and Fola must make your plans and whatever is your happiness will be ours." His skillful wooing got even better results later. "Indeed you may call me Mater or Mitter or Mother," Belle allowed after the marriage had taken place. "I like it."[45]

The ceremony of October 29 was a quiet family affair in the La Follette home with George's mother but not his father present. The short press release simply identified Middleton as "a well known young dramatist." The minister was a "nice, liberal, humorous-minded yet kindly gentleman," as Fola informed the groom beforehand. "He never uses *obey* in the service or 'thee with all my worldly goods.'" The newlyweds moved into a three-room apartment on West 12th Street in Manhattan. It had steam heat, electric lights, and a telephone, and cost forty-one dollars a month.

"Mid is so dear, mother," Fola bubbled, "and we are very, very happy."[46] And so she was. Love had, for once, conquered all. Marriage, even to so flexible a husband as Mid, would change Fola, as would life in general. The couple would shortly be involved in a "village scene" that modified her inherited views and practices. But at Christmastime in 1911 this was still ahead, and the sweet air was full of promise as Senator Bob's campaign and the express trains of progressive politics raced ahead on parallel tracks.

5

Transition Time:
The Family Completed
(1912–1916)

SENATOR LA FOLLETTE:
FROM CANDIDATE TO CONSCIENCE

"The scurrying feet of the stage hands"

The roadblocks that George Middleton had run into on the way to membership in the La Follette clan were partly the result of unfortunate timing. His engagement to Fola took place when the senator's nerves and resources were stretched to the limit by an open drive for the nomination at the Republican convention of 1912, some nine months in the offing.

For a brief and glorious moment it seemed that success was possible. But 1912 was to tell a different story. La Follette's presidential hopes were soon shattered by another man's ambition, by his own undiscriminating zeal, and by even broader forces stalking American history. The Progressive movement had its climax and turning point in 1912. Its center of gravity shifted away from the rescue of popular government from privilege and corruption and toward a redefinition of nationalism, national purpose, the nation's role in defining or promoting economic justice at home and influencing the current of events abroad. These last were not themes that La Follette had sounded. His roots were in the wave of moral indignation over inequality that ran through late nineteenth-century political protest. His voice was becoming that of a generation starting to move off into the wings.

132

The future would belong to those reformers who accepted, first of all, the new America rising around them. The signs of it were everywhere in such cultural and economic indicators as billion-dollar corporations, a navy fit for an empire, a national labor federation, thousands of automobiles on the roads, the growing telephone network, chain newspapers and retail stores, and motion pictures. So it was that when La Follette had his fling at candidacy, he was in effect taken up on the mountain for a view of the promised land of presidential leadership and then cast down to play a new part, not that of a Moses but of a prophet, speaking timeless (and usually ignored) truths about the meaning of free government.

The official kickoff was on October 16, 1911, when a conference of three hundred progressive Republicans from thirty states met in Chicago in answer to a call by Walter L. Houser, Wisconsin's secretary of state and Bob's campaign manager. The participants were the cream of the anti-Taft movement boiling furiously within Republican ranks. They unanimously adopted resolutions declaring that the record of La Follette made him "the logical candidate" for the presidency.[1]

But there was a shadow over the unanimity, and it had the unmistakable shape of the cartoon figure of Theodore Roosevelt, complete with Big Stick, Rough Rider hat, and flashing teeth. Still, it was not certain then that the shade would materialize into a flesh-and-blood candidate in the campaign for which the fiddles were tuning up and the partners being chosen. What *was* certain was that Taft would not be renominated without a fight, and that was La Follette's opportunity, especially if Roosevelt did not enter the contest. William Allen White wrote a special dispatch to the *New York Times* saying as much in plain English. "Wall Street sees that Taft cannot win . . . Wall Street's feet are so cold that its toes clink . . . La Follette sentiment is growing . . . Something must be done to stop La Follette's rise as Taft sinks. Something will be done. The scurrying feet of the stage hands behind the curtain foretell coming events."[2]

Bob would have appreciated the theatrical metaphor, and he was desperately at work preparing for his lead role when the curtain rose. Fola's wedding was a mere momentary distraction. Less than a week later, at a banquet in Taft's front yard in Ohio, Bob listened as Minnesota Senator Moses Clapp, one of La Follette's fellow insurgents, blasted "the reactionary leaders and champions of special privilege within his own party." The speakers' stage held pictures of Lincoln, Garfield, McKinley, Roosevelt — and La Follette, whose name was wildly cheered. Very quickly thereafter La Follette was set up for a busy December speaking tour to begin the hunt for delegates. He was excited and hopeful. "I believed we could do nationally with the Republican Party what we did with it in Wisconsin" was his later admission.[3]

It seemed possible, as insurgent speakers fanned out across the country. On a tour of the Far West, Clapp was stopped in mid-speech in Salt Lake City by an outburst of cheers at La Follette's name. George Norris was certain that his own Nebraska and Minnesota would go for La Follette by huge margins. Senator John D. Works of California, speaking at Los Angeles, predicted a close fight between Taft and La Follette. Gilson Gardner, political correspondent for the Scripps newspaper chain, reported after a swing through a farm belt infuriated by Taft's reciprocal trade policies: "If the rest of the country feels anything like this Northwest, it is a landslide. Taft can't get the nomination."[4]

Off-year elections in Ohio confirmed the onrushing energy of the reform tide. In Cleveland and Toledo progressive mayors Newton D. Baker and Brand Whitlock were swept into office, and progressives also won the majority of seats in a constitutional convention set for 1912. The magazines were filled with pieces that outlined a new agenda for politics: public health campaigns against tuberculosis and other diseases, workmen's compensation, improved juvenile courts, safer mines, cleaner tenements, pure food, battles against prostitution and the saloon. "Look now across the country," Ray Stannard Baker wrote. "Scores of cities have now adopted the new commission form of government . . . In the States a similar movement has been going forward. No fewer than nineteen governors out of the forty-six can be called militant progressives fighting for the new era. In no less than twenty-five legislatures the radicals hold the balance of power in either one or both of the houses. As to the National Government, [*sic*] . . . [n]ot two years ago Aldrich and Cannon and all that they stood for were in absolute control of Congress. Today, even in the last session of the old Congress, there are about forty members of the House of Representatives who may be called genuine progressives; and a dozen or more of the Senators." The country was seething, and Republican men and women battling for various reform causes would gladly look to an aggressive La Follette presidency that promoted their concerns to the national stage. With political weathervanes swinging in La Follette's direction, financial backing and political support would not be far behind.[5]

But there was still that shadow of Roosevelt. From his home in Oyster Bay, New York, he watched, theoretically neutral, as the anti-Taft movement threatened to turn into a La Follette boom. Not until the end of 1911 did he join the anti-Taft ranks and sound more and more like a prospective candidate himself. His thoughts in his early, above-the-fray period are still a matter for lengthy argument about contradictory pieces of testimony. Various memoirs tell different stories. One was that he approved the revolt against Taft but didn't want to widen a party split by taking sides. Another was that he would come out for the insurgents but back no particular leader to avoid charges of dictating to the party. Other versions had him eager to run but hobbled by the thought of attacking Taft, an old friend and his own 1908 choice for the succession.

La Follette himself—after it was all over—spent the rest of his life wedded to the most hostile view possible. Roosevelt, he insisted, had always intended to become a candidate, provided the "dump Taft" movement had a genuine chance. What was more, he quietly signaled his encouragement of a La Follette candidacy as a purely opportunistic way to test the strength of the revolt. Once La Follette had publicized the issues and collected enough pledges for a strong base, then he himself would move in. In his conceit Roosevelt was convinced that La Follette would step aside for him, recognizing that TR alone could win as a progressive Republican.[6]

Thus ran La Follette's version of the Roosevelt strategy. He said that he was on to the game and made it clear to Roosevelt that he was nobody's stalking horse. If he entered the race he was in it to stay and would never release his delegates to anyone. Especially not to the Colonel, who was, in his eyes, a sham progressive with no agenda but his own glorification.

Whatever the murky truth, two things are unmistakably clear. One is that many of Bob's early supporters—a glittering honor roll of progressivism including celebrated journalists, senators, governors, and publishers— were united as "Rooseveltians" who had "found life joyous when Roosevelt was in the W' : House, drab when he was out of it."[7] They would join La Follette in opposing Taft, but they would leave him the moment Roosevelt declared his candidacy (much as supporters of Robert F. Kennedy backing Eugene McCarthy in a "dump-Johnson" movement in 1968 followed their first loyalties as soon as Kennedy entered the primaries).

The second truth is that Roosevelt really was the stronger candidate in voter appeal in that dawning age of media politics. La Follette's base was still midwestern; Roosevelt's was national and even international. He had been a headline figure for at least a dozen years. He was among the first of presidents to make full and vigorous use of the enormous publicity-generating power of the office that he correctly called "a bully pulpit." And he had not been inconspicuous during the two years following his departure from the White House. In 1909 his game-slaughtering African safari had been an adventure story shared with the public. In 1910 in Europe, he had garnered degrees from Cambridge and Oxford universities, attended the funeral of Edward VII of England, dined with kings, and sat on horse-back at the side of Emperor Wilhelm reviewing the German army. His zesty physical exploits still delighted newspaper readers. His continuous stream of popular books and articles, plus weekly editorials in the *Out-look* (a magazine with a far larger circulation than *La Follette's Weekly*), gave regular expression to his informed, vigorous views on anything and everything. Though plenty of progressives were put off by his vanity and jingoism, or saw through to his basically conservative core, to millions he was still the embodiment of American vitality, idealism, and promise. As one reporter put it, "Roosevelt would be applauded for stoning his grandma."[8] If he decided to go after the nomination, Taft might still have a chance to beat him through regular control of the party machinery, as actually happened. But La Follette would be doomed.

He knew it. And he knew in many ways that it was coming, and it spread over his efforts in November and December—as Roosevelt edged closer to acknowledged candidacy—a miasma of anxiety. He felt as if he was being baited by Roosevelt's catlike waiting and it spurred him to in-crease his already hectic pace of activity. In December he was giving as many as three speeches a day and wrote to Gilbert Roe that "minutes are as diamonds." To other correspondents he reported that "I am . . . driven for every minute" and "I eat and sleep in the saddle these days." He an-swered a friendly invitation for a country weekend by saying, "For years all that sort of recreation has been crowded out of my busy life . . . For more than a year I have not had an hour at Maple Bluff." In addition to speechmaking, he was trying to keep up with his usual homework for the Senate session just beginning, and he faced strict copy deadlines for sec-tions of his autobiography.[9]

Meanwhile he and Roosevelt sparred through go-betweens. La Follette wanted the ex-president to clear the track by a definite withdrawal. Roose-velt would not do that; he seemed to suggest that he really would not run, but he wanted a statement that La Follette would support him just in case he should yield to the country's call and decide otherwise. There was ac-tually no chance of either adversary endorsing the other or even permit-ting joint slates of anti-Taft delegates in upcoming primary elections. But the mere fact of negotiation increased the stress on La Follette. He believed that people like Gilson Gardner, the Pinchot brothers, Illinois's Medill McCormick, and Ohio's James R. Garfield, his own Wisconsin associates Irvine Lenroot and Houser—all of whom were in frequent contact with the Colonel's people—were preparing to jump ship.

Either man might have been accused by objective onlookers of letting personal pique and vanity stand in the way of a united progressive front.

In La Follette's case his never-quite-slumbering sense of being the friendless underdog now broke through the restraints of political judgment. Given a chance to deliver a major campaign talk to an incomparably valuable audience, La Follette suffered an emotional collapse. He made a speech that was a media catastrophe, and in the space of two and a half hours destroyed his candidacy.

"My flunk at Philadelphia"

The story has been told many times, and no repetition can make it look better for La Follette.[10] The occasion was a banquet of the Periodical Publishers Association in Philadelphia on the night of February 2, 1912. It was a command performance for a declared candidate who would be addressing a table full of important opinion makers. That explains the presence both of La Follette and Woodrow Wilson. Taft and Roosevelt had been invited, but declined. The all-male guest list included Don Seitz, the publisher of the *New York World,* who was the toastmaster; Cyrus K. Curtis, whose publications included the *Saturday Evening Post* and *Ladies' Home Journal* as well as important Philadelphia dailies; John Phillips, publisher of *American* magazine, in whose sympathetic pages La Follette's autobiography had begun to run in installments; and virtually the whole editorial elite of the East Coast. Also on hand among the six hundred guests were notables like Admiral Peary and Alexander Graham Bell, writers like Owen Wister, Lincoln Steffens, and Ray Stannard Baker, and a good sprinkling of members of Congress.

La Follette's declared intention, he later said, was to speak as the publisher of *La Follette's Weekly Magazine* to fellow publishers and warn them that the growing centralization of control in the economy was beginning to infect newspapers and magazines, with damaging impact on honest debate. It was a theme entirely consistent with his insurgent record, and the speech, as later reprinted, was vintage La Follette in its thoroughness, with no surprises until close to the end.

I have sketched the growth and power of the great interests that to-day control our property and our governments . . . Rising up against them is the confused voice of the people. Their heart is true but their eyes do not yet see all the intricate sources of power. Who shall show them? . . .

One would think that in a democracy like ours, people seeking the truth, able to read and understand, would find the press their eager and willing instructors. Such was the press of Horace Greeley, Henry Raymond, Charles A. Dana, Joseph Medill, and Horace Rublee [of the *Milwaukee Sentinel*].

But what do we find has occurred in the past few years since the money power has gained control of our industry and government? It controls the newspaper press.

The people know this. Their confidence is weakened and destroyed. No longer are the editorial columns of newspapers a potent force in educating public opinion. The newspapers, of course, are still patronized for news. But even as to news, the public is fast coming to understand that wherever news items bear in any way upon the control of government by business, the news is colored; so confidence in the newspaper as a newspaper is being undermined.

Cultured and able men are still to be found upon the editorial staffs of all the great dailies, but the public understands them to be hired men who no longer express honest judgments and sincere conviction, who write what they are told to write, and whose judgments are salaried.[11]

Coupled with generous praise of muckraking magazines, it was a slap in the face to the newspapermen present, made worse by the fact, unknown to the senator, that the magazine publishers, in a special bid for harmony, had made them the honored guests of the evening. Even so, he might have escaped undamaged had his talk been brief and his manner reasonably gracious, as it often was. But that was not the case.

The La Follette of that night was at the ragged edge of total exhaustion. Besides the events of January, the long-range pressures of the campaign had been too much for him. "I have not had sleep enough in months," he told sister Josie afterward, and he was even more specific to his Madison friend Dr. George Keenan. He would go to bed between midnight and 2 A.M. and find himself unable to fall asleep for another hour or so. When he finally dozed off he would awaken in a little while and be unable to close his eyes again. By January's end he had begun to have constant, "dragging" headaches. Those hours of tossing in the darkness left his imagination too much time to play with new betrayals, enemies, and uncertainties. As the deadline for preparing his talk approached, Belle observed that he was "dreading" the dinner.

To top it off, twelve-year-old Mary was ill with infected glands in her neck and was scheduled for surgery in Washington to remove them on the morning after the speech. The serious operation would involve tricky work near the windpipe and major blood vessels (it actually took two hours and twenty minutes) and both parents were riven with anxiety.[12]

La Follette did not arrive at the Bellevue-Stratford in time to share the soup, roast lamb, sweet potatoes, peas, and frozen Boston pudding that the diners washed down with hot sherry and liqueurs. He took a late train from Washington, accompanied by Mid, John Hannan, and a few friends, and worked frantically *en route* marking cuts on the long rough draft of the speech, which there would be no time to retype. He ate nothing because he had been suffering from indigestion all day. At the hotel room reserved for him he drank a cup of hot chocolate and said it was "nauseating." Then, as was sometimes his custom when he was tired before a plat-form appearance, he threw a large shot of whiskey into his nearly empty stomach. Around 11 P.M. he walked down to the banquet hall, thick with cigar smoke, in time to hear the conclusion of a well-received off-the-cuff talk of some forty minutes by Wilson. Wilson had wisely abandoned his prepared script when he saw how late it had gotten.

La Follette should have done the same, but following his introduction, he made a gracious compliment—he hoped that if the next president had to be a Democrat Wilson would be the one—and got into instant trouble when he picked up his manuscript of fifty or sixty pages. Noticing the dismay of those immediately around him, he tried to explain and managed only to be insulting. "For fear there may be some here who will not report what I say correctly," he began, "I want to have a record."

It was all downhill from there, as the *Evening Bulletin* reported next day under the headline LA FOLLETTE JARS PUBLISHERS' FEAST BY 2½ HOUR TALK. Headachy, nauseated, possibly a little drunk, the man who was ordinarily a spellbinder totally lost audience contact. Trying to follow his own cuts and occasionally departing from the text to extemporize, he kept repeating himself and droned on in total disregard of the clock, meanwhile carrying on a running battle with the increasingly hostile banqueters. To some who were getting up to leave he shouted: "I have the floor; those that don't care to listen had better get out." Mocking answers were shouted to his rhetorical questions. When he described the march of monopoly and asked, "Is there a way out?" a voice called back, "We hope so." Eventually shouts of "Sit down" emerged from confusion "that took on the proportions of an uproar." Some time after 1 A.M. he collapsed back into his chair and sat mutely, head in hand, while Seitz got up and, in measured tones, apologized to the newspaper press for the "wicked, foolish and untruthful attack that has just been made upon it."

When the remaining speaker had finished, Woodrow Wilson, who had followed La Follette with sympathetic attention the whole time, chatted with him for a moment. So did John Phillips. Almost no one else spoke to him. In silence he took the elevator upstairs and immediately, as his loyal new son-in-law recalled, went into the bathroom to vomit. He barely acknowledged the presence of Steffens and Irvine Lenroot, who had come to console him, and left at once to catch a 4 A.M. train for Washington. There he would meet Belle, who had been at the hospital all night, just before the operation.

In the next few days he was condemned to read newspaper headlines that spoke of his "mental collapse" and his "breakdown." They sealed the doom of the already clouded candidacy, though the corpse would twitch and jerk through another few months. Seitz, still outraged on behalf of his profession, gave an interview in which he said that the senator "had simply wiped himself off the map." He believed that La Follette had been a temporary victim of "aphasia," the inability to articulate ideas in any form. Seitz seemed to have no political axe of his own to grind, and as a veteran lieutenant of Joseph Pulitzer was, if anything, usually inclined to side with hell-raisers. It didn't matter. His speculations were typical of those multiplying like bacteria in the press.[13]

The rumors were sinister. La Follette was desperately ill, he could not survive a campaign, he was in a sanitarium, he was "under restraint." He could spike these simply by showing himself in public, but he could not undo the damage that some of his associates, with or without malice afore-thought, committed in the seventy-two hours after the dinner. Houser, Gifford Pinchot, and others held two emergency meetings (without the senator) in Washington on Sunday. Out of them leaked tidings that La Follette was on the verge of getting out of the race. On Monday, February 5, a statement to that effect was drafted and taken by Lenroot, John Hannan (La Follette's secretary), and Houser to the La Follette home where, in Belle's approving presence, he declared that he would do no such thing. Nevertheless, Medill McCormick sent a wire to the Illinois Progressive Republican League, which the *Chicago Tribune* printed the next morning, to the effect that leaders of the anti-Taft movement everywhere had agreed that the time had come to unite in backing Roosevelt. On the same night George L. Record, a longtime La Follette backer, addressed a progressive rally in New Jersey with the electrifying news that he had been on the phone to Washington with Houser and that La Follette had definitely stepped aside in favor of "any other candidate" whom progressive Republicans might name; therefore, "we will be able to go into this fight under the united leadership of Theodore Roosevelt."[14]

Houser later denied saying anything so explicit, and either he misunderstood Record or one of them was lying. In any case, it was another stab to La Follette in the house of his friends, the very nightmare that haunted him. Dozens of backers leaped away in a matter of days. Even the conservative *New York Tribune* was shocked at the "haste with which most of the insurgent leaders are seeking to clamp the lid down on Senator La Follette's candidacy . . . He is being hustled ruthlessly inside the hearse."[15]

La Follette himself had recovered sufficiently by the morning of February 6 to size matters up. He wrote to Roe, "Since my flunk at Philadelphia, everybody here (outside of the immediate household) has been on my neck to force me out." To sister Josie he explained that his "mistake" at Philadelphia was in attempting to "compel" and "master" the audience outraged by his distasteful truths. His sense of persecution overflowed. "I am in a game where the cards are stacked and some 'friends' have a cold deck or two under the table."[16]

He ordered Houser to release a statement denying that he was quitting, but he also sensibly canceled speaking engagements for a while. "There is not a thing wrong with me," he assured Gilbert Roe, "excepting that I find myself dead tired. I think a couple of weeks spent mostly in sleeping will put me right." He put on a brave front for another friend. "I want to finish some literary work and also see this campaign, now that the deserters are weeded out, set going in a clean cut way. We propose to fight for delegates in Minnesota, North Dakota, South Dakota, Nebraska, Oregon and probably California . . . and before the convention meets in June the people of this country will understand the difference between the kind of progressives we are, and the sort that are ready to chase any old bandwagon." But the Roosevelt bandwagon was in high gear on the day after Washington's Birthday as the Colonel told reporters in the Cleveland railroad terminal, "My hat is in the ring, the fight is on and I am stripped to the buff."[17]

The next four months were filled with mingled sadness and irony. La Follette counted on support in those few states that had already provided for direct presidential primaries, the reform on which he had set his heart so unswervingly. He believed in them sincerely and without calculation. In November of 1911 he had written to Hiram Johnson, the progressive governor of California (one of his supporters who would desert to TR), urging him to push without fail a primary law in the upcoming legislative session. It would be dangerous because Taft had support in many parts of the state, and an honest vote might send a Taft delegation to Chicago. That would be "a very hard blow."

But, Governor, hard as it would be there is just one thing that ought to be and would be harder and indeed more harmful for us, and that would be to throw our principles to the dogs whenever an opportunity offers to gain a temporary advantage by so doing. If it would enable us to control the next national convention and the nomination for the presidency, we could not afford to do it . . . [So] put the presidential primary up to the very front . . . fight the reactionaries to the the last trench for the delegates . . .

If we stand for anything it is for a fundamental principle—the life, the soul of self-government. We can afford to be beaten, but we cannot compromise or juggle with the vital thing.[18]

Consistency in holding to "the vital thing" brought more heartbreak. On March 19, after a short campaign to spike rumors of his illness, La

Follette did beat Taft and Roosevelt in North Dakota in the first presidential preference primary ever held. Two weeks later he easily topped Taft in Wisconsin, where Roosevelt was not even on the ticket. But after that the weight of the colonel's wider exposure began to tell. La Follette lost to Roosevelt in Nebraska, Oregon, California, and Illinois, the other preferential primary states, as well as in all other contests he entered. He went into the convention where 540 votes would be needed to win with exactly 36 pledged to him.

The convention itself turned into a furious battle between Taft and Roosevelt forces, with party regulars in control of the committees that decided delegate contests. They awarded enough disputed seats to Taft supporters to give him a lock on the nomination. Roosevelt claimed fraud and instructed 344 of his own delegates to sit out the first ballot. Taft won it with 561 votes, after which Roosevelt bolted to form his own Progressive party.

Before that happened, however, his leaders made a last-minute effort to woo La Follette's delegates by supporting Francis McGovern, Wisconsin's governor (and a La Follette ally), for temporary chairman against a pro-Taft choice. La Follette was enraged at even the suggestion of a deal between himself and either one of the two main contenders. He had his manager, Houser, take the floor and bellow to the furthest reaches of the hall: "We make no deals with Roosevelt. We make no trades with Taft." McGovern lost on a slim vote, but La Follette never forgave him for agreeing to run nor Lenroot for later joining McGovern in supporting Roosevelt's third-party campaign. That resentment opened yet another serious rift among Wisconsin's progressive Republicans that led them to disastrous setbacks in 1914. The issues dividing McGovern and La Follette were deeper than the question of which presidential candidate to support. They were connected with the always ongoing question of how much control La Follette could, did, or should exercise over the development of independent progressive thinking in the state. But the rupture was one more disaster of Bob's dismal spring and summer.[19]

Debts continued to devour him. "I must cut off some of this drain or I will bleed to death," he told Alf Rogers, but he could not abandon the "magazine rat hole" because "[to] let loose of that now, in the midst of desertion and betrayal would be the end of everything and I'll die before I make such a finish." Even Belle's counsels were not enough to ward off the feeling of total isolation. "There is no one," he went on to Rogers, "*no one* with whom I can counsel. They have all stampeded . . . hounding me to . . . withdraw . . . and let Roosevelt get the entire vote—if he can.

Against this *I stand alone.*"[20] William Allen White, one of the stampeders, put it well when he wrote later that La Follette's "sense of betrayal mantled him like a neurosis."[21] And personal sorrow crowded on the heels of political repudiation. The very week of the convention, Belle's ailing father was buried after a final stroke finished him off.

There was no way of overstating how far he had fallen in national Republican ranks. The party was split, and each wing was under command of an enemy. At the Taft-dominated convention the Platform Committee simply ignored and tabled the radical planks proposed by his delegates, and he had no intention of any dealings with the Roosevelt Progressives. The nearest he came to that was in reluctant support for McGovern's re-election as governor of Wisconsin. His own feelings were those of Ray Stannard Baker who, like many other progressives, simply was not sure which of the many conflicting statements of Roosevelt to believe. Baker wrote to Bob: "If Roosevelt were not leading the new party, I should be with it heart and soul; as it is I shall vote for Wilson though I have no confidence at all in the old Democratic Party."[22]

La Follette could not, in his situation, go that far. He agreed that the progressive cause was in the hands of Wilson, whom the Democrats named at Baltimore at the end of June. He would have preferred Bryan, to whom he was similar in many ways. He had doubts about Wilson as a relatively new convert to progressivism who had not yet, as he put it to Gil Roe, shed his milk teeth, but Wilson was clearly the least of evils. Still, he could not see any sense in a total break with the party that would strip him of the Senate seniority he had already earned. "If I was a private citizen with no responsibility but my own role I might at once declare for Wilson," he reasoned, but it seemed sensible for "any of the real progressives who have taken such part in building up the . . . movement as have you and your humble servant" to "watch these newly hatched pinfeather leaders perform a little before we throw up our hats and 'holler our heads off' for any one."[23]

A few days afterward he wrote to a California friend, Rudolph Spreckels, with an inkling of more fully formed plans. Nothing would be gained by an immediate bolt to Wilson, but if Wilson won and really tried to implement a reform strategy, "he will need real progressive support in Senate and House more than he ever needed anything in his life . . . [I]t seems to me that building up and strengthening that little band offers the one field of activity in which I can be the most serviceable at the present time."

He was surprisingly philosophical after the storm had subsided. "Well," ended his letter to Roe about "pinfeather" leaders, "these be great times and are evoluting after their own fashion in large measure as is always the case with the working out of great events."[24] The great events of the summer culminated in a smashing repudiation of the standpatters. Wilson polled more than six million popular votes, Roosevelt just over four million, and even Eugene V. Debs, the Socialist candidate, got nearly a million—901,873 to be precise. Against this total Taft—who would himself have denied being a conservative—mustered only 3,484,956 votes. The Wilson total of the popular vote was less than 42 percent, but his victory in the electoral college was top-heavy with 435 votes to Roosevelt's 88 and Taft's paltry 8. There was good reason for Bob's terse telegram to Brandeis a few days after the election: "All happy here." It was, in the words of one later historian, "as much a political revolution as Jefferson's election had been."[25] Now it was now time for Robert M. La Follette and his family to find their places in that revolution.

"All things come to him who is patient and resolute"

The immediate problem before him was to respond to the initiatives of the reform program that Wilson called the "New Freedom." He did so with surprising adaptability for the first few years. During the campaign itself passion began to drain from him. His first rages of imagined abandonment had troubled Elizabeth Evans, who saw him during the summer and wrote frankly that when he spoke of Theodore Roosevelt he became another person. "Indignation is good. But to judge from the look in your eyes and on every line of your face, your indignation is shot through and lurid with *hate*. That is natural but it is not good. And I shudder when I see it." She had always defended Bob against charges of unreasonable rigidity, she added, but had to concede now that "perhaps your anger at the scurvy way you have been treated may have thrown out your judgment this time."

La Follette may have been swayed by this message. Or perhaps writing his own version of events for the final chapters of the *Autobiography* provided a necessary catharsis. In any case, by September he was consoling a Wisconsin correspondent: "All things come to him who is patient and resolute." And in October he was recovered enough to send Roosevelt a telegram of sympathy when a would-be assassin shot the Colonel in the chest just before an appearance in Milwaukee. (The deflected bullet lodged harmlessly near the breastbone and Roosevelt, in top theatrical form, insisted on giving his talk before letting himself be taken to a hospital.)[26]

The advent of Wilson (who was supported by such La Follette family intimates and backers as Charles Crane, Howe, Evans, and Brandeis) produced a third incarnation for La Follette. There had been the ten-year climb to the governor's chair and the paternity of the Wisconsin Idea. Then had come seven Senate years of building up to the expected climax as the insurgent liberator of the Republican party from reaction, and its candidate for the presidency. Realistically that hope was dead. The new Fighting Bob would be an independent progressive advocate on the minority side — occasionally soldiering for democracy under another chieftain and, back in Wisconsin, fighting to hold rather than extend progressive accomplishments.

And, though few realized it at the time, that was the beginning of the change in progressive enthusiasms; the point at which the machinery and management of reform began to prevail as the central theme in liberal thought rather than the worship of self-rule as a moral obligation. The prophetic voice of La Follette was going to be less audible than the clank and hammer of social engineers at work.

When the lame duck session of Congress met in December, things were already looking up for La Follette, who showed clear signs of relief from the strain of the past year. He sat at his desk, looking to Elizabeth Evans in the gallery "as jolly and as carefree as a college boy." His good humor was increased by the passage in the ensuing weeks of several laws that he had long endorsed. One created the legislative reference bureau in the Library of Congress, modeled on the one he had introduced in Wisconsin. Others regulated the hours of employment of women working in the District of Columbia, limited the use of injunctions in labor disputes, and gave the ICC new powers to evaluate the physical properties of the railroads. That was a good start, and more would come after the inauguration.

Wilson had courted La Follette followers during the campaign by describing the senator as one of those lonely figures among Republicans who challenged the reactionaries entrenched on the "ugly mountain of privilege." In a New Jersey speech after his victory he made another apparently sincere bow in La Follette's direction. "He is strong because he studies every angle of every question," said the president-elect. "When he gets up to speak he knows what he is talking about . . . The only way a man can justify voting against La Follette is to know more about the subject than La Follette knows." Ten days after taking the oath, Wilson invited the senator to his study for an hour of talk. It was the first time in three years that he had set foot in the White House.[27]

La Follette was ready to accept Wilson's friendship but he was also glad that he had not formally bound himself to the Democrats in any way. "I thank the Lord I had the foresight to maintain . . . independence," he told

145

Josie. "Now I am free, thank God, of every obligation to follow anything or anybody but the right." He came through for Wilson in the closely contested battle for a new and lowered tariff, supporting the president editorially in the *Weekly* against furious attacks by industry lobbyists. When the final Senate version of the measure came to a vote on September 9, 1913, his vigorous "Aye!"—the only one cast by a Republican—started an outburst of cheers in the gallery. He also stood behind Wilson's other groundbreaking measures to strengthen antitrust legislation and regulate the banking industry, but always reserved his right to be the cat that walked alone. He voted against the final version of the Federal Reserve Act because it did not prevent interlocking directorates among banks and corporations. He challenged two of Wilson's nominees to the ICC. And he was bitterly disappointed that Wilson failed to name Louis Brandeis as his attorney general, as had been rumored. "It breaks all our hearts," was his summation to Josie.[28]

Nonetheless, the fates were good to him in 1913; there was a sense everywhere that after long years of agitation, as one newspaper put it, "the public conscience is awakened."[29] In that climate Bob got through the Senate the only major piece of legislation to carry his name, the La Follette Seamen's Act.

The real begetter of the bill was not La Follette but a friend who had been introduced to him in 1909. Andrew Furuseth, president of the International Seamen's Union, was a tall, stooped bachelor with a craggy face and the piercing eyes of a Viking. He dressed in perpetually rumpled suits, refused to accept a union salary higher than that of an able-bodied seaman, and lived in monastic dedication to a single cause, the emancipation of sailors from the hellish conditions that prevailed in the merchant marine. Underpaid, overworked, and miserably fed, subjected to the absolute rule of captains at sea and forbidden to quit their jobs in port under penalty of jail, they were little better than slaves, chattels of the owners and masters. All this Furuseth knew firsthand from years of harsh experience since shipping before the mast in his boyhood in Norway. And all of it had been the target of his consuming efforts on behalf of remedial legislation.

He was almost exactly La Follette's age and the two became immediate friends. Furuseth joined that circle of Belle and Bob's familiars who came from widely different backgrounds but recognized and respected each other's character, selflessness, and diligence. Though Furuseth had little formal education, he had made himself an expert in international maritime law and conditions. The senator quickly became his willing and adept pupil and ally. In 1913, after three earlier failures, La Follette won a calendar

La Follette drew strength from friends in Progressivism's fellowship, like Lincoln Steffens (*right*), and Andrew Furuseth (*left*).

spot for his bill that would allow sailors to leave ships in foreign ports if they so chose and claim at least half their earned wages. It also mandated changes in the crews' living conditions and required that every vessel carry enough lifeboats for all passengers and crew, with each boat manned by at least two trained able seamen conversant with the language of the officers in charge.

These attached safety provisions improved the measure's acceptability, but the shipowners' lobby still resisted bitterly. The industry's practice was to recruit multinational crews from wharfside dives. They could barely communicate with each other under normal conditions, much less in emergencies, but they came cheaply. For the same pennypinching reasons the owners skimped on providing and maintaining lifeboats and life rafts. (Even the luxurious *Titanic,* when she went down in 1912, carried only 14 standard, safe, and seaworthy lifeboats, enough for only half those on board.)

In floor debate, with Furuseth watching from the gallery, La Follette vividly described the horrors of a panic-ridden scramble on a sinking ship in a storm, with passengers' fate in the hands of inexperienced and confused crew members, boats splintering against the vessel's sides or overturning in heavy seas. Innocent travelers' lives were endangered, and sailors' freedoms were torn away out of the same greedy motive, he said. Like past legislative battles for reform, this one was "another test of corporate power arrayed against human rights."

On October 23 La Follette's bill passed without a roll call. "Yesterday was really one of my best days in the Senate," he wrote to Belle next day. "That is, it brought probably the best results which I have achieved since I came here — the railroad valuation bill excepted — and on the human side it is far and away ahead of all else. I speak of it as my achievement. Of course, I would never have gotten into it far enough to have it seize hold on me if it hadn't been for Furuseth." Furuseth himself, on the final vote, ran into the corridor, tears streaming down his face, choking with happiness.

The legislative process being what it is, the story did not end there. A House version of the bill was bottled up for many months in committee. The Wilson administration made no effort to rescue it because the State and Commerce departments preferred to await the outcome of an international conference on safety standards at sea. It was not until February 27, 1915, that a final draft emerged from a House-Senate conference committee and was approved by both chambers. At that point, the president had decided not to sign it into law because he was advised that it would undermine existing maritime treaties with other nations. On March 2, La Follette got a White House appointment and brought Furuseth along to plead the seamen's case. Furuseth, "all aflame" by his own recall, went down on his knees and begged the president to make him a free man. La Follette told Gilbert Roe that he had never seen Wilson so moved. He stayed for another twenty minutes after Furuseth was sent outside and offered his personal promise to get Congress to allow time for the treaties to be reinterpreted or renegotiated. After he had left, Wilson telephoned his secretary, Joseph Tumulty, and said that he had "just experienced a great half-hour . . . That man La Follette pushed me over tonight on the Seamen's bill." He signed it on the morning of March 4 as the Sixty-third Congress adjourned, whispering to Bob as he shook his hand: "It's all right. I think you will be satisfied."[30]

Any serenity that La Follette felt in the fall of 1913, however, was transient. He needed to hit the paid lecture trail again. "Am anxious to go after some dough," was the way he put it to Bobbie. The very day the Seamen's Bill passed he headed south on a $250-a-lecture tour, telling Belle he would soon have "earned enough to beat the wolf, for a while anyway . . . Dear heart, if I live you won't feel the pinch any more." He said he liked the "feel" of being back in the harness, but like it or not, he was actually imprisoned in it because the bills of the farm and the magazine continued to be devastating.[31]

As his sixtieth birthday approached he passed more of the bittersweet trail marks of aging. Early in 1913 his older brother, Will, died. "It hit me pretty hard," he wrote to Josie in a loving tribute. "He saw the wrongs of the world and hated them—and fought them in his own way." Only a few months later Bobbie left the nest to enter the freshman class at the University of Wisconsin. Bob related what happened after they all saw him off from Washington. "When you left us at the station," ran his first letter to the new undergraduate, "no one wanted to go back to the house so we rode until bed time to drive away the 'lonesome devils.' You are close to all our hearts, laddie, and nothing but your own best good could reconcile us to losing so much of this part of your life out of town. Many times each day and in the wakeful hours of the night a blessing goes up from two of us here, for Uncle and Auntie. It lessens the jolt more than I can tell to feel that you are with them."[32]

More jolts—political and personal—were in store in 1914. War began in Europe, and Wilson drifted toward intervention in the three-year-old revolution in progress in Mexico. Bob saw both events as distractions from the business of progressivism. He likewise became increasingly disappointed with Wilson's domestic performance, especially when the president appeared to court conservative Democrats to win support for his agenda.

Worse still, the continuing split in progressive Republican ranks in Wisconsin once more threatened to undo much of La Follette's achievement there. Governor McGovern, now a confirmed anti–La Follette progressive, beat a La Follette–backed candidate for the Republican nomination to the state's other Senate seat, from which Isaac Stephenson (another former La Follette supporter now turned against him) was retiring. More important, the La Follette progressives were unable to agree among themselves on a gubernatorial choice. Two of them entered the primary, and by splitting the progressive vote between them gave the victory to Emanuel Philipp, a vigorous stalwart foe of the Wisconsin Idea. His election might mean, in Bob's words, "the end of progressive Wisconsin for a decade." There was, therefore, pressure on Bob to enter the race himself and play the savior, using his personal popularity to win the statehouse again and perhaps return later to the Senate, though shorn of important seniority. He agonized over the decision and finally said no, influenced by Gil Roe's brusque and sensible advice: "[T]he state of Wisconsin has got to stand on its own feet and be left to settle its own destiny. You cannot constitute yourself guardian of the state." Instead, the La Follette forces ran an independent candidate, John J. Blaine, and Philipp beat both him and his Democratic opponent in November. The predicted bad results for progressive programs followed, even though the voters sent a mixed message by electing progressives to the other state offices and a Wilsonian Democrat, Paul Husting, to the Senate instead of McGovern. Those results were small consolation, however. The progressive constituency in Wisconsin was divided and in trouble, with La Follette's own seat up for renewal in only two years.[33]

In addition, the *Weekly*'s financial woes persisted. Bobbie's academic performance in his freshman year was disappointing. Amid all these crises — or perhaps because of them, as often seemed the case — Bob fell seriously ill midway through the year. Once more, a defeat was followed by a confinement to the sickbed, one of the sure signs of the linkage between his personal and political fortunes.

Normally buoyant, even he was sobered by this latest attack, which had the characteristics of a mild stroke — partial loss of feeling on one side and a leg which dragged slightly on the other. He wrote to Fola that his attending specialists agreed the problem was not a blood clot or arterial leakage but some kind of poisoning of his digestive system that deadened the nerve centers but could be cured by diet. So for weeks he stayed at home, living on buttermilk, bran bread, and granola, unable to attend Senate sessions or fulfill lecture engagements, thereby deepening the financial abyss. Belle reluctantly left him to embark on a long, prearranged Chautauqua tour on behalf of suffrage. Bobbie, home for the summer, played housekeeper while Mary was sent to Wisconsin and Phil went on a trip to Europe with "Uncle David" Thompson. La Follette's doctors promised that he had "twenty years of reasonable work left in me," an overestimate of eleven years as it proved.

There was a difference in him after 1914. Sitting at home while Belle struggled with the rigors of the road was an uncomfortable new exercise in passivity. He was hurt by the foolish bickering, as he saw it, of Wisconsin's progressives and the faithlessness of their supporters. He wrote less about his own leadership prospects and more about the possible future achievements of Fola and Mid and Bobbie. He seemed resigned to indebtedness; "am so hard up that it don't make any difference any more" he told his "Dearly beloved ones" in August, though he promised he would get "*strong* and *sound* so I can work my debts off when I do start."[34]

When he finally did take to the stump again after Congress adjourned in 1915, he no longer filled his letters with descriptions of the gathering progressive tidal wave or the cheers of the crowd. He seemed to be fending off their expectations. "These dear people down here," he wrote from Winchester, Tennessee, in May, "nearly kill me with entertaining . . . They don't understand. They have the impression that I am to be president sometime and I have to stand to be shown the town and the surrounding county and to have receptions ad infinitum." A few weeks later, still in Tennessee, he showed a flash of the old interest: "I don't like to keep boosting myself but I do think I never made a more uniformly strong impression upon a section of the country than I am making this season on the South so far. If I were a Presidential candidate I could organize every one of these communities and carry this section. At least that is what they tell me." But he added with unusual diffidence: "I have to keep standing them off." There were few southern Republicans, but they did control state delegations, and some promised La Follette their help at convention time if he were interested. "I laugh it off," he said, "but it is gratifying as a measure of my work. And the Democrats just want to adopt me. There, that is enough of that. It is beastly lonesome," he concluded, "unless one wants to be talking to people and that is the hardest part of it all."

Those were not the remarks of an old campaigner. He found himself unable to sleep at night, fretful, impatient to return. Part of the problem was guilt. It was now Bobbie's turn to be seriously ill, and while he lay in Washington battling a near-fatal bacterial infection, his father was tormented by conflict over whether to continue earning on the road or return to stand with Belle at his boy's bedside. The guilt finally choked him off, literally, in South Dakota in August. Three quarters of the way through a speech in Minot, his voice abruptly quit on him for the first time in his life. But after returning to Madison for treatment he was soon back on the platform, flogging his battered system with more sleepless nights, days in unheated and smoky railroad cars, gobbled snacks, frantic baggage transfers. "Well, it's life—my kind and it's all right," he philosophized. But he was tiring, and he knew that the grand prize of American politics was out of his reach for the foreseeable future. The letters continued to be haunted by the subjects that raised his doubts rather than his hopes—Bobbie, money, and Wisconsin.[35]

He needed more than anything to hold his Senate seat in 1916. His future was there. No longer quite the loneliest man in the chamber, he occupied a special position as a man admired for his absolute immunity to political fear. He went on supporting Wilson at his discretion when their aims coincided. An administration measure of 1915, growing out of the wartime shipping shortage, proposed to create a federal agency that could build or buy vessels to carry American products abroad. Prominent Republicans denounced it as the entering wedge for socialism, but La Follette, after another White House visit, backed the president against the

By 1915, La Follette showed the fatigue of almost a quarter century of battle for his version of democracy.

shipping interests. He was the only Republican voting to rescue the bill from its eventual death by filibuster. "Every little while," Belle informed Bob, Jr., "your papa jokingly refers to his being read out of the party and I think he realizes that something may be sprung on him in that nature."[36] But it was not to happen; he had become too well entrenched for such a maneuver to succeed, and if some future election should produce a closely divided Senate the Republican leadership could not afford to throw away a member whom they might need to get or hold a majority to organize the chamber.

So they simply swallowed hard when he continued to thumb his nose at Senate perquisites and traditions by asking for things that were reasonable and unheard of—like open disclosure. During the 1913 tariff debate he demanded that all senators make public any holdings of theirs that would be affected by the rates imposed on any items, and refrain from voting on those particular schedules. To set the example he himself sat out the vote on the tariff on zinc, because he owned a few shares in a zinc mine—his only assets other than the magazine and the farm.

The following year saw a battle over the hotly contested nomination of Winthrop Daniels, an old friend and professorial colleague of Wilson, to the ICC. Some progressives—La Follette included—believed that he was too inclined toward the viewpoint of railroad owners in regulatory matters. The Senate debated the matter, as was then the custom, in closed executive session. Under White House pressure, progressive Democrats formerly opposed to Daniels switched enough votes to join with Old Guard Republicans in confirming him. Though La Follette was on the losing side in the vote, he used the occasion to mount an attack on the practice of conducting confirmation hearings in executive session. He led a group of nine senators who insisted that the secrecy surrounding the vote be lifted and, the next day, declared on the floor that he would publicly discuss all and any "legislation not affecting foreign relations." According to the *New York Times,* "The revolt created somewhat of a sensation," but in time, confirmation sessions were opened up to the public.[37]

But these challenges of a dedicated democrat no longer provoked violent floor battles. By 1916, La Follette was not seen as a threat. He continued to endorse the good causes of progressivism—health and safety regulations for workers, the prohibition of child labor—but not as the ambitious insurgent chieftain. He had lost in 1912, overcome by his own intensity and matched against a campaigner who played more skillfully to a public opinion that wanted the appearance rather than the substance of reform. In the ensuing years he had begun to carve out a new place for himself as the powerless but influential puritan of democracy, reminding its less committed leaders of their promises and holding them to judgment. The presidential bug destroys character. Once it was out of his system, he was a better senator and a better man.

He played the silent game in the national election of 1916, endorsing neither Wilson nor the regular Republican, Charles Evans Hughes. At one rally in Wisconsin during his own senatorial campaign, he answered a direct question on the subject by saying that every man "must decide his vote between himself and God." His real task was there in his home state, where the slow dismantling of his work by Governor Philipp had made him heartsick. As early as the autumn of 1915 he had promised a vigorous campaign in the year to follow. "The trouble with our whole political situation," he wrote Belle, "is that there has been no one to go out as I used to and make the people see what progressive government means to them. The old fellows have lost their pep and the young fellows don't know anything about it." He drowned himself as he had long been used to do in the reports of Wisconsin's regulatory commissions, which he had helped to create, groaning about his high-piled desk but explaining to Belle: "I have to wade through the stuff in order to know my ground." As election day itself approached he covered the state by auto, making seven or eight speeches a day, pulling big crowds, outlasting the "young fellows." For what it was worth, he had considerable editorial support from progressives outside the state. As William Allen White (who had abandoned him for TR in 1912) declared in his *Emporia Gazette,* La Follette was "truly and worthily a national public servant," and his record in the Senate "a guide . . . to the brave, wise, statesmanlike course in every crisis."[38]

The results were mixed. In the Wisconsin civil wars, Philipp had once again won the gubernatorial nomination and was reelected. Bob, running reluctantly on the same Republican ticket, beat his Democratic Senate rival by more than 115,000 votes out of some 385,000, the largest plurality in the state's history up to then. He ran well ahead of Hughes (who narrowly carried the state) and Philipp.

So he returned to the Senate in December of 1916, refreshed and secure but no longer near the center of the stage. He was older, wearier, still unbowed, but the spotlight appeared to be passing to others as a new generation took the stage. That was happening within his own family, too, as it responded to quick changes in society at large. As the new century grew out of infancy and started its second decade, it didn't resemble its baby pictures at all.

BELLE, FOLA, AND THE GENERATION GAP

"I should not have believed I had it in myself"

One day in the first week of April 1912, Belle, Bob, and Fola met on a train somewhere west of Chicago, each of them on the road for different, though overlapping purposes. Fola was on a tour of "readings" that took her to Nebraska. Bob was campaigning for primary votes in the western states. Belle, while along to help him, was also making appearances of her own on behalf of suffrage. The accidental convergence pleased all three, for their moments together were getting scarcer. In the next three years they would all be bound to long periods of their itinerant political preaching and livelihood-gathering. The crisscrossing flow of warm family letters would increase, augmented by the contributions of the younger children, now in their teens. Never had the network of correspondence that joined them been more heavily burdened or important. Their treasured, quoted, reread, and recirculated conversations on paper recorded the continuing story of family intimacy. But they also showed subtle and ultimately important shifts in perspective that divided Bob and Belle from their heirs-to-be.

The suffrage issue put Belle and Fola in march step with almost all of the enlightened souls enrolled in the armies of reform. But while mother and daughter fought for the ballot side by side, the experience affected them differently. During the final ten-year political offensive that won the Nineteenth Amendment in 1919, Fola and Belle were among thousands of women activists whose political frontline struggles led them toward new self-definitions in the aftermath of battle. For Fola, her travels in support of the cause not only divorced her from acting but in the long run began to alienate her from political reform and turn her toward cultural, *avant-garde* attitudinizing that distanced her from "the people" in whom her father had a bedrock faith.

For Belle, the old verities by which she lived did not disappear but took on new forms. Suffrage first shouldered scientific home management out of the central place in her thinking. It blended into a larger preoccupation with the improvement of governmental "housekeeping" through women's participation. After the fight for the vote reached its crest, her interests expanded even further. She became involved, early and along with very few other white women, in the fight against the color line. Then, when the world exploded in war, she joined other female reformers in a doomed crusade to restore and universalize peace.

But these were not departures from Belle's first principles. While racial justice could not easily be linked directly to family values, the peace movement, for her, was the final extension of woman's maternal role to the whole world. Who but mothers, the creators of life, could finally mobilize all of humanity's children to stop slaughtering each other?

Belle was still John Bascom's pupil, oriented toward service to society. She could still enthuse to her older son when the Seamen's Bill passed in

October of 1913: "It makes this life seem worth all the strain if something like that goes through, that is of real service to humanity."[39] Fola, by contrast, was on the way to a "liberal" politics of individual emancipation from the clutches of tradition. Social justice and democracy were important, but as necessary preconditions for personal growth, self-expression, inner change, and independent behavior. In shorthand, Belle remained an updated—that is, progressive—but earnest Victorian, while Fola became a cautious yet unmistakable bohemian. The differences in no way weakened the ties of love between the women, but they measured a distance between two Americas.

Belle continued to emerge in her own right from 1912 onward. She was becoming more comfortable writing under her own name, and the call of the suffrage lecture platform finally melted away some of the shyness that had kept her from pushing herself to the front since college days, especially if there were any suggestion of competition with Bob. He himself was amused and seemingly not threatened by the change. In 1912 they appeared jointly in Wisconsin before a number of audiences, he to plug the state Republican ticket and she to support a suffrage referendum (which he had long ago endorsed). In Madison on the night before election he joked with the crowd, saying that he was "allowing" Belle only half an hour to speak, "because they might otherwise find out who was the author of the speeches he had been delivering for the past twenty years."[40]

Actually, his recurrent health crises, each one leaving him a little weaker, strengthened her independent role—particularly in taking up the slack in earnings. She had nursed him through serious bouts of sickness in 1898 and 1901, from which he had emerged to thump the stalwarts with fresh vigor. But his gall bladder attacks and surgery in 1910, his collapse from exhaustion in 1912, and his nervous prostration in 1914 were more debilitating after an additional decade or two of cumulative insults to his system. She was becoming physically the stronger of the two, relatively speaking. Though she, too, was plagued by occasional illness, she took enough care of herself to have spare energies left for investment outside the home. As the children reached their teens, she had more time as well.

Not that she wasn't still a conventional mother. On April 7, 1913, a grand parade marched up Pennsylvania Avenue, the second in five weeks. This one escorted 531 women—two from each state, and one from each congressional district, carrying petitions in favor of the woman suffrage amendment. Belle wasn't in either parade; she was home taking care of Mary, who was quarantined with scarlet fever. No one seemed to question that she was the one for the job.[41]

156

But Fola carried the Wisconsin petition and presented it to a group of representatives and senators, her father included, who met the marchers in the Capitol rotunda. In the earlier parade, the day before Wilson's inauguration, Bobbie and Phil had buoyantly stepped along with the few men involved, thereby continuing a new La Follette tradition, for when a similar parade had taken place in New York in May of 1911 (with Fola carrying the banner for the actresses' division) Gil Roe and Mid (along with John Dewey, Oswald Garrison Villard, and Max Eastman) had joined the eighty-seven men who braved the jeers of male onlookers to join the ranks.[42]

Belle was so busy nursing her daughter, her column, and her political work in 1913 that she uncharacteristically forgot Phil's sixteenth birthday on May 8. The pace of domestic work did not slacken through the year. She spent an autumn of drudgery (and ran up furniture and decoration bills) getting the family settled in a cheaper, newly rented house at 3320 Sixteenth Street N.W. She was disappointed when the Senate buried the suffrage amendment for that year, especially when the defeat followed Bob's humiliation the year before. "In spite of the odds," she observed to Netha Roe, "I . . . thought luck might be on our side just once. But the fight for better things is all uphill." It was enough to shake her to the foundations. "[W]hat appalls me most," she continued, "is the thought that perhaps the results of these political movements just about measure the standards of the average man when put to the *test*. Bob never losses faith in the people—and I'm glad he does not. I wish I didn't. Like you, my faith in a *few* is what sustains me."[43]

She still had moments of self-doubt too. Late in June Fola wrote to her: "You're a wonderful person, mother mine. I don't think you have any idea at all how completely and utterly I adore you . . . I'm always wanting to tell you . . . but it is too overwhelming and all pervading." Belle replied: "It is helpful to me to know that you hold me so dear. There is a sustaining power in the thought . . . I am more conscious of my shortcomings and failures than I wish I were . . . I sometimes feel a great longing for my mother now, much as I did when a child . . . [Y]our appreciation was a comfort to me and a blessing."[44]

But such waves of uncertainty were getting fewer and were being replaced by a new, scrappy individuality. At the start of 1914 she took up the cause of two "colored" young women working with the Bureau of Printing and Engraving, one of whom had been fired for refusing to eat lunch at tables assigned to them when the Wilson administration started to segregate black government employees. (They had been enjoying immunity under Republican administrations.) In answer to Belle's inquiry, the director explained that two of the six tables in the lunchroom in question had been earmarked for the "colored girls for the reason that it would be better for them to associate together while eating their lunch." The "girls" had persisted in joining the whites at the other tables in spite of a "kindly" suggestion otherwise, which turned finally into "positive directions" when they did not take the hint.

Belle carried the matter to the secretary of the treasury and to Wilson himself. But William Gibbs McAdoo, the secretary, was Wilson's son-in-law and a native of Georgia. Wilson himself was from Virginia. Both were segregationists and refused to take the matter further. Belle, angry but helpless, became a convert to racial equality, though in earlier years she had thought it funny when little Bobbie dressed in blackface and amused the family by singing "If the Man in the Moon Were Only a Coon." Now, she addressed the NAACP and colored churches denouncing segregation in terms she expressed firmly in *La Follette's Weekly*. "Negroes" had submitted to discrimination in schools, public accommodations, and travel facilities and had suffered in silence when forced away from the polling places, hoping that time and progress would eventually bring a new dawn. "But to have the United States government take a backward step, to have the colored [*sic*] line drawn in places that they have won on their own merit, to be humiliated, repressed and degraded at the capital of the nation by their own government is a body blow to hope, pride and incentive." Continued violation of "fundamental human rights" would "corrupt our ideas and destroy our sense of democracy. Equality is in no way a matter of social privilege. It is a matter of civic right."[45]

These views now are standard and receive at least lip service from the staunchest conservatives, but they were strong meat in 1913, especially when Bob was getting lecture bookings in the South. The preceding fall he had written Belle, after a swing through Georgia, Alabama, and Mississippi, that if "the Lord would only let us out of the Phillipino [*sic*] mess and keep us out of Mexico we might in the course of time pay off the debt we owe to the black man,"[46] but that was purely for her private ear. That Belle would publicize her own unpopular feelings on the subject was a strong sign of how closely the issue touched her and how willing she was to be more than a mere facilitator of her husband's career.

The year 1914 found her tougher and more independent. It might have been the camaraderie of the suffrage movement that was stoking fires within her. "There is no tonic like loyalty," she wrote. "Many a woman, finding intolerable the restrictions placed upon her by society, has obtained relief only in joining other women to set their sex free." Almost certainly her newly expressed indignation at the resistance to the suffrage movement accounted for her sympathies toward the struggles of blacks. "This business of being a woman is, in many ways, much like the business of belonging to a despised race," she advised her readers.[47]

Anger stiffened her backbone, and the proof came when she embarked on a long, grueling lecture tour with Elizabeth Evans. The two were now the closest of friends, and in April Evans persuaded Belle to enjoy the unaccustomed luxury of a Caribbean cruise with her. She marveled at flying fishes in the Bahamas, clucked over the sight of women in Jamaica breaking rock for road foundations, hammering ten hours a day for twenty-five cents. She went on a horseback ride up the slopes of Mount Irazu in Costa Rica, ignoring the thin air and cold at five thousand feet, which chilled her Bostonian friend to exhaustion, and she got a look at the Panama Canal Zone only a few months before the waterway was opened to traffic.[48]

It was just as well that she returned well rested and brimming with positive energies, because immediately afterward Bob was stricken, and she then left on a two-month, sixty-four-appearance Chautauqua tour with Evans, mainly in Pennsylvania, Indiana, and Ohio. It turned into an emotionally grueling battle between two tired and cranky women.

They had gone on joint tours before without trouble, but this time the format called for each of them to alternate their lectures with debates against an antisuffrage woman speaker Belle referred to simply as "Miss [Lucy] Price." Evans seems to have felt that Belle did poorly in the debates and was hurting the cause. She wrangled with her constantly about points overlooked or missed, and the exchanges grew heated. Belle poured out her grievances in mail to Bob. Elizabeth had said "disagreeable things implying that I overestimated the importance of my name and position." She was "so aching to get at Miss Price herself that she thinks no one else can do the thing right." One morning "we had no more than started off on the train . . . than she began in a highly wrought up way to go for me." Among other things, "[s]he said she did not believe I had a bit of affection for any one except my own flesh and blood."[49]

After these clashes both of them would recoil. After denouncing Belle for coldheartedness, Evans fell on her neck and began "taking on." Belle, for her part, poured out her indignation and then begged Bob and Fola fruitlessly to burn the letters. The friendship survived and Evans herself wrote a thoroughly handsome letter of explanation and apology to Fola afterward, correctly guessing that it would be passed along.

The surprising thing was, however, that under the hammering, Belle grew in confidence. "I am getting adjusted and taking things in my own hands," she reported. "It is certainly great discipline. I fear I have lost in reputation, but I have grown in my own esteem. Isn't that funny? I often wonder if the nerve I have comes from long association with you or if it comes from within. Certainly I should not have believed I had it in myself alone to rise to the occasion as I have. I think the inner conviction that I am as nearly equal to the situation as almost any one could be makes me calm and if need be *hard*."[50]

Plugging the earnings gap and toughing out the rigors of travel completed the emancipation of Belle that had begun so tentatively with her law studies as a young bride and had taken off after 1910. While the two of them were in Mansfield, Ohio, on August 4, Belle took note of the start of the World War with a prophecy that mingled innocence and astuteness." Is not the world situation appalling?" she began, using a grammatical pattern, frequent in her letters, of writing out in full (rather than contracting) the "not" in a negative question. "It seems as though some mighty power must rise up to prevent the pending catastrophe. I do not see how the dynasties of Europe dare put their heads in jeopardy this way. It seems almost inevitable that if we have such a war as is threatened there will be revolt against Czars and Emperors and Kings."[51]

Six months later, the meat grinder of battle was mincing an entire European generation of Europe's youth, and the strongest focus of Belle's outside activities became the restoration of peace, or at least the preservation of it for the United States. She attended a mass meeting in Washington in January 1915 at which the Women's Peace Party was formed, with Jane Addams named its first chairman. The manifesto that came out of the sessions at the New Willard declared: "We understand that the planned-for, legalized, wholesale human slaughter is the sum of all villainies. As women we are especially the custodians of the life of all ages. We will no longer consent to its reckless destruction. As women we are called upon to start each generation onward toward a better humanity. We will no longer tolerate that denial of reason and justice by which war renders impotent the idealism of the human race."[52]

It was a late gasp of the spirit of progressive-era feminism that linked women's rights to a universe of uplift. It was "scarce heard amid the guns below." The specific goals and targets of the WPP were an immediate conference of neutral nations to mediate and bring an end to the war; the limitation of armaments and nationalization of their manufacture; organized opposition to militarism plus the education of young people in the theory and practice of peace; and "democratic control of foreign policies." From the distance of many years later, the last three still seem impeccable and heartbreakingly distant.

An additional condition was the "humanizing" of governments by giving the franchise to women. That has been achieved and changed nothing. Its position as almost an afterthought to the party credo showed how the war was already beginning to eat into the progressive consensus on what came first.

Belle shared news of her peace work with Fola, who certainly approved but did not participate. By the end of 1914, other concerns were dominating her thoughts. Nothing could make her less of a La Follette in character, but politically she was undergoing a metamorphosis.

"Just a gypsy rebel player"

"I want you dear one, close to me, all about me and within me. Tonight I detest the spaciousness of my bed because I have to lie alone." So Fola wrote to her husband of less than two months just after New Year's Day of 1912. She was in Dayton, Ohio, an itinerant for art and suffrage once again, but it was harder to face travel as a newlywed. Harder, yet all the more necessary; her lecturing income was indispensable. "Fola has . . . booked four weeks this summer with a guarantee of one thousand dollars *net* and all expenses," Middleton reported to his father-in-law. "She gets $250 per week in March also & has three readings or rather suffrage speeches next week in Connecticut. So you see how profitable that game will be for her." She would remain the chief breadwinner until the young dramatist became more established, and while he had no trouble accepting a wife who continued to call herself "Miss La Follette," he was uncomfortable staying at home while she put up with still more bathless hotel rooms, ovenlike auditoriums, greasy food, and boring welcoming committees. "Dear heart," she reassured him, "you mustn't feel that way. I am so glad to be able to make this contribution for *us* . . . It will all come out all right for both of us in the end."[53]

But it was a grind that began to take a psychic toll. It was not so bad in the cities, where she could end a performance by having a glass of beer and a sandwich with some friend of a friend who turned up in the audience, or find a hotel stenographer to whom to dictate an article or review, or mingle her political work with cheerleading interviews for a new, invigorated American theater.

But the tours in the hinterlands where she had begun as an enthusiastic learner in 1904 were now "hard, exhausting work," redeemed only by what they did for "the bank account." At Geneva she spoke to the Culture Club and the Eastern Star, but while people listened patiently to suffrage talk, her illustrative readings from contemporary social drama fell flat. "It's mighty discouraging," she lamented to George, "when you can't get a smile out of an intelligent high school audience . . . I think that [they] had expected something startling in costume . . . It takes the heart out of me to have them like the broad farce so much and get nothing from the high comedy and beauty of the other. Well, I suppose building dreams is hard work."[54]

The theme continued as she made her way westward into Nebraska. "I don't feel as if I get my audiences much; it's an awful heavy lift all the time. I feel as if I were carrying a thousand pound load over a sandy road." In Beatrice, one of her meetings turned out to be in a church and they insisted that she talk about citizenship rather than theater. "I'll be glad to get where I don't have to be a reformer no more but can just be an actress. I'm glad I'm not a preacher." She was repeating with emphasis what she had written only a couple of days earlier: "Oh, I get so tired of arguing! . . . I'm sure no reformer at heart, just a gypsy rebel player."

At Fremont she was cheered to find four hundred people from the Eastern State Teachers Association, where she "had them all the way through," but ran into early manifestations of mass culture's effect on taste. "In most of these other places I think they come expecting me to recite pieces and sing little songs and do imitations and that they are bored by a simple reading of a play where they have to think all the way through instead of little patches of laughter and little patches of tears. They want a concert company entertainment and I ain't it."

At Lincoln she "became unwell," a common euphemism for menstruating, two days ahead of time "and was mighty glad to find the bed, my bottle of gin and hot water bag when I got to the hotel here." In her weariness she politely turned down a dinner invitation from William Jennings Bryan. But the very same afternoon Emma Goldman, who had spoken in town the previous night, came over to visit her. "I'll be glad to see someone who . . . doesn't measure virtue by whether you believe in Temperance or not. I certainly don't belong in the ranks of the respectable." Goldman, like Bryan, was a friend of Bob and Belle, which says a good deal about their warmth and their world in 1912. She arrived with flowers and told Fola that her father was "the finest, most inconsistent anarchist" she knew.[55]

At York she complained about meager reports of the Wisconsin primaries, and while waiting for a three-hour-late train scribbled: "I've travelled some pretty rocky working roads, but this takes the Geist out of me faster than anything . . . The people are so good and so *Christian* and so afraid of joy and mirth and laughter that it drives me nearly frantic. Oh what our Puritan inheritance burdens us with."

Her loneliness deepened each day. "Last night . . . it just seemed to me as if I couldn't endure being away from you . . . You've done what you wanted to, dear—bound me to you with the complete bondage of freedom and love."[56] It was a delicious imprisonment. Between speaking dates that summer she and George spent a few weeks at Maple Bluff, where he sat under the wild grapevine reading Carlyle's *French Revolution* and Charlotte Perkins Gilman's *Women and Economics,* wrote and revised plays on "the woman question," and drafted his regular column as literary editor of *La Follette's Weekly Magazine.* They read some Balzac and Defoe's *Moll Flanders* aloud to each other. In September they went off for a private vacation at Siasconset, on Nantucket Island, where they would walk over the isolated sand dunes and plunge naked into the waves. They were, in George's words, "altogether happy." Fola freely described the nude swims by mail to Belle (whose reaction, if any, is unrecorded) and tried to explain what was happening to her: "[S]omehow I can't get the same kind of thrill and return joy from speaking, no matter how good the audience is to me, that I can from acting . . . When I dance I come nearer to the same kind of inner content that I do when I am playing a role I love . . . [T]here's a rhythm in beautiful words and tones and movement that I hunger to be a part of, and no amount of reforming argument seems to satisfy that particular hunger."[57]

There was no talk of the presidential canvass in her letters that fall. Mid voted for Socialists in New York state elections and apparently split his ticket to vote for Wilson as president. He loved the Washington ringside seat that life with his in-laws provided, and his primary enjoyment was as a playwright-spectator, finding new characters and situations in the theater of politics.[58]

Fola could not be completely detached from politics, not so long as the suffrage struggle was unfinished and other causes snatched at her attention. In February of 1913, thousands of workers in New York's "white goods" industry (women's blouses, nightgowns, and underwear) went on strike. Most of them were teen-age immigrant girls who got two and a half to five dollars a week for fifty to sixty hours' work—"the youngest, the most ignorant, the poorest and most unskilled group of women workers" ever to strike, as one writer explained, and very likely the hungriest. Like the walkout of textile workers in Lawrence, Massachusetts, the preceding year and the silk workers' strike in Paterson that would shortly follow, the strike attracted wide sympathy from middle- and upper-class progressives—especially women—whose eyes were opened to the savage conditions under which the poor worked and lived in order to provide them with cheap ready-made clothes.

The Women's Trade Union Educational League of New York set up feeding stations for the pickets, and among other forms of support asked Fola to go down and read poetry to them. Looking at their pinched faces she stopped in mid-phrase and said: "I only wish there was something I could *do*." A girl volunteered a suggestion: if Fola joined the picket line, police and strikebreakers might be less likely to beat them up. Fola did so and watched a picket being roughed around all the same. Fola's protests only resulted in the arrest and conviction of the victim for disorderly conduct, despite her supportive testimony.[59]

This was a different kind of political activism from the old Wisconsin fight against the bosses and the machines. Fola, in an industrial city, was seeing a new aspect of who was protected and who victimized by a crooked system. It was a radicalizing experience, intensified by her move with Mid, late in 1913, into the heart of prewar Greenwich Village at 158 Waverly Place, just south of Washington Square. The Village was, Middleton recalled, "a state of mind . . . hard to define but recognizable." Unconventional freedom was the watchword. Unmarried couples lived together openly, and the neighbors included every variety of critical thinker, some of them as genial personally as they were fiery in their politics. Reporters like Steffens, Hutchins Hapgood, and John Reed (and his consort Mabel Dodge) were there; Max Eastman and cartoonist Art Young of the Socialist *Masses* magazine; Floyd Dell the novelist; Walter Weyl and Randolph Bourne, economic freethinkers; Big Bill Haywood, head of the Industrial Workers of the World; Elizabeth Gurley Flynn, his cohort in that anarcho-syndicalist labor confederation, and her lover Carlo Tresca; sculptor Jo Davidson, Emma Goldman, and many others.

Fola and Mid were relative moderates in that group, happy to watch the show in intervals when they were not each working on plays, articles, and speeches from the spacious comfort of individual studies in their ground floor apartment with fourteen-foot ceilings. (The actor George Arliss had the top floor and was succeeded there later by Walter Hampden.) Because it was so congenial, the Village such a yeasty, hopeful, comradely place, Fola suffered the pangs of hell when she once more traveled westward in the summer of 1914.[60]

For her, as for almost everyone in the family, it turned out to be a particularly significant year, in which she suffered a crucial loss of political faith. Progressive setbacks in Wisconsin shook her up, much as the conservative 1980s would later harrow survivors of the seemingly golden age of liberalism that ran from the New Deal through the Johnson administration. As future governor Philipp, a wealthy man in his own right, appeared to be garnering support for his candidacy through promises to cut back on the "socialistic" Wisconsin Idea, Fola pondered (as Gil Roe had done) whether or not Daddy should rush to the rescue and reached the same conclusion, that he should not. She argued the case in an extremely thoughtful letter to Belle that deserves lengthy quotation as a perfect example of the family philosophy, and one which calls into question the repeated charge that La Follette deliberately worked to make reform in Wisconsin a one-man show. She began:

Never before have you had a situation like this. Dad's whole fight has been toward restoring their government to the people. Toward securing for them the instruments whereby they could *express themselves* . . . He has never advocated, never wanted to *govern* the people but has stood unflinchingly for them to be allowed to govern themselves. Always before, when he refused to abide by a convention decision or some legislative action it was because, as he expressed it . . . the people had not been allowed to express their will [because] the instrument of government had been twisted to the use of special interest. Now the situation *is* an expression of the will or *lack* of will of the people . . . It isn't that the will of the people *hasn't* been expressed because of some failure in the machinery . . .

[I]t seems to me entirely true to Dad's faith and philosophy in spite of this instance that the will of the people, even when free, isn't always for good govt . . . [but] if he bides these two years and makes a straight and stirring campaign two years from now he will find them re-bounding, re-awakened.

She was overly optimistic about the extent of the reawakening that might follow two years of a stalwart governorship, but her analysis of what happens to liberals and their followers when they have been long in power was astute.

If they get two years of bad government as an expression of their own free will that will seem a splendid battle cry, rousing them again to the fact that the kind of government they have rests with them, that it isn't the burden of any one man to give it to them or to take it away from them but that it is the burden all the time and that the price is eternal vigilance . . .

A year and a half from now he could start in with a perfect old fashioned whirlwind campaign . . . on the *offensive,* and it is a long time since the progressive element in Wisconsin has had that kind of campaign. It's what they need. For too many years they've had the defensive position of those in power—no real *issue* except explaining how wise and good their actions have been and how dreadful the other fellows would be or used to be years ago—and it looks as though the people in Wisconsin had forgotten.[61]

It was hard for her to keep the faith, however, as she returned to Minnesota, Iowa, Nebraska, and the other heartland states that had begun to dismay her two summers earlier. "I dread Kansas," she wailed to Mid late in July, "and Nebraska is awful. Oh, it's so desolately Puritan and self-righteous that it just takes all the heart out of me." (Like Sinclair Lewis, H. L. Mencken, George Jean Nathan, and other scolds who would soon be attacking the people and values of Main Street, she inaccurately equated puritanism with whatever was drab and morose in America's soul.)

But how, then, could she account for the fact that everywhere she went people would approach her to say how much they admired Old Bob? Her answer was to perceive a division between the way people voted and the way they behaved outside the polling booth: "The people are, many of them, so fine and noble in so many things . . . Progressive politically. But when it comes to sex or economics—wow! Conservative isn't a word for it." This was by way of explanation to Mid who, as a city boy, could not "realize what my mental isolation is." She observed, "You've always lived and worked where you could be yourself or where you could find your own kind as one can in a city."[62]

Slowly she was being uprooted, as a gap widened between the personal habits and moral outlooks of urbanized liberal political thinkers and millions of "the people" whom they were defending. The wrench, which wrecked her dream of doing her father's work through her onstage activities, was painful. Her letters spoke in anguish about the "great wastes of sunbaked fields," the "terrible glare," the two-foot-thick dust of Kansas. Like all the La Follettes, she quickly converted mental miseries into physical ailments—headaches, indigestion, irregular periods. "Feeling wretchedly in body and mind—blue and depressed and miserably weak and fainty," she struggled on against "the desolation, the wretched isolation of spirit and this terrible suffocating self-righteousness." Her physical yearning for George became more tormenting at night. "I wish Nature took care of females as she does of males in that regard." He could do nothing about that from New York, but he could and did send her cigarettes in plain wrappers to puff in secret.[63]

The dream of an uplifting "people's theater" was fading fast in the face of dead audiences. She lamented that she felt and probably looked like an old hag and warned Mid that "[Y]our Peter Pan is growing old and battered." What was she to do when "that damnable longing for expression won't die? . . . Oh. If I'd been given the gift of writing or painting or sculpturing or 'musicking' then I could register my little dream & get it out of my system . . . I think the summer has robbed me of my last illusion in that direction. I haven't any faith left in the people when it comes to art."

She was "tired of being a 'reformer'" and could not "grind out suffrage speeches for the rest of my life," but nothing seemed to be opening in the theater. In her deep blue mood her faith in the political wisdom of commoners, if not their artistic judgment, went up in smoke as well. A newspaper article on Theodore Roosevelt's future plans sparked the comment: "My lord, what's the use striving for the dear people and sticking to principle if all that can be discussed out of it, even by keen observers, is a desire to get office or gain personal advancement. La, la, I sometimes wonder why and how Dad has kept at it and kept his faith and purposefulness all these years."[64]

The war news only made it worse. France, Great Britain, and Russia went to war on August 1; Britain joined on August 4. The news, which she read in Phillipsburg, Kansas, left her "appalled and heart sick . . . It is unspeakable, unthinkable and unbelievable that all Europe can be on the verge of such wholesale murder." Unlike Bob himself, she was not neutral in thought; the German victories of the first month frightened her with their prospect of "all Europe caught and converted to this awful destructive, wasteful militarism that has been Germany's." But she wanted no part of the fighting and thanked God that "T.R. isn't President . . . [W]e would have been embroiled . . . before now had he been."

But it was less the death of Europe's peace than of the people's appetite for politics that upset her. "I've been through eight states this summer," she wrote to Belle, "and everywhere the lack of political interest was appalling; people were tired of investigations, of discussion even." It hurt most in Wisconsin, but the best and only thing that could happen would be that "the people of the state" should "drink the good, bitter medicine of their own indifference."[65]

The burden of progressive idealism was too heavy to carry through the dust and heat of reality. Could it be that the people were unreachable both artistically *and* politically? She could not say yes to both propositions and survive. Embers would be left, but they were embers, not flames. After 1914 Fola did not become a political dropout or turn, as other disillusioned democrats would do in the future, to authoritarian solutions. But she functioned as an unexpectant agnostic rather than a prophet's daughter. She would make her own peace with the possible.

Middleton understood it—he was having his own problems reconciling his serious work with the fluff that brought in money—and he consoled her in a long letter that appeared to advise a kind of stoic withdrawal into a private universe. "I do know that what the public wants is not what I can give them," he admitted. So "[l]et us grow more and more to know that only in the small circle of kindred souls can we find the atmosphere in which to breathe." Fola's letters and the war had, together, hardened his tentative conclusion that the people at large had no sense of art. "And why should they have," he asked like a good democrat, "since they don't feel the need of it?" It seemed to leave artists without purpose, perhaps:

But if two people can come together as you and I have . . . then there can be a meaning to individual lives . . . I have often marvelled at your wonderful faith; yet I have seen it lessen more and more. And let me tell you a little secret dear; it may be a platitude to you but it is a living truth to me: the great courage for the artist as well as for the worker is when he learns to live and work without faith . . . Only another week after you get this you will be coming back to me and I shall love you so that there is nothing left in the world but you and me.[66]

He was not quite right; there was nothing left but him and her and the other La Follettes, but they were not in themselves the models and substitutes for an entire world. That was the hardest lesson for each of Bob and Belle's children to learn, the price they paid for growing up in their sheltered nest, full of their parents' aspirations for them. In 1914 Bobbie, the older son, would also learn some hard lessons about what those expectations meant.

"BOBBIE" BECOMES "YOUNG BOB"

"I am so homesick"

When Belle left the three children at the Hillside House boarding school in Spring Green in the winter of 1906, Mary was barely six and not yet started on letter-writing. Phil, going on nine, was solidly matter-of-fact in his letters. "Dear Father: I want to know whether that dollar was meant to take us home or whether it was meant to spend for different things. Your loving Philip."

It was very much otherwise with Bobbie, nearly eleven. "Dear Papa," ran his first letter to Washington, "I am terobley homesick and I cry every night but I be brave I am so homesick that I can hardly write but I most be brave cause it cant by [be] eny other way O papa you doen't now how mouch I love you and Mama but otherwhize I like it it's all right in the day but when it comes to braving it at night I cant but I try my hardest to cape it to myself . . . Phip and Mary do not mind it much compeard with me but I think that Mary takes it prity hard at night."

The childish misspellings (deliberately preserved here, though not elsewhere in this book) make the letters the little boy wrote in that cold January even more touching. A few days later he said that "I doen't like the langu[a]ge thay use and I am afrayd Phil will learn bad langudge and enyway Mary last night you ought to have seen her it was pitt[i]ful . . . Oh mama right [write] Aunt J quick and let us get out of west cottage oh *please mama* . . . oh mama and papa 5 months seems 10 years."[67]

"Aunt Jen" and her sister "Aunt Nell" were not running a Dotheboys Hall; they were well known to the La Follettes as was their brother, Jenkin Lloyd Jones, a progressive clergyman. That made no difference to Bobbie, who begged to be allowed to go to Madison and visit Uncle Bob and Aunt Josie Siebecker for his birthday weekend: "If you cant get a letter back in time wire at my expence please let us all go we are so homesick that it would do our homesickness good to see some relashyson I hope we will never haf to be parted mama and papa for we miss each other so mouch [,] that is [,] at this end of the line oh Mother and Father if you onley new how hard it is for us but it cant be helped but I hope it will never come ageyn."

Josie confirmed Bobbie's observations. Mary, she noted, had begged to stay when the weekend was over. "I hope you will let them come up as often as you can," she wrote Belle. Bobbie was a "manly little fellow" who took care of his baby sister and put her to bed every night "because she wants him to." As for Phil, he was "as happy as can be. He was eager to go back." Bobbie explained to his aunt. "Phil wouldn't be homesick at the north pole."[68]

Bobbie was the more emotional of the two boys and the more closely attached to the family. He was gregarious, fun loving, and hungry for approval. It was he who clowned and pantomimed to entertain the clan at holiday revels; it was he who, as he reached adolescence, seemed to have more of the profile of the "regular fellow." He followed the University of Wisconsin's football team with a dedicated rooter's agony and ecstasy. He asked for and got (over parental reluctance) a motorcycle when he was sixteen. He caused a mini-crisis when he began to smoke prematurely, and he wrote slangy letters to both younger siblings in the terms that were considered sporty in the heyday of vaudeville. "I wish you could see me in a green hat," he confided to Phil in his freshman year at college, "I look like Fatty Spencer when he was three years old. It is fierce but such is life in a big school. I have been to a few dances and everybody is doing the grapevine . . . How are all the Wash. girls? I sure do miss them, especially Ety. She can't see me for dust but I am sure nuts about her."

With Mary, Bobbie was playful and affectionate, keeping up his protective role long after she had abandoned her six-year-old insistence on being tucked in. He enjoyed dropping into dialect humor with her. "Dearest Mary, How is dat you'm got pinched?" he asked when she had apparently received a speeding ticket in Madison. "You must be some speeder an all. What you trying to do . . . You'm think you'm Barny Oldfield mid a Fort. You'm must be a rich lady. $10 is lots money for one drive on Sherman Avenue." "I tell the world that I am blessed with two wonderful sisters," ran another letter. "Each so different and yet each so talented and loveable—I am sure proud of the judgement that I showed when I picked out my whole damn family."[69]

With Fola he was the protected rather than the protector—an adoring little brother, starry-eyed about her involvement in "the theater," and appreciative of her gifts, uncondescending letters, and occasional interventions on his behalf with Belle and Bob. "I must bid good night my dear, dear sister," one letter written when he was thirteen ended. "You don't know how much I love [you] and how much I think and try to make the start of a man like you are [a] woman." When Fola became embroiled with the parents over the engagement to Middleton, his sixteen-year-old loyalty to her overrode even his attachment to Bob and Belle:

You know how I love you and how many hells I would go thru for you just at your say so (or without). But among all the men I have met in my young life I never struck one that came within a hell of a long ways of being good enough for you . . . Do you get my point? In other words I LOVE YOU and looking thru my eyes, somewhat blinded, I suppose, by the aforementioned, I can't see Mid for your mate. Still, you ought to be able to pick your own pardner and if he's the one I am for him just because you own me. I *like* Mid and will gladly give him the glad hand. As for my clairvoyant powers with Dad and Mother I can't see how you can get any prescription that will make them see Mid. It seems to me pretty darn small of them if they won't even get acquainted with him to see if they like him.

"Take it slow," he concluded, "and see how things turn out but keep on trying to make them get acquainted with Mid. After you have tried that and if it don't work, go ahead anyway, don't sacrifice your happiness . . . I have spoken plainly and without padding so you know just how I feel . . . I love you."[70]

Affectionate and cuddly, Bobbie was more approachable than the rest of the clan. He lacked the driving intensity that Bob, Belle, Fola, and Phil translated into achievement but that also seemed at times to build walls between them and all but a very few intimates—the quality that Elizabeth Evans had criticized when she accused Belle of having no affection save for her own flesh and blood. Bobbie, in contrast, gave and inspired verbal hugs. Belle herself could not resist clucking at him as late as his twentieth birthday: "I will talk to my tootsie, wootsie, baby boy who wrote such a funny letter to his mammy-pappy," she said. "There trudges along beside you in mother's memory a beautiful sturdy little boy with golden curls and big blue eyes with long curling lashes."

The radiant likeableness that made him instantly popular caught Old Bob's attention, too. Visiting the boy in Madison in 1915 he observed that "you seem to have more friends than I ever had. It almost makes me jealous."[71]

The father realized how easily such popularity could be turned into political currency, and it threw him into dynastic musings. He truly loved Bobbie and was taken with the idea of passing down the political mantle to his eldest male heir. But the trouble was that the boy could not put on Fighting Bob's armor without possessing the old man's toughness and passion to outsmart, outtalk, and outstudy the enemies he saw everywhere. And he did not. Bobbie at eighteen, when he went off to the University of Wisconsin, was neither studious, hard-driving, nor combative.

That is not to say that he was lazy, stupid, and noncommittal, or a pampered second-generation child spurning hard-won opportunities. He totally shared his parents' values. He had grown increasingly self-reliant, taking a widening share of the responsibility and hard work of running the pony ranch and other operations at Maple Bluff on his own during vacation months (as did the other children in their turn, just as Bob and Belle had planned). He enjoyed and was a knowledgeable onlooker in the game of politics. But he could not do what his father clearly wanted him to do: launch a Wisconsin career with a brilliant record at the university where his parents and older sister had starred, the university that Old Bob had given a central part in the democratic regeneration of Wisconsin and from which it was assumed that the next generation of progressive leaders must come.

Accordingly, the record of his first year and a half at Wisconsin was written in misery. He produced a lackluster academic record and learned by his parents' violent reaction — as Fola had learned in 1911 — that they loved much and also expected much. He was savaged by a desire to please his parents that he could not fulfill without subverting his nature. Meanwhile Old Bob and Belle — but especially Old Bob — themselves battled conflicting desires for their son to excel but to be happy, too.

The struggle ended with the young man's breakdown, and with an outcome in which neither "side" won or lost clearly — an unresolved chord that stilled Bobbie's campus crisis, a year-and-a-half-long family chorus of conflict, frustration, love, and pain.

"That is what you are there for"

Bobbie—he was never referred to as Junior—did not especially relish going away from home to attend college, although he recognized the inevitability of the University of Wisconsin in his plans. Seemingly out of place amid the relentlessly itinerant La Follettes, he not only remained more homesick than the others but wrote letters that were less frequent and less discursive than those of Old Bob, Fola, and Belle, natural correspondents who enjoyed and even welcomed the chance to "talk" on paper.

At the end of the summer of 1911 at Maple Bluff he did ask permission to stay on and finish high school in Madison, but that was because he needed fewer credits there than at Western High School in Washington and could graduate sooner. "It means I will graduate from the University a year sooner and begin my fight to do something worth while," he petitioned—in vain—but a deeper motive was probably to get his life in classrooms over with more quickly.[72] He was adequate but little more, unlike Phil, who groused conventionally about the hard and boring work of "the blamed school" but had a natural academic bent. The difference between the boys was encapsulated in what each of them did with a small legacy from Belle's mother. Bobbie used his for his Harley-Davidson; Phil went to England in the summer of 1914 (with David Thompson) where he visited the houses of Parliament and got the signatures of leading British politicians for his budding autograph collection.

Bobbie's true enjoyment was the political game that he had watched all of his young life, and he was able to understand at eighteen that nothing in a university catalog could compare with the seminars in democratic government that took place around the family dinner table with guests like Howe, Steffens, Furuseth, Baker, Roe, Bishop, and Evans, the political and communications elite of the progressive generation. "I don't think I will ever be contented except at home," he railed in the middle of his sophomore year; "I miss the politics and the big men that come to the house. I got more out of one conference with Mr. Brandeis and John Commons than I will ever get out of a year's work in Geology . . . I don't care if England has to import most of her foodstuffs and . . . Norway has more ships' tonnage per capita than any other country . . . I'd even rather talk with the French ambassador's wife!"[73] He was deliciously happy in the summer of 1912 when, after motoring out to the Chicago convention with Mid,

172

Fola, and the other two children, he worked in the office of *La Follette's Weekly Magazine* for fifteen cents an hour and had an insider's view of the Wisconsin campaign.

Bob and Belle treated him with an alternation of loving and "shape-up" messages that made it clear that performance rather than complaint was what they expected from him. Bob occasionally scolded the boy in routine father-to-son fashion for errors and omissions of one kind and another, especially if he felt a "raw deal in the matter of correspondence." Each parent nudged him to write more on behalf of the other. "Write," was Belle's command when Bob was hospitalized in 1910. "He has a great heart hunger for you . . . Do you not remember the dear beautiful letters he used to write us on his long, hot wearisome trips?" Bob, in his turn, ordered Bobbie to smile bravely when he turned down the boy's request (on financial grounds) to visit Washington during a brief spring break. "I just want you to write a nice cheerful letter to Mamma and tell her that you are going to save up all of your heart hunger for a return to Washington just as early in June as your examinations will release you."[74]

A hint to Belle that he found the academic going difficult after his arrival as a freshman in September of 1913 only brought Bobbie a little comforting and a large dose of the inspiration that was inseparable from Belle's love. "Of course I am sorry you find your German hard," she told him, "and as always I am not able to understand why. It seems to me you know a great deal of German and I feel it ought to begin to be easier for you. Who is your teacher? I hope you passed your English exam. But I am not going to worry about anything so long as you are working your best and are interested. That means growth — and that is what you are there for."

Bobbie compounded his classroom problems and tried to escape from them at the same time by plunging into an election for freshman class president, which, he believed, turned into a mini-referendum on the 1913 standing of the La Follette name in Madison. He won, but Belle's reaction was curiously cool. Before the voting she told Gilbert Roe's eight-year-old son that Bobbie "knew how to lose and that was the greatest preparation." After the victory, her brief statement of happiness was tempered with the comment: "I expect you to have troubles ahead of you as every executive is sure to have. But I know your standards of justice and democracy will guide you and you have the other qualities that ought to carry you through your difficulties and enable you to meet your responsibilities." Fola said much the same but in a way that suggested a better handle on college student feelings: "I am so glad . . . Good luck to you in everything. Keep your firm hand on the study helm as well as on politics. No, I'm not preaching. I just love you and want *everything* to go well." And as for Robert M. La Follette, Sr., he wired from Alabama: "Congratulations from Dad. Be nice to the fellows who were beaten. And now remember what your real job is. With worlds of love I am yours to count on."[75]

For the rest of the academic year Bobbie became more of a social animal than a serious student. He dated, danced, played cards, partied, rooted at football games, cut classes. The time bomb did not explode until September of 1914, when Belle and Bob were informed by the dean that their son was on academic probation and would not advance to sophomore rank.

Bob wrote at once to Bobbie's professors and learned that the evil decree could be canceled if the record improved. He told Bobbie to "buck the line from the start to end early and late every day," to get right with the faculty "and *wipe out the record before it gets set in their minds.*" He sent him twenty-five postal cards for the month of October, each carrying the initials of Bobbie's subjects for the term (American history, psychology, French, philosophy, and economics) and demanded a daily report on each recitation.

Then he learned that in the semester's first week, before classes had begun, Bobbie had been "rushed" and invited to join a fraternity. "You start from the *first day on school work* and *nothing else*," he scrawled at the bottom of a typed letter. "*I mean business* . . . [S]end me the full name and address of *each one of the professors or instructors to whom you recite.*" A few days later he wrote that "you must not think me hard or driving. This thing is very close to my heart. It has cost me much pain and suffering. It has cost your mother more . . . You are in contact with thousands of men who will settle in Wisconsin and in other states. They are forming their various estimates of you and your future." Inexorably, Bob—the former governor of the state and the university's most distinguished alumnus—sent to the dean of students blank report forms of his own design, on which he requested from each instructor a weekly evaluation of his son's work.[76]

Belle herself traveled out to Madison for a combined reconnaissance of the political situation, the condition of the farm, and the depth of Bobbie's troubles. She talked to Uncle Robert, at whose home Bobbie had been living, to the dean and all of Bobbie's professors, and to her classmate President Van Hise. She lunched at Beta Theta Pi and spoke with one of the senior brothers, one "Chickering," a star student, who agreed to have Bobbie room with him to be tutored and watched over so that he might improve his record and be pledged.

Belle showed something of her state of mind in a letter to Bobbie after she returned home. "Make up your mind . . . and get started on the new regime with that inner power which you disclosed when you were two years and a half old and decided one day . . . to break the habit of sucking your thumb." If Bobbie felt any sense of humiliation over this public infantilization it is not recorded except for a pathetic outcry the following February on the eve of exams that he dreaded: "If the worst should happen please be nice to me because I love you all."[77]

He did make an honest effort to take hold and improved briefly. But in late October his instructors reported some new cuts. "Oh, Bobbie," came Belle's letter, driven back into the country slang of her childhood, "this is a critical time and *you just must come out right.* When Papa got those discouraging reports it seemed to take the gimp out of him."

Bob had enough "gimp" left to lash his dearly beloved with two more guilt-inducing letters. On November 9, after commanding him to cut out all entertainment and social affairs and reduce his smoking to three pipes a day ("It is dulling your wits and undermining your will") he cried out: "Oh, Bobbie, Bobbie! If you have no interest, no zeal, no ambition for yourself, no pride to make good with the faculty and your student friends, do it for your mother—if you have to work eighteen hours out of every twenty-four for the balance of the year. Everybody loves you. Everybody knows that you have the ability. Everybody wants to help you. But *you* have got to do *this thing* for *yourself.*"

Nine days later he started a new letter with: "It is just forty-one years ago today that I drove a farm team hitched to a lumber wagon, loaded with cordwood—a cow tied behind—from Primrose to Madison . . . so I could go to school.

"It seemed tough," he continued, "when I looked about and saw other boys having it easy—nothing to do but get their lessons. But oh it was fine to *make myself* go over the rough road with a big burden on my back. You don't have to make yourself do outside things in order to buy wood and coal and clothing and supplies and pay house rent—but you have a chance to make yourself do your *job* and do it better than any man in your class."

He ended with a sincere "You'll make it laddie if you set your jaw and go after it. With a heartful of love, always and ever, Dad."[78]

In fact, Bobbie did improve enough to be off probation by the beginning of the spring semester of 1915. It was Fola, as always sympathetic, who understood his real problem.

I can't but feel that would all change when he has what he feels "innerlich" is real work to do. I think it is that, though perhaps he knows he *ought* to, he cannot make his school work seem real work and at that I don't wonder so much. He has lived so maturely, even as a child . . . that it would be strange rather than otherwise if his school were a wonder world to be conquered. It can't captivate his imagination and he doesn't seem to be able to will the work without that . . . [W]hen it comes to the test of life he will show his metal and rare quality. He has real power but it evidently takes *reality* to enable him to focus it.[79]

"Dreams in which he is struggling to climb mountains"

Reality for both Bobbie and his parents took the unexpected shape of crucial illness. He completed the autumn semester with satisfactory grades in everything but French and embarked on the new term's work without the sword over his head. But he suffered from persistent colds and sore throats and on March 22 awoke with a face "swelled tight." The doctor in the college infirmary said his system was "loaded with poison" and put him to bed. Bobbie reported this to his father in a letter ending "I love you more than I can tell."[80] Presently painful lumps developed under the skin of his cheeks and on his hips. By the beginning of April he was so seriously sick that there was no question of his finishing his classes, and Bob, on the way back from a speaking swing, collected him and returned with him to Washington.

For nearly five months he lay bedridden, struggling with what was apparently a major, probably streptococcal, infection that could possibly prove fatal. His doctors, in a pre-antibiotic era, treated his symptoms and struggled with his diet, uttering conventional wisdom about the necessity of strengthening his system's power to "assimilate" nourishment or guarding it from being "overloaded." His temperature, faithfully reported by Belle in letters to Bob and Fola, swung between 100 and 104. His eyes swelled shut; he was racked by vomiting; his gut, shoulders, and neck ached; his white cell count wavered up and down on the charts. Belle nursed him until she was weary. Fola came to help in August. Outside nursing help was required. Between these bouts of agony the emaciated twenty-year-old, overdosed and groggy, tried gallantly to joke with his sickroom attendants. The disease finally ran its course at the beginning of the fall, but there was no question of going back to school the next month. It was November before the convalescent, bundled to the ears, visited Fola and Mid in New York for a football game and a bus ride on Fifth Avenue.

Psychosomatic illness is still too controversial a subject for easy generalization, but it is hard to avoid the conclusion that at the very least, Bobbie was especially susceptible to systemic breakdown as a result of the strain he had been under. The evidence of Old Bob's behavior suggests that he may have believed that and felt responsible.

176

For him there were six months of guilt over his absences from the bedside and probable remorse over his earlier treatment of his beloved first son. The boy's brush with death restored a sense of priorities. "How other things fade away when one of the family gets on the downgrade," he told Belle. "It makes a fellow feel he has fooled away most of his life chasing phantoms."

One way or another, he chose to interpret Bobbie's courageous battle as a substitute for the academic "victory" that had eluded his grasp. "It seems a cruel thing to consider a bed of . . . pain and confinement as a place in which we grow," he wrote to his "dear Bobbie," but "a fellow takes stock of himself in a long stretch of sickness as he never has before." And Bobbie had, in his father's eyes, proven his grit. As friend after friend of the family sent messages testifying to their affection, it seemed that somehow the boy had emerged from the shadow of disgrace that Old Bob had feared for him and made himself even more politically viable than a *summa cum laude* degree would have afforded.

And on his own! "I just marvel at Bob whenever it all comes over me," was La Follette's judgment in October, and it is worthy of note that he did not say "Bobbie."

To have gone to the mat with such a relentless antagonist in a deadly grapple—sixty minutes out of every hour, twenty-four hours out of every day, thirty days out of every month for six—going on seven—months—to beat it a score of times and have it come back and come back again . . . and to face it every time with a courage that never falters—well, you can't find anything like it very often in this life to say the least. Give Bob back his health and he is a winner in anything he goes after. It's the stuff of which dead game fighters are made.[81]

In his suffering, Bob had won the approval he needed, but that was not the final extent of his gain. He returned to the campus for part of 1916, but in January of 1917 the doctors agreed that he should not return to the campus but instead flee Madison's winter climate and the risk of colds, grippe, or influenza. As it turned out he never did go back (though he later received an honorary degree). While deciding on his future, he went to work as assistant clerk in La Follette's office.

It was a providential decision. He was out of the academic world that he disliked and into the real world where he functioned best. Dad's office became his university. He grew in time to master the routines, know the personnel of Capitol Hill, take on more and more responsibility for constituent service and campaign planning—to serve an apprenticeship that would end in time with his own succession to the La Follette seat.

In the Capitol, to avoid confusion, people now spoke of "Old Bob" and "Young Bob." Even in the family, it was recognized that "Bobbie" had come of age in a hard way.

There was still a problem. Being his father's successor had enormous benefits for a boy raised to think of governing well as a future occupation and a citizen's greatest obligation. But when the father was a super-figure, the thought of filling giant footprints subtracted from a sense of security. What the job rendered in self-esteem with one hand it took away with the other. So much was expected of a La Follette (and of the American people) by other La Follettes! Once in that busy and fateful summer of 1914 when he was taking care of his sick Dad and Belle was on the road, Bobbie's heart had overflowed when writing her, into a kind of despair: "I love you so much I almost swell . . . and bust when I think of you, which is *constantly.* If you two dear parents don't stop behaving so bravely, courageously and general[ly] splendiferously, we kids will just throw up our hands and say 'nothing doing!'"

A year later as Young Bob lay desperately ill, his father wrote to Aunt Josie about how he was faring. "[T]he night sleep is somewhat disturbed by dreams in which he is struggling to climb mountains with the ground slipping under his feet, or dreams of like character."

Old Bob chose to interpret that as "showing . . . how his resolution to fight his way up to higher, firmer ground has been a fixed habit in his waking and sleeping hours as well." But it was possible to look into the soul of a boy who had threatened to throw up his hands at the thought of equaling his splendiferous parents and reach a sadder conclusion.[82]

6

The Catastrophe:
Alone and at Bay
(1917–1919)

THE MOST HATED MAN IN AMERICA

"Cave men under the surface"

On the second of August, 1914, a day when, in Sir Edward Grey's unforgettable phrase, the lights were going out all over Europe, Bob commented on the news to Belle, an active pacifist, in words that reflected the tranquillity of a Washington abandoned by Congress for the summer recess: "Of course this whole thing may quiet down," he said, "and the war dogs be sent growling back to their kennels inside a week. It would seem as if it could not be otherwise."[1]

Then an unprogressive thought insisted on forcing its way into the uncompleted sentence. He added, "[B]ut we are all cave men under the surface, I guess."

Neither La Follette nor any of his forward-looking political contemporaries imagined how close to the surface the primitive emotions were boiling, or how readily they could be manipulated by nations at war. A benign outlook on the future had become part of the mind-set of 1914 modernism. It fed on democratic, scientific, and humane accomplishments in all the "advanced" countries. They were visible in Great Britain, where Liberals, Labourites, and intellectual socialists were active champions of laws to benefit the working class; in France, where the republicans had won firm control of the schools and the army from the clergy and the royal-

179

ists; even in the Kaiser's Germany, where Social Democrats and labor unions were hammering at the landed and industrial aristocracy for increased benefits and voting powers in the Reichstag; and even in autocracies like Czarist Russia or imperial Austria-Hungary, whose wiser leaders were recognizing that they could not indefinitely postpone the demands for stronger, broader-based parliaments and greater rights for subject nationalities.

The United States was part of that world scene. The wave of progressivism was rolling onward from 1912, carrying on its crest woman suffrage, restriction of child labor, industrial health and safety codes, and other evidences of what the editor of *World's Work* described as "the growth of our interest in one another." An even more enthusiastic journalist predicted, in *Collier's,* that future historians would label "the ten years ending about January 1, 1914" as "the period of the greatest ethical advance made by this nation in any decade."[2] America, it appeared, was well on the road to reconciling a giant, centralized economy with the spirit and practice of democracy. Whatever Bob's presidential disappointments, he and Belle, their children, and their circle of intimates could share a sense that the extended "family" of progressivism was due, after the long struggle, for a serene maturity spent in reviewing and strengthening its triumphs.

Then the world beyond the Atlantic went berserk. The gains of European liberalism had concealed the ugly and enduring realities of life in a world of "great powers." Imperial cruelties and ambitions; struggles for markets and territories; the creation of conscript armies and modernized navies armed with terrifying weapons of mass destruction — all these were barely restrained forces beneath the benign surface, and they broke through peacemaking efforts in that summer of 1914. Between August 1 and August 6, France, Great Britain, and Russia declared war on Germany and Austria-Hungary. Two mighty alliances collided with each other in a tragic grapple whose length, devastation, and millions of deaths no public spokesman of an overconfident "civilization" had imagined.

In the United States, reactions to the struggle were a kaleidoscope of shock, dismay, disdain, and then fascination. At its outbreak, not one American in a hundred predicted or desired involvement. But a year and a half after the war's outbreak, pressures were building toward an American diplomatic rupture with Berlin. Two years later the country was in the midst of a "preparedness" campaign of military buildup. And two years and eight months after the fatal August of 1914, Congress formally declared that a state of war existed between the United States and Germany.

Robert M. La Follette fought against America's march to war every step of the way, leading a doomed and dwindling handful in the Senate. Fellow progressives, for reasons that they considered good and sufficient, came to embrace the idea that joining the Allies to defeat "Prussianism" would in the long run enlarge the prospects of freedom everywhere. But La Follette remained certain that American participation could only wreck progressivism at home and be hurtful to the democracy he believed in with his whole being. When war came in spite of him, he learned how furiously that democracy could punish those who misjudged its temper. Universally reviled and condemned, ostracized and muzzled, he narrowly escaped expulsion from Congress only five years after being a presidential contender.

He had never needed his family's sustaining love more, and he got it in full measure. With it, he could renew the raw courage that allowed him to stick to his principles in the face of the tempest, and he did so consistently and unswervingly. But the struggle turned him into an old man, a survivor in a regimented country, a brutalized world. Though he kept his flags flying, he and the rest of the La Follettes carried on their souls the multiple scars of catastrophe.

"The thought of these German victories"

The war was not at the center of La Follette's focus at the outset. In the last half of 1914 his attention was claimed primarily by the antiprogressive revolt in Wisconsin. In 1915 Bobbie's illness and the unrelenting struggle for money dominated his family correspondence. In 1916 he had to be preoccupied with his own reelection campaign. It was only slowly that the battle for neutrality assumed importance in his mind. Like the nation as a whole, with few exceptions, he assumed at the war's start that nonintervention was the only possible, the unchangeable American policy.

So did Woodrow Wilson. He and La Follette began with the same principled premises—that war was needless folly. La Follette was especially pleased when Wilson, at the start of his first term, resisted pressure to intervene in the revolution then racking Mexico in order to protect the lives and properties of American individuals and corporations who held a generous share of Mexico's mines, ranches, and other assets. Later on, events would push the president toward a more aggressive posture south of the border. But in August of 1913 he called for an arms embargo against both the rebels and the government and urged American citizens to leave Mexico rather than assume "unnecessary risks." Bob commented with pleasure in *La Follette's Weekly* that Wilson's message on the subject was "a state document . . . that will assuredly prove a beacon towards world peace." Belle echoed his enthusiasm; Wilson's approach would bring in a "new era—not of sentimental talk about peace but of *actual enforcement of the peace principle.*"[3]

When Europe went to war a year later, Wilson's first response was to urge Americans to be neutral in thought as well as name, and again, La Follette praised his "high statesmanship and splendid patriotism." Staying aloof appeared hard, at first, for a populace swelled by more than twenty years of mass immigration. By some estimates one American in three was either foreign-born or the child of foreign-born parents. In the first days of mobilization, newspapers carried photographs of sober-faced foreign army reservists lined up for steamer tickets to get home to active duty.

But the overwhelming majority of "new" and old Americans lacked any strong commitment to the quarrels of relatives in the nation-states they had willingly left. They thought of the war at first as a characteristically European affair from which they were happy to be exempt. If they chose sides at all it was as watchers of events that were historically important and, in certain circumstances, personally inconvenient, but not related to an American future. The La Follettes themselves were directly involved because seventeen-year-old Phil was in the middle of a trip to England with David Thompson and Nellie Dunn, one of the senator's secretaries who had lived with them in Washington and was virtually a family member. Thanks to a letter of introduction from one of his father's friends, Phil was admitted to the visitor's gallery of the House of Commons on August 4 and heard Grey, Viscount Herbert Asquith, Winston Churchill, Lloyd George, and Ramsay MacDonald debate the declaration of war on Germany that was passed that evening.[4]

Even as a high school senior Phil grasped the fact that he was "witnessing a world event of vast magnitude." But on the other hand, the original plans for visiting the Continent were canceled and it was impossible to get a ship home without a long wait in Liverpool that exhausted every cent of travel money. Old Bob himself urged the boy to stay longer if he liked and offered to send more funds; "[i]n an affair of this sort," he advised, "when you are once embarked you must *finish right* . . . I would *see things* and cover as much country as you can properly take in." La Follette in fact wanted brother Bobbie to visit England himself and spend two weeks "right in the heart of the greatest events of the world's history," but his firstborn male preferred instead a planned auto trip home to Madison that had "got hold of him hard."

Bob and both sons discussed the war by long distance letter as they might have compared rooting interests in intercollegiate football. For unspecified reasons Phil described himself as "very much pro-German" in

September, though his primary emotion, like that of generations of American tourists, was one of anxiety "to get back home to the only country. I am an ardent American indeed."[5]

La Follette was surprised, as he had assumed Nellie and Phil were "[p]robably . . . pro-English as you are in that atmosphere." As for himself:

Bob and I just at this time are for the Germans—because everybody is against them and they are so in the minority. Of course I wanted to see the French take back that patch of country they lost in 1870. But when Great Britain jumped in and then pulled in the Jap it was too much for my proclivity to fight with the underdog. I don't want to see Germany carved up by the Russian. Of course if the Kaiser cleans up the whole bilin' lot in a month I am going to reserve the right to get on the other side and root for the underdog again but I don't much expect to have that put up to me.

Fola was already on the other side. "I can't endure the thought of these German victories," she commented as the Kaiser's troops swept into northern France. "Think what a sacking of Paris would be to the world." Mid, however, like Belle, was truly neutral in thought, and he alone of the group in 1914 had a sense of the dimensions of the universal tragedy. "All indications point to a cataclysm," he warned Fola two weeks before hostilities actually began. "Lord knows where it will all end . . . It all means dear heart that the one true, abiding world for you and me is that which rests in ourselves."[6]

Time proved him the most farseeing in his doubts. The collapse of all the belligerent nations' plans for a quick victory confounded prophecies and put soldiers and events rather than statesmen and policies in the saddle. Evenhanded American neutrality might have lasted throughout a short war such as nineteenth-century experience suggested. (There had been no general European war since 1815, and none involving major powers ran for more than two years of intermittent battles.) But as the large-scale fighting that started in 1914 ground on inconclusively, month after bloody month, without any sign of diminishing commitment by the warriors, basic forces began to change American public perceptions—to La Follette's disadvantage.

That requires a word of explanation that temporarily diverts the spotlight from La Follette.

"The great evil of war itself"

In general, members of the opinion-making elite of the United States—editors, writers, preachers, and professors, especially in New England and the Atlantic states—were almost entirely of British descent and held firmly to the idea of an "Anglo-Saxon" bent toward democracy and progress. They were instinctively inclined to accept the Anglo-French version of the war as a pure struggle against "Prussian militarism" rather than the contest for territories and spheres of influence that secret treaties among the Allies later showed it to be.

The pro-Allied view was strengthened by the circumstances of wartime journalism. The British navy controlled the seas and cut underwater cables linking Germany directly to the United States. Firsthand war reports rarely came from the huge eastern European and Balkan fighting zones. For Americans the war news flowed mainly from the trenches of the deadlocked western front and through French and British capitals and censors. It was not a major factor in undermining neutrality, but it helped London and Paris in their appeals to American public opinion.

The German case in American eyes also suffered from the arrogance of Germany's military leadership that began the war with the invasion of Belgium. The kaiser was less of an absolute ruler than his cousin, the czar of Russia, but was known to the world (and to Fola) as a saber rattler. All of the bemedaled generals on both sides who shoveled troops into the furnace of battle believed in the cleansing virtues of war—as did Americans like Theodore Roosevelt. But the cartoon image most tightly connected with "militarism" was that of a Prussian with monocle and shaved head.

Of course some well-educated and progressive Americans were familiar with German achievements in public health, engineering, education, literature and, music. Ordinary Americans—especially in midwestern states and cities—also knew their German-descended Lutheran and Catholic neighbors as hardworking and family-centered folk whose genial contributions to culture included beer gardens, kindergartens, delicatessens, gymnastic clubs, and oompah bands. Belle confessed to her readers that having grown up in a "strongly German" county she had "a faith in the German character and regard for the German people which has never been shaken." Becoming the sister-in-law, through Bob, of German-stock Judge Robert Siebecker did nothing to diminish that regard.

Nevertheless, the harsher side of Germany's national profile was the one that emerged most strongly in the wartime light. "The Dutchman" was transformed, with incredible speed, into "the Hun," making it much harder for neutralists to question the virtue of the Allies without acquiring the taint of appearing to defend blood, iron, and mailed fists.

And nothing sped along the demonization of Germany like the brutal emergence of the submarine. The changing fortunes and technology of war quickly undermined the hopes of American pacifists that their government might sustain evenhanded efforts to stop the fighting. It was a perfect example of the constant destabilizing and demoralizing triumph of the unexpected in what was supposed to be not only the newest but the best of centuries.

Both Germany and Great Britain, in mortal grapple, tried from the moment of the war's outbreak to strangle and starve each other by blockades that flouted traditional "laws" of maritime war as they applied to neutrals. Under them, blockades could be enforced only by actually stationing warships at the entrances to enemy ports. Only "contraband" goods, usable by armed forces, could be seized. Other kinds of property and all civilian passengers had to be allowed free passage. On the high seas, surface raiders could sink unarmed enemy cargo ships but only after removing travelers and crews to places of safety.

The British broke most of these regulations. They could not safely patrol close to defended German harbors, so instead they sowed the North Sea with floating mines, thereby restricting travel to cleared channels in which they could stop anything bound for Germany. They included food, medicine, textiles, and industrial materials in their lists of contraband. They commandeered goods consigned to neutral merchants that might be transshipped to Germany. They took ships into British ports to have their cargoes judged by Admiralty prize courts, and there they stayed for weeks or months, while the frustrated owners lost time, customers, and money. The United States was one of Germany's important trading partners and American shippers were directly and painfully hit. But nobody drowned, except for unlucky crew members of a very small number of neutral ships that were sunk by mines that broke away and drifted into their paths.

It was not so with the German submarine blockade of the British Isles. The small, lightly armed U-boat could not take on passengers for transfer. It could not even, without great risk, surface to give an "abandon ship" warning to a freighter it was about to sink because the British soon began to arm and escort merchantmen. The sub's real weapon, therefore, was concealment and surprise. Without warning it fired the lethal torpedo and merchant sailors and passengers not killed in the explosion scrambled for the boats. Only the lucky ones got away.

The submarine, like the bombing aircraft, was one of the new instruments of total war that killed civilians as well as soldiers. In 1914 and 1915 people could still be horrified by that idea, especially when the civilians were not Africans or Asians. The kaiser's government, when rebuked, first spoke of dropping submarine warfare in exchange for British concessions on blockade rules, but no such deal was possible as the struggle got ever more savage. Ultimately Berlin fell back on the argument that a nation has the right to do anything needed to survive. In time all "civilized" nations would use the same excuse to bomb crowded cities.

But American public opinion did not accept the German argument in 1914. Wilson was undoubtedly angered by British infringements of American neutrality rights (despite the pro-British leanings of his ambassador to London). But he and Secretary of State William Jennings Bryan called Great Britain to account with diplomatic protests and warnings of economic retaliation. Berlin, however, from whence came orders that drowned the innocent, was treated with implicit threats of broken relations and, if necessary, war. Wilson, whatever the degree of his personal neutrality, believed that conscience left no other choice, and the public undoubtedly shared his sense of outrage.

But however understandable, the different responses to the two belligerents carried the United States steadily further away from real impartiality. And when the British blockade restricted American wartime trade to the Allies, the imbalance became greater. A torrential flow of war goods to the French and British swirled threateningly around the foundations of the United States' neutrality.

La Follette watched with dismay. He was against American involvement, not because he was opposed to the use of force under any circumstances, but because he saw no possible benefit in it to the American people. Though other progressives would in time disagree, he saw war as the negation of all they stood for and everything he lived for. It would bury progressive gains by exalting efficiency over democracy. Its profits would fatten bankers, arms-makers, industrialists, and their lawyers and lobbyists, while ordinary citizens would only reap wounds, death, and bereavement for their share. It would bend the Constitution out of shape by inflating the powers of the presidency. It would exalt conformity over informed debate. As he saw it, the moral supremacy claimed by the Allies was the camouflaged wrapping on a sordid free-for-all among greedy dynasties and their supporters in both camps.

His skepticism about that may have had many sources. Critics then and later assumed that it was politically convenient in Wisconsin, with its heavy German and Scandinavian population. Undoubtedly it was. But mere expediency could hardly account for his willingness to assume the unrewarding role of senatorial antiwar leadership, much as he liked playing the underdog. Belle's pacifism may have been an influence. Whatever his motives, they were stronger than reason, powerful enough to override prudence, and shaped by a deep inner conviction that his faith in democracy could not be wrong and in the long run the popular temper would prove to be on his side. Despite the setbacks of 1912 and 1914, he still believed that his whole career was proof of his prophetic grasp of the people's will.

Such being the case, La Follette saw the submarine issue in a different light from Wilson. He was no defender of murder on the seas, but like Bryan he believed that going to war was a disproportionate remedy. Its massive sufferings and injustices would infinitely outweigh the original crime. What he wanted was for Americans, as much as possible, to stay out of the submarine's way. At best only a small number of wealthy tourists and businessmen had reason to go abroad. Let them avoid traveling on belligerent ships, doing in effect what Wilson had cautioned Americans in Mexico to do in 1913, to wit, "avoid unnecessary risks." Let the State Department seek indemnity for the owners of sunken cargoes and families of drowned passengers in courtrooms of international law. And let the United States claim its rights impartially from all belligerents.

This was not as stirring a position as insisting on national honor and rights of unrestricted travel. But smaller maritime neutrals like Holland and Norway followed that course out of sheer necessity and, in La Follette's view, were the better off for it.

But in the superheated climate of wartime it was hard for such an argument of self-restraint to prevail for long. La Follette was certain that the great mass of voters did not want war. So was Wilson in 1914. Both were right; only a bellicose handful like Theodore Roosevelt called for war as a response if the German sea war should cost any American lives.

But the public at large was also unwilling, however inconsistently, to forgo judgment on the sinkings. Few Americans stood behind Belle's no-fault pacifist view that it was "folly to try to place the blame for the war. In the last analysis Society is to blame for *tolerating* war . . . [T]he rights and wrongs of the great war now raging are but incidents of the great evil of war itself."[7] That was—and still is—a rare viewpoint. It was far more natural to see the use of the submarine as especially villainous, and to identify more and more with those fighting against the villains. If, therefore, the sinkings multiplied, which they surely would as the war intensified, and if, as was inevitable, Americans should become victims, a growing war fever would be hard to check.

Therefore, for pacifists and neutralists (not always synonymous terms) the best option for keeping America out was to end the fighting as soon as possible. The war was just six months old, and barely settled into an obvious standoff, when La Follette made a first move in that direction. But neither he nor anyone else opposed to the war anticipated how hard it would be, and how little breathing room the rush of events would leave them.

"History will hold us accountable"

The small peace movement in the United States was a loose alliance of organizations well supplied with eloquent progressive leaders—people like Jane Addams, Frederic Howe, Florence Kelley, John Haynes Holmes, Rabbi Stephen Wise, and Belle La Follette—but lacking the political clout embodied in a significant number of elected supporters. True, many congressmen routinely praised the virtues of peace and scolded the "militarism" of other countries. But few risked their political necks by criticizing the institution of war itself or by taking a leading part in trying to end the carnage in Europe. Bob was one of the few exceptions.

He wanted to get the United States, as the strongest nonbelligerent power, to work actively for a settlement of the war. It could do so either by offering its own good offices or calling a conference of neutral nations that would encourage the warring governments to state their conflicting aims, and would then propose and negotiate compromises—a kind of *ad hoc,* temporary international peacemaking body. The flaw in the conception was that rulers had become the prisoners of their own rhetoric. Like the new machines of war, mass propaganda was carrying the conflict to levels of unmanageable intensity. Each side had saturated its own people with the argument that the struggle was between good and evil, national safety or national extinction. Neither, therefore, could comfortably haggle in public about concrete objectives. It would look like calculating how many lives they were willing to spend for spoils. The odds against negotiation were prohibitive.

All the same, in the short session of Congress that began in the winter of 1914–1915, La Follette made his first try at a peace policy. On February 8, 1915, he introduced a resolution that called for the United States to sponsor a convocation of neutrals to offer mediation and to make long-range proposals for limiting the scope and destructiveness of war itself. Possible examples might be arms limitation, controls on the export of armaments, neutralization of some trade routes and safeguards for neutral rights, and the establishment of a permanent international judicial body to which quarreling countries could refer disputes.

La Follette claimed neither originality nor novelty for any of these ideas, and at least one version of the international court—the Hague Tribunal— had been in existence, for the most part impotently, since 1899. The time was not ripe, as Bob undoubtedly knew, and the resolution was buried in the Foreign Relations Committee until the adjournment date of March 4. One chance to put peacemaking on the agenda had gone by.[8]

At the State Department, meanwhile, Secretary Bryan was trying to nudge both the British and the Germans toward a greater commitment to freedom of the seas by abandoning their more offensive practices. Having successfully negotiated a number of international arbitration treaties in his two years, he still had hopes of reversing the juggernaut. But the clock was running against his efforts as well as La Follette's as the spring fighting began in earnest. First came the sinking of a British ship on which an American was killed, and then of a United States–owned tanker.

Then, on May 7, 1915, American neutrality received its most gigantic shock of the nine-month-old war. The liner *Lusitania* was torpedoed off the coast of Ireland. She was only a few miles from land, and the sea was calm, but the great ship's bottom was ripped out by a mysterious second explosion that followed the torpedo's detonation. She sank in eighteen minutes, not nearly enough time to evacuate nearly 1,500 passengers and crew; 1,198 of them lost their lives, including 128 Americans.

Indignation burst from almost every platform and printing press in the country. The barbarism of murdering innocents—over sixty of the drowned were infants—confirmed the worst Allied propaganda stereotypes of the Germans. The president's intimate and decidedly pro-British adviser, Colonel Edward M. House, assumed that war was inevitable and cabled, "[W]e can no longer remain neutral spectators." Wilson, however, did not answer with an immediate threat of war. He called for calm and said there was such a thing as a man (and by implication a nation) being too proud to fight—to the infinite frustration of Theodore Roosevelt who denounced his "milk and water" diplomacy as a concession to "the solid flubdub and pacifist vote . . . every soft creature, every coward and weakling."[9]

La Follette clearly agreed with the president but took no outspoken stand on the affair until more than two years later, when it landed him in the worst trouble of his political life. He did believe, however, that Americans were taking unwise risks to travel through war zones on the ships of belligerent nations, especially when they carried cargoes of military value. The German Embassy had published a warning in New York newspapers on the day the *Lusitania* sailed that her passengers were at risk. La Follette, too, had heard and believed that the ship had explosives aboard. It was, in fact, later learned that 1.5 million rounds of rifle ammunition were in the cargo hold.

Bryan felt much the same but quickly found himself outflanked within the administration. Though Wilson resisted a rush to hostilities in 1915, he was anything but indifferent to the ramifications of the sinking. He drafted diplomatic notes demanding German reparations, and more important, absolute guarantees of the safety of American passengers traveling anywhere on any ships. This was an impossibility without virtually abandoning submarine warfare. Nonetheless, Wilson declared that Germany's refusal would be an unfriendly act and that the United States would take all and any steps necessary to protect its citizens. He did not say what they would be; he was still trying to preserve neutrality while accommodating angry public opinion. But his words were strong in the conventional diplomacy of 1915. There was little precedent then for undeclared or limited wars between major powers in which they might kill each others' citizens or bomb each others' territory while still technically at peace with each other.

But for Secretary Bryan, even the president's restrained note was too strong. He read its terms as implied threats and could not concur in them without undercutting his hope that the United States would work most effectively for peace as a true neutral. Having no support for his position in the cabinet, he resigned on June 9, amidst a chorus of "good-riddance" editorial comment that denounced his "pro-German" efforts to water down Wilson's protests. The eastern press had always considered him naive and uninformed about international affairs—he owed his appointment to his political following within the Democratic party rather than to any foreign-policy experience or expertise—and his biblical brand of near-pacifism, based on the simple conviction that nation should not lift up sword against nation, had invited the kind of mockery that always surrounded his career. The La Follettes, who understood and shared his instinctive faith in what Belle called "the plain folks" (without embracing his religious fundamentalism), watched him go in sadness. "I think the attitude of the papers has been terrible towards him," Fola expressed herself to Belle, her 1914 distaste for the kaiser submerged in her opposition to American belligerence. "I have felt very sympathetic with his actions and I cannot understand how they find it possible to so question the integrity of his spirit."

Bryan's ouster was a bad long-range omen for La Follette. Once again, we depart from the main story for a few words of explanation.

The *Lusitania* crisis had an inconclusive diplomatic ending. Neither Germany nor the United States would abandon its official position, but neither nation wanted to push the other over the edge. Yet by the end of 1915 the situation had changed dramatically for the worse from a neutralist point of view. The chances of America's staying out had been severely reduced. Any quickening of the submarine campaign could bring her into war against Germany.

However carefully worded his warnings, Wilson had in effect put the key to the situation in Berlin's hands—if it ignored his first protest he would have to respond more strongly. In his new position he had severely reduced his own options for becoming a neutral mediator, as Bryan feared. The president's wartime mentality has been a fertile source of debate among historians, with no final resolution in sight. He was too sophisticated to endorse any black-and-white notion that the kaiser had "started" the war. Whatever his distaste for "Prussian autocracy," he understood the broader causes of the conflagration. During its bloody course he became taken with the idea of the United States leading the world to a long-range settlement that would eliminate them. But with every month that passed after 1915 it became clearer that the only way this was likely to happen was if the United States took part in the action, and that realistically, she could do so only on the Allied side.

Wilson disliked war and was well aware of its baleful effects on progressivism. Nevertheless, he followed policies that pushed him toward involvement and gradually convinced himself that he could control the monster and shape the outcome of all those savage years to his liking. Like all the chief actors in the drama of progressivism, particularly those who later followed his call to help make the world safe for democracy, he operated from a mixture of innocence, good faith, and arrogance.

Precisely when this conversion began to take place is arguable, but one early sign of it was Wilson's endorsement, at the end of 1915, of a campaign of "preparedness" that involved the creation of military training camps for civilians and a large buildup of the army and navy. The movement had wide political support from manufacturers interested in the economic boost it would provide. It was loudly acclaimed by vigorous supporters of the Allies and by patriotic organizations and leaders who still thought of war as a strengthening test of national fiber. It seemed only appropriate for a certified world power such as the United States was clearly becoming. And it had a certain almost romantic appeal to a public largely innocent of the realities of battle. The cruel sacrifices of the Civil War were already half a century in the past. The vogue of preparedness also coincided with the decision of a consortium of American bankers to grant half a billion dollars in loans to the French and British, whose treasuries were reaching the exhaustion point. Although it is simplistic to claim that this was a "cause" of intervention, it was part of an overall tightening linkage of United States interests with the fortunes of the Allied powers.

What this meant overall for La Follette was that by mid-1916, the peace movement, potentially the best-organized opposition to intervention, was being marginalized. It was less likely to be seen by the public as an important element in the progressive crusade, and more likely to be condemned as an unpopular fringe faction. To support it became a political liability, and it took a powerful mixture of optimism and stubbornness—La Follette's mixture—to stay on board, particularly when other progressives were beginning to argue that the pathway to a better world was for the United States to win influence by playing a part in the war itself. The clash between preparedness and pacifism became in part a civil war among progressives. La Follette took the losing side in 1915, though in the long run there were no winners.

A sign of the times occurred in November of 1915 when Henry Ford chartered a Norwegian vessel, the *Oskar II,* and funded an expedition of peace movement leaders to accompany him to Oslo, where they would meet European counterparts and try to lay the basis for a conference to end the war. The idea met with an avalanche of ridicule. Ford, at the height of his reputation as a productive "genius," was making one of his first ill-advised forays into public affairs to show the politicians what a little common sense would do. He was so undeniably quirky and simplistic that the real benevolence of his wish to have the troops "out of the trenches by Christmas" was ignored in a flood of jibes at the "Peace Ship."

Bob and Belle were among those whom Ford invited to come along. Bob took it seriously enough to wire her from Madison, where he had speaking dates, and ask her to go in person with John Hannan to Ford and explain why he believed that he could do more good staying in Washington to look after "big things coming on in Senate, tremendously urgent." It was no mere gesture to a possible future backer. La Follette's follow-up letter to his wife expressed honest regret:

When Ford's telegram came yesterday it really struck me awful hard. There may be a *chance* to help do a *great big thing* to halt the slaughter. I wired you as I did because it seemed the right thing to show him how much we would like to help and I felt you would deeply impress him with your sound thinking on the subject. Also I felt that there was a possibility that you might think the chance to help out on one of the *biggest pieces of work* in the *history of mankind* might warrant our packing up and leaving everything here (Wisconsin and Washington) for a month or six weeks—let happen what might.

But I feel too that it would be hard to decide to absent myself from Washington and Wisconsin where a fixed obligation exists. I tell you, dear, I sometimes wish I was as free as Bryan is—with never a thought but to respond as an individual with all that would mean.[10]

192

It was unquestionably the right political decision. Bryan himself did not go but showed up to give his blessing at the sailing and gave reporters a field day when he innocently spoke to them while holding a cage meant either for a squirrel or a dove that someone had thrust at him. He was on his way to the diminished status of his last years, an outsider whose views were increasingly seen as naive if not narrow. The expedition was a failure, too. The various participants, who certainly did include a number of eccentrics, inevitably quarreled among themselves. Wartime restrictions thwarted the plan for getting pacifist delegations from the warring countries to attend the conference. Ford became discouraged and left early. Eventually the whole project was called off. What could have been a promising private effort to bring the neutral world to the rescue of the stalemated warriors collapsed.

But though the public-relations stock of pacifists and noninterventionists was declining, they continued the battle. Congress reconvened in December for the second time in the war, and a few weeks later, on January 27, 1916, progressive Senator William Kenyon of Iowa presented a petition favoring an embargo on the export of weaponry. It carried more than a million signatures collected by the Organization of American Women for Strict Neutrality. On the very day of its presentation, however, the president, who was now arguing that only a militarily strong America could have any influence for peace, was beginning a speaking tour for preparedness. In its course he would call for "incomparably the greatest navy in the world." He would also expose the dangerous flaw in his existing policy by cautioning one audience that while they could "count upon my heart and resolution to keep you out of war . . . you must be ready if it is necessary that I should maintain your honor."

Under the circumstances the petition was slated for the usual interment in committee, but several senators spoke for it, La Follette included. He berated the administration for its apparent indifference to ending the war. "I believe," he said, "that history will hold us accountable for our contribution to the general holocaust, and I think it will be hard for future generations to understand why the neutral powers kept aloof; why they did not unite, under the leadership of the United States, in an effort to restore peace and order . . . [I]f one-tenth part of the energy and time now directed in agitation . . . of preparedness were to be turned toward other means of settlement of international problems for the future we should restore the confidence of the people and redeem our place in history."[11]

A couple of weeks later, two neutralist Democrats, Senator Thomas Gore and Representative Jeff McLemore, introduced complementary resolutions to avoid further clashes over the theoretical rights of Americans to travel with impunity in battle zones. One would have banned passports for Americans taking passage on ships of belligerent nations. The other directed the president to order American citizens off armed merchant ships, which were considered fair game for subs.

Both measures had a chance of picking up support from members on whom it was beginning to dawn that war was a genuine possibility. And both rekindled the continuing constitutional struggle between the president and Congress over who should control foreign policy far more than the La Follette resolution of a year earlier urging a conference of neutrals. Now, Wilson was carrying on his post-*Lusitania* argument with the Germans, threatening to hold them to "strict accountability" if they ignored his insistence that Americans had the right to travel in safety anywhere and by any means. The message implicit in the Gore-McLemore resolutions was the last thing he needed. As would any president, he argued that if Congress undercut his negotiating efforts by suggesting that he did not speak for a united people, peace would be less likely. He passed the word to the leadership of the foreign relations committees in both House and Senate: the resolutions must not even get to the floor for divisive debate. They must be buried by whatever parliamentary maneuvers it took.

La Follette stubbornly fought against the burial on March 10. He made the classic and still-valid case for the congressional right to a share in diplomacy. If Congress must be silent during diplomatic negotiations, the president can create crisis situations in which there is no choice but to support him. If, in the name of national unity, all of the president's foreign-policy initiatives had to stand unchallenged, then democracy was a joke. He argued that "[i]f the President is clothed with such unlimited power, if in conducting foreign affairs he can go unhindered to Congress to the limit of making war inevitable, and if the Congress has no alternative but to accept and sanction his course, then we have become a one-man power, then the President has the authority to make war as absolutely as though he were Czar of Russia." He concluded that "democratic control of foreign policies is a basic principle of all organized effort looking for the future establishment of permanent world peace." The "plain people," the "saner people" of the warring countries were organizing to make sure that their autocratic rulers would never again, through secret diplomacy, produce another world catastrophe. The United States would make an enormous mistake in allowing "that exclusive Executive control over foreign affairs that the people of Europe are now repenting amid the agonies of War."[12]

They were vibrant words that Wilson would later utter in his postwar pleas for open diplomacy, but they were in a lost cause in defense of the Gore-McLemore resolutions, which went to their inevitable doom, as the drift toward war continued. In April, the French ship *Sussex* was torpedoed in the English Channel and three Americans died. This time Secretary of State Robert Lansing, Bryan's more militant replacement, was authorized to say that any more attacks would bring on a break in diplomatic relations, at that time an almost certain prelude to war. When Wilson asked for congressional support for this tough stand La Follette, in debate, had a counterproposal—an advisory mail referendum on the question of war or peace that could be set in motion by a petition of one percent of the qualified electors in each of twenty-five states. It, too, disappeared into the black hole of the Foreign Relations Committee, as scornfully dismissed as most such proposals continue to be, in spite of the argument that was compellingly set forth in *La Follette's Magazine*. "The day is coming when the people, who always pay the full price, are going to have the final say over their own destinies . . . They themselves shall decide what questions of 'defense' of 'aggression,' or of 'national honor' may be involved, compelling enough to make them desire to kill and be killed. They who do the fighting and the dying will do the deciding."[13]

The *Sussex* crisis was defused early in May by a partial German backdown. Berlin pledged not to sink unresisting merchantmen without warning, though it reserved its freedom of action unless the United States compelled Great Britain to modify its own blockade. Wilson rejected that reservation, but the attacks stopped exactly in time for the 1916 election campaign.

The Democratic National Convention met in St. Louis on June 14. That day—which ironically was La Follette's birthday—was officially proclaimed as national Flag Day by Wilson, who celebrated by leading a monster Preparedness Parade in Washington, stepping along in dapper light trousers, blazer, and straw boater with a flag carried like a rifle on his shoulder. The following evening he was renominated by a convention that tumultuously cheered a keynote speaker who contributed the winning campaign slogan by his insistence that the president's policies had "kept us out of war."

There was clearly ambivalence in the national mind, and it was enough to encourage La Follette to keep up his peace agitation as he headed into his own reelection campaign in Wisconsin. In debates on the huge naval appropriation bill passed in July, he opposed the huge new tax burdens it would add and vainly offered an amendment that no American ship of war should be used to collect private debts. It was a vintage La Follette performance, replete with documented summaries of expert testimony on why a big navy was unnecessary, plus attacks on the "financial imperialism" that had "converted almost all of Europe into a human slaughter pen." It earned the amendment a total of eight votes.[14]

He won easily in Wisconsin after a campaign that saw him whipping around the state at speeds of forty miles an hour in a new Ford driven by one or the other of his sons. He was encouraged that his antipreparedness stand had not hurt him and that the vote for Wilson was a sign of a people's mandate against war. With his usual indifference to Republican partisanship, he still supported Wilson on some issues—on not invading Mexico (save for a small and temporary "punitive expedition" against Pancho Villa) and on domestic legislation like the Adamson Railway Labor Act that legally standardized the eight-hour day on interstate lines. Coming back to Washington after the elections, for the third opening of Congress during the Great War, La Follette even found one final occasion to applaud Woodrow Wilson. It came about in this way.

The end of 1916 offered a brief, tantalizing moment of opportunity for serious negotiation. On the western front the ghastly and inconclusive battles of Verdun and the Somme had been mass blood sacrifices—millions of French, German, and British young men killed and wounded in futile charges against barbed wire and machine guns. The Italian front was deadlocked. In the east, Russia was on the brink of collapse, but her antagonists, Austria-Hungary and the Ottoman Empire, were also close to bankruptcy and revolution. The war was so obviously a failure thus far in terms of achieving anything worth its cost that pro-negotiation groups within the warring nations were emboldened to put pressure on their own governments for new initiatives. The Germans extended a feeler through Wilson, who in turn sent notes to all the belligerents asking their peace terms and proposing a mediator's role for neutrals.

It came to nothing in the end. Germany rejected neutral involvement. The Allies insisted on prior agreement to territorial adjustments that they had not been able to win in battle. Essentially, those nationalist leaders on both sides who clung to the hope of total victory instead of unsatisfying compromise prevailed over the peace-seekers (as they had in 1914) and were not dislodged from power. Each side's would-be victors had some ground for hope—the Allies that the United States would finally come to their rescue, the Germans that Russia's imminent collapse would give them a huge temporary advantage. Both prophecies were correct, and connected. With the political "peace offensive" repulsed, the German high command convinced the kaiser that an all-out submarine offensive against the Anglo-

French trans-Atlantic supply line would provide the winning edge when coupled with new drives on the western front. It might bring in the United States, but the Allies would be forced to surrender long before American power could be mobilized and projected to another continent. January 31, 1917, was set as the date to unleash the U-boats again. The last chance for peace was gone; the carnage would grind on for another twenty-two months and victory would finally go to the side that, in French Premier Clemenceau's words, held on for another quarter of an hour.

But no one knew this on January 22, 1917, when Wilson addressed a joint session of Congress and unveiled his own idea of what the end of the war should bring: freedom of the seas, the self-determination of nationalities, government by the consent of the governed everywhere, the "moderation" of armaments—all foreshadowing his Fourteen Points of a year later. Wilson ambitiously declared that these were "American principles, American policies [and] the principles and policies of forward-looking men everywhere." They were "the principles of mankind and must prevail." Their establishment would benefit all the former belligerents alike, so that the final result of all the suffering would be "peace without victory." When he uttered those words, the packed House chamber and galleries burst into applause. Leading the demonstration on the floor was Bob La Follette.[15]

If Wilson could have pursued these goals as a neutral, their on-and-off collaboration would never have turned, as it did, into violent hatred. It was not to be, as events drove Wilson to the decision that "peace without victory" must be preceded by Allied triumph on the battlefield with American participation. Five days after the president's address, however, they were not yet enemies. La Follette, who was staying alone in Washington, was invited to a White House dinner. He described the evening to Belle in a final glimpse of a provincial Washington on the eve of the storm. In the late afternoon he came home—by streetcar as always—from the Capitol to the rented house he shared at 3320 Sixteenth Street with his cousin William La Follette, who was a U.S. Representative from the state of Washington, and with an army captain on duty at the War Department. Discovering that the vest to his formal suit had come back from the dry cleaners stinking of gasoline, he rode to the White House on the rear platform of another streetcar in order to let the sharp January wind blow the fumes away. His outfit included Bobbie's silk hat and the army captain's borrowed formal scarf. The evening passed pleasantly and included a friendly chat with Louis Brandeis, recently confirmed to the Supreme Court, as they sat on a couch enjoying the concert provided for the diners.[16]

Then, on the second morning after the dinner, the German government exploded its surprise. Neutral ships, armed or otherwise, would henceforth be attacked without warning in waters around Great Britain. A clumsy exception would be made for one American vessel a week, if it followed a prescribed course and was conspicuously lit and marked. Wilson's hand had been called, as he had long known it could be. From then on he had, in his own mind, no choice but commitment to war, hoping—if one gives him the benefit of the doubt—that he could to rise above the passions he was about to release. He did not; he became their prisoner. La Follette, meanwhile, once more became the principled, suffering loner that he constantly believed himself to be, but this time with a fearful reality. The "war" between the two men symbolized the unhealed wound in American liberal thought about the uses and limits of world power.

La Follette knew from the moment of the German announcement that neutralism was in devastating trouble. The White House had gone into round-the-clock preparations in deepest secrecy. Rumors buzzed, editorialists shouted for "firmness," Democratic leaders held closed-door meetings with the president, and Bob's own efforts to see Wilson were stopped cold. "The White House and State Department," he wrote, were "sealed up tight as a drum." He scribbled to Belle: "[A]n awful crisis [is] impending. You can only stand and grimly wait for a chance to fight the devils off."[17] Grimly, he waited for the opening of the ordeal.

"Bob, they'll crucify you"

On Saturday afternoon, February 3, Wilson appeared before still another joint session of Congress to announce that he had broken diplomatic relations with the German empire. On Monday morning a resolution approving the president's course sailed through the Senate with 78 ayes to only 5 nays, one of them Bob's. The other four were split between two Bryan Democrats and two progressive Republicans. On the majority side party lines were swept away as pro-war Republicans rushed exultantly to the colors, led by Senator Henry Cabot Lodge, whose close friend Theodore Roosevelt had recently written him that La Follette was "considerably inferior, in morality and capacity, to Robespierre."[18] It was one of the milder comparisons that Bob would soon have to endure.

Bob was fighting for time, hoping for a backlash of peace sentiment to form. To give it a focus, he had resolutions ready to submit, calling for a temporary embargo and for mediation. Belle was back in Madison planning emergency meetings of the Women's Peace Party. He missed her badly.

"It is hard not to . . . talk things over with you," was his message. But "[n]othing matters so long as we are doing what is right."[19]

He could not have Belle, but he did get Bob, Jr., who, exiled by doctor's orders from wintry Wisconsin, showed up at this moment to be signed on as his delighted father's clerk. There were no more paternal thoughts of a great academic record as an overture to political climbing. Instead, during the bitter weeks and months of 1917 Old Bob was grateful for the hardworking elder son at his side to share his living quarters, his office, and his struggles.

On February 26, Wilson addressed Congress again with his proposed answer to unrestricted submarine warfare. He asked for legislative authority to arm American merchant ships and to employ "any other instrumentalities or methods . . . to protect our ships and our people in their legitimate and peaceful pursuits on the seas." It was Monday and the Congress would automatically be adjourned at noon on March 4, the following Sunday. That left only six days to study, debate, and vote on the measure—actually five, because La Follette immediately refused unanimous consent to move it ahead of another bill slated for an early vote.[20]

La Follette believed that the president's haste was an ominous signal of his intention to run a war entirely on his own and to whip up an irresistible sentiment for "unity" that would snuff out free discussion. There was no legislative need to ram through the armed-ship bill in less than a week. It was obvious that a special session could be and would be (and was) called soon after the regular term of the Sixty-fourth Congress expired. He also was convinced that the substance of the bill was unconstitutional. In pitting American against German gunners by Wilson's order, it amounted to a presidential declaration of war. The issue was important enough in La Follette's eyes to make a symbolic counter-assertion of congressional rights by stalling the bill to death.

La Follette and a handful of other objectors had the necessary parliamentary tools, furnished by the Senate's tradition of unlimited debate. But the pressure brought against them would be enormous. It was increased on March 1—with suspiciously convenient but actually unplanned timing—when the administration released the text of a wireless message between German Foreign Minister Arthur Zimmerman and Germany's ambassador to Mexico, which the British had intercepted in January and turned over to the State Department on February 24. The "Zimmerman Telegram" said that if the United States made war against Germany, Germany would propose an alliance with Mexico and would back Mexican demands for the return of the territories she lost in the Mexican War of 1846–1848.

The idea was farfetched and heavy-handed, a propaganda disaster. Though in essence it only said that Germany, in the event of war, would try to find allies on America's border—hardly a diplomatic novelty—it was taken as the final proof of Hun perfidy. It proposed to bring war to the Western Hemisphere, in violation of the sacred Monroe Doctrine. Worse, it also suggested a later approach to Japan, the "yellow peril" that haunted the imaginations of some sensationalistic editors on the West Coast.

Something close to hysteria followed. On Friday the House rushed the armed-ship bill through, 403 to 14, and its came to a Senate anxious to show its patriotism and martial readiness by a swift and similar lopsided vote. But La Follette and eleven other senators thought otherwise. Through the waning hours of Saturday, March 3, they kept the debate going, with the understanding that La Follette, their leader, would reserve the final three hours for himself to make a stirring appeal to reason.

The bill's sponsors originally intended to avoid the floor in hopes that its opponents would exhaust themselves talking before the gavel fell. But they soon realized that it would not work and that they were in fact beaten. They then switched strategies and used as much time as possible to go on record with bellicose speeches. As a special point, they planned to run out the clock themselves and keep La Follette from speaking.

There was no sleep for the senators on Saturday night, as the debate raged on before galleries that were full despite the late hour. Tempers were short and traditional courtesies toppled before the gale. At 3 A.M. Senator Gilbert Hitchcock of Nebraska, Wilson's floor leader, appeared with a "round robin" signed by seventy-six senators who protested that they were ready to vote at once and denouncing the obstructionists. But North Dakota's Asle Gronna was angered by that senatorial discourtesy. The rules were the rules, and he for one would not be bulldozed by an obvious appeal to the crowd, designed to embarrass the minority into silence.

Around dawn, La Follette was at his desk preparing to take the floor, by prearrangement, at 9 A.M. A pink Senate memorandum form was brought to him with an unsigned note scrawled on it. It said simply that the presiding officer had already agreed not to recognize him and to rush the bill to a vote.

It was his first inkling of the plan to silence him, and it drove him into the same self-destructive frenzy that had overcome him at the Philadelphia newspaper banquet when he thought he was being ignored. Part of his fury was sheer vanity; he was convinced that his speech could actually redirect the tidal wave of pro-war opinion. Part of it was the desperation of feeling a threat to his power of expression, the very core of his existence.

200

Awful scenes now took place. He rushed to the presiding officer's desk and learned that he had been bumped down the speaker's list, behind two pro-bill senators, Robert Owen of Oklahoma and Hitchcock. Boiling, he asked Bob, Jr., to bring up a traveling bag that he kept in the office and leave it near him. Young Bob knew that the bag contained a gun for protection on late-night waits in lonely depots. Using excellent sense he quickly conferred with Hannan; the two of them quietly removed the gun before delivering the bag.

The decision made them both nervous, however, since rumors were circulating that some members would try to overpower La Follette physically if there were no other way to keep him quiet. And he seemed incapable of quiet. He warned the presiding officer that he had rights and that "someone would get hurt" if he was denied them. When Senator Owen finished his remarks, he tried to pass the floor to Hitchcock. La Follette leaped to his feet simultaneously with Hitchcock and demanded recognition; for a moment he, Hitchcock, Owen, and Delaware's Willard Saulsbury, the presiding officer, stood screaming at each other. There was a stirring on the Democratic side led by the gigantic Ollie James of Kentucky, a ripple of movement toward La Follette. Bob, Jr., open-mouthed, expected "a riot right there on the floor of the Senate." Harry Lane of Oregon, one of the filibusterers, slipped behind James. He told Bob later that he knew James had a gun, and if he made a move toward it he, Lane, intended to plunge a rat-tail file kept ready in his pocket into James's throat.

Someone broke the tension with a quorum call. Hitchcock was recognized and began to speak. La Follette rose with a parliamentary inquiry. Joseph Robinson of Arkansas interrupted with a "point of order" that La Follette was making a speech and should be forced to sit down. "I will continue on this floor," La Follette roared, "until I complete my statement unless somebody carries me off, and I should like to see the man who will do it." He and Robinson stood nose to nose in the aisle, red-faced, Saulsbury banging the gavel. Finally La Follette did agree to sit down where he remained, enraged and helpless as Hitchcock continued to use up the flying minutes.

He kept trying to break in; there were sharp exchanges with other senators, accusations of falsehood, sarcastic jibes. Nebraska's George Norris went over to calm him down but Bob said that he would get recognition one way or another, if he had to throw a spittoon at the rostrum. Young Bob sent him a frantic note: "Please, please be calm—you know what the press will do. Remember mother." Another note followed: "You can not afford to get into a physical argument or be arrested by the Sergt. at Arms for misconduct. You are noticeably and extremely excited. For God's sake make your protest & prevent passage of bill if you like, but . . . do not try to fight Senate physically. I am almost crazy with strain."

Finally, twenty-two-year-old Bob dashed up to the family gallery where Gilbert Roe was looking on and asked advice. Roe told him to tell Bob that "the way to meet those fellows is to smile at them." This advice of an old friend, relayed by note, got through where other counsels had failed. The actor in La Follette took over. He glanced over at his son, smiled, and for the rest of a morning filled with fencing and bickering in attempts to force a vote, he gazed at Hitchcock with an ironic smile of mock attention. Perhaps it had occurred to him at last that Woodrow Wilson, who had come down to sign last-minute legislation, was sitting in an adjoining room, impotent like Bob himself, and fuming in defeat.

The clock struck, the bang of the gavel resounded, and it was over. Bob rose from his seat, walked alone to the back of the chamber where he joined Hannan and Bob, Jr., and continued on with them to his office, ignoring spectators and reporters. Gil and Netha Roe, Fola, and Andrew Furuseth were waiting for him there. Furuseth put his arm around his friend. "Bob," he said, "they'll crucify you. But God bless you."

He wired Belle: "Fought it through to the finish. Feeling here is intense. I must take the gaff for a time." But he believed that he had postponed "aggressive action" until the crisis had passed and the country might be spared entry into the war. "If it does work out that way it will be the greatest service which could be rendered our country and humanity."

Belle's letter was already on the way to him. These two knew each other so well that they answered questions which had not yet been put. She gave him the approval that she had been supplying for his many years of charging dragons. "You have used the power and opportunity that was yours for humanity and democracy . . . I am filled with a deep sense of thanksgiving beyond all words to express. You are sure to be terribly maligned and misunderstood and probably the general public will never get on to the absurdity and dangerous trend of Wilson's usurpation of power." She did not know the half of it. "Maligned" was a major understatement.[21]

"There will come an awakening"

The filibuster actually bought very little time. Within a few days the attorney general rendered an opinion that Wilson had the inherent authority to arm merchant ships without congressional consent, lending weight to the notion that what he had wanted was not legal sanction but public arousal. The actual arming of ships began on March 12, a day on which the American merchant ship *Algonquin* was sunk without warning. Inside of another week there were three more sinkings, and the president issued the expected call for a special session to meet on April 2. It was assumed that its first order of business would be the issue of war or peace. On March 15 the pro-war forces got an unexpected boost when the czar of Russia abdicated. The war could now be packaged as a crusade for democracy without his inconvenient presence among the Allies.

La Follette had hoped that time would cool down war fever, but he underestimated the power of the press to keep it burning, especially when encouraged from the top. Wilson set the tone by a furious public reaction to the filibuster. He called it the work of "a little group of willful men, representing no opinion but their own," who had "rendered the great government of the United States helpless and contemptible."[22] His inflammatory language was echoed almost unanimously by the nation's editors who seemed to compete to see who could be most indignant. The *New York Times* said that "the odium of treasonable purpose" would dog the filibusterers forever. The *New York World* declared that La Follette and the others had denied "consciences and courage in order to make a Prussian holiday. Shame on them now and forever!" Others referred to the twelve as "knaves" and "perverts." Since pictures were already becoming more powerful than words in the arsenal of mass persuasion, one of the worst blows was a Rollin Kirby cartoon in the *World* that showed La Follette standing at the head of his little group while a mailed fist pinned the Iron Cross on his lapel.[23]

Denunciation came from other sources, too. Sixteen members of the Wisconsin Senate signed a round robin regretting that La Follette had helped to give "the impression abroad that we are not only helpless against attack from foreign countries but divided and disloyal at home." At a mass meeting of the American Rights League in New York's Carnegie Hall the audience howled "Traitor!" each time La Follette's name was mentioned. These feelings were expressed while the country was still at peace. In the week immediately following the filibuster La Follette was shunned by fellow senators during Wilson's second inaugural and spat on in a streetcar.

The Senate itself quickly adopted a new "cloture" rule, providing that by a two-thirds vote, debate on a question could be limited to one hour per speaker. Only three members of the world's greatest deliberative body voted against it.[24]

Almost no one defended Bob publicly, though he took comfort in the fact that his constituent mail was running about nine to one in favor of his stand. The Reverend Walter Rauschenbusch, for example, a pacifist and spokesman for a reform-minded "social gospel" theology, assured him that in spite of the "hateful and vindictive" messages he would receive, there were "others who appreciate what you have done." Rauschenbusch assumed that some "spiritual compulsion" was behind Bob's course; "certainly there was no outward gain to be had by it."

The most generous words were those of close friends who were on the other side but respected La Follette's character. It is easy to understand Bob's deep affection for Louis Brandeis in the light of the note he got from the justice on March 8. "Dear Bob: I think you are wrong, but I love you all the same. Won't you come and dine with me this evening?"[25]

But his position was still a lonely one. He had always gloried in standing isolated against "the interests." Now, however, his cherished "people" seemed to be turning against him. On the morning of Monday, April 2, he awoke in a Washington tense with expectation of the president's message slated for that evening. Parades and meetings had been banned to prevent clashes between pro-war demonstrators and pacifist delegations arriving to present final petitions. Around eight, the president arrived in a light rain, behind a jingling cavalry escort with drawn sabers. The senators had marched two by two to the House chamber to await him, many with tiny flags tucked in their lapels. The officeholding elite of Washington, the cabinet members, the Supreme Court justices, the foreign ambassadors—all rose to their feet in storms of applause as Wilson entered. Reporters took note that La Follette, too, got to his feet, but silently and without joining in the handclaps.

Wilson's speech lasted thirty-six minutes, punctuated by cheers and demonstrations. He reviewed German provocations, vowed that the country "would not choose the path of submission," and pledged that the war would be fought not to gain sordid or temporary advantages but to make the world safe for democracy. As he swept to his final words, "America is privileged to spend her blood and her might for the principles that gave her birth and happiness . . . God helping her, she can do no other," wave after wave of applause rocked the Capitol. Bob La Follette stood silently, arms folded, chewing gum, ready to confront the war express hurtling down on him because he, too, could do no other.[26]

He held up the war vote for twenty-four hours by refusing unanimous consent for its immediate consideration on Tuesday morning. That night in New York a Columbia professor, in a public lecture, linked the names of La Follette and Bryan with other such "immortals" as Judas Iscariot and Benedict Arnold, while in Boston, M.I.T. students set a dummy figure of the senator aflame and danced around it in the glow.

The resolution came up on Wednesday at 10 A.M. and was debated all day. Most of the hours were consumed by seventeen pro-war orations, urging the Senate to unite in supporting the president upon whom war had been forced by German militarism. Only six senators voted no, and one of them, Harry Lane of Oregon, chose not to speak. The four other resisters besides La Follette who took the floor were, one way or another, heirs to the populist tradition. They made forthright class appeals, arguing that the rich would prosper and the poor would die in the coming battles.

One of the opponents was Mississippi's former governor James K. Vardaman, a striking figure in white suit and long hair, who traveled his state in ox-drawn wagons, fighting the battles of poor white farmers—and also preaching rabid racism. He had served in Cuba in 1898, but in his constituents' eyes that did not excuse his lack of patriotic spirit in 1917. They threw him out the following year.

Asle Gronna of North Dakota was a Norwegian social democrat, bred in the prairie political hothouse that sprouted the Nonpartisan League and the Farmer-Labor party after he was gone. "We criticize European monarchies for forcing their subjects into war," he said, "but . . . refuse to ascertain by a referendum . . . of the American people whether they desire peace or war." He too never served another term.

Nebraska's George Norris concealed stubborn independence behind a noncombative personal style. Though a Republican, he was much influenced by William Jennings Bryan, and his words almost directly echoed Bryan's celebrated speech of 1896, repeated by him hundreds of times on the Chautauqua platform, which concluded with the words: "You shall not crucify mankind upon a cross of gold." Norris thought that the lobbyists for manufacturers and bankers with a stake in the Allies' survival were behind America's sudden belligerence. "We are going into war upon the command of gold," he announced. "I feel we are about to put the dollar sign on the American flag."

Missouri's William Stone was a tragic case, a Democratic defector who had actually stepped down from the chairmanship of the Foreign Relations Committee to stand against the war on principle, putting his neck in a political noose rather than toy with the lives of millions. Like Vardaman he was an ex-governor. He was nearly seventy, a man of fading strength who had begun to study law when Grant was in the White House, and he spoke for less than five minutes. The heart of it was in two sentences. "Mr. President, I fear that the Congress is about to involve the United States in this European war, and when you do that, it is my belief that you will commit the greatest national blunder in history. I shall vote against this mistake, to prevent which, God helping me, I would gladly lay down my life."

These were La Follette's handful of Senate allies. They were all, Lane and Vardaman included, from areas still heavily rural, and their opposition may have been driven in part by lingering, frontierlike suspicions of the coercive power, the upper-class biases and manipulative contrivances of a modernized nation playing a great power's role. As progressives they were not necessarily afraid of government, but they were concerned, among other things, that war and preparation for war made government more the master and less the servant of its citizens. It mobilized them, preached at them, lined them up in step behind a strong president. Stone summed up the feeling in a remark to a colleague who warned him that he was committing political suicide: "I won't vote for this war because if we go into it, we will never again have this same old Republic."[27]

La Follette himself had the last word that he had been denied on March 4, speaking this time for three hours. Once again he laid out the case he often made in the pages of *La Follette's,* that we had not enforced our rights impartially between Britain and Germany and so wasted our influence as real neutrals. Whatever our injuries from the submarine campaign, they did not justify the agonies of combat. "[W]e should not seek to . . . inflame the mind of our people by half truths into the frenzy of war." His credo was in his closing words.

There is always lodged, and always will be, thank the God above us, power in the people supreme. Sometimes it sleeps, sometimes it seems the sleep of death; but, sir, the sovereign power of the people never dies. It may be suppressed for a time, it may be misled, be fooled, silenced. I think, Mr. President, that it is being denied expression now . . . The poor . . . who are the ones called upon to rot in the trenches have no organized power . . . but oh, Mr. President, at some time they will be heard . . . I think they may be heard from before long . . . there will come an awakening; they will have their day and they will be heard. It will be as certain and as inevitable as the return of the tides, and as resistless, too.[28]

There was silence as he gathered up his pages and walked to the rear of the chamber. Mississippi's other senator, John Sharp Williams, secured recognition. He was a lawyer who sparkled savagely in debate, Disheveled and hard-drinking, a graduate of a military school with ancestors who had fought in three wars (including a father killed at Shiloh), he had, in earlier remarks, urged Wilson to deploy a million-man army in France while the bands played "Dixie." "We have . . . heard a speech," he choked, flinging senatorial courtesy out the window, "which would have better become Herr Bethmann-Hollweg of the German Parliament, than an American Senator . . . pro-German, pretty nearly pro-Goth and pro-Vandal . . . anti-American President and anti-American Congress and anti-American people." No one interrupted to protest, as his voice rose to a shout, hoping to catch La Follette's attention. But La Follette ignored him and walked into the cloakroom. Later, after the 82-6 vote for war, Bob walked to his office through ranks of silent colleagues and hostile spectators, one of whom handed him a rope. The next day, the *Boston Evening Transcript* editorialized: "He is an example of the self-destructive effect of the basest form of egotism. Standing against his own country and for his country's enemies, he is gone and fallen . . . Henceforth he is the Man without a Country."[29]

La Follette was not that quite yet, and for a while he tried to fight on as a kind of loyal opponent, supporting war appropriations but resisting measures that he thought compromised democracy or fattened profiteers. He pointed out to one friend in Madison that in all of 1917 the administration submitted some sixty war measures of which he had objected to only five. These included the Conscription Act — he believed it unconstitutional and wrong in principle — and the Espionage Act, which clamped a gag on free speech in the interests of unity.

His stand on financing the war was consistent with his past record. When the first War Revenue Bill came from the administration it called for raising $7 billion in loans against $2 billion in taxes (a total that quickly proved inadequate). La Follette tried to amend it to pay for the war mainly through current revenues, which were to be increased by a 50 percent income tax. Pennsylvania's conservative Republican Senator Boies Penrose, known for a genial candor that sometimes terrified his friends, leaned over La Follette's desk at one point and said: "Baub, if you keep trying to tax these war profits, you're gonna make this war darned unpopular." But there was little danger of "Baub's" efforts succeeding, especially given his unpopularity. Hiram Johnson, La Follette's onetime progressive ally, complained that "[h]is attitude upon the war . . . has tainted him so that his leadership even in a just cause . . . will militate against that cause."[30]

La Follette made himself a thorn in Wilson's side in other ways as well. In mid-1917 desperation was cresting among the exhausted ordinary people of Europe; the year would see mutinies in the French army, revolution among Russian soldiers and sailors, demoralization and rout in the Italian ranks. Peace advocates tried yet again to get the belligerents to formulate terms for a nonvictorious peace that might be universally acceptable. In the United States a People's Council of America, comprised of distinguished progressive scholars and activists (like the tireless Jane Addams, Stanford University president David Starr Jordan, and Rabbi Judah Magnes), tried to sponsor conferences on the subject in the teeth of state bans on such gatherings and post office rulings that blocked their mailings. Bob introduced a resolution on August 11, affirming the right of Congress to declare the war aims of the United States, which should include the repudiation of annexations and indemnities and a general fund, with contributions from all the belligerents, for repairing the devastation.

Wilson had no intention of sharing the definition of war aims with anyone. On August 27—the same day that the State Department refused passports to American delegates to an international Socialist congress—he torpedoed hopes of negotiation by a statement that he approved peace without victory but would enter into no agreements of any kind with the existing government of Germany. Meanwhile, the newspapers had responded to Bob's resolution with fresh attacks. Madison's *Wisconsin State Journal* said his plan would "defend, comfort and help the greastest criminal the world has ever known." When Charles Edward Russell, a former friend and Socialist turned war enthusiast, said that every member of Congress introducing peace resolutions was doing more harm "than a million German soldiers on the battle line," the *New York Times* commented: "One can imagine how Senator La Follette's eyes glisten as he reads that. More harm than 'a million German soldiers' . . . better than he dreamed."[31]

La Follette was sure that there would be organized attempts, especially by war profiteers, to shut him up. He was trying to follow the advice of Steffens ("Be very patient, Bob"), especially in *La Follette's Magazine,* now reduced by financial constraint to a monthly. ("I suppose they are laying for a chance to put us out," he advised Fred Holmes. "They should not be given the slightest chance . . . Let us be very careful about what we print.") But on September 20 he was trapped into an extemporaneous exchange that was easily distorted to get him into real trouble.[32]

He was rarely getting invitations to speak by this time, but one did come to address a convention of the National Nonpartisan League in St. Paul. The League was a left-oriented farmer-labor organization with origins in North Dakota where, as in most of the northwest, antiwar feeling still fertilized the grassroots. La Follette had planned a talk on war revenue but discovered that Idaho's Senator William E. Borah had already claimed that topic. So he agreed to make some "off-the-cuff" remarks on popular rights in wartime to the ten thousand listeners in the auditorium.

He began by praising nonpartisanship in the defense of popular rights and moved to a discussion of his own position on military appropriations, which he would support in the interests of the troops, though he had not favored the war. To clarify the last point he went on: "I don't mean to say that we hadn't suffered grievances; we had—at the hands of Germany.

Serious grievances!" To be sure, the last remark was somewhat sarcastic, because when a voice from the audience shouted "You bet," La Follette continued: "We had cause for complaint. They had interfered with the right of American citizens to travel upon the high seas—on ships loaded with munitions for Great Britain."

He was fudging the issue himself, since not all the sunken ships carried munitions. But he repeated that he was not denying the existence of grievances, or the "technical right" of Americans to sail on ships carrying munitions below decks. He thought it a bad idea to exercise the right because the consequences could be "so awful."

There was an exchange with a heckler who called him "yellow," to which Bob, showing his old-time fire, answered that anyone who hid in a crowd was himself yellow. Calls rang through the hall to throw the heckler out, but he begged them all to calm down and give him their attention in the few minutes he had; he could deal with interruptions perfectly well. Then someone shouted: "What about the *Lusitania?*" and La Follette answered with a statement that he had heard from a newspaperman and that he believed to be true. Just before the *Lusitania* sailed, he said, Bryan warned Wilson that she had six million rounds of rifle ammunition aboard and that, therefore, Americans booked on her were violating an old statute banning travel on "vehicles" with "dangerous explosives." (Bryan denied the story of the warning later, but the *Lusitania* did have 1.5 million rifle rounds in her cargo.)[33]

La Follette finished to brisk applause and rushed for his train. But next morning's papers brought the bombshell. An Associated Press dispatch flatly (and perhaps deliberately) misquoted him as having said "We had *no* grievances against Germany," although there had been three stenographers on hand who made official transcripts that could have been checked. One was furnished by the League; the other two were from the Justice Department and from a vigilante group, the Minnesota Commission of Public Safety, both sniffing for treason.

The AP did not acknowledge that its version was wrong until seven months had passed. Meanwhile its subscribing papers ran the story that La Follette had denied the existence of American grievances—the precise opposite of his actual words—and some added, in their headlines, an additional misrepresentation: "La Follette Defends Lusitania Sinking."

The storm now broke more furiously than ever. The Minnesota Commission of Public Safety voted that his speech had been "disloyal and seditious" and petitioned the Senate to expel him. The idea was attractive to almost everyone who had come to hate the embattled little critic of the war. Roosevelt, who had already referred to him as an "unhung traitor," "the grand American neo-Copperhead," and a man who was "loyally serving one country—Germany," now declared that he would be ashamed to sit in the Senate if some way could not be found of ousting this spokesman for "the Huns within our gates." William Howard Taft, TR's rival of 1912, joined him in this call, and Nicholas Murray Butler, the distinguished president of Columbia University, was quoted as saying that "you might as well put poison in the food of every American boy that goes to his transport as to permit that man to talk as he does."[34]

Eventually, the Senate's Committee on Privileges and Elections took cognizance of a flow of anti–La Follette petitions based mainly on the misreported St. Paul speech and named a subcommittee to investigate whether or not there were actually grounds for expulsion. In the fashion of such "disciplinary" bodies within the Senate to this day, the subcommittee practiced a form of torment by delay that avoided hard decisions and left it free for convenient changes of direction, all in the name of thoroughness and justice. But while the weeks slipped by, the accused dangled in limbo, neither found guilty nor cleared. Bob's "case" was taken up in December of 1917, but repeated postponements (despite his entreaties) stalled the decision until after the 1918 elections. That turned out to be to his advantage, but it meant that for the entire year he was a pariah, neutralized and muzzled, the nightmare of gagging fully realized. He might as well, for political purposes, have actually been expelled.

His last important Senate appearance before that curtain fell was in October, and it was a sturdy defense of free speech in wartime. He challenged the campaign of intimidation launched against himself and the other antiwar senators. "[T]he right to control their own Government according to constitutional forms," he protested, was not "one of the rights that the citizens of this country are called upon to surrender in time of war." More than ever, citizenship required a watchful eye on military encroachment and untrammeled debate in order to shape a peace based on "a due regard for the rights and honor of this Nation and the interests of humanity.

"Why should not the American people voice their convictions through their chosen representatives in Congress?" he asked. "Have the people no intelligent contribution to make to the solution of the problems of this war? I believe that they have, and that in this matter, as in so many others, they may be wiser than their leaders and that, if left free to discuss the issues of the war, they will find the correct settlement of those issues."

It was one of his best speeches ever. Bobbie, bursting with pride, wrote to the family: "I would have given almost anything if you had been here yesterday . . . It was GREAT . . . I think I am not being carried away when I say that it is one of the great addresses of all time."[35]

He was not the only one to think so. Eugene V. Debs, the Socialist party's admired leader who would himself go to jail a year later for antiwar utterances, sent him a letter marked "No answer!" (to spare La Follette any further pressure on his time). "You have had the central part in the great drama of the past few weeks and you have borne yourself with such absolute rectitude, such uncompromising courage, such lofty bearing as to win the admiration and love of the honest people not only of your own country but of the whole civilized world . . . The people are with you in every hour and every moment of your trial and history will do you justice."

La Follette believed that. He could not have endured otherwise. His answer ran: "From my heart I thank you for your beautiful letter. It will always have a cherished place with those which have come to me from other great souls in these mad days. In this chaos I do not see very far ahead. I do try to face the right way, keep my feet on the ground, and my faith in the people . . . What is done to me does not concern me so much as what, if anything, I can do for democracy. The need is very great."[36]

Belle was always amazed at the persistence of her husband's confidence in the eventual wisdom of people. "Bob never loses faith in the people," she reported to Netha Roe in 1913 after the 1912 campaign, "and I'm glad he does not." When the progressives were trounced in Wisconsin in 1914, she reassured Bobbie: "[N]othing could ever make your papa believe that Wisconsin or the country is going to be always reactionary. He says one better die than lose faith." Now, during the war, she told the children once more: "Nothing phases [*sic*] Bob or destroys his faith in the ultimate outcome of all this malign feeling."[37]

But no one's faith since Job's was more sorely tested. He had scarcely taken his seat after the speech on wartime civil rights before Senator Robinson was responding: "There are only two sides to this conflict—Germanism and Americanism; the Kaiser or the President." He suggested that La Follette should leave the Senate and apply for a seat in its German equivalent, the Bundesrat.

The rage against all things German, against the slightest hint of "disloyalty," was enough to dismay anyone convinced of the reasonableness of people at large. It was fed by a massive effort from the top. A Committee on Public Information was created that flooded the country with posters, pamphlets, films, cartoon strips, advertisements, speakers, and syllabi denouncing the beast of Berlin. Voluntary censors and self-appointed watchdog groups operated with governmental blessing to destroy any vestige of independent thought. German language courses were banned in many schools. Learned historians taught college-level "war issues" courses that twisted European history into approved anti-German patterns. Ministers of Christ like the Reverend Newell D. Hillis said that he would extend Christian forgiveness to the people of Germany "just as soon as they are all shot." With the intellectual elite so maddened with what Steffens, in a letter to Bob, called "war insanity," who could blame the uneducated for outrages like forcing suspected pro-Germans to kneel and kiss the flag? Or, in one case, actually lynching a young immigrant in St. Louis? The legal machinery of federal and state governments bulldozed away at dissent; the antiwar Socialist magazine *The Masses* was kept from the mails; Eugene Debs was jailed, as were the leaders of the antiwar syndicalist labor federation, the Industrial Workers of the World.[38]

All of it went on with the consent, or at least the public silence, of Woodrow Wilson. Whatever his other virtues, he set the tone for a government that not only failed to calm war hysteria but accepted it as an organizing tool and used it as a weapon—a weapon that was powerful and effective and used with unrelenting devastation against La Follette. By mid-1918 he was used to the articles that compared his work to the operations of German spies; the cartoons showing him forcing a German spiked helmet on the head of a ravished-looking female figure named "Wisconsin"; the headlines that explained how he "Would March to the White House to the Tune of 'Die Wacht Am Rhein.'" He had the energy to fight back with libel suits against some of the newspapers in Madison accusing him of treason. He could even try to ignore being thrown out of the Madison Club. It was much harder to take rejection from the university. Four hundred twenty-one faculty members signed a petition protesting against his utterances that "have given aid and comfort to Germany and her allies." Worst of all was the public letter of Charles Van Hise, his classmate and friend and now university president, to the president of the Wisconsin Alumni Council, calling La Follette's policies "dangerous to the country."[39]

Yet he believed that the propaganda barrages fired by the government only proved that there was no real popular will to war, that consent had to be manufactured quickly and fiercely before truth began to dawn. To him, it was the great majority of fellow progressives, closing ranks behind the war, who really did not trust the people at large. Many of them, later frightened by the success with which the manipulation had worked, began to entertain doubts about the capacity of "the masses" to think for themselves without wise leadership and direction from above. The war had some effect on what one scholar calls "the rise of a substantial nagging fear of the people among modern liberals."[40]

La Follette had no such fears, but his confidence was maintained at a price. He needed the sustenance of the family more than ever, and he got it in full measure, even though they were not as assured as he was of an eventual happy ending. They walked through the flame together, tasting despair and aging, and without the old sustaining sense that America was right behind them.

THE FAMILY UNDER DURESS

"This horrible thing is with one day and night"

The strain La Follette was under showed in his forthright private confessions of discouragement and fatigue. He admitted to being "tired, depressed and lonesome" in the first week of February, though "nothing matter[ed] so long as we are doing what is right." Just after the armed-ship filibuster, still frantically trying to organize an antiwar front, he told Belle: "[L]ittle sleep last night . . . no time for any tonight . . . I must work as long as I can stay awake. Lordie, but I have needed your counsel and help these days. It has been an awful trial . . . [but] I couldn't have done anything else unless I went down and slipped into the Potomac and the water's too cold for that now."[41]

By March 10 he could no longer stand to be without Belle. "If things at the farm are so you could leave on an early train," he begged, "I would be glad to have you come." She did and stayed until late in May. Then she went back to Maple Bluff taking Mary, freshly graduated from high school, with her. At eighteen, Mary offered a short and sharp summation of current events "I am so sick of this war I can't stand to think of it."

Young Bob went back to Maple Bluff for part of the summer of 1917, too, leaving La Follette to unburden himself of still more gloom to Belle. "Life here — and I suppose there, too — is very depressing. This horrible thing is with one day and night. It is said that they go mad in the trenches. It would be a blessing from God if they could go mad before they reach the trenches."

But the senator stayed in his own trenches, getting older and wearier. "We work every day at the office and I get to bed at 1 or 2 in the morning . . . I am like a hack horse and go at a shack. I don't feel the whip or anything — just shack along." He was looking older than his sixty-three years. Middleton noted to Young Bob, "Your father has grown grey and remained poor in his fight — how many have both distinctions?"

In the past Bob had gone for many months without Belle at his side, but that was when he was traveling, earning money, and hearing the murmurs and stirrings of coming progressive victories in every hamlet and lecture hall. Now it was different, and before August was over he was warning the children in Madison that "I shall have to steal Mamma at least part of the time or I'll go nutty down here all alone."

What Bob meant by "alone" was without any member of the immediate family. Cousin Will and wife were with him at 3320 Sixteenth, and so was their young daughter Clara La Follette. Later, taking the first name of Suzanne, she would become a well-known radical writer and commentator on her own. In 1917–1918, she kept a secret journal to which she confided her enormous admiration for Cousin Bob, "the most magnificent fighter I ever imagined." On the rare occasions when he was neither too busy nor too tired, "Cousin Bob" would read aloud to the group. He also kept his grip on reason by sometimes shelving war talk to send Belle and Phil long-distance advice on running the farm; likewise by reminding himself of how blessed he felt in the children. In his enforced isolation he seemed to realize, as if for the first time, some of the difficulties that his chosen way of life made for them. How wonderful it was for Mary to graduate

as though she hadn't had knock-outs year after year from every sort of sickness and then first in one school and then another until she couldn't tell whether she was coming or going. God bless her, she is a girl in a million. And Phil—to have gone through the earthquake that tore the University from its foundations and threw the faculty into hysterics—and to have preserved his sanity and finished his year's work with credit fills me with the greatest satisfaction. The Lord has been good to us in our children.

"Good night, beloved ones," Bob scrawled late one night. "I love you with every drop of blood that my old heart drives through my tired old body."[42]

"This war mad university of ours"

Bob's praise of Phil for surviving the "earthquake" that shook the university in the spring of 1917 was well deserved. He was only a nineteen-year-old sophomore, caught in the middle of what he later recalled as a "violent emotional storm" blowing across the country as a whole, but in Madison precipitating "a holocaust of abuse and assault." During those years, he wrote, "I never heard the name La Follette spoken in public places without flinching and bracing myself for some epithet."[43]

Phil's problems were compounded by a second son's battle for recognition and separate identity. Though he loved Young Bob, it was not always easy to accept an implied preferential status for him. Bobbie was, for better or worse, the apple of his father's eye, whereas Phil had closer emotional ties to Belle. He reflected her own introspective, work-dominated and studious side. But at the same time he had much of his father's platform magnetism and not a little of his combativeness, which led the two of them into occasional angry confrontations. After one of them in the spring of 1916, Phil wrote a stormy note to Young Bob, then in Washington, saying that since Dad seemed to "resent anything in the way of friendship from this kid of his, . . . he shall never see it in me again." He threatened to drop out of school rather than continue to take Dad's money, but couldn't help adding a characteristic note of prudent reasoning: "But I'll not do anything rash, spectacular or sorry-for-later. I take it mighty slow." There was a pattern in Phil's life of headstrong drives wrestling with the mind's advice to go slow.[44]

The quarrel did not last long. Phil apologized; the matter was soon forgotten, and Dad shortly thereafter began to "look on me not as a youth but as a young man who in certain respects might be more like him than Bob was." Phil won the Freshman Declamatory Oration contest and got a bear hug and a kiss from Old Bob, who had tears in his eyes. He also continued to forge the shining academic record that had been expected of the older brother. Moreover, living steadily in Madison now, he took on more and more of the work of farm manager. Only a well-organized and diligent youngster could have combined campus and work responsibilities so successfully and left time—carefully allotted and measured—for hiking, reading, and a reasonable amount of socializing.

Yet Phil still had the La Follette second-generation problem of finding some sense of himself as a separate being while trying, in his words, to meet "the honor and responsibility of trying to live up to the greatest name in our history." Belle and Bob had worked hard and successfully to make their children independent, yet bound them to frustrating inner struggles. "I know that it will take an almost superhuman effort on any of our parts to even approximate living up to you," Phil told Old Bob after the armed-ship filibuster. "I love you so for your courage, your bravery . . . Oh I pray to God that I may in some small way be worthy of you. I do so want to make my life worth while, but you have set an almost unattainable goal for me." He adored Belle, too. "The hours of life go clinking by," ran his letter to her on his own twentieth birthday, "but my thankfulness of having been born to you increases with each hour at compound interest . . . Till the clock of time stops ticking . . . you'll find my loving ever increasing." The relationship with Belle was easier than with his father; as a young male he did not feel that he needed to match or excel her.[45]

The war, for all the anguish it brought Phil, offered him an opening to create a sharper self-profile, by taking a part in it. He knew how his father opposed the war, but he hoped, correctly in the event, that a well-argued independent choice of serving in it once it became inevitable would win respect. As early as January of 1917 he wrote, asking permission to join the American Ambulance Corps in France. "I really do not believe in war," he explained, but the experience "would make a man out of me . . . I need something to bracen me up—to make me stronger morally and physically—something that will give me . . . assurance that I have the real stuff in me."

Bob's answer was either lost or not confided to paper, but the question was made moot by the double-time march of events. By mid-April, the country was at war, and Phil, like college boys everywhere, especially those who leaned toward pacifism, was having serious talks with his friends about what duty dictated: enlistment, waiting for the draft, or nonparticipation to whatever extent possible. Phil's intimates seemed to agree that "doing their duty" would enable them to speak against future wars with greater authority. Belle countered with the reminder that enlistment would give tacit approval to the war actually in progress. Phil responded by repeating that a veteran could "fight against war with so much more influence and vigor, BECAUSE one has been a soldier, and knows what trench digging is, what it means to live with vermin, rats, *etc.*" He also raised a political consideration with a hint of future plans in it. He was tempted to take officer training because "one would have more influence as an officer, after the war."

In any case, enlistment offered an escape from a campus that seemed to have lost sight of its academic purpose. "[W]ith everything so torn up, the profs all chasing around like a bunch of stuck pigs, and about the only cool thing in sight Old Lake Mendota," Phil judged, "there isn't going to be much studying for anyone."[46]

Worst of all, the merciless public drubbing of the elder La Follette made what should have been carefree student life an ordeal to escape as much as possible. He moved out of his fraternity house after a local newspaper, taking note of his presence, described it as a "hotbed of sedition." He tried to ignore cuts and snubs from old family acquaintances. "Don't worry about me," he wrote bravely. "Most people [are] fairly friendly and the others I don't give a damn about." But he needed getaways. After Bob and Belle talked him out of immediate enlistment in the spring of 1917 he kept himself away from the campus. He plunged into dogged work in the arbor, the yard, the fields of potatoes, corn, oats, and alfalfa, and, for a break from the farm, the office of *La Follette's Magazine.* He visited out-of-town friends and holed up at the farm on wet spring weekends with a few earnest pals. He signed on for summer school to accelerate his progress toward the diploma, eager to be done with the grind.

Yet Madison was in his blood. Phil turned out to be the one child of the four who would never leave the town of his birth (except for a few unsatisfactory years toward the end of his life). He offered to go to school in Washington if it would help Bob to have him nearby but made it clear that he would "rather stay here in this war mad university of ours and sort of 'stick to my guns.'"

And in a perverse way, the ordeal became, in Phil's eyes, a rite of passage that proved him both independently strong yet worthy of La Follette-hood. "If I ever amount to anything of any account," he decided near the end of 1917, "it will be due quite largely to this crisis. Bob, Mary and I had come into our life of realization at the time when Dad had become 'respectable'—we had not been through what Fola had—at the early time of our struggle—we had become . . . inculcated with the idea that the life of a reformer was easy . . . That kind of thing doesn't make men . . . [T]his crisis is something to make us go on our own fibre. We have to paddle our own canoe . . . I love you all dear ones. The corn is getting into the silo today—the colts are back and look mighty fine."

So Phil entered 1918 poised for takeoff in some unknown direction. Then new calamity struck; Bobbie became seriously sick again, and Phil's enlistment problem dropped from the center of family attention.[47]

"Bobbie is plucky"

If the essence of being a La Follette, as Phil's letter suggested, was to expend oneself in a worthy cause against all odds, then Bob, Jr., was proving his right to belong with every desperate hour of 1917. He took on an enormous load of political and personal chores. He dictated replies to the stacks of mail that arrived for his father each day. He prepared a weekly column from Washington that was mailed to a number of small papers around the country whose publishers were still willing to hear what was going on in Senator La Follette's office. He was also the liaison with the managing editor of *La Follette's Magazine,* which remained Old Bob's muffled but much-needed outlet. There was, in fact, some thought given to sending him out to Madison to take over as editor and business manager. Belle seems to have vetoed the idea, possibly because she believed that a more experienced hand than her son's was needed to keep off both the creditors and the sedition-hunters. Unfortunately, Bobbie took her failure to be "prostrated with enthusiasm for my coming out to the magazine" as a sign that somehow he had been weighed and found wanting again. "I regarded it with great apprehension," he wrote her; "nevertheless I also felt that should the decision be made giving me the chance I would take it as I looked upon it as the greatest opportunity yet offered to me . . . There is important work to do here, however."

The fact was that Bobbie was growing swiftly, temporarily taking the stabilizing role in the family that neither his beleaguered parents nor Fola had time for. He dropped cheerful notes to Fola when she was "somewhat depressed" and fed Mary's need for approval, which was all the stronger because she tended to get lost in the whirlwind of activities into which events sucked the others. "How is dat?" he teased her after her high school graduation in June. "De wonderful woman wid bumps and all is learned to paint and make geometry and English and de history and got de well known sheep skin to prove it . . . I am de proud brother this day . . . You see I am as crazy as ever in spite of the war . . . [T]he part about your graduation that I like to think about most is the way you came through all by yourself." That fall, having decided she was not ready to go to college, Mary stayed on at Maple Bluff while taking secretarial courses in Madison. When she complained to Bobbie that she was slow and "stupid" in her shorthand courses, he jollied her along. Everyone had trouble learning it; "I have heard many other stenographers say the same thing . . . I love you, honey."[48]

Young Bob was managing the checkbook, too, and it was a grim job with the senator's lecture income evaporated. "Please send all the bills for this month on promptly," he asked Phil, "so I can get my list up and select the favored few." The situation was so tight that he asked his younger brother, already burdened with full-time studies and the work of the farm, to do any needed mechanical and maintenance work on the family car himself rather than going to a garage. "I know how busy you are," he sympathized, "and how tired you must be at the end of the week but you see, dad's income is limited to the salary these days and we must all try and help."

He was himself pushed to the edge of exhaustion by the brutal regimen. "I am so tired," he confided, "that I could sleep standing on the toes of one foot." It was, in the long run, too much for his system, which had never really overcome the bacterial infection of 1915 and now fell before it again. "I am surprised how well I stand the strain,"[49] he wrote buoyantly late in 1917, but the new year had hardly started before he was once again flattened by a high temperature. Very quickly his case became so severe that he needed round-the-clock nursing, and in February he was rushed to the hospital for surgery to drain pus from his lung cavity. Once again the cycle of three years earlier was repeated—critically high temperatures, swellings, severe pain, and total enervation. This time he was in bed so long that the muscles in the backs of his legs became atrophied and contracted; so long that it was August before he could gamely report his joy at again being "able to wipe my own rectum"; so long that convalescence would take almost a year of additional pain, rehabilitative exercises, and a slow return to walking with the help of crutches and cane.[50]

But the family was relieved that Young Bob got better at all, after many crises when they feared he would die. In a perverse way his son's desperate condition was a salvation for Old Bob, who hovered at the bedside, often administering medicines with his own hands. The siege took all of his attention during many months of his political exile and kept him from brooding his own way into serious depression or rash public outbursts. It was the kind of challenge he needed. "[A]ll we can do is fight on," he wrote to Phil at one point. "We are bound to win. Bobbie is plucky and so long as he can keep his fighting spirit we can stand these battles." At the same time, the doctor bills remorselessly piled new debts on old ones which were already large enough so that Belle, on learning of them, wrote to Bob that "it seemed to me I would have to give up the ghost, but after a few days I recovered as I have for the past hundred or more years and went ahead."[51]

When the summer heat of 1918 blasted Washington, the family escaped with the invalid to Hot Springs, Virginia, for a couple of weeks. Then in September, Belle took him to California for nearly a year of recuperation in the mild sun and crisp Pacific air of La Jolla, where they lived in a cottage rented for forty-five dollars a month. Mary went along to help with the nursing and to occupy her time with college-prep courses in a private academy that became Scripps College. By then Phil was in service and Fola, who had helped valiantly in nursing Bobbie in Washington, returned to Middleton's side in New York. Old Bob was now left truly alone in the capital. The family had never been more scattered, and ironically the cause was in Bobbie who, almost more than any of them, hated the separation. "Each year," he had declared in Madison at the start of 1917, "we have said we must not be separated and yet we have. If we are again it will only be after I have exercised all my 'influence' and persuasive power to prevent

Young Bob, in California with Belle in 1919, showed the ravages of his long illness.

it." When sickness struck it was another in a string of depressing blows to his hopes and self-esteem.[52]

"The maze of doubt that engulfs us all"

Phil finally made his own decision at the end of his junior year when Bobbie was out of immediate danger of dying. Left to his own devices in Madison for the most part, he was gnawed by uncertainty about how best to further his ambitions in an unfriendly environment. He had already shown plenty of energy and organizing capacity in his work on and around the farm, the training school in responsibility for both boys. But to what end? Whom would he lead? And where? What was his mission as a reformer's son in wartime? In a world with shaken confidence in eternal progress? What was the future of a La Follette without public portfolio? Reading and nature walks deepened the confusion. Shakespeare's "reactionary and basically unhelpful view of humanity," he reported in a passage that wonderfully reveals the frame of mind of a youthful progressive, "undermines all of our faiths in the ultimate success of mankind." But the progressivism was not rock-solid; given what was happening around him, he was not so sure of mankind after all. "How much saner and wiser are the mere bugs," he ruminated a few weeks later. "They create and work to bring new and more life rather than to destroy . . . We must make our civilization come back to drink at nature, fountain of true wisdom."

So few things remained certain in a clouded time. Phil was grateful for the steady beacon of Belle. On his twenty-first birthday he wrote her with the note of melancholy that sounded in the background of all the family letters in May of 1918: "Through the maze of doubt which engulfs us all, nothing is of as much strength as to know I am your son."[53]

Finally, Phil went into action. Faced with the draft (though a slight heart murmur might have excused him), he shopped among choices and signed up for a summer officer's training program in Fort Sheridan, outside of Chicago, still half apologetic to his parents about becoming part of the war machine. But it was an excellent decision for everyone. He was adept in training, was commissioned, and was then sent on to the Student Army Training Center on the campus of the University of Oklahoma at Norman as a personnel adjutant. It kept him out of France and harm's way (not by his choice), which was a relief to Bob and Belle. And he proved to be a first-class, diligent administrator who adapted to and enjoyed staff routine and even considered extending his enlistment at the war's end. He relished the independence of his own room in a rooming house off base, the independent salary— which he overspent, to Belle's horror—the praise of his superiors, the sense of success achieved without reliance on the family name.

Because of Bobbie's illness, Phil had outgrown the role of kid brother and they both knew it. He visited the sickroom once in Washington just before his enlistment, to say good-bye. Not trusting himself to speak, he left a note for Mary to hand to Bobbie. "You are one in ten million . . . my love for you permeates every fibre of my body." Poor Bobbie's response was to rate himself even lower. "Phil has such a wonderful future before him," he confided to Fola after the visit. "He will amount to so much and I shall never amount to anything." He felt no better about it a few months later, sitting in his wheelchair on the porch at La Jolla and watching the Pacific surf pounding the rocks. "They tell us that sickness means growth, but I fail to see or feel it. Perhaps I am the exception that proves the rule."[54]

Yet even Phil's success in the army, which set him apart, was a temporary interlude in the wartime bleakness that enveloped the driven family.

"The dark cloud that has hung over one's heart"

The women suffered in their own fashion. Mary, dogged by feelings of inferiority in any case, lamented her academic shortcomings in California even while she was reading Galsworthy, Romain Rolland, and Balzac at home. Simple, intelligent literacy was merely taken for granted in families of the La Follette type in that era of yet-undwindled intellectual expectations. Mary believed that she was letting the side down. She wrote to Belle once that "I know that every day I do things which must hurt you and disappoint you and that you overlook them in your big, fine, wonderful way."

Belle did overlook them. "I want to tell you not to worry one little bit about your work," she answered. "Just keep at it in your own way, doing your best without any nervous strain." There were no pep talks, no exhortations, no rallying cries. Mary was permitted to drop college plans. Having a gift for drawing, she asked if she might study art in New York or Washington when the war was over. The answer was yes. For whatever reasons, Mary would not be expected to vindicate the educational investment made in her by some larger service.

Belle had become more tolerant, or perhaps more resigned, less the crusader and more the protective mother. The betrayal of antiwar principle (as she saw it) by progressive friends had toppled her unswerving confidence in the educated elite as the vanguard of freedom. But oddly that made her more of a populist democrat. When Phil wrote about the spasms of superpatriotism racking the campus, she responded: "It is a clear indication to me, since the universities and schools are the worst nests of intolerance and ignorance . . . that there is something wrong in the training . . . The men who toil with their hands seem to be better balanced and to arrive at sounder conclusions and to have less egotism and prejudice."[55]

Barred from the lecture platform—and with the suffrage battle virtually won anyway—Belle found most happiness when the family was united and when Bobbie was on the mend. There was a brief moment in August when everyone had gathered at Hot Springs except Phil, and she captured a rare moment of tranquil togetherness in a letter to him. Fola was trimming a hat, Mid reading French, "Daddy" napping, Bobbie enjoying the air, and even Bud, the family bulldog, snoozing happily in a cool spot. This was the best that could be hoped for from life now. She mentioned the political scene less and less, though it thrust itself into her mind in spite of her now and again. "Oh, if this war would only stop! How has it been possible for the world to endure it so long."[56]

Fola was as unhappy as Belle and less philosophic. The political alienation that had begun for her on the hot plains of Kansas and Nebraska in 1914 was nearly completed by her family's travails. She directed more of her social energies to Greenwich Village life and to helping George, whose career was doing well. He had two successive hit collaborations with Guy Bolton, *Adam and Eva* and *Polly with a Past.* Money was coming in during midsummer of 1917, which was soothing, and yet "I find myself the victim of such overwhelming bitterness against what *is,*" Fola cried out, "that it's hard some times." Even Siasconset, her vacation refuge by the sea, offered no escape. Everyone was knitting or digging in victory gardens, and the atmosphere was "jingo jingo."[57]

So the next fall, after a spring spent deeply involved in the care of Bobbie, she and Mid chose an even more remote escape than Nantucket. They went to Moosehead Lake in Maine and spent September and October at the home of a friend, Gardner Hale. It was a sylvan idyll. She enjoyed the freedom of "trousers," the days spent in cutting firewood and fishing, the triumphs of Mid and Gardner when they bagged a deer for the pot. "I am very happy in this wild forest," she told the scattered clan. "Should like to live in here until the world becomes a different place."

News of the fighting, the flu epidemic then raging, and even the approaching end of the ordeal seemed distant. German peace overtures only reminded her of "how every fibre of one's being is yearning for the word that the world will cease its hideous carnage." As it happened, the actual date of leaving their getaway island of "green pines and red and gold leaves" was November 11, Armistice Day, and they got the news as they debarked. She shared the joy of it with her two brothers. "I hope that life may become a little more tolerable," was her word to Phil, "and that some of my complexes about old New York may be resolved and dissipated through the lifting of the dark cloud that has hung over one's heart this last four years." With Bob, she was playful in a Thanksgiving Day note. "Are I thankful this day? Well I are as I haven't been for years—the war over, and you welling up and walking with a cane . . . Phil soon on the free—Mary, Mummy and Dad well and all our hearts freed of the terrific world burden that has shadowed everything. Are I thankful? Well I are from the soul of my foots to the crown of my head."[58]

It was a joyful time all right, thanks to the winds of politics. In the fall elections, Wilson had prematurely thrown wartime nonpartisanship overboard and asked for the return of a Democratic Congress. What he got, even as victory was only days away, was the first wave of reaction to the draft, the taxes, the casualties, the shortages, the high prices, and the other aspects of wartime life left out of the recruiting posters. The Republicans won control of the House and enough Senate races to give them 49 of 96 seats. But Bob La Follette was one of those 49. If he were not allowed—or did not choose—to vote with the Republicans to organize the Senate and went instead with the Democrats, that would create a 48-48 tie, to be broken by the Democratic vice president.

La Follette, the pariah, held the key to Republican control of the Senate. Revenge was no less sweet for being unexpected. Not surprisingly the Committee on Privileges and Elections swiftly dismissed the charges against him when Congress reconvened in December, and an actual courtship of his vote got under way. He was grateful and satisfied, above all because he was convinced that at last the voters had seen the light. Yet he knew that it was not that simple; that he and his family, the country, and the world were altered past recognition by age, by time, by history. Events would show that as the La Follette story rolled toward unexpected conclusions. On New Year's Eve, 1918, he wrote to his loved ones: "One of the hardest things about the last two years is the feeling of repression we have had to carry around with us. It is an awful strain on one's poise and control. I know it has made me a very different person to live with. Sometimes I wonder if I will ever be just the same again."

7

In Another Country: Old Bob's Last Campaigns (1919–1925)

VINDICATION WITHIN LIMITS

"Does it not seem possible . . . the hatred was not real?"

The anticipation of a celebration often makes people bubble over even before the happy event itself takes place. On November 7, 1918, two days after the elections put the key to Republican control of the Senate in his hands, Bob La Follette exulted that old enemies were "indicating quite a mellowness towards a certain much despised member." Technically, he was still facing expulsion, but in political reality the threat was lifted, and he was not going to be expelled.

And on that very Thursday afternoon, a false armistice report reached Washington, a city still at war but completely aware that with the kaiser's abdication and flight, German surrender was imminent. Like La Follette, the people of Washington glowed in premature exhilaration. Crowds spilled into the streets, hugging, singing, cheering, and weeping. Bob reconstructed the scene from newspaper stories next day. "It was all clean ecstatic joy," he told the family, and in the midst of it all "a young man—a *wonderful* whistler" began to whistle the German anthem, *Die Wacht Am Rhein,* to cheers and applause. Two hours earlier, he would have been mobbed, but now, "Peace had come and hatred seemed suddenly to have died the death. Does it not seem possible that the hatred was not real; that the war enthusiasm was a sham; that with the *restraints off* the thing that has been cowed and repressed found natural expression[?] May we not get back to the normal sooner than seemed possible and find that the *great mass* of our people were not war mad? Let us hope and pray that it will prove to be the case."[1]

In hoping to "get back to the normal" La Follette divined the country's mood. Two years later, the voters would elect Ohio's Warren G. Harding, a fellow member of the Senate, to the White House on the strength of his pledge to restore what he called "normalcy."

But there was a difference in what the two midwesterners meant by the term. For Old Bob it meant a time in which resources and attention could be turned again to the permanent fight for improved popular government. He had no interest in Harding's "normalcy," which turned out to signify the right of business to expand without regulation and wage earners to borrow and spend freely on attractive new consumer products like autos and electrical appliances, while they largely ignored civic responsibility and the plight of the hard-up.

The majority of the electorate, however, found the Harding version irresistible, and La Follette was again a minority voice when he returned to the Senate floor. But this time—in contrast to the progressive springtime of 1908 to 1912—there were no comforting indications that the long-run tide was flowing his way. His fighting spirit, even in a weakened body, was still strong. Nonetheless, he and Belle, with their ideals of uplift and service, were outsiders in the new world.

"The damned war changed everything," George Norris, an old insurgent comrade in arms, lamented to Bob.[2] But it was not simply the damned war. Gasoline and celluloid and electromagnetism—Ford and Hollywood and Radio Corporation of America—had changed things, too, not to mention Freud and Lenin. Along with his old political and economic enemies like "the bosses" and "the interests," these invisible forces would confront Bob in his final battles. They also meant that his sons would never be able to fight on against wrong and oppression in quite the way that he had expected when he taught them as boys to forge their armor by hard study.

All this, however, was not immediately clear in 1919. It was an up and down year for Bob, a time of mood swings when his inherent optimism would struggle toward revival and then crash into the immovable realities of conservative control of the Congress and his own weariness. The hottest, though not necessarily the most important, political debates were sparked by the Treaty of Versailles and the Russian Revolution. He commented privately on these and other issues with unaccustomed fullness because of the special circumstances of his life in the nine months following the armistice. From November through March he was without the company of any member of the immediate family. Belle, Bobbie, and Mary were a continent's width away, while recently demobilized Phil was completing his undergraduate work in Madison, and Fola continued to live in New York. Desperately lonely for them, Old Bob wrote a family letter, sometimes two, almost every night after dinner. "I let *nothing* stand in the way," he said proudly.[3]

It was not until late in March that Mary joined him, and only in mid-May that Belle finally got back to his side. After that he kept posting frequent reports on the political scene to his two boys now grown into young men. Finally that, too, became unnecessary because they both arrived in Washington in the fall, Young Bob to serve as chief office assistant and Phil to begin law studies at George Washington University before going back to Wisconsin to finish them.

Then and then only was "Dad" truly and immensely happy. "I wouldn't give one damn to be alive and have the family all spread round over this hemisphere for a steady thing" was his opinion.[4] But in that long, lonely 1919 interim, during which his letters, taken together, would have added up to a small volume, he was witness and chorus to the beginning of a new age.

"There is so much lying that one gets fooled"

On New Year's Day of 1919, he went "swelling around" like an "old dude," sporting new cuff buttons and a stick pin that were the Christmas gifts of his loved ones. He was swelling inwardly, too. "I find myself day by day more and more eager to lash out," he had already confided, "like an old horse that has been confined in a box stall all winter . . . I snuff the fresh air and feel the freedom. I want to kick the bars and go racing unrestrained over the field." But he was aware of the limits. "There is real danger that I might run up against the barbed wire fence for it is *still there.*"

So it was, and it consisted of multiple strands. The return of a Republican majority in the Senate was good news for La Follette personally, but not for the progressive agenda. Conservatives dominated the party machinery and would control the voting on domestic affairs. In foreign policy matters La Follette expected little from a wartime Republicanism that had surrendered to Wilson and "become a mere prostitute and camp follower for the last twenty-two months." If it were not for that, he thought that there would "be a chance for real service." He took what he could get, however. When the Senate was reorganized he requested and was allowed to stay on the Committee on Finance, where he could continue to fight for stiff taxation of war profits and on the Committee on Manufactures, where seniority made him chairman. That potentially opened doors to investigate monopoly and price-gouging—if the national will and energy were there.

That was questionable. La Follette's faith would not allow him to doubt entirely, especially as he emerged from nearly two years of being "shut up with dark thoughts until I had a twist in my mind." But he could not ignore the realities around him. When Louis Brandeis congratulated him on being able to resume his "leadership for democracy" in America he answered bitterly: "Democracy in America has been trampled under foot, submerged, forgotten. Her enemies have multiplied their wealth and power appallingly." In a follow-up note to the family he added, "There is nothing to lead. The forces . . . which we had been organizing for twenty years have been scattered to the four winds by this mad stampede for democracy in Europe."[5]

But still . . . he could not quite be downed. Not too long afterward, excited by the preliminary results of an investigation of concentration in the meat-packing industry, he wrote Belle that if "the right man" put in six months of hard work on the testimony and presented it graphically enough, "it would shake things to the very *foundation*. It is my kind of job. I wish I had the time to give to it." He had visions of hitting the trail again. "I am coming back into my own before very long," he predicted early in 1919, "and will have an earning power possibly greater than I ever had." He was woefully wrong about that; neither he nor the public lecture circuit had their old-time strength. But he was free to speak his mind again in *La Follette's Magazine,* with a faithful core of some 32,000 subscribers who paid him a dollar a year in exchange for his thoughts, and that, too, was encouraging.

The trouble was that the magazine's motto, "The Truth Shall Make You Free," meant little when truth was inaccessible. The major stories of 1919—the Versailles treaty, and the attempts to stamp out the Bolshevik revolution—were swathed, just as the war news had been, in official secrecy, censorship, and propaganda. "Don't it beat H—— that we can't know what is being done to us and with us?" Bob asked in disbelief at the news blackout from the peace conference. He was eager for "everything from Russia that smacks of the truth. There are tons of lies." The worst of it was the uncertainty. "There is so much lying that one gets fooled—for there is always a bare possibility that the thing you read may be true."[6]

La Follette was racked by the conflict between the conviction that his cherished "people" would correctly judge their own interests and his clear observation that, in the preceding three years, they had been frightened and fooled. The press had succeeded with the preparedness crusade, the bond drives, and the "campaign of atrocities and hate," and La Follette feared that [w]e shall have the same thing on the treaty . . . [T]here is no way to meet them on anything they resolve to put over." Uneasily, he anticipated the new power of propaganda. "Some psychologist might make, maybe has made, a study of the effect of repeated impressions upon the mind through the eye in overcoming and subduing all resistance even against one's positive knowledge and settled convictions," he mused. "Just how the public is to protect itself against this thing I am not able to see at present. If the mass wasn't so large it would be a very simple thing to do it through the spoken word—that is, it would be so if you had absolutely free speech."

Confronting the growing reality of skilled manipulation of mass emotions, La Follette was justifiably depressed. "We are afloat on a sea of BUNK," he wound up writing one night, "and no one can see the rocks ahead or sense the gathering storm . . . This is a gloomy letter I know." He would not stop fighting, and he would win some victories, but after 1918 there was always the haunting knowledge that nothing could cancel even half a line of what the moving finger of history had written. "Oh, if this country could have been kept free and clean of the horrible infection of war!" he lamented. Things could never be the same, not even old friendships with supporters of the war who had stuck by him. He told Belle as much before a dinner party with the Brandeises and Elizabeth Evans in February. The common vision of the world binding them together had vanished, probably beyond restoration. It would take time—"a long time and new events not related to this world-crash that has gone to the very foundation of all things human. It has changed our country, our government, our life."[7]

So as he made his way back he was somewhat sadder and mellower as a person, less the confident prophet of a better tomorrow. But that only showed in private. In the arena he looked and sounded like the loved and detested battler of old.

"I am still to be reckoned with"

The final "short" session of the lame duck Congress met in December. First there was the painful business of dealing with the expulsion resolution. The Committee on Privileges and Elections had already voted, 9 to 2, to report that the charges should be dismissed because Bob's St. Paul speech (especially once the Associated Press had confessed to misquoting it) "did not justify any action by the Senate." The holdouts were two Democratic senators. One was Atlee Pomerene of Ohio, a solemn and devout man, customarily clad in black suits, who was still outraged by any deviation from the standards of patriotism set in 1917. The other was a different case. Thomas J. Walsh of Montana shared La Follette's own lawyerlike thoroughness and stubborn independence and in fact agreed with him on such issues as woman suffrage, child labor, and disarmament. But he, too, had been a true believer in the war, and he thought that before charges were dismissed La Follette should do some explaining to the committee about the sources of his information on the *Lusitania*'s cargo and on discussions within the State Department about the subject.

When the report came before the full Senate on January 16, it was adopted 50 to 21, with 25 (more than a quarter of the Senate) not present or not voting. Only one Republican opposed the dismissal. Presumably more would have joined the twenty Democrats—Walsh included—if it were not for the public cordiality already being shown La Follette by the likes of Senator Henry Cabot Lodge, who was to become majority leader in the incoming Sixty-sixth Congress. La Follette did not hold it against Walsh, and the two would later become respectful collaborators in the investigation of the Teapot Dome oil-leasing scandals.

It was another story, however, when John Sharp Williams, as he had done on the day war was declared, launched into a violent personal attack on La Follette, unrebuked by the presiding officer. He insisted on taking the floor so that, as he said, his children and grandchildren should not misunderstand his attitude. He branded the St. Paul speech as a series of "everlasting lies" about why America had gone to war and a defense of the murderers of the passengers on the *Lusitania*. "I have no glad hand of welcome to extend," he said, "to any man that slanders my country, that tells falsehoods about it, and I do not care whether he is a Senator or whether he is a plowboy, except that I can forgive the plowboy because of his ignorance." Shouting, shaking his fist, wandering into the center aisle, and peering down at La Follette in his seat, he continued for at least half an hour. He speculated that if La Follette had "thought anything at all" in making his speech, "he thought that the self-seekers, the sloth lovers, the peace worshipers . . . would finally control America and that somehow or other he or somebody else advocating that sort of doctrine would come out in front." Some men in crisis behaved like fighting mastiffs and brave watchdogs, he said. Others—and it was clear who was meant—

behaved like "common clay" and "vultures." He declared that Bob lacked "the moral courage" to apologize for his falsehoods and wound up with a ringing announcement that he, for one, would not overlook a speech "disloyal in spirit, disloyal in words, disloyal in intendment [*sic*], disloyal in effect, and disloyal with a set purpose."

Through it all, La Follette gazed steadily ahead, never once taking notice of Williams or speaking a word afterward, on the advice of his friends. It hurt, especially when he thought about it alone in his room that night. "I felt as if I had been publicly horsewhipped by some fool woman," he told Belle, and he added a wistful note. "If, after you read Williams' attack you think it would be all right for me to make a brief '*reply*' outside the Senate when I meet up with him *just let me know* and I'll do it properly." Belle answered soothingly "I know what you must have suffered. But I am sure you adopted the wisest course."[8]

It was the last direct personal assault stemming from the war that La Follette had to face, though he continued to receive hate mail. But the worst was over, and throughout the remainder of the session he was in what seemed old-time form. He had already submitted an amendment to a war revenue bill in December that would have raised the amount to be collected by taxes. "Why do you not stand up to your duty here," he asked the senators, "and take as much out of wealth as you take out of the blood and flesh of the people of this country? . . . [Y]ou did not hesitate to take not only the income of the poor family but the capital that is producing the income—the father and the sons—and putting them into the service of the government. All right, but by the God that is over us, if you want to do justice do the same thing by capital."

La Follette's amendment got exactly five votes not counting his own. "There is such a thing as people getting used to being robbed," he philosophized to the family.[9] Then he girded up his loins for another familiar fight on conservation, reminiscent of his clash with Theodore Roosevelt in 1906. The House and Senate had passed slightly different bills, providing for leases of federally owned coal and oil lands and waterpower sites. They were greatly desired, for development purposes, by western members of Congress, including Washington's Representative William La Follette, the Cousin Will with whose family Bob was sharing the house on Sixteenth Street. The measures were also popular with oil and gas companies for the liberal terms that were slipped into them in the conference to reconcile the two versions. La Follette opposed them as the entering wedge for massive corporate raids on mineral-rich parts of the public domain. "These coal and oil vandals . . . have the gall to write it into the conference report," he fumed in one letter, "that they can take claims and become owners of coal mines in the Grand Canyon and the Mount Olympus monument . . . They would blow up the Holy Sepulchre in their scramble for dirty money. Go and see the Grand Canyon as God made it while you can."[10]

The bill's supporters expected the conference committee's report to be rushed through in the closing hours before March 4. It was time for another filibuster. La Follette—with others—took the floor on March 1, and together they fought it off through four long, sleepless, late-night sessions filled with parliamentary bickering. Bob argued that the conferees had violated Congress's own rules by adding new material to the bills. He also raised his voice against the general practice, which still exists, of delaying action on important laws until the final, frantic rush to adjourn, when there was no time for close examination of giveaways to favored constituencies. It indicated "a pretty flagrant disregard of the principles of representative government and of the principles of democracy," he added sarcastically, "of which we have heard so much in recent years."[11]

The delaying tactics won; the legislation died as the gavel fell. This time, however, there was no tidal wave of outrage directed at La Follette and no attempt to invoke the brand new cloture role adopted two years earlier in a fury after he beat back the armed ship bill. The reason was that another issue, having nothing to do with conservation, was hidden behind this particular filibuster.

As always, there was no absolute necessity for an expiring Congress to wrap up important legislation by March 4. The president could always call the next one into immediate special sessions. But Woodrow Wilson had no wish whatsoever to do that. He had gone to Paris in December to participate in the peace negotiations. He had returned the last week in February just to sign bills, and he would board the liner *George Washington* and steam back to France immediately after March 4 to finish work on the treaty. He did not want to deal with Congress until then, especially a new, Republican Congress.

Republican leaders naturally felt otherwise, as did a number of senators of both parties who were having anticipatory misgivings about the results of the peace conference. These doubters, Bob among them, insisted on honoring the constitutional provision that calls for the president to make treaties with the Senate's *advice* and consent. They were already dismayed that the cloak of secrecy around the peace proceedings made it impossible for them to do any "advising," and they resented Wilson's stated intention not to call a new session until he had the finished product to hand them. Therefore, they had no objection to putting pressure on him by leaving unfinished business on the agenda. The filibuster was acceptable.

La Follette was in a minority in his views on western "development," but the Senate had come around to his side on asserting its powers against the president. The victory was a signpost on the comeback road and buoyed him as much as personal gestures of cordiality. "I feel very good over my work," he reported to La Jolla; "I made them all feel that I am still to be reckoned with."

Returning spring brought small daily doses of happiness that rekindled the will to live and drove the shadows back further. On St. Valentine's Day La Follette emerged from the Capitol at 7 P.M. and stood in the darkness and rain, contemplating a long wait for a streetcar. Suddenly a handsome red chauffeured auto pulled up to the curb, carrying Senator Boies Penrose, the steadfast political opponent who nonetheless had the gentlemanly courage to keep up his public friendship with Bob during the "exile." "Won't you let me take you home?" he asked cheerily, and indeed Bob would, so they rode off together in the back seat in symbolic postwar harmony.

A few weeks later, on the eve of St. Patrick's Day, Bob playfully addressed his "Dear Micks." "I wish I could drop in on you tonight with Darby O'Gill under me arm . . . and make ye acquainted with . . . King Brian O'Connor and the Good people. But bein' only a common mortal I haven't the power . . . to cover long distances in a wink of yer eye," he joked. Then, eight days later came the best moment yet of the ripening year: "Well, what do you think happened to me this afternoon? I was moping away up here in my room when there came a faint tap at the door . . . I opened the door and *there stood Mary—my Mary!* Do you know what I did? I just cried! That's what I did. I'm an old man all right. Ye Gods but it was good to have my arms around her and hold her in my lap—my baby . . . Say, *I feel, just as if I had been demobilized.*"

Mary was the vanguard of the return from La Jolla. It had been an isolated spot for a pretty nineteen-year-old (even with what Belle called "soldier boys" calling on her), and she was ready to come back east as soon as she could be spared from helping to care for her convalescing brother. Abandoning plans to enroll at the University of Wisconsin, she intended to study art either in New York or Washington; she would work temporarily for Dad as office help while deciding. She stopped off in Chicago for a "date" with Phil, who, armed with fifteen dollars sent by the senator, showed her the town.

Mary and her father temporarily made a happy and curious couple. He worked in his bedroom in the evenings and she in hers, but they would run back and forth to trade comments, discoveries, and opinions of which he, at least, had a limitless variety. A few nights after her arrival she decided to shampoo her hair. He wanted to do it for her, thinking he knew the best way. She refused, but as he told Belle, "I stood around and criticized until I made her see, even if she didn't admit, that I knew a lot about it."[12]

April, a lovely month in Washington, brought vistas of pink and white redbud and dogwood blossoms, green grass and leaves, and an old-boy visit from former and present partners. Gil Roe came from New York, and Alf Rogers and "Billy" Evjue from Madison. Evjue, a former state lawmaker, was editing the Madison *Capital Times,* founded during the war as a pro–La Follette voice. They drove around the suburbs, visited the zoo and the monuments, and talked politics. "As we didn't have our knitting," Bob explained, "we smoked some so as not to seem altogether idle." In a relaxed mood with only the demands of the magazine to answer, La Follette made his peace with Cousin Will, who had not been speaking to him since the waterpower filibuster. Finally in early May came the best news of all—Belle was on the way.

Bob had urged Belle to rest in California until the winter was well over, building up her own health, weakened by months of strain and work, with horseback rides and ocean swims. But he couldn't resist telling her that without anyone to "council with" he floundered along simply hoping to avoid serious blunders, and at the end of March he said forthrightly: "I never needed you close to me more than I will when the battle [over the treaty] opens." So on May 6, leaving Bobbie in a smaller and cheaper cottage to take care of himself and mull his future, she started back to Old Bob's side. Like Mary, she stopped in Chicago to visit with Phil. It is a small record of how ravaged the family finances had become that she left with $3.50 in her purse. She neglected to telegraph her arrival time in Washington, but the senator and Mary checked every incoming train and finally caught her, as he put it in his next letter, "trying to slip through the gate" at the Baltimore and Ohio terminal. "She surrendered with[out] a fight," he related to the boys, "and we now have her securely in hand." Belle was dismayed at first to find him looking tired and aged, though it was she herself who went on the sick list next, with a major infection from an abscessed tooth late in July. It gave her a violent systemic shock that prostrated her and required several weeks of recuperation in a sanatorium. The relentless grind of years was showing in both of them, and each was especially aware of it—but mainly in the other![13]

The special session finally called by Wilson opened on May 19, and for six months the Capitol rang with debates that volleyed and thundered until the Treaty of Versailles was finally rejected. La Follette was against it from start to finish. He hammered away steadily in the magazine and delivered at least four antiratification speeches in the Senate. But the defeat of the treaty was not a victory for La Follette's principles. It was engineered by a peculiar coalition that conformed, as Fola wrote years afterward, "to no party, factional or sectional lines" that the Senate had known before. The opposition included both conservative and progressive Republicans and a few Democrats who, for different reasons, abandoned Wilson on key votes along the road to the final outcome.

It deserves to be said that everything in La Follette's hostility was consistent with his previous democratic practices and ideas. He saw the war that had "made the world one house of mourning" (his phrase to a bereaved mother) as a cruel hoax upon the plain people of the fighting nations. "God in Heaven," he cried out at the sight of long pages of casualty lists, "what is the world to get for it all?" To his mind, the answer that came back daily from the conference table in Paris was "nothing."

Both in public statements and in those revealing, sometimes confessional letters to the indispensable family, he reeled off his list of objections to the treaty itself and the League of Nations. None of his arguments was rooted in some "isolationist" philosophy of a special American innocence that would be spoiled by involvement in foreign wars. He hated the treaty for what he believed were its concrete betrayals of the powerless that only prepared for "another harvest of hate and bloodshed." These could have been reduced to a series of sentence-long propositions, barbed to puncture Wilson's "shipload of flim flam for suckers." The treaty, negotiated without the Senate's participation, violated the Constitution. It likewise trashed the Fourteen Points on which basis the German people had overthrown the kaiser and surrendered. It was not an "open covenant of peace openly arrived at," but crafted in deepest secrecy. It did not deal at all with freedom of the seas. Its only disarmament provisions destroyed the armed forces of the losers and left huge, burdensome and murderous fleets and armies in the hands of the winners. It did not liberate peoples colonized by the victors, such as the Egyptians, the Indians, the Koreans, and the Indochinese. It redrew the map of central Europe not in accordance with "self-determination of peoples" but to fulfill secret prewar agreements. The new nations that it created—Yugoslavia, for instance—were forced marriages of unwilling peoples. It was a peace engineered by the very governments that had imposed war's agonies upon their deluded or voiceless peoples— a peace of vengeance forced on Germany by starvation because the wartime blockade was continued in force until she signed.

And the League of Nations that could theoretically right these wrongs? It would be dominated by the governments of those same Great Powers, who would use it as a cover to protect the new *status quo*—with the help of the United States if she were foolish enough to join. The one Allied power whose government *had* changed significantly and had rejected the old diplomatic and military system was Russia. And Russia's revolutionary government was the one that Britain, France, Japan, and the United States were doing their best to stamp out. What were they afraid of? In America, wartime espionage and sedition acts were being used to harass and muzzle anyone who simply dared to speak out in favor of anything thought to be pro-Bolshevik. So much for saving the world for democracy.

Whether or not these arguments had merit—and post-1919 defenders of Wilson's internationalism have never really confronted them—they were signs of how deeply the war and the postwar climate had radicalized La Follette. His basic beliefs were unchanged. He could not ever subscribe to such ideas as the necessity of revolution and the dictatorship of the proletariat. However tortoiselike the pace of middle-class reform, it was the only road on which he trusted the footing. He asked rhetorically: "While reform by the ballot is slow and discouraging it would seem that in a country where every citizen has the ballot, if there is not intelligence enough to *use* it to *reform* the government, would there be intelligence enough *successfully to conduct a real democratic government* after they had established it by force?" And one of the last letters he ever wrote became an unwitting political testament, part of which reads: "I am not for a class party or a party composed of organized labor and organized farmers and organized socialists or any other form of group organization . . . I think the citizen should be the unit of any political organization."[14]

But the "surging revolutions" around the globe seemed understandable to him in places like Russia, where the ballot had been denied too long. He did not share right-thinking Americans' visceral terror of "Reds" in 1919 any more than their hatred of "the Hun" in 1918, and he was naturally sympathetic to political outsiders. He hated repression and was dismayed that the Supreme Court (his friend Brandeis included) sustained wartime jailings and censorship under the Espionage and Sedition Act. "Not a word of suggestion," he fumed, "that there are any wrongs to right, any evils to cure. Force, jail, the firing squad—that is the program to give us a happy and contented people."

For all these reasons he seemed to move toward the left as the country itself tilted in the other direction. He had a serious and respectful discussion of socialism with his Milwaukee friend Victor Berger, a Socialist who was actually tried and convicted under the sedition law but escaped jail. Afterward he explained to the boys that there would still be plenty of room for private ownership in a socialistic system that would only nationalize enterprises vital to the common life of the nation. He joked about it after a walk through the National Zoo with Belle:

The park was filled with people enjoying themselves hugely. One couldn't but think of what it really means for everybody to have an equal share in property commonly owned. If we can have community-owned parks why not community-owned transportation, light, heat—and a lot of other things. If it was possible for *private* enterprise to corner the shade and the lawns that nature furnishes in abundance, then we should have plenty of people arguing that you could not maintain public parks *economically* and that it would be a dangerous and harmful interference with "individual initiative" to set up such a socialistic scheme as a Bolshevik park.[15]

As 1919 ended, foreign affairs no longer took stage front in Congress. Reconversion to a peacetime economy pushed pocketbook issues onto the calendar after a hard year of strikes and other protests against escalating costs of living. La Follette found himself heavily engaged with labor and consumer questions. Early in the year young Phil had picked up the trend and suggested making *La Follette's Magazine* more appealing to "the laboring classes (farmers, small business men, and laborers—in the latter word's strict industrial interpretation"). Political reality moved Old Bob closer to alliances with unions and farmer-labor organizations, organized pressure groups that had not been conspicuous in progressivism's earlier leadership. The hardening conservatism of Congress made him more willing as well to look for links with any group that accepted democratic premises, socialists included. And he was becoming open-minded about some forms of public ownership. It was all part of the process that would make him the captain of an oddly assorted army of hard-up "working stiffs," "hayseeds," and discontented idealists in 1924.

The coalition did not jell without problems along the way, but its formation was helped by a losing battle on the Esch-Cummins Transportation Act of 1920. It restored the railroads, taken over by the government during the war, to their owners with handsome bonuses and advantages. They were to be guaranteed a return on investment of 5½ to 6 percent (at a time when government bonds were paying 4 percent), and the basis of calculation was to include their watered stock. They would be guaranteed a large jump in freight rates that would squeeze farmers and shippers. And finally they would be allowed to restrict some forms of competition without interference from antitrust laws. The Interstate Commerce Commission, now controlled by conservative appointees, could override state regulators who were less generous to the rail corporations. "Nothing could be lovelier," in Bob's wry words; "the public is to be satisfied with a Commission with 'enlarged powers' and the railroads satisfied with an obedient Commission."[16]

This giveaway, for which the owners had lobbied hard for a year, convinced La Follette of the urgency of organizing a new kind of rebellion, especially since many of his progressive allies of ten years earlier were out of Congress or had gone soft—like the bill's author Albert Cummins, himself a 1909 "insurgent."

But it was important first to test the waters at home, and to see if the La Follette name was still magic in Wisconsin after the storm of war.

"Longing for the time when I can get back"

As early as May of 1919 Bob had expressed interest in finding out how well his name and organization had survived wartime attacks in his own backyard. "I am longing for the time when I can get back into Wisconsin," he advised Young Bob. "I don't want to do it until I can do some talking . . . I am satisfied that we have got as much real rock bottom loyalty there among the people as we ever had."

But it was not until early in 1920 that Bob returned to find an uncertain situation. Wisconsin reflected in microcosm the great shifts in the bedrock of culture underlying political life. The farm population was declining. Rural life was less isolated, small towns ways and wisdom no longer unchallenged. More of the state's people worked in offices and factories; more of them belonged to unions. New issues separated old political comrades. Socialists, already split by the war, divided over whether to follow the Bolshevik road. Those who did so left to form the Communist party. Immigration restriction drove a wedge between foreign and "native"-dominated labor organizations; the revived Ku Klux Klan would hammer it deeper. Friends and enemies of joining the League of Nations could be found among both stalwarts and progressives. Prohibition, too, was not a clear litmus test between these two rival camps. (On that issue La Follette, with unusual circumspection, took no strong position either way but privately asked Phil in 1919—it is not clear how seriously—to "work the Pabsts for a couple of barrels of beer for the cellar at Maple Bluff . . . We are in for a terrible drouth and ought to prepare.")[17]

The question was whether, in these realignments of thinking, the La Follette organization could still deliver votes for La Follette causes. That there was such an organization is undeniable. Every county and congressional district had a network of La Follette friends and advocates, which he had built up over years through frequent visits, cultivation by mail, and the dispensation of such patronage as a governor and senator could bestow. At election time the network produced a substantial number of party and state officials and lawmakers who would respond to Old Bob's direction.

Opponents raged that this was nothing more than a machine and that La Follette was a Republican boss of exactly the type he professed to be fighting. That is at least arguable. The conventional machine delivered votes that benefited important business interests, which paid for the favors in cash; the cash was then distributed among the leaders to keep the wheels going. La Follette was never caught with a questionable dollar; his operations were low budget and scandal-free; and his whole taxation, regulation, conservation, and public-control agenda was resolutely anticorporate. The conventional machine preferred small and unpublicized primary elections that were easy to control. La Follette's whole career was dedicated to widening the voters' choices at every stage.

As for his being a "boss," he was unblushing and overt in his efforts to have his followers in the legislature line up behind his favored measures. When he was not in Madison to lobby them in person, he did so through intermediaries like his law partners, his wife, and his sons. That was what leadership meant. Many who criticized his "arbitrary" rule simply found it politically easier to denounce his methods than to oppose the democratizing results they brought.

Where La Follette *was* actually high-handed was in not tolerating much disagreement within the ranks. He was quick to see someone else's dissent from his own definition of progressivism as betrayal. When former allies like Irvine Lenroot or Francis McGovern broke away, he was as bitter toward them as he ever was to any bred-in-the-bone stalwart, and he showed no sign of ever sharing the role of spokesman for the Progressive movement in Wisconsin. Nor did he appear ready to relinquish control of it someday to any lieutenant—other than possibly Bob or Phil.

Despite all that, however, his "rule" was anything but absolute. His side lost Republican primaries again and again, sometimes because he could not keep the players together. Phil remembered how, in that very February of 1920, three La Follette supporters wanted to be the Republican candidate for governor. All of "Dad's" entreaties in conferences in his second-floor Madison law offices (the ground floor was occupied by a grocery) could not keep two of them from entering the primary and splitting the Progressive vote.[18]

But as it turned out that rebuff was not crucially important. John Blaine, the candidate for governor whom La Follette finally endorsed, won the Republican nomination, although the increasingly conservative Lenroot beat out Bob's choice to run for the Senate, James Thompson. It was the second time he had beaten Thompson; the first was in 1918, when a special election had been held following the death of Senator Paul Husting, and Lenroot had then won in the general election, too, and gone to the Senate. But Lenroot's primary triumph could not overshadow the magnitude of La Follette's return from the wartime shadows. In the voting for delegates to the GOP national convention, La Follette men virtually swept the board, getting twenty-two of twenty-six. Next morning he opened a telegram from Belle and Phil in Washington: YOUR FAITH IN PEOPLE JUSTIFIED. VERY HAPPY HERE. The Washington *Sunday Star* ran a photo of La Follette captioned, "Holds Vote of Wisconsin in Hollow of His Hand."[19]

That was an exaggeration, but the delegate near-sweep was still a major reversal of fortune in his favor. In practical terms it meant not merely a favorite-son vote for La Follette at the convention but a chance to have his delegation present a minority report on the platform as it had done in the three previous conventions. This time the La Follette planks, thoroughly publicized during the primary campaign, included a League for Peace comprised of nations that would reduce their armies and navies to a minimum; eventual public ownership of railroads, stockyard terminals, and large packing plants; the abolition of injunctions against strikers; the restoration of all civil liberties abridged in wartime; and finally a progressive overhaul of the machinery of the national government. Federal judges were to be elected, and the initiative, referendum, and recall would be used to let citizens, by petition, get a vote on measures blocked in Congress and "fire" unresponsive officials.

To no one's surprise the reading of these proposals was greeted from the hot, crowded floor with hisses and hoots, cries of "Bolshevik!" and petitions to "Throw him out!" This was, after all, the same convention that went on to nominate Harding and Coolidge. La Follette himself was not present. He was, at that moment, in the Mayo Clinic recuperating from the removal of his diseased gall bladder, which had intermittently prostrated him for months. While his painful recovery continued, two other conventions were held in Chicago by miscellaneous opponents of Harding who also rejected the Democratic nominee, Ohio's Governor James M. Cox, an uncritical Wilson supporter.[20]

One of these was the work of the Committee of Forty-eight, which represented a substantial number of veterans of the 1912 Progressive party—the remnants of Theodore Roosevelt's Bull Moose forces, deprived of their leader who had died in January 1919. The other, meeting at the same time, was dominated by the Nonpartisan League—the agrarian socialist organization centered in Minnesota and North Dakota that had sponsored La Follette's damaging 1917 speech—and the four Railroad Brotherhoods, unions free of the conservative hand of the American Federation of Labor's aging chief, Samuel Gompers. Bob had pungently expressed in the family correspondence his certainty that the "reactionary element" would dominate the AFL "until Gompers is either overthrown or gets his harp and halo."

Both conventions liked the idea of running La Follette for the presidency, but he made it clear from afar that he was not interested unless they could unite on his platform—the one so rudely and recently trampled by the Republicans. This proved impossible and the idea fell through. The Committee of Forty-eight more or less vanished. The other and much more powerful gathering of rebels organized itself as the Farmer-Labor party and ran a man named Parley P. Christensen, who got about 265,000 votes—some 665,000 fewer than the Socialists' Eugene V. Debs, who was still in a cell in the Atlanta penitentiary.[21] These totals were of little significance in the general Republican sweep that put Harding in the White House and gave the Republicans 301 out of 435 House seats and 59 of 96 Senate seats, including Lenroot's. (But in Wisconsin, Blaine won, too, riding the Republican wave.)

Nothing could have better illustrated the postwar political picture. A core of at least a million and a quarter radical voters remained unsubdued after the war, plus an uncounted army of potential defectors from the business-as-usual major parties. But there was no way to get laborers, farmers, middle-class reformers, Socialists, and various discontented or shut-out groups into the kind of cohesive alliance that had produced the progressive surge of 1900 to 1914. Most of them could agree on only one thing: they liked La Follette, who had battled for so long against their various enemies.

La Follette, however, would not be their candidate on sentiment alone. He knew that a protest constituency needed to be unified, organized, funded, and ripened before it had the smallest chance to make a difference—if it could make a difference at all in the new America. And he was old and sick, driving toward seventy. His body would no longer take the old-time punishment.

But his spirit was that of the younger man who had enthralled the standing crowds for long hours in the heat and dust of a quarter century earlier. His voice was that of a passing generation but it still had power. In March of 1921 he returned to make his first major public appearance in Madison since the war. The intention was to kick off his reelection campaign for the following year and to let any wavering progressive legislators know that his eye was still on them. Friends offered him practical advice. "Spread balm on the scars," they told him. "Let your old friends who deserted us in the war days come back to our camp." He listened, nodded, kept his counsel.

On March 25, 1921, La Follette appeared before a packed Assembly chamber full of people he had known, embraced, and denounced for so many long years. He opened with formal and gracious acknowledgments to those who had invited him, his sentences flowing in the nineteenth-century cadences learned in the hot little debating rooms on the university campus in the heyday of an ornate and embroidered rhetoric that disregarded clocks. Then he paused, drew himself up to his full five feet six inches, and pounded the point home with his outstretched, clenched fist: "I am going to be a candidate for re-election to the United States Senate. I do not want the vote of a single citizen under any misapprehension of where I stand: I WOULD NOT CHANGE MY RECORD ON THE WAR FOR THAT OF ANY MAN, LIVING OR DEAD."

There was stunned silence, according to Phil's remembrance, then the realization that this aging man who had been politically buried alive was now standing, with the dirt still on his clothes, before the gravediggers, asking no forgiveness and showing no repentance. Wave after wave of applause rang out. A member of the state senate who had all his life fought La Follette sat with tears running down his cheeks, sobbing audibly: "I hate the son of a bitch, but my God, what guts he's got."[22]

The jam was broken. La Follette worked the state through the rest of the year, stoking old fires, damning the return of the railroads to monopoly, the Harding tax schemes that favored the rich, the rush to gobble up the public domain. Back in Washington for the new Congress he continued his floor fights against naval expansion and the refunding of the war debt on terms too favorable to the banks. And it was he who, at the start of 1922, took a leading role in following up rumors that something odd was going on with important naval oil reserves in Elk Hills, California, and Teapot Dome, Wyoming. First they had been mysteriously transferred from the custody of the Navy Department to the Interior Department; next, drilling rights had been leased to an oil consortium headed by Harry F. Sinclair. As April of 1922 ended La Follette had, with his characteristic dogged completeness, dug up enough evidence to propose a resolution for a major investigation, which was quickly passed. The ultimate results of the probe, chaired by La Follette's former foe Thomas J. Walsh on his recommendation, uncovered a tale of bribery and betrayal reaching into the highest circles of the Harding administration.

And so, when La Follette entered the final stage of his fourth run for the Senate, he was to outward appearances the head rebel once more, drawing to himself all the various currents of protest against the dark underside of the "business civilization" that had succeeded progressivism. The question was: How would that affect him in his home state? And what did that portend for the national elections two years later?

The first question was answered in the decisive Republican primary of September 5, 1922. Robert La Follette carried seventy of seventy-one counties, and he lost that single one by 481 votes out of 7,785 cast. He outpolled his opponent in the popular vote by more than 220,000. Reelection in November, also by record-breaking margins, was a certainty. Vindication after five years of what Phil called "abuse by political bullies" could not speak in sweeter tones. Some time afterward Middleton reminded his father-in-law of wartime days when he had not expected to live to see such an hour. "Yes, Mid," La Follette beamed, "the circle is complete: all the rest is velvet."[23]

It seemed even more velvety when voters in Minnesota elected Henrik Shipstead, the Farmer-Labor candidate, to the Senate. That unseated Frank B. Kellogg, who had led the fight to expel La Follette. Bob spoke for Shipstead in St. Paul the weekend before election day and was greeted by a packed, cheering auditorium, with thousands waiting vainly for seats outside. It was still another personal victory. And more than that; the national midterm election results were a rebuke to Harding. Republican majorities in the House sank to 17, and in the Senate to 11—meaning that a core of old and new progressive members might possibly again hold the balance of power.

But those promising indications were not the first signs of a new progressive springtime or of a new life for Robert M. La Follette's ambitions and expectations. Too many things were changing, some of them in the very bosom of his family. The old loves endured, but the old certainties were changing shape.

LAST HURRAHS

"The chatter of birds against a hurricane"

The La Follette women gradually came down, after the war was over, from the thin and rarefied atmosphere of a constant struggle for principle and into the warmer climate of domesticity, each in her own fashion. After a year of being fully occupied with the care of an invalid son, Belle devoted herself more and more to preserving the strength of her game but physically faltering husband. Fola was enjoying, with George, a period of affluence and foreign travel. Mary, unable to find a career path for herself that would satisfy a La Follette conscience, married at twenty-one and shared in the politics of the 1920s mostly through her husband.

Belle's long isolation by the pounding Pacific breakers in the winter of 1918–1919 was a vacation from politics that gave her time for reflection. Her letters, especially to Phil, were more personal and reminiscent, less preoccupied with righting wrongs and discharging duties. She was no longer certain of her power to find clear moral solutions to problems. One January night she debated with herself whether or not the United States should give food aid to foreign countries — especially if Germany were excluded — while there was hunger at home. "Don't take this letter too seriously," she concluded. "I have no settled convictions and have not thought below the surface and am woefully unread." Her interest in peace and disarmament broadened the framework of her thinking and made her aware of complexities. She did not completely agree with Bob's resistance to the League of Nations. Indeed yes, she told him, its purpose was to fortify the "intrenched power" of the Allied governments and it was backed by the "moneyed and property interests" of the great nations. "And yet the idea itself is sound," she added. "At least I cannot see how we can escape the conclusion that the world today is a unit."

And, as a unit, the world was not nearly as manageable as she might have thought in her youth. The storms that had swept over it had blown away landmarks in her own life, and she sensed a link between the family's personal and political uprootings and dispossessions. Both were due to irresistible forces. The apostasy of progressive friends who had joined in the crusade for war cut deeply, so deeply that even Maple Bluff was spoiled for her, as she confided to Phil. She had never before minded the work and expense, she said, but "now something is gone and I don't feel that I can ever care so much even for the Farm as I once did. I don't care to go there even to pack up." But all the same, to persist in anger against others who were caught up in the passions of the time seemed wrong, even to this daughter of New England Unitarians and believer in the sacredness of individualism and individual responsibility. She wrote as much to Bob, soon after he told her that he was having a hard time composing a condolence note to the widow of classmate Charles Van Hise, who, as University of Wisconsin president, had denounced him in 1918: "What shall we do? Shall we disassociate ourselves from everyone who disappoints us and with whom we disagree? If we would preserve our sanity . . . if we are to have any chance for usefulness, must we not co-operate where we can . . . and keep faith in the outcome? . . . I find it very hard to convince myself any effort of individuals will avail. The forces set loose seem so beyond control. All we can do or say seems like the chatter of birds against a hurricane."

She was not lapsing into passivity. But woman suffrage, her major invigorating cause for so long, was now a completed battle. On June 4, 1919, when the Senate passed the Nineteenth Amendment and started it on its way to ratification, Belle herself was in the jubilant galleries and Bob started the applause on the floor that spread in reverberating waves throughout the chamber as it celebrated, in her words, a "great event in history." With that victory won, the fight for peace and disarmament became the core of Belle's writing and speaking activities. It was much slower and more discouraging work.[24]

Work was taking its physical toll, too. Illness in the fall of 1919 was one long spell of misery. It began when Belle went to a mountain cabin in West Virginia with Fola to recover from the extraction of an infected tooth. There she had been racked with spasm after spasm of violent diarrhea. Afterward her poisoned system caused sores to erupt inside her nose and mouth. It was long before anything like old-time vigor returned; neuritis, toothaches, and a "trick knee" continued to plague her. "I seem to be slowing down," she observed to her loved ones early in 1921. "It takes me so long to get anything done." But she was still Belle and added, "And yet I am always trying to do something." At sixty-two, "something" included packing, moving, and getting resettled in a cheaper rented house, supervising Mary's wedding, and being Old Bob's chauffeur and postsurgery nurse, in addition to letter-writing and public activities. By the fall of 1921, Young Bob expressed his alarm in a letter to Phil: "I do not think any of us realize how hard on Mother this life is here [in Washington] especially since she sort of dropped out from active participation in things following her illness. This leaves her with only one outlet for her energies beside her house work and that is through Dad's work. This of course is trying to the extreme as both she and I have so closely identified ourselves with him that we are constantly trying to make him do things as we would, and when he does not it is very hard on us."[25]

The triumphant Wisconsin campaign of 1922—plus a few needed vacations—restored Belle slightly. She helped with drafts of the platform, drove Bob to meetings that drew "fine crowds," made doughnuts and coffee for strategy meetings at the farm as if it were old times, and was delighted that the State Central Committee now included women. It was so *right* that they should be politically involved. "I have always worked for suffrage on that theory," she enthused, "and yet I can hardly realize that my theory is actually working." There was even some good news on the peace front in the form of a five-power naval disarmament conference in Washington for which peace organizations had long lobbied. (The success was slightly illusory, however, for the goal was not so much to end the arms race at sea as to regulate it in the interests of sparing the treasuries of the major players, Britain, the United States, and Japan.)

Such events brought temporary happiness but could not offset the adversities of advancing age, such as the death of brother-in-law Robert Siebecker, or the inevitable slowing down. Spring of 1923 found Bob and Belle both taking a needed rest cure at a sanitarium in Battle Creek. Between sessions of being "rolled and pounded, shaken and slapped and spanked with electrical apparatus" in the "mechanical Swedish treatment room," Belle the reformer, the teacher of using oneself to the fullest for the future benefit of the entire human race, wrote to Mary with a different message. "Get all the joy you can out of each day for after all, living day by day is what counts . . . Most of us . . . miss the value of accumulated happiness—of being happy day by day—*as happy as we can be,* that is."[26]

As for Fola, who had worked so hard for suffrage and the cultural irrigation of the wasteland, her life was taking on a different tenor. Mid was doing well. In 1918 he wrote a hit, *Adam and Eva,* in collaboration with Guy Bolton, and the two followed it up in 1919 with another, *Polly with a Past.* He was also beginning to tap into the bonanza of Hollywood money. He got $2,000 for a script and gave $250 to Fola for her help. She promptly used it to buy a typewriter on which to do her own articles. Then, in December, actress Ina Claire bought the film rights to *Polly* from the producer for $75,000, of which Mid got a share that was promptly invested in Liberty Bonds.

Life was more generous and relaxed. Politics were felt intensely but were no longer the substance of daily activities. Fola was becoming more of a critical onlooker and less of a participant. The Middleton–La Follette friends in the Village included men and women who had direct contact with developments in Russia; Old Bob recorded in February of 1919 that "Fola and Mid are quite active on all radical lines in New York and are in touch one way and another with most everything going on with the different groups." Yet Fola wrote to Bobbie one June night, after a leisurely horseback ride in Central Park, in a vein far different from that of the committed revolutionary:

246

I still enjoy the pace of the four-footed beast . . . it soothes my spirit and sort of swings me back into other days when the world was not quite so full of gasoline and submarines . . . [T]he air all about is seething with raids, exposures, charges and counter-charges. Some way it's so overwhelming and colossal that it makes individual effort seem rather futile—and drives one back into a yearning for the foolish little things of personal life. Just petty gossip and little trifles far removed from the "great social questions." Perhaps it's just the warm weather but true it is that at this present moment I've a great spleen on reforms and reformation.

But that was not all. She was recasting her life, as she neared forty, in patterns far removed from the rational and optimistic progressivism of her still-adored parents.

I've been doing quite a bit of reading in psychoanalysis and find it most absorbing and fascinating. I think that if I were 15 years younger I'd study neurology and go into the psychological side of medicine. It seems to me that in these transition days that are coming, when the old order is passing and a new economic adjustment coming and coming with considerable violence, too, if the Bourbons continue their present methods, that occupation in the scientific field would be the most satisfying work one could have. It would satisfy this instinct of workmanship which is in us all and needs expression and activity. It is an occupation which would be useful and creative irrespective of whether the new order prevails in our time or whether we only have to live through transitions.[27]

Fola had gone from actress-reformer to Village radical, anticipating inevitable revolution. And while waiting for Lefty she was searching her soul with the help of psychology. It was a long step for the midwestern governor's daughter but one that thousands of children of the American small-town heartland were also taking. Some did it with pretentious breast-beating, but Fola had a natural healthiness of mind that spared her from feeding on gloom. She was able to escape the ever-threatening La Follette trap of taking oneself too seriously (as Phil, for example, was prone to), and she kept urging the others to follow her example. She hoped that Bobbie might stay on in California another winter, doing "some outdoor work in a warm, happy climate." And she begged Belle, without hope, to suspend earnestness and loaf. She threatened to send her a copy of Robert Louis Stevenson's *Apology for Idlers*. "You and Dad both preach the gospel of rest and relaxation . . . but lordy you both do hate to take even a small dose of your own prescription. Now if you only had a few of the lazy bones—just a wee bit of the parasitic marrow that lies in my bones and which my mind always has to fight—you'd get a lot of fun out of playing lady or gypsy for a little bit."

Fola had no problem in taking her own prescription. After nursing Belle through the summer's illness she returned with Mid to Aquiden Lodge in the Maine woods, writing, loafing, and eating lustily right through the end of October. Mary, meanwhile, stayed in their empty New York apartment, and Fola counseled her: "Have a gay time . . . but conceal your crimes from the respectable neighbors and treat my booze with gentle consideration as it's hard to get more. When I get my private still going I'll give you carte blanche on all fire water that I can manufacture."[28]

Next summer Fola and Mid went to Paris, stayed until late in 1922, and returned frequently thereafter to an apartment on the Rue Jacob, visiting with other expatriates like Steffens and sculptor Jo Davidson and exploring the European theater scene. In the spring of 1923 they rambled around New England in a Ford and oversaw the production of another pair of Mid's plays (*Collusion* and *The Road Together*). On the day she became precisely forty and a half years old, Fola told Belle to keep it to herself but "all the indications are that I am pregnant." The letter carrying this announcement has the bottom snipped off, for reasons unknown. The subject is not alluded to again, but Fola and George were never to have any children.

In the fall and winter they were back in the New York swim, going to the Metropolitan Museum of Art to look at the Cezannes, dining with historians Charles and Mary Beard, lamenting the sad state of political life under Coolidge. Then Mid sailed for Europe on business, with Fola remaining behind this time. In a letter to him in May of 1924, she dropped a hint of a story not shared, for a change, with the family.

I went to the group meeting last night. It is proving an exceedingly stimulating and interesting association. It gives one a chance to carry on in relation to others many of the problems which one has had to meet in one's personal analysis. There one could, of course, only deal with them in relation to the analysist [sic] who, because of the inevitable relation to the patient, can not react. Here one gets the reaction of oneself on others, but on others who have worked with analysis—and therefore one can deal with these reactions in different terms . . . I am getting something out of it which is very vital and will, I think, prove helpful.

Mid apparently had not been converted to the gospel of analysis and would have preferred more inside dope on the presidential campaign. "I know that this subject irritates you," Fola said in winding up her report from the collective couch. But a couple of weeks later she said again that she had an "exceedingly interesting session" at the group meeting. "And so I go on, you see. The quest continues absorbing."

The conclusion seems inescapable that Fola had undergone at least some analysis, but whether in New York in the preceding year or in Paris, or for how long, is not revealed in her saved letters (which are much fewer in number in the 1920s). It is fascinating to speculate on what she and an analyst together would have made of her family life. But it is also useless, of course. At all events, her relentless turning inward was one more sign of the gap between the first and second generations of La Follettes. Perhaps, too, it supports Phil's assessment of the 1917–1918 agonies: "There were deep scars within each of us that we would carry as long as we lived."[29]

Mary's scars seemed to predate the wartime turmoil during which she came of age. Her talents were nonverbal to judge by the brevity of her letters, and in that family circle of taken-for-granted eloquence she suffered deep uncertainty about her own vocation and her place in the La Follette group portrait. Her parents, her brothers, and her sister all reassured her constantly, perhaps not only from simple loving-kindness but also from sincere conviction that her reticence was a novel (for them) form of wisdom. It was another sign of post-Progressive change that they were willing to credit her with qualities that did not manifest themselves politically, and to encourage her to find them.

But Mary was unable to share in their generous view of her. "The dear girl always depreciates herself," was how Old Bob put it to the boys in May of 1919 after Mary had struggled with a long depression, telling him one tearful evening that "she didn't amount to anything, is awful looking, did not have anything to live for, and a lot of that kind of stuff." He urged them to write her cheerful notes but to "pull it off in such a way as not to tip your hand—or mine." Part of the problem, he explained, was "our damned social customs," which did not give girls "the same things to look forward to" as boys, and "the same rights to take the initiative . . . and make a good time for themselves."

Although there were some testy father-daughter exchanges, Old Bob tried hard to brace up Mary's self-confidence. When she despaired because her art teacher said that her work was original but lacked technique, he scolded her lovingly. Technique could be learned, but talent was a "precious thing—to be nourished and cherished—not a thing to be disparaged by one's own self." If Mary believed in herself, his letter explained, she would "begin to do strong things . . . which will carry the impress of your individuality—your soul. I believe in you, Mary, just as I used to believe in myself. And I do love you, dear girl."

Phil and Young Bob also came through valiantly. "You have so much sweetness and kindness in you," Phil wrote her, "that it cannot but seep out and through your hand onto canvas." As Bob thanked her for putting her own life on hold to help his California recovery, he cheered her on:

"Mary, you are a truly wonderful girl. You are going to make your mark just as sure as shooting . . . Goodbye, sweetheart, I am with you through thick and thin."[30]

But it was not enough. Mary's ugly duckling syndrome could not be exorcised by any amount of family encouragement. She abandoned her college plans in March of 1919 because she feared flunking out, and art school might at least equip her to make a living. Her next plan was to work in her father's office part time for an extended period, while she saved up money to finance art study in New York. She quickly decided, however, that she was of no help. "I get so very little done down there . . . I am not able to do one half the amount I ought to do anyway. You know how Papa is—he thinks just because it is me it is all right but I don't want him or anyone else to have that attitude about it." After fewer than four months in Washington she left for New York, to Old Bob's explicit disappointment. In a sad and guilty letter she explained herself to Phil. "I certainly shall not stay a minute or spend a penny after I find that I can not succeed," she said, "but feel that I must try it out." She added that happiness was an impossible state to attain, because it required being true to oneself, and that, in turn, sometimes required one to be cruel to others, so "consequently in the very act of trying to attain happiness one shatters it." A few weeks later, temporarily settled at Fola's, she had recovered somewhat. "I am apt to see the darkest side of things, you know," she confessed. "There isn't another girl in the world as fortunate as I am. Each member of my family is so beautiful."[31]

Mary was ripe for marriage when Ralph Sucher came into the picture in the fall of 1919. He was a Wisconsin graduate, a veteran, and a classmate of Phil's. He came from Illinois (his grandmother remembered listening to one of the Lincoln-Douglas debates), had worked as a stringer for Peoria newspapers, loved politics, and was uncertain whether to establish a career in law or journalism. Words spilled genially from him (as in his nineties they still did during an interview) on almost any subject. His pen and typewriter were facile but well informed, and he and Phil hit it off so resoundingly that they decided to go to Washington together to begin legal studies in the fall of 1919. Ralph would live with the family, paying nothing for his room and a dollar a day for breakfast and dinner. Likeable, serious, and plainly devoted to Old Bob and Belle's politics, he endeared himself to everyone, including the family bulldog, Bud.[32]

Inevitably Ralph became part of the La Follette entourage and then of the family. He and Mary began to see each other on her trips home. The romance progressed to a point of open discussion in September of

1920 after a summer that Mary described as "beautiful." The following March, Mary announced that she would not finish her courses at the School of Fine and Applied Arts and that she and Ralph intended to marry in June. Ralph had no job, and Belle expressed what was presumably her own and Old Bob's mutual distress, though in a low key compared to her tempestuous reaction to Fola's announced engagement ten years earlier. "There is no telling, Mary dear," she urged, "what a little forbearance and self-discipline may mean for your future happiness. Think it over, my dear Mary." Both parents hoped that Mary would continue in school "for your best good and largest ultimate happiness." But though Mary adored Belle no whit less than the others (she said she could no more express her feelings on the matter than describe what she felt in looking over the Grand Canyon) she would not be moved. And Belle quickly capitulated this time. "Daddy and I agree that since you and Ralph have decided . . . you are welcome home and our arms are open for you whenever you wish to come now and always . . . [W]e want to do all we can to make you happy."

Fola, writing from Paris, had concurred: "[P]erhaps the emotional contentment that she would find in having her life with Ralph and in having a home of her own . . . might give her a serenity and bring out the reserve strength which we all feel so much in her." The ceremony, simple and virtually private like all the La Follette weddings, took place in Washington on June 15, performed by a former Senate chaplain. The young couple moved to an apartment on S Street, Ralph started a press service, and Mary, the first La Follette woman to reach voting age after the fight for suffrage was won, settled into domesticity. Private claims took first place with her as they did, in somewhat different ways, with her sister and mother.[33]

It was not so with the brothers in the immediate postwar period. They completed their own apprenticeships and entered political life as adults — independent and grown men but stamped unavoidably as "the La Follette boys," the old lion's cubs, and therefore never quite possessed of identities all their own. They wrestled with themselves about it and toyed with thoughts of other careers, but in the end each followed his fate and became an elected official.

Yet neither one would grow white-haired and die in political harness like Old Bob. Neither would show the Father's stubborn resilience in defeat. Why? At least some partial understanding can be gained from reading the letters in which they occasionally revealed their hearts between 1919 and 1924.

They were not unwilling to follow in Bob and Belle's footsteps. But they came of age in a different era, and they could not share the vision that so moved Bob and Belle, of the progressive heavenly city, the just society of conscientious individuals governing themselves on the best "scientific principles." Their expectations were trimmed by the collapses and disasters that their own youthful eyes witnessed. In 1926 their old family friend Frederic Howe wrote of that fellowship of prewar reformers: "We were evangelists."[34] La Follette's sons were not evangelists.

Politics rewarded their egos in many ways. They loved carrying on for Dad. They were honestly committed to fighting conservatism and privilege. They were skilled and comfortable with the familiar details of managing a campaign, a bill, an appointment—the planning, the maneuvering, the tension and crises, the sweet applause, even the bruises. But lacking Dad's missionary zeal and inner need for powerful enemies, they never got the fulfillment that he did from the game. Politics gave them a great deal, but never quite enough.

"Standing on my shoulders"

The spring of 1919 was, for Young Bob, almost literally a rebirth. Snatched from death's grip, he had a chance to weigh the prospects of returning to his father's office and orbit against other possible opportunities. There was no doubt of what the senator wanted. On his firstborn's twenty-fourth birthday he wrote to Belle that the "boy-baby" they both remembered in sweater, cap, and curls was now better prepared for public life than he himself had been at that age. To Bob he wrote: "You will start life as a man, Bobbie, standing on my shoulders. You have your mother's brain, my boy—the best brain in the world. With established health, what a service you can be to your community, your country and humanity. I greet you. Take one on me! Here is my check for ten."

"Bobbie" answered guardedly. He appreciated the compliment but thought that his father overlooked the advantages of making one's way up from the bottom. "Dad," he argued, singing a familiar refrain, "I don't start on your shoulders by a long shot. If I did I certainly would set the world on fire. You have accomplished so very much and cut such a figure that I sometimes think you have blazed too straight and steep a trail for one as unfit as I to follow."

Thoughts of unfitness were put behind as the joy of returning health filled him. He lived out Belle's earlier advice to Fola when Middleton's plays started to click. "Squeeze all the joy there is to be had out of good fortune," she had written. "We make the most of the dregs of unhappiness but not enough of the sugar left in the cup." Bob smacked his lips over every grain of sugar. Good spirits bubbled through the letters he sent to Washington, with carbon copies for Phil and Fola so that the endless intra-family dialog might not lapse. In a small car that he and Belle had bought he drove to Long Beach, to the ferry to Catalina, to Hollywood. He took up golf and was swallowed in its pleasures and frustrations. He described himself as "getting to be a beach lizard," danced with the daughters of local families, wolfed down huge breakfasts that got his weight up to 152 on a drugstore scale in La Jolla, and strolled the streets in the freedom of grass-stained and greasy tennis shoes. He spent and needed little, sustained by a small allowance from the salary that Old Bob had banked for him during his months in bed.[35]

Young Bob appeared to be a caricature laid-back Californian. "The little mind I had when I came here," he reported in May, "has surely gone to seed but somehow I just revel in the doing of nothing . . . I do not know the day of the week and what is more I don't care a damn." When Phil soberly recommended a reading list to him that included Galsworthy, Shaw, Ibsen, *Les Misérables,* and Romain Rolland's huge novel series of a musician's life, *Jean-Christophe,* he answered: "I wish I could find the time and the inclination . . . but it does not fit into the atmosphere of the life here." Gregarious and outgoing ("you all know that I like to have company for my fun or work," he told the clan), he projected a lightweight image that was deceptive. One would not have tagged him for the child who was devastated by separation from the family at the age of ten, much less an adult who might make a final suicidal surrender to depression.[36]

Yet his "dark melancholy," as Phil remembered it, was there, and so was a seriousness of purpose fused with his very being. He read little for pleasure (though actually he had *already* read *Jean-Christophe* in 1919) but was thoroughly informed on the political issues and events that absorbed him, despite his disclaimers. His running responses to Old Bob's almost-daily reflections on Wilson, the treaty, and other matters made it clear that he missed nothing in the papers that bore on issues before the Senate. And however happily he wore his independence, he was actually more than willing to get back. "I feel that the time has come to get out in the open and begin to talk," he said in April. "We"—the La Follette collective first-person plural—"have been silent too long." On the very day after reporting his alleged mindlessness he was noting that "[t]his is going to be a mighty interesting Congress" and he would have to concentrate on his golf and swimming in order to keep from rushing back. But a month later he was packed and on the way east via a long, circuitous route through San Francisco, the Pacific Northwest, and the Canadian Rockies, ending with a stop at the Mayo Clinic to get a final medical okay for work.

From there he went to Madison and registered the most basic change of his hard experience. "[T]he war-mad patriots here have succeeded in killing any attachment I had," he told his father. Coming in on the train, "I did not have the thrill I used to that I was really getting home." There were no interesting unmarried girls left in town, the farm looked terrible, and there was "absolutely nothing for a 'stranger' to do in this town." Old Bob answered him in a way that throws a blazing light on the difference in their temperaments. "Don't let that feeling against our home place take hold of you for a moment," he shot back. "It is the same crowd that always fought me . . . I whipped them; I forced them to lift their hats to me and eat out of my hand. Eighty per cent are our real friends . . . They have been bound and gagged . . . But *there is another day*." But Bobbie, while not nearly as pugnacious, was more stubborn in his conviction that the bridges were down for good. He would return many times, but always and only, even when a vacation was squeezed in, in connection with a political campaign for his father or himself.[37]

When he and Phil got to Washington in August the exact shape of his future was still fuzzy. He had spoken early in the year of studying law himself, but it was Belle's opinion that he merely wanted to humor his father in this. She wrote to Old Bob that "Bobbie seems to me singularly susceptible to environment and suggestion . . . [H]is problem seems to be to take the initiative, to assume the big responsibility of . . . deciding what he shall do and be . . . I think it would be of immense value to Bobbie to *earn a dollar* doing something he really wanted."[38] Her husband apparently did not take the hint that he should leave "Bobbie" alone and, as is so often the case, the issue was settled by unexpected circumstances that called for a quick decision. La Follette's longtime head secretary, John Hannan, a former Milwaukee newspaperman who had been with him since the governorship, decided to quit at fifty and work in private industry. Young Bob immediately and without discussion stepped into the older man's place.

That sealed his vocation. Young Bob became to Old Bob what Joseph was in the house of Potiphar, the brilliant doer of whatsoever was to be done. He was researcher, speech drafter, press secretary, legislative liaison, and general emissary. In addition he kept the family checkbook and accounts and tried, fruitlessly for the most part, to get both of his workaholic and unwell parents to rest. He wrote columns and articles for both *La Follette's Magazine* and the Madison *Capital Times*. From time to time his letters alluded to other job prospects in journalism or management, or to the old project of legal study, but there was always something else to do for Old Bob. He was needed to organize the delegate campaign in 1920 and then to be his father's eyes and ears at the conventions; he was needed to help win the senatorship in 1922; he was needed in the odd years to help Dad carry on the fights for conservation and labor rights and railroad regulation, or in one case to go back to Wisconsin and negotiate compromises on a tax bill between quarreling La Follette progressives in the legislature after things had reached what Old Bob called "the knifing stage." He was getting a thorough training course as an apprentice senator, though he firmly insisted to Phil as late as 1923: "I have no political ambitions."[39]

Young Bob's only biographer believes that he was a reluctant conscript, unable to stand up to the pressure and outright manipulation of his father. The evidence of the letters is by no means clear on that. Bobbie believed in what he was doing. He enjoyed the contacts and the action. When he was discouraged it was either because progressivism was losing or because his personal life was unsatisfactory. He somehow made time for parties and dates both in Washington and New York and, especially in his letters to Phil, referred jokingly to an ongoing sex life, or at least romantic life. But he was the last of the children to marry. "Real girls are few and far between" he complained, and the search for "someone upon whom one can center their affections" left him restless and unsettled. His problem may well have been that of the other La Follettes—that no outside relationship could quite equal the intensity of those within the clan. The happiest possible marriage might leave a taste of second best.

Politics was sometimes an actual relief from private emotional stress. It was definitely not a burden that Young Bob carried unwillingly. It only made him unhappy when it failed—inevitably—to achieve the high purposes and goals that he had been taught to expect of it. What he disliked, however, was trying to get himself elected, and that was because his own speaking and crowd-pleasing abilities were far short of his father's and he knew it. That was why he disclaimed "political ambitions."

With Phil it was otherwise, so much so that the two men appeared to be direct opposites. Brilliant and bookish, he was, in private life, far more introspective, isolated, and broody than his brother. But he sparkled on the platform, and where Bob was a facilitator and compromiser, Phil shared his father's desire to star and to lead and therefore *appeared* to be the more politically ambitious of the two. But he enjoyed winning more than governing. And unlike Bob, whose nonpolitical prospects were always speculative, Phil could demonstrably have had a brilliant legal and teaching career had he stayed on that track. He did not. Like Bob he was drawn, in his formative twenties, into following Dad's political path, and when it took uncomfortable turnings, Phil complained the louder of the two. The seemingly simple "brother act" had layers of complexity.

"To Hell with politics and law"

Where Young Bob's 1919 letters shone with crisp good humor, Phil's were intense and wordy. In his final undergraduate semester he composed long, typewritten meditations on the materials of his courses in contemporary world politics, American literature (concentrating on Poe and Whitman), and philosophy. The last was taught by a stimulating professor named Max Otto who became a close friend and admirer of the La Follettes. Otto's course "Man and Nature" was especially popular with liberal students set afire by his humanist belief that philosophy was meant to serve social needs and could provide the basis for "creative bargaining" within conflict-ridden communities. "Life is a sort of a highway," Phil wrote to his father. "[T]here appear to be many short cuts to the goal we have set ourselves. The radical wants to hurry us down his bye-way which he is sincerely sure will get us to the goal quicker; the conservative wants to hold us back, and believes that the status quo is what we want . . . I believe that the surest and MOST PERMANENT progress comes by going straight ahead and not trying to take short-cuts, or by stopping for rest and enjoyment of the status quo."[40]

Old Bob encouraged Phil's expressed enthusiasm for Shakespeare and the Bible. Belle, learning that he enjoyed Emerson, confided that she had not read the Yankee sage much when young, though as a good Unitarian she had thought she should. Only later in life had she come to appreciate him. Phil himself attended and enjoyed Unitarian services on Sunday mornings, part of a generally disciplined regimen of life filled with classes from nine until three (minus a lunch hour), study from then until nine or ten with a two-hour break for a walk and dinner, and general reading until he turned out his light. His dissipations—on a seventy-dollar-a-month allowance—were cigarettes and an occasional movie. He recorded his expenses punctiliously by habit. It gave him pleasure to calculate them to the penny. He carefully weighed the cost of driving to Washington with Bob against the costs of shipping the car and going by train, and did not forget to include depreciation at two cents per mile in the car expenses. He was also a clipper, filer, list-maker, and card-indexer without peer. He wrote neat little memoranda to himself, like the one on his birthday in 1920:

1. What are my Aims:
   (a) As to character
   (b) As to career
   (c) As to marriage
2. What do I think:
   (a) About the Treaty, and why
   (b) About Russia, and why
   (c) About Wisconsin politics, and why
   (d) About the University, and why
3. What Is My Programme for the Future
   (a) In American politics
   (b) In American Industry
   (c) In American Judiciary[41]

Although Phil did have friends and dates, the tendency of this semi-monastic style was to reinforce his emotional dependence on the family. "My heart is full with the joy of our all being together," he declared just before coming to Washington in August of 1919. "Our family contact has, I hope, kept us sweet in all our troubles. It has made life worth living alone. The idea of still another year of it means a great deal." His loyalty to Old Bob was undivided, and on Dad's sixty-fourth birthday he pledged "that so long as I live I am going to keep scrapping for the same things you have, to the best of my ability."

Phil's feelings about Belle were even stronger. He considered her to be, even more than Bob, the essential creator and guide of his spirit. On one birthday he wrote a private meditation: "[F]our and twenty years ago I was conceived in my mother's womb and after a period was wrenched forth from her warmth through her blood and pain, and so I was bound. There passed into me part of her—to be true to that gift is the divine purpose of life." It was devotion that bordered on the incestuous, and he made no bones about it. "The real reason I have never been in love with a girl," he told her, "is because my love for you is so profound that love for a girl (right now—perhaps some time I'll meet 'Her') seems so insignificant beside it." And in another extraordinary letter he lamented:

It is certainly tragic that the creator of all things didn't make the world with a relationship that would keep mother and son together always. The relationship between a man and his wife is tinged with sex. Sex is founded on banter—that is, in youth. There is this playing back and forth—this courting and rejecting; this high-planned teasing. After one is married it becomes prosaic and if followed by the proper function of life, propagation, is taken place by motherhood and fatherhood. But there is always the remaining element of selfishness . . . which mars it . . . But the really sanctified and human relationship is that of Mother and son:

there is all the element of the opposite sex—without the lowering (NOT degrad-
ing, mind you, but just lowering) of sex fulfillment; there is that understanding
which comes only between two opposite poles of comprehending sex; then there
is absolute devotion; and, at least on the mother's side, there is real unselfishness.[42]

It is unfair to subject an historical figure, on such slender evidence, to
prescription-counter psychoanalysis. The quotation possibly says more
about the sexual confusions of a healthy young man with puritanical ideals
than about Oedipal yearnings. All the same, it is one more reflection of
Phil's intensely inward-looking nature, so at odds with the conventional
good-fellowship of the "born" politician.

Despite Phil's professed difficulty in falling in love he did exactly that
while finishing college, but the course of the affair exposed new problems
in his development. His "girl" was Betty Head, a doctor's daughter and
a childhood friend. They agreed to become engaged on a balmy spring
evening in Madison, and in December of 1920, very definitely with Belle's
blessing, she came down from a post-graduation job in New York to join
the La Follette Christmas celebrations in the house on Sixteenth Street.
It was not a happy holiday for her. Phil treated her distantly and, on the
morning of her last day, left her alone while he slept hour after hour. It
got him a scolding from Young Bob that ran: "I think you little realize what
your absorption in the law for the past year and a half has cost you temporarily, or rather what it has cost your friends. You have . . . the gift of
sociability, which you have allowed to lie dormant these many months . . . I
wanted to say too what I tho[ugh]t of your attitude towards Betty while
she was here. Not that I objected if you were really expressing what you
felt inside because if you were then of course the sooner she knew it the
better, but somehow I was sure you did not feel the way you acted and
I hated to see you hurt her needlessly."

But Phil did, in reality, feel unable to make a genuine connection with
Betty or anyone else, and the engagement ended soon afterward by mutual
friendly consent. He explained the problem to Belle by saying "I have never
'let-go' of my affections, or of my temper, nor of any of my emotions. It
isn't because I haven't them—but because I sense their force and dislike
to let them out of my control."

Phil's uptightness outside the family walls was reinforced by what his
brother rightly called "absorption" in the legal training that he returned
to finish at the University of Wisconsin in 1920. He devoured law books,
digested cases, memorized opinions, and listened intently to arguments
before the Supreme Court, especially when Brandeis tipped him off to a
worthwhile case coming up. He seemed to be headed for a donnish life

on some law faculty, or a quiet practice in Madison, which greatly appealed to him. But other currents were stirring, too, a restlessness that would erupt from time to time in proposals to take off for a vacation in South America, enter the diplomatic service, or work full time on the magazine, and an itch to excel. "I am deeply ambitious," he wrote of himself just after his break-up with Betty, and La Follette public ambitions were not easily held within the boundaries of campus and courtroom.[43]

He broke out of his shell, thanks to two enormous discoveries during the last year of relentless study that ended with admission to the bar in 1922. He found that he had his father's golden gift of speech, and he met a woman who could be a political helpmeet equal to his mother. Politics, always beckoning, thereupon claimed him fully for its own.

The initial push came out of the needs of the postwar senatorial contest. Phil was already a veteran of the backstage conferences and the unglamorous legwork of campaigning. It was only in 1920, however, that he had been given a small speaking part. It was a talk to an audience of some fifty people in the hamlet of Rome, Wisconsin, in a hall lit by kerosene lamps. "I found I could swim," was his brief summation. But in 1922 he was trusted to set out with a borrowed touring car and the responsibility for stumping the entire western side of the state by himself. He came alive on the platform, holding audiences "in the hollow of his hand," radiating Dad's magnetism and conviction.

Old Bob was not yet entirely aware of his younger son's gift. But after the Wisconsin primary, the two of them went together on the brief speaking tour in Minnesota to support Henrik Shipstead's Senate candidacy. In Mankato, Phil took the floor first to warm up the audience. He "started in like a rocket" and poured out the pent-up rage of five years in a flaming defense of the handful of senators who had held out against the war. After La Follette's own speech the pair returned to their "dingy" hotel room. The old man, ecstatic tears rolling down his cheeks, took Phil's face between his palms. "You are *my* boy," he sobbed.[44]

The unveiling of Phil as a second political heir—and one with a charmed tongue, to boot—was stunningly important. Old Bob's "machine" ran on personal appeal. It demanded steady contact with the small towns that were his base, and now a healthy young La Follette was available for the job. Phil began a killing pattern of existence. Six or seven days a week he would work all day at his law practice, and two or three evenings a week he would drive forty or fifty miles, deliver a speech, drive back, and fall into bed. This would continue off and on for twenty years. Thus taking over the field command of the Wisconsin progressive forces loyal to the

The La Follette boys hit the road for Dad as soon as they reached young manhood.

family name almost guaranteed that Phil would have a political career within the state. Despite occasional private murmurs of wanderlust, this was essentially what he wanted. Madison, despite the aches it had inflicted in 1917–1919, remained the home of his heart.

His balancing act between political and intellectual life might well have been impossible, however, if he had not joined fortunes with Isabel Bacon, almost universally known by her nickname of Isen.

They came into each others' lives in 1921 when Isen was an undergraduate senior at Wisconsin. The daughter (one of five) of a civil engineer in Salt Lake City, she came of the same deep-thinking Yankee stock as Belle. Relatives on her father's side helped run the Boston educational publishing house of Allyn and Bacon. At her high school commencement she

"Isen"—Isabel Bacon La Follette around the time of her marriage to Phil.

had delivered an earnest and endearing speech on new womanhood. It was a summary of all the gains and accomplishments of women in the preceding half century, culminating in "the educated woman of today" who "sees evils and threatening conditions in the heart of her city and country . . . [and] has formed into clubs, leagues, and federations, to remedy this wrong." Of course there were still men who objected and feared the loss of woman's cheering influence in the home, but eighteen-year-old Miss Bacon brushed them bravely aside: "[T]he day of the spinning wheel and the loom in the home is over. The woman has more time for outside interests. Why should she not expend her surplus energy for the public welfare!"[45]

Isen had, and would in time need, plenty of "surplus" energy. Her fizzy letters home were full of enthusiastic underlinings. She was *crazy* about a law course, "learning stuff that absolutely everybody should know"; a visiting ballet troupe was *heavenly;* some toilet water and "eats" sent from home were *marvellous* and the folks were simply *peaches* to send it. In her senior year she took a course in political ethics and explained: "It deals with the causes of the war, its results and problems, and how to deal with them. Doesn't that sound great?" She was impatient to fit her learning into real life. "Sometimes I get so anxious to get out and to work that I don't know what to do," she burst out, "but then I calm down and think of the opportunities I'm getting right here."[46]

Isen met Phil at a discussion group and reported him to the family to be "about as fas-kinating as you could wish for" and "quite a flirt." He began to "rush" her, as he called it, and a few months later astonished her with a proposal that mixed "Gallic fire and Scotch caution." Would she marry him, he asked, sometime in the future when he could earn a living? She would and did, but the process was somewhat more drawn out than she had expected. After graduation she went east to teach in a settlement house in Bayonne, New Jersey, while he was supposedly laying the foundations of a law practice to support them, but he never seemed to feel that they were deep or solid enough. Two years went by with no plans made, while Phil wavered and agonized. "When I get all the trappings of matrimony . . . waved at me . . . I get panicky," he admitted to her. Brief vacation reunions in Washington or on Nantucket were broken by long spells of separation when he continued his pattern of round-the-clock work, reading, and speechmaking.

Then, at Belle's urging, Isen joined the editorial staff of *La Follette's Magazine* early in 1923, and a wedding date of April 14 was set. The week before the wedding, the barn at Maple Bluff burned down. Isen was in

Salt Lake City visiting her parents when Phil called to suggest postponing the wedding, which was to take place in Chicago in the apartment of the officiating minister, Dr. Eustace Haydon. There was a puzzled silence. "We weren't planning on living in the *barn,* were we?" she asked. "Oh, no," he answered sheepishly, "but I thought I ought to tell you." Isen's practical father had put her aboard the train with this advice: "If Phil isn't there to meet you, go to a movie and come home." But the ceremony took place as planned.

Despite the hesitation it was a good marriage. Belle was delighted that the new Mrs. La Follette could simultaneously write progressive editorials for the magazine, lobby state legislators to ratify the child labor amendment, and make a comfortable home for Phil. "You are a daughter after my own heart, dear Isen," she rejoiced. Isen in her turn was fully committed to the La Follette candidates and causes, though she was in for a number of surprises. There were jagged divisions in Madison society between those who accepted her new in-laws and some who hated them beyond reason and would attend no social gathering where they had to sit with a La Follette. She was also unprepared for the uncritical solemnity with which Bob and Phil idealized and defended each other. Luckily, she was more amused than hurt. As Ralph pointed out, she and he and Mid might be accepted but were not "of the blood royal."[47]

Isen was a fine balance wheel for Phil, who loved her genuinely but unhesitatingly unfolded his ambivalent moodiness to her in the almost daily letters that he wrote during the engagement. "I've got a complex on power all right," he told her in the first summer of engagement. "Frank as I appear to be," he warned, "[I] am yet frightfully constrained about my personal self . . . Too tied up in a knot inside." Periodically he was too much for himself. "I want to kick over the traces . . . and start out for the East, where my dreams are located" he confided once. Presumably he meant further east than New York, because shortly before the wedding he "hit a spell when I've felt like chucking, and beating it for China or any damned place where one wasn't continually hampered by the worries and problems of life." Hard at work in the 1922 campaign, he complained of missing his fiancée, but immediately rebuffed her suggestion to join him for her summer vacation on the grounds that she would get no rest. Then he groused: "At times I want to throw up the sponge and say to 'Hell' with politics and law. Let's just LIVE." But his itchy-footed spells more often than not were tied to dreams of glory. "Every once in a while," he observed in 1921, "I get a 'call' of the wanderlust . . . [I]t's always accompanied by a desire to 'lead the folks into the promised land.'"

All of these apparent waverings may have some explanatory bearing on Phil's later life. But in the spring of 1924 there was no possible doubt that, like brother Bob, he had been enlisted in Dad's political wars for an indefinite term of service. As Isen phrased it, that year as always they were all "soldiers in a cause"—herself, Ralph, and especially the two La Follette "princes." The cause of the year was Old Bob's campaign for the prize that had gotten away in 1912, the presidency. It was only twelve years since then, but it might as well have been a century.[48]

"I want to die . . . with my boots on"

The 1924 campaign was the third in less than thirty years in which rebels had tried to break through the steadily hardening concrete of two-party political domination. It was a touch of theater in the "roaring twenties," the so-called golden age of film and sport spectaculars, as well as a farewell tour for La Follette, the old actor and fighter, a final defiant fist shaken in the face of the swarming enemy hosts, a last appeal to the capricious gods of popular favor.

It was foredoomed to defeat, of course, yet it was not a suicide charge. "None of us thought for a moment we had any chance to win," Phil later admitted, but there were prospects beyond the short term to consider. The young Coolidge administration did not look invulnerable. The scandals of the Harding regime were fresh in the public mind. There was an odor of decay from the buried underside of "prosperity"—the mortgaged wheat farms, the shuttered factories and bleak mill towns, the coal mines and logging camps where men still worked and were treated like animals. The postwar economy and culture were breeding a discontented bipartisan multitude without a political voice, since conservatives seemed to have a firm grasp on both the Democratic and Republican high commands. That being so, it appeared possible that a vigorous independent campaign for the presidency would siphon off enough progressive voters from both parties to lay in building materials for the future—if not a new party, then a bloc of votes that the old ones would have to appease.

The independent nominee, to make any showing, would have to be widely recognized and respected by almost all of the country's dissidents, a spectacularly heterogeneous tribe. Only Robert M. La Follette had those credentials. The trouble was that he was a very sick man, of indomitable spirit but with a body slowly being drained of its remaining vitality.

In the spring of 1923 he had willingly gone to the Kellogg sanitarium at Battle Creek at the urging and as the guest of William T. Rawleigh.

Rawleigh was one of those rarities, a millionaire devotee of Fighting Bob. He had moved from his native Wisconsin to Illinois and done well in patent medicines and "health products," and now made it his mission to be La Follette's financial angel, much as Charles Crane, the progressive plumbing heir, had been twelve years earlier. After Bob and Belle had undergone a regimen of whole grain dieting and physical therapy in Michigan, they were persuaded to let Rawleigh pay for their first and only trip to Europe.[49] It was not precisely a vacation. They were accompanied by Young Bob and Basil Manly, another new supporter. He was director of the People's Legislative Service, a bipartisan progressive research and lobbying organization begun in 1920 to supply insurgent lawmakers with data and support services.

The itinerary took them through England, Germany, the Soviet Union, and back to France. It was scarcely a restful trip since La Follette made it an occasion for gathering information and writing newspaper articles. It began in irony, when, on the third day at sea, news was received that President Harding had died, and Bob, as ranking public official on board, led a memorial service for the amiable, corrupt, and reactionary figurehead of his party. In London he met with prominent Labour party politicians and intellectuals. In Germany, surveying the economic devastation wrought by hunger and inflation, he renewed his public assaults on the Versailles treaty as a sure breeder of future wars. In the USSR he got red-carpet treatment and reported fairly on what seemed to be progress, but he was unrelenting in his rejection of one-party rule in the name of the proletariat. "If I were a citizen of Russia," he wrote on his return, "I should resist this communistic dictatorship as vigorously as I have endeavored to resist the encroachment upon our democratic institutions in America. I hold that government by one class denying to other classes the right to participate, is tyranny." That put him at odds with his old friend Lincoln Steffens who, at that time, believed that Russia was the future that worked. On a swing through Italy Bob met Mussolini. His opinion was "What an actor!" but he had no more sympathy with Il Duce's suppressions of free discussion than of Lenin's. The trip ended with a visit to Paris and his Wisconsin friend sculptor Jo Davidson.

Bob enjoyed it all and lamented not having visited Europe until the twilight of his life. "It is a crime to have waited so many years to see this beauty," he told Davidson as they stood in front of the Crillon and admired the Place de la Concorde.[50] From the point of view of a rest cure it was a flop. Travel, sightseeing, and stair climbing took their toll; Bobbie reported home that Dad's heart was "kicking up didos." And inevitably, some weeks afterward, La Follette fell ill again with disabling chest pains. Under the circumstances, he was unable to assume field command of the progressives preparing for the opening of the Senate, much less to begin thinking about the 1924 campaign. Bobbie put it bluntly and confidentially in November: Dad was incapable of work for another six weeks at least, and he, Bobbie, hoped that the old man would let him announce "that he cannot be a candidate for President under any circumstances."

But even on nitroglycerine tablets and morphine shots, Dad would do no such thing. He was needed to strengthen Norris and the insurgent band, and he would be needed in 1924. Advised bluntly that the race might kill him, he told Phil: "I have had a wonderful life. I'd like to live it all over again. But I don't want to—I just can't—live rolled up in a cotton blanket in a damned wheelchair. I want to die, as I have lived, with my boots on." Go on with the plans he ordered, "with a full head of steam in the boiler."[51]

And they did, while he cast off the bedclothes and went back to keep the heat on the administration in the Senate. That exertion promptly gave him pneumonia, which he had to cure with a May rest in Atlantic City. By the start of June, thanks to frantic work by quickly improvised state committees, two hundred thousand signatures had been collected on petitions urging him to make the run. A coordinating committee of liberals calling itself the Conference for Progressive Political Action (CPPA) slated a meeting in Cleveland for July 4 for the clear purpose of nominating him, so all was in readiness.

This time he kept firm control of the process. First he fended off a nomination by a Farmer-Labor gathering that was open to Communists, with a public letter issued before its meeting on June 17. Communists, it stated, did not intend to cure evils by the ballot but to "establish by revolutionary action a dictatorship of the proletariat, which is absolutely repugnant to democratic ideals." This repudiation gave him some protection from predictable campaign Red-baiting. Meanwhile he arranged as usual to have the Wisconsin delegation to the Republican convention present his platform as a minority report. That it did, amid the customary howls of scorn. This time, however, it had a "free" audience of impressionable radio listeners scattered across the land. Finally La Follette made it clear that he would not yet be the choice of a new *party* with a full national slate of nominees, who would only divide the progressive vote and knock out sympathetic Republicans and Democrats running for congressional and state offices. He would go it alone this time.[52]

All of these pre-curtain-raising arrangements cost Young Bob, Phil, Ralph, Manly, and a team of Wisconsin lieutenants weeks of all-night work in railroad cars and hotel rooms. The only item that could not be managed was a monopoly on press attention for the CPPA gathering. July 4 came five days after the Democrats in convention had begun their balloting in New York, and ordinarily they should have been finished. Instead, they disemboweled themselves in a fight between their urban-immigrant and southern-fundamentalist adherents and suffered through 103 roll calls before compromising on July 9 by a dip into their small cadre of conservatives. They chose a pin-striped "lawyer's lawyer," John W. Davis, best known for skilled efforts on behalf of J. P. Morgan and other international financial syndicates. The La Follette convention had to share billing with the Democrats' free-for-all, which might not have been entirely a drawback. For many, the total lack of any CPPA opposition to the La Follette "steamroller" was a refreshing contrast to the anarchy in New York.

It was a colorful rally of outsiders that met in Cleveland's Public Hall, with the improvisational spontaneity that surfaces on the rare occasions that a convention is not controlled by professionals. There were some twelve hundred delegates and nine thousand onlookers in the hall, mainly young and all enthusiastic. The chairman, William Johnston, was the president of the International Association of Machinists, but there were delegates — with weighted votes according to the size of their organization — from labor federations, farm cooperatives, the National Association of Colored People, the Committee of Forty-eight, church groups, women's organizations, college political clubs, the Food Reform Society of America, and the Davenport (Iowa) Ethical Society. "There in one room," wrote a reporter, "sat side by side hardboiled Socialists from the East Side of New York . . . mildly liberal businessmen from Cleveland and Detroit . . . clothing workers from Rochester, professional men from all the large cities of the East, and youngsters in knickers who had 'hitch-hiked' to the convention as representatives of the Youth Movement."

It was a low-budget operation; no band was hired and collections were taken from the floor to meet expenses. The crowd furnished its own noise with group singing and applause for a long list of speakers such as Peter Witt, an old follower of the saintly single-taxer Tom Johnson; gaunt and dedicated Andrew Furuseth; Edwin Markham, whose poem *The Man with the Hoe* was a favorite declamation piece of radicals with its defiant challenge to the "masters, lords and rulers of the earth"; William Pickens, a black Yale graduate adding the voice of the NAACP to La Follette's tributes; and fiery Fiorello La Guardia from New York, who shouted "I would rather be right than regular" and meant it. Others on hand were Populist veterans like Jacob Coxey, who had ridden boxcars from Ohio to Washing-

267

ton as the general of Coxey's Army of unemployed in the Depression of 1893.[53]

Young Bob, showing surprising platform ease, read his father's statement of willingness to run. On July 5 the nomination was made by acclamation and the delegates agreed to leave the naming of a vice president to the national committee. La Follette wanted Louis Brandeis but the justice declined with thanks. As Belle reasonably commented, "With Bob it is the logic of his life. With Louis it would be stepping into a new field."[54] The choice went to Montana's Democratic Senator Burton K. Wheeler, a sturdy enemy of the copper and other trusts, who said that when his party went to Wall Street for a candidate, he refused to go with it.

The platform was, in the prevailing style of the time, a long list of catch-all demands that included cleaning out spoilsmen, developing public power resources, government take-over of railroads, a lower tariff, easier credit for farmers, guarantees of the rights of unions, and the outlawing of child labor. It horrified conservatives anew with a call to elect federal judges and make Supreme Court decisions subject to a congressional override. It condemned financial imperialism in Central America and demanded disarmament and a popular referendum on war. All of these ideas had been aired since 1920, and some went as far back as the antimonopoly crusades of the preceding half century. What knit them together was the broad theme that economic justice was reachable through the voluntary cooperation of intelligent citizens. Its declaration of general principles declared: "Free men of every generation must combat renewed efforts of organized force and greed to destroy liberty . . . It is our faith that we all go up or down together—that class gains are temporary delusions and that eternal laws of compensation make every man his brother's keeper . . . The nation may grow rich in the vision of greed. The nation will grow great in the vision of service."[55]

And so the crusade was launched. A collective biography of those who joined it would frame, all by itself, a history of progressivism and liberalism. Bob was supported by John Dewey and Jane Addams, Florence Kelley and Arthur Garfield Hays, W. E. B. Du Bois and Harriot Stanton Blatch, Oswald G. Villard and John Haynes Holmes, Fiorello La Guardia and Harold Ickes, Helen Keller and Ernest Gruening, Morris Hillquit and Norman Thomas, and Frederic Howe and Felix Frankfurter, whose article "Why I shall Vote for La Follette" in the *New Republic* summed up La Follettism as well as it ever has been done with the statement: "His aim has been consistently to . . . make the commonwealth more secure and enduring by resting it on a broad basis of independent, trained, contented citizens."[56]

Because few issues of substance separated Coolidge and Davis, and both were speakers guaranteed to cure insomnia, the mere fact of La Follette's candidacy was the most exciting thing about a basically torpid campaign, its "one dramatic, colorful spectacle," according to reporter Frank Kent. Given the articulate voices and visibility of his support among the intelligentsia, La Follette's prospects did not appear too dismal at first.

His own campaigning was limited by his waning strength and empty pockets. His speeches were well received, though already a little archaic—sadly—in their length and heavy content of facts. He was aware of changing realities and plunged $3,500 of scarce campaign money into a radio speech to start the ball rolling—not a broadcast address to a live audience but a studio talk. Asked how it felt to speak to invisible listeners, he said wryly that he "never had a more respectful hearing or fewer interruptions." He did not easily make friends with the new technology in public appearances. He liked to roam the platform and raise his voice, but crude early microphones did not let him do either. Once his radio listeners heard a plaintive murmur: "I wish I had some straps to put my feet in."[57] He worked major centers of the industrial East and Midwest—Boston, Baltimore, New York, Rochester, Cleveland, Detroit, Cincinnati, Chicago, Kansas City, and St. Louis—but went no further west than Minneapolis, Des Moines, and Omaha. At every stop of his campaign train the crowds were loud and lusty in their approval. People flocked to see the little white-haired old man who, almost on his own, was taking on the two national parties. When auditoriums were jammed full, overflow crowds clustered like bees around outdoor amplifiers.

But it was not nearly enough. Elections are won by organization and money, and there was very little of either. There were no cadres of party workers to parade, leaflet, ring doorbells, bombard the press with letters and ads. (Most major papers, owned by rich publishers who turned purple at the mere mention of his name, opposed him.) Money was raised in driblets by such shifts as selling half the seats at his appearances. Sometimes he could not proceed to the next stop until the hat was passed to buy railroad tickets for his entourage. In all he had some $220,000 to work with, as against contributions, probably underreported, of $820,000 for Davis and $4.3 million for Coolidge.

So the weeks dwindled down toward election day. Belle came along on some trips, talking to outdoor meetings where men arrived in dusty flivvers and women held babies in their arms while they listened. She charmed reporters, joked that she was "more radical" than Bob, admitted freely that she was keeping a jealous watch over his health.[58] When she

The spirit was there, but old age showed as La Follette wooed his few supporters for president in 1924.

herself became ill in October, Fola took her engagements for a while. The strain was hurting them all. Belle tried to shield Mary from visiting Maple Bluff in the midst of her first pregnancy, fearful of the "stress and distraction" of the contest. Phil begged Isen to ignore her "nervous irritable husband and his antics" during speaking tours. (Besides campaigning for his father, he had cast the die for a Wisconsin political career and entered the contest for district attorney of Dane County.) In October Bob, Jr., advised Rachel Young, one of his office staff, that "we are all tired to the bone." Only Old Bob, whom everyone knew to have the shortest life expectancy of them all, seemed tireless.[59]

After the last big meeting in Cleveland, Bob took the train to Madison, by way of Chicago. A crowd of over three thousand supporters met him at the station and escorted him to the capitol steps for a few words. He told them he hoped to "last long enough to see the nation freed from its economic slavery and the government returned to the people." And he told those too young to remember that it reminded him of the great day in 1879 when the same kind of throng waited to lift him on their shoulders when he came home with the oratorical prize. That had been the beginning, and now the story was ending the same way in the same place.

On election night, Bob and the boys listened to the returns over the

big radio in Governor Blaine's office. Belle was back in Washington awaiting Mary's imminent delivery, so she was spared the effort of keeping a
brave face while the news grew darker hour by hour. They had hoped to
carry a few states, but only Wisconsin delivered its thirteen electoral votes
to Old Bob. Coolidge had piled up 382, and Davis got only 136, every
one of them from a southern state (if Oklahoma is counted as southern).
The only dim cheer of the night was provided by Phil's election to the district attorney's office.

In August Lincoln Steffens had predicted, "The American people may
feel the impulse to support Bob. But the least little thing will stampede
them. Some banker will pass the word that a vote for La Follette will be
a vote wasted and they will chuck Bob and vote for Coolidge." That had
been pretty much the case. The Democrats argued in October that only
their man had a real chance to win so that any vote denied to Davis was
a *de facto* vote for Coolidge. The Republicans warned that a big La Follette vote could deny either major party an electoral-college majority and
throw the election into the House of Representatives, where anything could
happen and the economoy could collapse from uncertainty while awaiting the result. "Coolidge or Chaos" was their slogan, and it played well
with a huge majority of the working public, even though the union movement, including Gompers's AFL (though somewhat tepidly), had endorsed
Old Bob.

Driving back to Maple Bluff late that night, Phil and Bob berated labor
for its defection. Dad rebuked them, "You have never known real poverty,"
he snapped. "We have had hard times but never the haunting fear of losing
your job, of losing those paychecks that are all that stand between starvation for those workers and their families. Don't blame the folks. They just
got scared."[60]

He had put his finger on a key change. America's politics were now
those of a nation made up overwhelmingly of wage earners. Taxes, trusts,
and the tariff might stir them up, but their essential identity and security
were in the job. Whatever deals protected it and enlarged its rewards were
acceptable; whatever reform movements threatened it — and they had been
persuaded that La Follettism did so — were not.

Considering the odds, in fact, he did remarkably well, incredibly well
in fact for a man who had been a national pariah seven years earlier. He
got 16.5 percent of the popular vote, some 4.8 million. His popular vote
was slightly larger than that cast for Theodore Roosevelt in 1912, but a
smaller percentage of the total (and Roosevelt collected 88 electoral votes).
In eleven western states La Follette and Wheeler came in second, ahead

of Davis. In ten major cities he got almost every fourth vote. His tiny electoral total somewhat distorted, as it often does, the actual preferences of the voters.

These facts kept his faith in the people alive. They had been submitted to "economic thumbscrews," he argued in *La Follette's Magazine* in the final campaign days, with threats of foreclosures and firings if Coolidge were not elected. There would be another day, he promised. "The Progressives will close ranks for the next battle." But it was not a battle that he would live to fight.[61]

"There is a lot of work I still could do"

He went back to the Senate with a brave smile but admitted in a touching letter to his sister that it was all show. "It was not easy," he confessed, "to face the old gang with the election just over and every state lost except Wisconsin. But I sailed in with my head up and all smiles. You [can] be sure I would not give any evidence of the taste in my mouth."

He admitted to being "unfit for good hard work just at this time," but told Josie that he was looking ahead to an organization meeting of progressives coming up in February in Chicago that might finally launch a new Progressive party. The trouble was that there would be an unavoidable fight over which founding *organizations* would swing the most weight in it. That was the shape of the future, but Bob the individualist did not like what he saw. He laid out the reasons for Josie in what was, for all purposes, his political will and testament.

I am not for a class party or a party composed of organized labor and organized farmers and organized socialists or any other form of group organization . . . I think the citizen should be the unit of any political organization and I hope such a party can be formed . . . which will appeal to every American . . . who believes in a government of the people by and for the people. I cannot go into any new party movement upon any other basis. I believe in democracy. It is a religion with me. I don't say we can win the next election on those principles. But I do say that it will win in the end and it is the duty of every man and woman in America to give out of themselves each a part of the best that is in them to this cause.

Then he turned back to his daily battles with the Republican Old Guard in the Senate. It punished him for challenging Coolidge by stripping away his seniority rights and putting him at the bottom of the list on the Finance, Interstate Commerce, and Indian Affairs committees. It was a sign of how much they still feared a man who was physically slipping downhill week by week.[62]

The La Follettes had not come out of the fight in good health. Belle had a tonsillectomy in December, Fola had infected sinuses, and Bobbie came down with grippe. The good news was the birth, on November 11, of Robert La Follette Sucher to Ralph and Mary. But Bob's enjoyment of grandfatherhood was abruptly cut short by fresh attacks of bronchial congestion. The doctors ordered him to go to Florida and "bake the remnants of the pneumonia out." He and Belle stayed at an inn in Fort Lauderdale through the winter, two old-timers dutifully taking walks, naps, and sunbaths and writing letters to the children. He got back to Washington in time to join in one last winning fight. A coalition of Republican progressives and Democrats rejected Coolidge's nominee for attorney general, Charles B. Warren, a lawyer closely tied to trusts that he might have to prosecute under the Sherman Act.

The session ended on March 18. Bob sat in Washington, thinking of new projects for the summer and haunted by a sense of roads untaken. Bobbie got away for a short vacation in Europe, and Bob noted in his diary, "I am awfully dependent on the lad—and feel guilty at taking so much out of his life to keep me company as the years come on me." He wrote Phil, who was struggling overtime to do his official job and wrest more dollars out of private practice: "I am sorry to see you merge yourself so wholly in your professional work. It is all very well . . . to think that it is only a temporary thing you are doing, this going to the office nights and Sundays. How much I would give if I could make over that part of my life. It is very wrong . . . narrowing in its effect on the cultural side . . . besides being mighty hard on home life."

But another voice said to him that there was no time to spare. "When the last night comes and I go to the land of Never Return," he had written in 1919, "what an awful account of *things undone* I shall leave *behind*." That tug between love of home and the call of duty had dominated him all his life, and his family, for better or for worse, was never free of its influence.[63]

But in the end he came home for good. In the small hours of May 18 he woke up with a chill and shooting pains in his heart. It was a major attack, and he was told to stay in bed for a month. He played with his new grandchild, read detective stories, joked, and pretended that he was not dying, but he knew better. "I am at peace with all the world," he told Young Bob, "but there is a lot of work I still could do. I don't know how the people will feel toward me, but I shall take to the grave my love for them which has sustained me through life."

Four days after his seventieth birthday a final seizure came at eight in

Old Bob, home on his shield at last, drew his final crowds.

the morning. He died early that afternoon with the family around the bedside.

Next morning they accompanied the casket to the train for Madison. None of them wore black; he had never liked it. He lay in state in the east rotunda of Wisconsin's capitol for two days while the condolence messages poured in from the movers and shakers, and somewhat over fifty thousand plain people from every part of Wisconsin and neighboring states jammed the roads and shuffled past the bier to say good-bye in lines that snaked clear around Capitol Square. Eustace Haydon, the Unitarian minister from the University of Chicago's Divinity School who had married Phil and Isen fourteen months earlier, officiated. "The old enemies against which he fought still are in the field; the causes which he championed still call for battling, heroic hearts," he told them all. "The future democracy of which he dreamed is still to win . . . We say farewell, but we shall always remember him."

Then the crowd, inside and out, broke into "America" as the casket was carried to the hearse. "Sweet land of liberty," the voices quavered, and the procession of autos inched away on its three-mile crawl through the

June heat and dust, past silent, bareheaded onlookers, to the family plot at Forest Hill Cemetery. The final words and rituals were completed. And Fighting Bob had rest from his enemies round about.[64]

"The spirit of Mr. La Follette's work will go on"

The immediate question was the succession to the unexpired Senate term. Governor Blaine set a special election for September 29, but the Republican primary two weeks earlier would be the definitive contest. Blaine removed himself from consideration; he wanted time to prepare for a Senate run against Lenroot in 1926. His fellow progressives knew whom they wanted instead, and they lost no time in offering their support to Belle La Follette. On every ground of sentiment and practical experience, Belle would have been perfect and probably invincible. She would have become the first woman senator (though in 1922 a Georgian, Rebecca Felton, had briefly held an honorary and token appointment). That was undoubtedly a temptation for her—to be a pathbreaker for other women candidates.

But she was sixty-six years old, tired, and still the Belle who had always preferred the background. Messages, editorials, resolutions of endorsement and exhortation rained on Maple Bluff, but she stood firm in the knowledge of who she was. She issued a public statement of thanks, but no thanks. "At no time in my life would I ever have chosen a public career for myself. It would be against nature for me to undertake the responsibilities of political leadership." She wasn't giving up the good fight; she was heartened by all the popular tributes that showed a public feeling guaranteeing "[t]hat the spirit of Mr. La Follette's work shall go on. To this end I hope to contribute my share." But her major share, as she later revealed, would be to complete her husband's life story, begun in his 1912 *Autobiography,* as an inspiration for the coming generation.

That left the progressive leaders eager to have the La Follette name on the ballot with a choice among the sons, and only Bob, Jr., who had just turned thirty, was eligible. He declared his candidacy on July 30 and won easily.[65]

Some students of Wisconsin history believe, in hindsight, that Bob was reluctant to take the seat whereas Phil, two years younger, chafed with hopeless ambition for it. But nothing in the family letters or memoirs unambiguously sustains that drama of jealousy. Phil did more openly than Bob acknowledge dreams of eventual grandeur, but he was not necessarily itching for Washington in 1925. He knew Bob was far better prepared for the Senate than he was, and he loved him unrestrictedly.

Bob himself expressed frustration with political and Senate life often enough to warrant the suspicion that he needed a push. It is a safe bet that he initially preferred being his father's assistant to his father's successor. But the record he made for himself on Capitol Hill in the fullness of time was too good to be the product of a man who had to scourge himself to work every morning. At all events, hesitant or not, he took the job. Therefore, in the autumn of 1925, a curious fact was inscribed in the political record books. Phil was holding the first political job that Old Bob ever held. Bob was installed in the last.

So the succession had taken place, but in a world that the royal family had neither created nor anticipated, and that would dictate many surprises in the chronicles that were yet to come.

8

The Succession That Wasn't
(1925–1941)

"Forgive me for letting my mind rot"

Late in December of 1938, an official of a Washington bank wrote a letter to Young Bob's office, apologizing for failing to credit his account with a check made out to "Robert La Follette," without the "Jr." added. Wouldn't it be a good idea, the official suggested, for the senator to drop the "Junior" and avoid future confusion? Back came an icy letter from secretary Grace Lynch. The senator wished his name to remain "Robert M. La Follette, Jr.," on all the bank's records. It was "rather stupid of Mr. Turner to make this check to Robert La Follette because the Senator never signs his name that way." Thirteen years after his father's death La Follette still wanted to make it clear to the world that he was succeeding but *not* replacing him.[1]

No one could. Not even Bob and Phil in combination. The two brothers were neither the first nor the last state politicians to carry a controversial name into a second generation of tumult and shouting. But the timing of their own careers was special. They took up their father's political burdens with an especially devout sense of fulfilling his mission, and they also faced changes so sweeping as to all but guarantee that they could not succeed in carrying it out, no matter what else they might achieve. For La Follettes, that was not merely frustrating. It was the stuff of personal tragedy.

It was Bob who faced the problem first as he slid into the "old man's" vacated Senate seat. From time to time, especially knowing that *Hamlet* was the senior La Follette's favorite play, he may well have imagined whisperings in the night from a paternal ghost, materializing in his chamber to remind him of his "almost blunted purpose." For he was unable to do very much to advance the cause of progressivism in his first four years, and he sometimes appeared reluctant to try.

He had run on a 1925 platform basically derived from the expired La Follette presidential campaign. Its planks included progressive taxation, vigorous antitrust action, antimilitarism (including an end to sending marines to Central America as debt collectors), economic relief for farmers, fair treatment in the courts for labor unions, federal development of the waterpower facilities on the Tennessee River at Muscle Shoals, Alabama.

It was a program with something for everyone shut out of the supposed prosperity of America under Coolidge, whom Bob referred to as "the codfish in the White House." But it was essentially reactive to specific grievances, its parts not fused together by the heat of Old Bob's democratic passions. However, even had Young Bob had a tongue of fire, the time was out of joint. La Follettism in Wisconsin had meant restoration of government to the people, and in Old Bob's day those who had stolen it were clearly identifiable individual villains — bankers like J. P. Morgan or trust-builders like Rockefeller and Carnegie, or legislative allies of the "robber barons" such as Senator Aldrich and "Uncle Joe" Cannon. Those easy targets were gone. Corporate leaders were, for the most part, anonymous organization men. The most notable exception, Henry Ford, was generally regarded as a productive genius and national hero. A temporary majority of voters seemed to have decided that they were less concerned with recapturing control of the government than with getting a continued supply of the cars, the appliances, the material goods that had become part of an "American standard of living."

It was hard, therefore, for the new Senator La Follette to arouse an army of rebels when the population was far from rebellious. His youthfulness was also a handicap and gave him special problems in relating to the handful of progressive senators who had followed his father's leadership. They were middle-aged men who in some cases had literally known him when he tagged into the chamber behind Dad wearing short pants. They liked him, but he lacked the standing to push stubborn loners like Hiram Johnson or William E. Borah into line to present a common anti-Coolidge front. The job belonged by seniority to a generally noncombative George Norris, who, in Young Bob's own 1927 assessment, was "not in a frame of mind where he is willing to give the necessary time and energy" to the cause.[2]

These were good enough reasons in themselves to back away from active legislative leadership, and besides, Young Bob was still nursing a deep, unvoiced hurt at the electorate's rejection of Dad in 1924. "I seem to have had my fill of politics for the time being," he told his girlfriend, Rachel Young, soon afterward. When Old Bob, sick unto death, sent him as representative to an exploratory post-election conference on setting up a national Progressive party, he went with a bleak heart. "It is a burden greater than any one man should be asked to carry," he objected, "but under the circumstances I see no other way out and I trust you will be lenient in your judgment." The words echoed his plaintive lament to the family in 1914 on the eve of his first semester exams: "if the worst should happen please be nice to me because I love you all." Ten years older, he was still afraid of letting the family down by failure that he saw coming. His anticipation was sound; quite as he expected, the temporary coalition of unionists, farmers, socialists, and reformers quickly fell apart, leaving nothing to build on.

In 1926 Young Bob was tempted to drop out, at least informally, and his shaky health gave him a perfectly legitimate excuse. That year his legs began to pain him again and the old, frightening swellings returned to his face. In the autumn he spent several weeks in Rochester, Minnesota, at the Mayo Clinic while the staff poked, probed, took cultures, ran tests, and finally opened his leg to remove an inflammatory blood clot. No clear verdict on his general condition was announced except that he should not hurry back to Washington for the brief Senate session due to end in March of 1927. He did not, and spent part of the winter golfing in North Carolina. He was restored enough to conduct a second winning campaign for his seat in 1928, but the primary was hardly over before he was back in Rochester for another prolonged period of lying on his back while the cause of a flare-up of the old symptoms was again pursued with various injections. He seemed not to mind. He read a good deal of fiction and biography, listened to University of Wisconsin football games on the radio, and, when finally released from the doctors' clutches, took another long and therapeutic southern vacation. He wrote to the family early in 1929: "It has been good for my body though it has put my mind in a coma . . . You must forgive me for letting my mind rot as I am doing, but even that seems a relief. I am not thinking a serious thought from one day's end to another . . . [T]hink of what a story it will make when the world learns that a rising young senator has decided to become a beach comber for life."[3]

For the first time Bob paid serious attention to his personal emotional life. At thirty-four he was still unmarried and in his own words "playing the field" where women were concerned. As the only remaining single child he felt a special responsibility for watching over Belle, who was living with him. She apparently worried that she stood in the way and told him so. He assured her it was otherwise. "I would not hesitate to tell you if and when I ever feel that I want to marry," he promised. "I knew before you wrote that you want as much as I do to have me follow the course which promises the most for happiness in this life." It may only be coincidental but that letter was followed very quickly by a commitment. For several years he had been dating Rachel Young, and writing her warm but relatively impersonal letters when he was traveling. But in July of 1929 he went to visit Mid and Fola in Hollywood, where they had temporarily settled. Under the influence of the California sunshine in which he toasted his still-sore leg, things began to move quickly. Rachel seems to have suggested breaking things off, because he wrote her late that month asking, "Would you throw away all the progress we have made during the past two years?" Her answer is not recorded, but less than two weeks later he was on the Santa Fe Chief rushing eastward to a rendezvous in New York, and writing to her that hours and minutes were dragging by until they could be reunited. "Darling, I am almost beside myself with longing for you," his letter on railroad stationery protested, "I love you, love you dear, with my whole being."[4]

Like Phil, Bob was less than impetuous once he had proposed. He did not marry Rachel for another full year, but his decision seemed to fall in with a general tendency in 1929 among all the La Follettes to give serious consideration to cultivating their personal gardens for a change. Fola had become the most withdrawn of all from mainstream politics. Her outrage over the 1924 election was the culmination of a ten-year embitterment that got steadily blacker through the years of war and reaction. She let it explode to Mary:

It is too bad that the election went as it did. I can't see much consolation in it from any angle. It seems to me quite completely disillusioning as to the capacity of "the people" to stand by anything or anyone who works in their behalf . . . from my point of view they failed in almost every direction. They have shown themselves spineless and even worse than that muddleheaded . . . [T]he American people would rather identify themselves with a winning candidate than . . . with someone who was making a long fight for them.

Fola went to work teaching English and theater at the City and Country private school in New York, and in the summer of 1928 joined a group that visited Russia under the leadership of John Dewey to study the Soviet educational system. She found it "a thrilling country," and after a three-week tour of classrooms, factories, nurseries, and theaters concluded that no one could "come to this country with a half open mind [and] see what we have seen without being convinced that this country should be given every opportunity to carry on the work that they are doing." Her enthusiasm, however, only drove her as far left as endorsing the platform of the Socialist party at a dinner for Norman Thomas back home. Then in 1929 Mid joined the writers' trek to Hollywood on a two-year contract, and before long the two of them were middle-aged Californians, enjoying sunbaths, the sea, the mountains, and the company of a visiting parade of international stars and directors who were old friends. Politics was remote, and even artistic intensity took short breathing spells, as for example when they tuned in regularly to *Amos 'n' Andy* on the radio. Of course they listened as well to symphonic recordings on "the Victrola part of it," so good that it was "hard to believe the music is coming from the box." The days of suffrage and seriousness, the social drama and Greenwich Village revolt faded further into the background as age and arthritis advanced on Fola.[5]

Mary and Ralph had moved, in that last bright afternoon of the 1920s, to suburban Bethesda, where he played golf and she painted in what time she could spare from five-year-old Bob. (A second child, Joan, was born in 1930.)

Belle, too, was finding herself more and more absorbed in her biographical labor of love. She turned aside from the path of duty for some 1928 campaigning on "Bobbie's" behalf that brought out the old fire. "I would not have believed that I could get into the game again and keep up as well as I did," she exulted to Fola. But early in 1929 she was groaning under the accumulated weight of an historian's problems—how much use should she make of Old Bob's speeches and writings, how much background should she provide, where was the balance point between distracting genealogy and anecdotes and "sidelights" that brought the story to life, how much fact-checking was enough? Middleton sent her a few suggestions, and she answered wearily that she was "getting on slowly and realize more every day that I must be patient and keep plodding . . . It seems as though I was climbing a steep hill that I cannot see the top and must keep going or fall down altogether." Young Bob finally saw that she needed bailing out. "I did not realize," he told Fola, "how the biography has been weighing on mother's mind . . . She broke down completely three different times when we discussed it . . . [W]e must all do what we can to help her make the best possible working arrangements." A series of researchers, editors, and secretaries was eventually hired, including Ralph, but no matter how much they burrowed and drafted, they could not liberate Belle from her conscience.[6]

One bit of "help" for her came inadvertently. *La Follette's Magazine,* without its founder, sank lower and lower in the water until it could no longer be kept afloat by the family alone. It was recapitalized and reorganized as *The Progressive,* owned jointly (for a time) by the La Follettes and William Evjue's *Capital Times,* with Evjue taking most of the editorial burden from Belle. She and the boys continued to write for it, and at Belle's urging Isen blossomed into a regular columnist, her monthly contribution consisting of a woman's-eye view of current issues, entitled "A Room of Our Own." Even so, the magazine's twenty years of insatiable drain on the clan's bankbooks and energies were largely at an end.[7]

Finally the president of the University of Wisconsin offered Phil the deanship of the law school on the day before his thirty-second birthday, in 1929. Though he appeared to have made his choice for a political life five years earlier, he now gave the offer to leave it his earnest and self-absorbed consideration. Being a La Follette, he naturally did so in a joint letter to Bob, Mary, Fola, and Ralph:

There is a side of me that this appeals to very strongly *especially as I contemplate the likelihood of disappointments and defeat in the world outside.* [Underlining supplied.] When one puts his effort and personality into the academic field . . . he can see and sense the results of his effort more easily and more immediately . . . If he reaches out beyond the academic world in his work and thinking, he may have quite as important results. If one considers and assesses the relative value of men like Karl Marx, William James, Kant, Voltaire, etc., with Jefferson, Lincoln, Bright, Dad, etc., one's first reaction is that perhaps the former have a more profound and lasting influence.

At that point, he seemed to waver, and for a suspended moment in 1929 it looked as if the political momentum created by Old Bob's first run for office almost exactly half a century earlier had finally run down. If Phil dropped out to become a seminal thinker, Bob was unlikely to go on beating his head against the wall for more than another term. But Phil swept on to a conclusion toward which his life thus far inexorably pointed.

The fact that the academic group does not deal primarily in the world of reality enables them to avoid the necessity of compromise — and thus to appear as individuals who laid down profound and inflexible plans . . . From this, if it be correct, it follows that the greatest job of all is the leadership which preserves itself in the conflict of the open field unprotected by the softer influence of the University World.

If the choice could be made I should like to spend some years in this atmosphere of reflection. I would welcome an opportunity to write, think, and act, so that when and if the time came for me to return in some way to public affairs I could come with better preparation. But that choice is not possible . . . because my accepting this position now would leave our forces with a sense of being left somewhat without leadership . . . I . . . doubt whether I have the qualities which they hope I have . . . [but] if those inherent qualities are not in me now, . . . [they] . . . will not be developed by a period of incubation in a university. I don't need to add that I have concluded not to take it, and that I am ready to take what may come in the world of politics.[8]

It wasn't a specific declaration of a particular candidacy, but a general statement that he was awaiting the toga whenever history should drape it around him. Hungry to lead, he accepted the judgment of old friends that he was "made for politics," and simply chose, as he told Isen a while later, to wait for events.

And in the autumn of 1929, events came with a rush that swept him and Bob both back toward the center of progressive action. The fountains of the great deep were broken up and the flood of the Great Depression swallowed the land.

"The relief of human suffering"

The stock market crash, the country's long tumble into economic stagnation, and the mounting toll of desperation galvanized both La Follettes, starting with Bob who was already in office when the economy began to unravel. From the young man wondering whether to be or not to be Old Bob's legatee, he suddenly became the chief contender for the role of his party's conscience, the very role that Dad had played for so long. On a stumping tour during the 1930 congressional campaign he began to call for a major program of relief, something decidedly unpopular with President Hoover and his supporters. The repulsion between the two men was mutual. Young Bob had not endorsed Hoover in 1928, but merely kept a prudent silence, unlike his colleague George Norris, who openly backed Alfred E. Smith, and much unlike sister Fola, who had publicly pledged allegiance to the platform of Socialist candidate Norman Thomas. But even this neutralism did not endear La Follette to "regular" Republicans in Congress.

Then a change in the political weather opened up new possibilities. The voters in 1930 gave control of the House to the Democrats and cut the Republican Senate majority to one. That meant that the party leadership would need every vote to retain control and would be amenable, however grudgingly, to dealing with the small group of liberal-minded Republican senators. It was a great opportunity for someone in the group to take charge and hammer out a unified negotiating position. This time, Bobbie,

Phil, running for governor, inherited Dad's style and Wisconsin loyalties.

the reluctant heir of 1925, was ready. "I am going to try to get the progressive group together soon," Bob promised the family, "to see if we cannot outline our position and a legislative program for this session." In the expiring session of the Seventy-first Congress he introduced a resolution calling for heavy federal outlays to help states feed and shelter the swelling armies of the unemployed, who in many areas numbered a disastrous quarter of the work force or close to it. The relief effort was to be financed in part by stepping up the income taxes, especially in the upper brackets, which had hitherto been generously favored with light burdens by the grace of Treasury Secretary Andrew Mellon. "The relief of human suffering," Bob's statement proclaimed, "should take precedence over the interests of wealthy income-tax payers."

The resolution failed, but it now put Young Bob publicly into conflict with President Hoover, who continued to insist that local governments and private charities should carry the relief burden until private investment put the economy back on the rails. But La Follette was stung by the injustice of that approach. The cities and states had not caused the crash. The federal government had done that by neglecting farmers and workers and coddling the bull market. Hoover's "calloused indifference got under my skin," Bob steamed. "[N]o one else in Washington appears to feel as keenly as I do about the shameful manner in which he had neglected his responsibilities in this economic crisis."[9]

There was undoubtedly political advantage to be reaped in courting the gratitude of state and municipal officials of both parties, but La Follette's anger was not mere window dressing. It was deep enough to turn him at last into something resembling a new "Fighting Bob." He mobilized his fellow progressives, including Norris, Idaho's William E. Borah, Burton K. Wheeler of Montana (Dad's 1924 running mate), and two more recent arrivals in the Senate, Bronson Cutting of New Mexico and Edward P. Costigan of Colorado, and persuaded them to join him in convening a conference of some two hundred progressive educators, journalists, and other leaders that met in Washington in March of 1931 to consider all and any remedies. It was a cast of thinkers as varied as the passenger list of Noah's Ark — Lincoln Steffens, Lillian Wald, Charles and Mary Beard, and Stuart Chase were some of the better-known names — and like any such group it naturally produced nothing but speculative and conflicting proposals that had no hope of enactment and were loudly damned by reactionaries and revolutionaries alike.

Yet it was important that one senator was trying to get the country to think its way past the administration's clichés. Bob next offered another idea to Congress — the formation of a permanent fifteen-member economic council drawn from the leadership of industry, finance, transportation, agriculture, and labor. Its job would be to monitor economic changes, anticipate problems, and suggest solutions in regular periodic reports. It was possibly an outgrowth of Bob's private suggestion to Fola in mid-May: "I believe a real service could be rendered by calling the industrial and financial leaders and putting them 'on the spot' to tell what they plan to do if anything to solve the critical economic situation." Despite the fact that the council would be drawn from established leadership ranks, it was a bold advocacy of regular economic planning, and therefore it fell on deaf ears among congressional listeners who smelled socialism in it. Though nowadays routinely embodied in the President's Council of Economic Advisers, the concept was premature and stillborn in 1931. Merely advancing it, however, moved Bob further along the road to recognition. Perceptive reporters began to recognize him for the intellectual that he was when he had a problem that focused his attention (just as Fola had predicted when he was a floundering college boy). One story even predicted that the next House and Senate, due to meet in December, would constitute "Little Bob's Congress."[10]

Meanwhile, back in Wisconsin in 1930, Phil had seized the moment to run for the governorship. He said that it was by default, to fill a vacuum in the ranks of attractive progressive candidates, but he acted like someone who knew the troubled times offered the perfect moment for his move. He was at his best as a campaigner, sweeping energetically through county after county to rekindle delighted old-timers' memories of his father. He made, by his own count, some 260 speeches in sixty days, usually at outdoor gatherings without loudspeakers. He shook so many voters' hands that his own swelled to half again its normal size. Isen took an active part, too, organizing the women voters behind her youthful spouse. Hers was the follow-up task of the generation of women that came along after the battle for the vote was won. It was pragmatic duty, less idealized by linkage with the general cause of human liberty, and therefore easier to write off as "women's work," but mundanely necessary all the same. Nonetheless she did it, by all accounts, willingly and well.[11]

Phil's stalwart opponent, Walter J. Kohler, was a plumbing tycoon who had won the primary and the governorship in 1928, aided by excellent name recognition—hundreds of thousands saw it several times daily when they went to the toilet—but La Follette outpolled him in the primary by a generous margin. The day after the balloting, Phil and Isen were the only witnesses as Bob married Rachel at Maple Bluff. The new bride was promptly introduced to life as a La Follette when all four of them left for a honeymoon at a lodge in the northern part of the state. Phil could not bring himself to stay more than a couple of days and rushed back to begin work on his legislative program, sighing to Belle that "people expect so much of us." He was the embodiment of youthful energy, rounding up progressive legislators weeks before inauguration, "trying to get a program for presentation lined up the minute we get into office instead of waiting around." Like Bob, he was committed to early planning. He had his adherents divided into groups, one dealing with issues on which immediate legislative proposals were available (taxation, corrupt practices, public power, and the like) and another with questions "where we have a policy but don't know how to attain it," which, in December of 1930, embraced unemployment, banking, and education.

The aggressive program called for restrictions on chain banks and retail stores; stronger state control over power companies; a shifting of tax burdens from real estate to incomes—that is, from farmers to urbanites and businesses, programs of reforestation and building of overpasses at railroad-highway crossings to create jobs; and enlarged appropriations for outright relief, paid for through higher taxes. As he wrote to Bob, it wasn't really big enough: "In order to really help to start things we would have to put about 10 billions to work in the country as a whole. But irrespective of the final outcome politically, people in our position do owe a duty to use every power we have to prevent people from suffering whether it wins their votes or not." Not all of it got into law because progressives did not control the legislature, but enough of it was enacted, especially the increased taxes, to cost Phil a good deal of political capital.[12] Both he and Bob were driven by the same imperative, however: to take quick action because they felt morally obliged to deal with what they perceived as popular need, and to calculate the costs later if at all. Though the two young politicians were palpably different in style and personality, they were their father's—and mother's—sons.

By the beginning of summer 1931, Belle had reason to glow. When Old Bob died, Louis Brandeis had written to Phil and Bob to say that their father, in one of the last serious conversations the two old friends had, expressed the opinion that democracy within the states needed constant vitalizing and that he himself might have made a mistake leaving Wisconsin for Washington.[13] Now he had a son carrying on his work in each place while the stalwarts gnashed their teeth in vain. And she, Belle, had lived to see it happen.

Then, almost at that moment of fulfillment, Belle died in a needless and tragic medical accident. On August 16, 1931—Mary's birthday—she entered a Washington hospital for a checkup that included a proctoscopic examination. When the instrument was inserted it punctured her colon. A defensive doctor explained later that it was like inserting one's hand into a silk stocking expecting it to stretch, and having it tear like paper instead. Peritonitis set in, and in that pre-antibiotic era it killed seventy-two-year-old Belle within three days.

Words could not possibly measure what the loss meant to her children. In 1920 Phil, worried about Old Bob's impending gall bladder surgery, had written a midnight meditation: "Whenever death strikes our family it is going to be bitterly sad. We have all lived so close together, so much a part of each other, that the passing of one of us will be like the going out of a part of ourselves." Many weeks after Belle's death Fola, cleaning up her effects at the farm, wrote to Mid that she was still "trying to find my way back into my life." Young Bob's cry was most poignant of all. "I spare you," he told Fola, "any details of the struggle I am going through, adjusting to Mother's death. You sense it because of your own problem and it does not help me any to be articulate about it . . . I am so lonesome all the time."[14]

They never were quite the same family again. The world that formed them was gone, and in more ways than one. Biographers need to beware of seeing too many huge, cloudy symbols in their stories, but Belle's death in the lengthening shadow of the Depression coincided almost exactly with a great, dividing moment in the history of the entire country. Once past it, her generation's progressivism could not survive unaltered.

"The alternative is the goose step"

America of the 1930s cannot be understood without taking into account the Great Depression, and the impact on those who endured it cannot be overstated. Hard times had ravaged the country before within the memory of living men and women, notably in 1873 and 1893. But then the country was visibly growing; anyone with eyes could see the advance of settlement, the crowded immigrant steamers, and the rising cities and know that democracy had a future. But when the wheels came off the economy between 1930 and 1932 there was a sense that the very foundations were perishing. The country was physically undamaged yet paralyzed. The truly haunting question that rose at the sight of breadlines and shantytowns and foreclosure sales was not "What happened?" but "What now?" As Bob put it somewhat redundantly in a speech, "Certain basic, essential, fundamental and sweeping changes" had taken place. He spelled them out: "Immigration has stopped. Natural population growth is slowing down. Free land has disappeared. Economic nationalism is closing economic opportunity in foreign trade. All these things have resulted in a curtailment of individual economic opportunity which presents fundamental problems of solution." What, then, would restart the engines of production? What repairs to the broken-down system of distribution would create the steady demand to keep them running?

For many despairing Americans there was a fleeting temptation to believe that totalitarian states had the answer. That created the second indelible brand on the politics of the thirties—the allure and threat of communism and fascism. The dictatorships, with their uniformed and marching masses, seemed at least able to mobilize their peoples to productive effort in a unified spirit. It is easy to see now (as of course it was for perceptive people then to understand) that, all issues of justice aside, suppression was no answer. An economy run by fiat money, commandeered capital, and drafted labor would also break down in the long run. A society that hoped to trade freedom for food wound up without much of either. But that is the wisdom of hindsight, and back then, hungry Americans caught in the sharp jaws of want looked like candidates for revolution. The mood of the time was suggested by Robert Scripps, one of the speakers at Bob's 1931 conference of experts. "If wealth is not fairly shared," he said, "the alternative is the goose step, one way or another, and Lenin or Mussolini makes mighty little difference."

Under these circumstances the efforts of reformers in the day of the La Follette brothers had to focus on keeping democracy's heart beating more than improving its character. In Bob's words in a newspaper commentary in 1937, the "curtailment of individual economic opportunity" presented "fundamental problems for solution. Speaking in broad terms, those problems require us to apply the same intelligence to the creation of a measure of equality of economic opportunity as the generation of the Revolution of 1776 had to apply to the problem of creating a measure of equality of political opportunity."

He went on in the same column to sound like Old Bob, warning that "[w]hile the American people have always been vigilant against governmental tyranny, they have been slow to observe a greater tyranny in the growth of unrestrained private economic power over the life, property and labor of a once free people." Phil, too, in his campaign speeches, would continue to hammer at the "interests" who, for selfish reasons, resisted efforts at relief for families ravaged by hard times. Nonetheless, the concern of both brothers with increasing the income and purchasing power of the broad masses of people separated them from the main thrust of their father's thought even though their campaign styles were still warmed by his uncompromising intensity. The elder La Follette's economic arguments always had political roots. He wanted changes in the tax system or regulatory commissions primarily as part of a broad crusade against privilege, not simply as devices to stimulate growth and circulate wealth. Economic legislation was a moral as much as a managerial question. That was why progressives of his day could at one and the same time denounce railroad and banking cartels, sweatshops, prostitution, and the saloon instead of putting them on separately labeled agendas. They all threatened a republic of free and virtuous individuals.

The "liberals" of the thirties did not universally drop the moral and political assumptions of the "progressives," but the circumstances of the Depression concentrated their minds on engineering mass rescues from economic disasters. Increasingly, their remedies required heavy input from the central government on behalf of organized groups lobbying for their share. James Causey, a Wisconsin liberal banker friend of Bob's, put it very well in 1939: "We must strive to build a true *economic* democracy. This new attitude must be based on simple ethical values — equality of opportunity and cooperation for the common good. Government must be accepted as the chief instrument for social, political and economic self-improvement, and must be given adequate power to play this role successfully. At the same time there must be extensive and effective community organization to keep such a Government responsive to the wishes of the citizenry." Or as Phil put it more simply in his first gubernatorial address to the Wisconsin legislature, "It is by no means clear that the American experiment of self-government will succeed. We must be prepared for genuine, profound readjustments, not merely of institutions but of mental habits, if it does." Co-operation and community would have to replace self-regulating individualism as cherished traits.[15]

That did not happen quite according to plan. No golden age of cooperativism emerged from the crisis. On the other hand the worst fears of the alarmists were not realized. There was no revolution from either the right or the left. Instead, Americans united in the thirties behind an interventionist government that saved capitalism, and with it representative government, by pumping money directly into the economy in one way or another.

But the leader in this redemption was not one of the Wisconsin brothers. He was a flexible politician who learned new rules quickly, profoundly changed the entire federal system by personal impact, and became in time a political colossus who cast a shadow over the remainder of the century. For the second time in twenty years, a Roosevelt thwarted La Follette political ambitions and was never forgiven.

"If he is the man his most ardent supporters believe"

The La Follette–Roosevelt relationship did not begin too badly, especially for Bob. During the final year of the Hoover administration he kept up the pressure on the beleaguered president, working with a new set of senatorial allies, notably Bronson Cutting of New Mexico and Edward P. Costigan of Colorado. With Costigan he tried in vain to get $375 million in relief funds sent to the states, and he also fought a losing battle for a public works bill with the then unheard of price tag of $5.5 billion. Hoover's answer was to get behind the creation of the Reconstruction Finance Corporation, which would lend money to businesses on the verge of shipwreck. It was better than nothing, but Bob publicly doubted that "tinkering with the credit structure" would do much. What was needed was a huge and immediate shot of purchasing power, nothing less.

It was obvious to everyone that Hoover would be beaten in 1932, and equally clear that Bob would be happy with the result. The only drawback was that the rising national Democratic tide would also wash Phil out of office, which it did. Wisconsin had a crossover system that allowed for a vote in either primary, and for years progressive Democrats, discouraged with the dinosaurs who ran their state party, had become Republicans-for-a-day to help La Follette–backed candidates. Now, energized by an exciting pre-nomination battle between Al Smith and Franklin Roosevelt, they stayed in their own ranks. Phil lost to Kohler, loathing the feeling of defeat but taking what consolation he could in Kohler's own whipping at the hands of Democrat Albert Schmedeman in November. Meanwhile, he and Bob both endorsed Roosevelt. After the election Phil and Isen went on a brief trip to Europe. It was his third—he had gone in 1914 and again in 1927. He visited the USSR as well as Germany, where he arrived in time to watch Hitler sweep into power, something that he saw as the tragic result of "economic disease." He would later become a notable "isolationist," but the term is misleading in its suggestion of a political cave dweller whose awareness and concern stopped at the water's edge. He was, on the contrary, eager to learn as much as he could from a steady round of interviews with political counterparts abroad. He returned to write articles on his experiences, and to find himself being wooed for a cabinet post by Franklin D. Roosevelt.[16]

The brothers had backed the incoming president without being entirely certain how they felt about him. Meeting him in April of 1932, Phil recalled nothing beyond the impression of FDR's magnetism and jauntiness, along with his unwillingness to disagree forthrightly with whoever was talking to him. Bob waited until mid-October before offering his support, confiding to Cutting that he wasn't sure of the "depth and breadth" of Roosevelt's progressivism. Fola, observing from the outside, was slightly more generous. "I can't hope for quite as much from R. as some of his

291

more enthusiastic supporters appear to," was her post-election comment. She thought correctly that he would have trouble with conservative Democrats in Congress, many of them southerners entrenched in seniority. But "if he is the man his most ardent supporters believe," she went on, "[he] may be able to . . . whip them into line."

The president-elect, for his part, was more than willing to make himself more independent of standpat Democrats by courting progressive Republicans like the hard-charging young Wisconsin governor with the already legendary father. Saying that he wanted Phil in his "official family," he made a somewhat conditional offer of the attorney generalship on which he later reneged. Subsequently Phil was felt out about his willingness to work on the Federal Trade Commission or to become chairman of the Federal Power Commission. Phil testified afterward to other nibbles—he counted eight in all. None attracted him. Roosevelt's attentions extended to Bob as well. He invited him to a private meeting (the first of many to come) at the Mayflower Hotel in January, and a few days later down to his winter home in Warm Springs, Georgia, along with Senator Cutting, before whom the post of secretary of the interior was dangled. Cutting decided, after consultation with Bob, that he would not go into the cabinet unless Phil did, too. A single progressive Republican would not be able to have much influence against conservative Democratic advisors to the president, whereas two might. In the end, Cutting stayed in the Senate until his death in an airplane crash in 1935.

Phil's reaction to the episode was in character. He really preferred to stay in Wisconin and was unquestionably planning to try to regain the governorship in 1934, where he could fight for his own, modernized version of Old Bob's Wisconsin Idea. Besides, he said, he recalled too well his youthful disappointments at Theodore Roosevelt's "watered-down or at times even shabby progressivism," not to mention Wilson's decline from "progressive achievements" in his first term to "disappointments in his second." He was true to the family faith that only La Follettes could truly define progressivism. Bob, too, behaved as his father's son. Norris spoke with him and expressed the idea that they should stay in the background and work for the legislation they favored by striking alliances with what Bob called "the reactionary Democrats." But Bob, as he told Phil, rejected the idea. "My training and experience convince me," he wrote firmly, "that the only way the Progressives have ever succeeded in writing their principles into law was by fighting for them in season and out."[17]

That is precisely what Bob continued to do, but all the same, despite unhesitating criticism of Roosevelt when he felt it appropriate, he was a valuable and important ally in winning congressional support for the New Deal. The arrangement helped them both. Bob freely expressed to the family his sense that FDR was not moving fast enough on farm relief, public works, home loans, and other measures to boost purchasing power. His letters to the family were strewn with doubts about the president's course. "Unless the administration comes forward speedily with a large program for re-employment . . . I anticipate a sharp recession," one ran. Another lamented that "I have given up hope that the President will sponsor an adequate program to restore purchasing power." While the country believed that Roosevelt's first months were full of action, La Follette found them wanting—"no action on public works, farm refinancing nor home loans . . . [U]nless Roosevelt cuts loose on this recovery program . . . his administration is going to fail tragically." But he gave a willing "aye" on roll calls that established key New Deal measures such as the Agricultural Adjustment Act, the Wagner Act, the Social Security Act, and other building blocks of the welfare state.

The National Industrial Recovery Act of 1933 (later invalidated by the Supreme Court) gave him a problem, with its emergency approach of stabilizing the economy by allowing industrial associations to act together to restrain price wars and other forms of competition. "Once industries are permitted to come out from under the antitrust act and to integrate themselves for the purpose of enforcing codes," he told a radio audience, "it will be a physical impossibility ever again to break them up into their integral parts . . . [O]nce we break these eggs into the frying pan . . . we shall never be in a position to unscramble them." He told a labor convention that creating the NRA would be "one of the most drastic peacetime measures in our history." All the same, he voted for it and even boasted to Fola of having swung an important committee vote in its favor. Later, however, he backed away by voting against a final, amended version.

Bob was much happier pushing for bigger public works programs than the president would support; in 1935, when Roosevelt proposed $4.8 billion in such appropriations, he introduced a bill to spend $9.8 billion. It failed, but it broke ground for the smaller sum to pass. La Follette was not, however, in favor of large-scale deficit spending. He wanted to pay for the new programs by higher taxes on wealth, which allowed him, in debate, to enjoy himself by rolling out the heavy artillery of Dad's old arguments against the plutocracy. He consistently fought for more progressivity in the tax code and especially for heavy inheritance taxes. "Those who are most anxious to balance our budget . . . [by cutting spending] are often those who protest vociferously against any attempt to increase taxes upon wealth and income in accordance with ability to pay."[18]

Roosevelt had no objection to a Republican gadfly on the spending issue who made his own smaller appropriations requests look prudent by contrast. He also was grateful for Bob's votes on key points of his program. He repaid the support by discreetly, indirectly encouraging Wisconsin Democrats to vote for Bob in the 1934 Senate campaign. As the drift of progressive thinkers toward the Democrats continued, there were even rumors that the La Follette "boys," or Bob, at least, might jump the fence, give up the unending battle with the Republican stalwarts, and seek Democratic nominations.

For Bob the choice was immediate as his seat was coming up for renewal, and there were arguments in its favor if in fact—it could never clearly be proven, of course—the La Follette prospects in the Republican primary really depended on the cooperation of Democrats who might no longer be available. Bob could secure those votes by a shift of party and take a comfortable number of Republican progressives with him. But it went against the grain of tradition and had other drawbacks too. There would be a new set of Democratic reactionaries to fight, and meanwhile he would fall to the bottom of the seniority ladder in Congress even if he got elected.[19]

Another alternative, however, was to corral Wisconsin progressives from all sides into a new, third party that would be glad to have his name on the ballot. The only trouble was that the brothers could not be so sure of keeping a new, differently minded generation of rebels—labor activists, agrarian critics, and socialists—in harness with their old methods. The choice might not be entirely theirs to make, as pressure began to mount for a new party, particularly from progressives increasingly radicalized by the hard times, especially Thomas Amlie, a former progressive member of Congress inclining toward embracing the socialists. If Phil and Bob ignored the movement it might take over their constituency.

Bob's own instincts were nevertheless against the jump. Like his father he believed that parties only worked when built up from the bottom, layer by geological layer of local organization over the years. Moreover, Belle's almost-final words to him in a letter written ten days before she died had warned against such a move. It would be "inconsistent with the calm, balanced judgment you have shown since you entered the field of politics." She admitted that the two-party system seemed to be inefficient and a failure, but "the symptoms of a revolt" against it were not obvious to her shrewd old eyes, though in August of 1931 things had not yet reached the lowest point of desperation.[20]

Phil, however, was strongly taken with the idea that two and a half years after Belle's passing, the time was ripe for a realignment of the old parties. As he read the omens, if progressives and reactionaries were divided into identifiable parties, the more numerous progressives would win elections every time. He did enormous amounts of preliminary legwork among the polyglot array of unhappy Wisconsin progressives that included advocates of every economic panacea being hawked to the public. He fended off Amlie and others of like mind who wanted to turn the new grouping into a far left, class-based Farmer-Labor party. And he finally got Bob's last-minute consent to be one of the midwives of the Progressive Party of Wisconsin—the title itself the sign of Phil's victory over the far left—in May of 1934, and to be its senatorial candidate.

But Bob at first held firm on one point; Phil must not yet run for governor. Two La Follettes on the same ticket would be too much, and they would both lose. It was not a question of jealousy; the loyalty of the two brothers to each other was absolute at that time, though years later it would be stretched to the limit on this precise question of the Wisconsin Progressive Party's future. In 1934, however, Phil finally convinced Bob that no gubernatorial candidate was in sight who was any less controversial or better known than he himself was, and who would not be more rather than less likely to divide and weaken the new party in its first outing. So they did run together, and Phil won the gamble, though barely. Phil edged Schmedeman, the Democrat, with only a two percentage-point edge of 14,000 votes; moreover, he would not have a majority in either house of the state legislature even though the Progressives did well for a new party, taking 45 out of 100 Assembly seats and 12 of 33 in the Senate. But Bob beat his opponent by a landslide.[21]

All the same it was a double win, the high point of La Follettism in the state. Phil had been right and Bob wrong in guessing the outcome in 1934. But Bob was sounder in his feeling that eventually the stirred-up silt would settle back into old Republican-*versus*-Democratic patterns. The victory may have been an expensive one for Phil in first implanting in his mind the idea that he could duplicate the Wisconsin feat on a national scale—Old Bob's dream renewed once again. But to do it Phil would have to unhorse Franklin D. Roosevelt.

He had no declared idea of doing so in 1934, of course, and for the next two years the boys got along well with Roosevelt and with each other despite their divergent views about the best way to preserve Dad's legacy in Wisconsin. Bob's fortieth birthday fell two months after the election, and Phil wrote him: "I hope it is needless for me to tell you what your

Though Bob had misgivings about a separate party in Wisconsin, he accepted it and both brothers won on its ticket in 1934—the high tide of La Follettism in the state.

judgment and above all your companionship personally and politically has meant to my own life. I love you profoundly and am everlastingly grateful for you, as my brother." Bob's answer ran: "You know that I return with compound interest all the feeling which you have for our mutual love, companionship and association in life. You are one of the chief factors in making life worth living. So long as I draw breath you may depend on me."

"Man can have work AND be free"

Soon after his second inauguration in January of 1935 Phil went to Washington where he and Bob were welcomed in the White House by a beaming President Roosevelt. There were further cordial meetings that year, including one at Hyde Park in the fall to plan the imminent 1936 campaign. The three leaders seemed to be on the same track. Roosevelt was about to launch the Works Progress Administration, a major national public works undertaking whose aging airports, bridges, and post offices still dot America. Bob and Phil thought it was sound but badly underfunded. According to Bob, only lusty public investment could provide the growth incentives that had disappeared with the frontier. A hundred billions' worth of useful, income-generating work waited to be done and all it would take to begin was a temporary willingness to unbalance the budget. Phil had a recovery program of his own for Wisconsin. It would involve using a federal relief grant as a loan of "seed money" to set up a state authority, in effect a development bank, that would in turn grant credit to communities. They would hire private contractors to carry out a program of desirable physical improvements planned by politically untainted state experts. Part of the builders' profit would be regained in taxes and used to repay the state, which would then finance new undertakings. FDR gave a tentative commitment to put up a starter sum of a hundred million in federal funds, but the Wisconsin legislature failed by a single vote to enact Phil's scheme.[22]

Nevertheless, they were all thinking alike. Bob kept on with his string of pro–New Deal votes in the Senate, and what was more, in 1936 he organized a Progressive National Committee to support Roosevelt's reelection, using the strength of the family name to bring together many of Old Bob's graying allies behind the president. Roosevelt won in the landslide of the century up to then. He lost only the eight electoral votes of Maine and Vermont and got 60 percent of the popular vote. Republican membership in the Senate sank to a pathetic sixteen. In Wisconsin, Phil was triumphantly reelected and even better, the Progressives this time got working control of the state senate and assembly.

The meaning of the Roosevelt victory was enormous. It ratified a revolution not in the economic but in the governmental system. Conservatives who grumbled that FDR had spent his way to success were actually understating the case. This was more than a one-time phenomenon. New federal programs, such as forest and soil conservation, power development, rural resettlement, and urban housing would become embedded in the social texture. They would centralize power in Washington, from whence came the money. Governors busy administering federal largesse had less chance to become innovative leaders as Old Bob La Follette had been in the progressive heyday. One side effect of the new order was to diminish the chances of future "Wisconsin Ideas."

Another consequence concerned the people's perception of the federal government. Direct payments and services to individuals—home loans, pensions, relief checks, farm subsidies, help in organizing unions—made the recipients more likely to think of government as a faraway and impersonal fountain of benefits. When it collected taxes to pay for them, however, it became a distant enemy. La Follette's turn-of-the-century progressivism had begun with the idea that citizens in local communities should act together for the common good. It was much harder to do that when, for many economic purposes, the country was becoming one super-community run by faceless machinery that individuals felt unable to control.

These two developments, which shook the ancient bedrock of progressivism, were not necessarily clear to FDR voters (or FDR himself) in 1936. A third major change was eminently visible. Anyone could see how Roosevelt had changed the presidency of the United States. His skilled use of radio to go directly into the homes of the plain Americans, whom he called "my friends," gave them a voice and a face—the president's—that they could identify with the impersonal government that was helping them. His ability to hold the stage kept him at the center of action, appearing to set things in motion or slow them down even when very little was happening. He created the "personal presidency" that all his successors, whatever their politics or stature, have adopted as their model. And with it he overshadowed Congress so thoroughly that the possibility of a powerful senator successfully picking a public fight with a president—as Robert M. La Follette and his following of Senate insurgents had done with Taft—shrank dramatically.

For all these reasons, the 1936 election guaranteed an eventual end to the political climate in which Robert La Follette, Sr., had been able to employ his particular skills and drives to become a nationally recognized rebel and reformer. There would be no succession. In one sense, however, Roosevelt himself completed the elder La Follette's work. Ironically, he rallied behind himself millions of urban workers, immigrants, women, blacks, socialists, intellectuals, farmers—all of those whom La Follette had courted in his own presidential bid—and he did so by denouncing, in La Follette-like language, economic royalists and by standing behind the policy of regulating business for the common good. He won the election of 1924 as well as that of 1936, and he did it within the old party system. Phil himself was later to say that "for the first time in nearly two decades the great mass of people *became* the Democratic party, embracing it as the only available instrument for change and progress."[23] It was, unfortunately for him, an insight that he did not reach until after he had collided head on with the national Democrats and been wrecked.

Yet in the immediate aftermath of the landslide the inconsistent collaboration of the La Follettes and Roosevelt was in a positive phase. Phil's work in launching the Wisconsin Progressive Party did the Democrats in the state no harm; it opened up new political opportunities for them by breaking down a long period of virtual Republican monopoly on victory.

Moreover, during the campaign Bob had been especially helpful with his pro-Roosevelt Progressive National Committee, despite the fact that by then many members of the older generation of progressives were turning against FDR for various reasons. "However well intentioned" such men and women might be, Bob warned, they would be responsible "if the reactionaries obtain control of the government." He went even further immediately after Roosevelt's second inauguration, when the president proposed legislation to "pack" the Supreme Court, which had been standing in his way, by appointing additional justices. The measure provoked furious charges of dictatorship and was ultimately beaten, but Bob La Follette sturdily supported it. His position was consistent with his father's well-recorded resistance to judicial conservatism, but more important than the substance was the evidence that Young Bob would back Roosevelt even in an unpopular undertaking.

His own reputation was rising steadily. Elmer Davis, the astute Washington correspondent of the *New York Times,* had noted in 1933 that La Follette had been calling for all-out economic mobilization since 1931 and that finally "there was an administration that had caught up with him." Davis was also profoundly impressed once when he dropped into the Senate and heard Young Bob beginning a speech and realized that he had "stumbled onto something historic." Young Bob's style was drier than his father's, Davis recorded, but "he was not talking merely about the troubles of Wisconsin; here for the first time a man in high office was looking at the troubles of all the sections of the country as a problem that was all of one piece." Another veteran capital journalist, Marquis Childs, said that the senator came "closer to being an intellectual — a theorist — than anyone elected to the Senate in his generation." Rexford Tugwell, a key Roosevelt adviser, believed that La Follette "of all the progressives of that time had made the most complete transition to modernism."[24]

The interest in La Follette even sparked discussion of the prospect of a presidential candidacy as a Democrat. One newspaper story of 1937 quoted Senator Royal S. Copeland of New York as the source of a rumor that "if FDR felt it was impossible to get the third term that he wanted in 1940 he would support La Follette instead, with John L. Lewis as his next choice." Harold Ickes confided to his secret diary an astonishing suggestion that Roosevelt wanted to neutralize Bob's presidential chances in order to guarantee his own viability in 1940. "He has it in mind," said the interior secretary, "as 1940 approaches, to make overtures to the La Follettes . . . He would be willing to make a deal . . . Bob La Follette could go into the next Cabinet as Secretary of State . . . and then Phil could go into the Senate and this would take care of both of them . . . This talk about Bob La Follette rather negatives the idea that the President is think-ing of supporting him for the Presidential nomination on the Democratic ticket in 1940." Whether from fear of him or some other motive, Roose-velt did continue to woo La Follette, inviting him on a cruise on the presi-dential yacht in the spring of 1938 to ease rumors of strained relations between them.[25]

There is not the slightest indication in anything said or written by Young Bob that he wanted or expected serious consideration as a presidential possibility. He was, in fact, moving in another direction by his well-publicized activities as chairman of the Senate Civil Liberties Committee, which spent much of 1936 and 1937 looking into the use of labor spies and strikebreakers by employers. The dramatic and shocking findings of the deceit, coercion, and naked thuggery used by some bosses to prevent the organization of their workers helped to rally support for the administra-tion's backing of unionism, and what was more, they made a solid reputa-tion for La Follette as a diligent, patient, and keen investigator. In taking on that role La Follette was following a long tradition of congressional investigations and solidifying one of the major powers of Congress (sometimes well used, and sometimes abused) to influence the course of events. After eleven years on the Hill, he was looking more and more like a congressional veteran, an insider who was part of a near-permanent government. He neither sounded like — nor was — a presidential aspirant, but that did not give him the sense of being powerless.[26]

It was not so with Phil. In 1937 he was becoming more restless and more convinced that Roosevelt was an obstacle to progressivism whose removal was necessary and possible. FDR had disappointed the brothers in the immediate aftermath of his 1936 personal triumph. Instead of pro-ceeding with still bolder spending initiatives in 1937, he backed away from his "pump-priming" strategy and gave his sanction to cuts in the WPA and other relief programs, believing that the worst was over. It turned out to be the wrong decision when the economy slumped and the unemployment curve shot upward in 1938. Phil in particular saw the move as a sign that the president was "drifting and confused,"[27] unsure whether he should con-solidate and enlarge his achievements or retreat from them. He had always been suspicious of Roosevelt's tendency to keep an eye on the weathervane of public opinion. it looked to him like lack of principle, a cardinal sin among La Follettes. Besides, Phil's own tidy mind rejected the improvised and patchwork nature of the New Deal. All in all, he managed to convince himself that the president was backsliding and the conservative wing of the Democratic party was resuming control. That meant that progressives throughout the nation would again be without a major-party home in 1940 as they had been in the twenties.

Unless—unless they could be organized into a powerful third force in 1938 that would siphon more and more forward-looking voters out of the old, reactionary-controlled parties and finally win in 1940 or perhaps even in 1944. It could be done with the right kind of intelligent program and dynamic leader, and Phil La Follette was reasonably certain that he saw such a leader in his shaving mirror each morning. The Phil who had written in the 1920s that he sometimes felt a restless urge to lead people to the promised land was surfacing again.

He was somewhat behind events. In 1934 there were constant murmurings about political realignment, all of them much in the vein of old Andrew Furuseth's observation to Bob that "the big majority of the people are now voting not for parties but for measures and men and are therefore ready for the reorganization of the old parties or their funeral." But 1936 had changed that. Phil should also have been warned of the dangers of *hubris* by his own experiences in 1937. Riding the wave of the statewide Progressive victory, he went to the legislature with two important programs. One was his Wisconsin Development Authority, a fresh version of the permanent public works plan defeated in 1935. The other was a change in Wisconsin's constitutional system that would allow the governor to re-arrange executive agencies and initiate programs on his own. The idea was to change the governor's role from passive to active. Instead of simply "executing" laws passed by the senate and assembly, he would take the lead, and they could rein him in if they chose by refusing to go along.

In Phil's view this enhancement of the governor's power would still preserve the checks and balances of the system. It was very much in line with the modernizing trend, visible in other states as well as Wisconsin, of focusing responsibility and streamlining the procedures that enabled government to be more expeditious in transacting the public's business. (In 1938 Roosevelt would unsuccessfully attempt to launch a similar reorganization of the national executive department.) But in the eyes of many legislators, Phil's proposals gave the executive the power to set up situations in which he could confront them with unchangeable situations, bribe their constituents, and generally lead them by the nose. They called his plan dictatorial and threatened to reject it. He responded in the summer of 1937 by calling them into a limited special session. He held them in Madison, used every scrap of influence he possessed, and got parliamentary rulings allowing him to override "obstructive" members until the bill was passed in the form he wanted. It was a costly victory because it set a great many people to wondering if Phil's craving for leadership had not gotten out of control.

Another development of 1937 caused rumbles of discontent with Phil's performance as governor. He played a part in getting the regents of the University of Wisconsin to oust Glenn Frank at its president. Frank was a controversial figure—arbitrary, extravagant, egotistical, and manipulative—who might well have justified the regents' action. But it was known that his appointment in 1926 had not pleased the La Follettes, who felt a proprietary interest in the university of which they were alumni and which Old Bob had done so much to advance. Frank himself, a conservative Republican, was quick to complain that he was being done in for political revenge. He found sympathetic listeners and, what was more, he was able to convert the issue to one of academic freedom and recruit support even among old La Follette friends. As Elmer Davis said, the precedent was bad and could be used against any university head for more sinister reasons.[28]

It was against this background that Phil launched his new movement— not yet a nationwide party but the nucleus of one—in the spring of 1938. It was to be called the National Progressives of America. Its economic platform was not entirely clear, but as Phil explained it, it was to steer a course between the reactionaries who wanted nothing to change and the radicals who wanted to change everything. It called for an important role for the state in directing resources and capital toward productive work, while scrupulously preserving the right of the people to choose who should govern. He put its objective in the form of a slogan: "Man Can Have Work AND Be Free."

Phil had not gone entirely off the rails. He assumed that the existing New Deal measures had not gotten to the root of the Depression since it seemed to be returning with a roar in 1938. Phil's criticisms, therefore, were not entirely unreasonable, and he held careful and prudent consultations with a number of progressive figures across the country and got qualified endorsements and signals to proceed. One of the major doubters, however, was Bob, who smelled trouble and had reconciled himself better than his brother to the idea that Roosevelt's leadership of American reform was, at least for the time being, unshakable.

The metaphors Phil used in various interviews to characterize his proposed new order kept changing. Sometimes he spoke of pumping "blood" into the arteries of the economic system, sometimes of regulating the economic "thermostat" so as not to be freezing one moment and perspiring the next. In a review of the whole episode, Davis suggested that it was more of an artistic than a political conception, and that Phil should have presented it in the form of a novel.

The way Phil did choose to present it was particularly maladroit. Perhaps from his experiences in Europe he recognized the power of symbols in a new age of mass communication. They could unify, inspire, and energize. He chose one for the NPA that seemed to make great sense — a blue X in a red circle on a white background. The X, Phil explained, stood for the multiplication of wealth. Placed in a circle, it also represented a voter's marked ballot. Freedom and productivity were not alternatives but partners, joined in an endless ring.

It sounded persuasive — but it looked to too many people in 1938 like the Nazi swastika, shorn of a few strokes — "circumcised," as some unkindly called it. Moreover, Phil unveiled his program at a grand rally in Madison on a late April night, in a huge pavilion usually used for judging livestock. There were massed flags bearing the new symbol, marching bands, and spotlights that converged to bathe him in a halo as he stood before the throng. The effect was exaggerated by newspaper and magazine photos that focused on Phil's outstretched arms, mane of hair, and rapt expression as he hit full oratorical stride. It looked altogether too much like what newsreels from Hitlerian rallies at Nuremberg were showing. Forewarned, hundreds of early supporters of the NPA stayed away from the event. Bob, loyal brother that he was, announced his support a couple of days before the great event — but he did not attend, pleading urgent business in the Senate.

Phil had made one other mistake. He was running as a candidate for a fourth term as governor himself. Even his titanic energies — and even Isen's faithful support — could not enable him simultaneously to organize a national movement, attend to his own campaigning, and govern effectively. Given the bitter battle of 1937, thousands were persuaded that Phil, driven by power hunger, had become a fascist in fact.

It was almost certainly an unfair characterization. The thrust of all Phil's writings and personal letters is that he believed he was leading the way to a new kind of progressivism in the state that would be a model for the nation, just as he believed his father had done thirty years earlier. He believed in democracy, but he wanted to cure what seemed to be its sickness of soul in the Depression era by infusing it with what he saw as the healthy public involvement of the citizenry visible in the organized activities of the totalitarian states. Somehow he failed to realize how much of that loyalty to the state and its ideals was coerced, or else he thought that Americans

303

Newsreels showed Phil as he launched the NPA—isolated, spotlighted, rallying the masses below to a symbol.

could be persuaded to do voluntarily what Germans, Italians, or Russians were doing under threats.

What probably happened was that two sides of Phil's personality had been forced apart and the "wrong" one was in control. The Phil of the NPA was the student who had written long and moony letters dreaming of new worlds to conquer. He was not the young politician who loved long drives to hick towns where he could speak for two hours with his jacket off to his "old man's" followers. What he needed was Belle to tell him that he was being a fool—something that no one else in the family could or would do. What he needed was Old Bob to thunder that one didn't address "the people" in massed ranks in a stadium; one spoke to the farmer, the housewife, the preacher, the editor, the worker, the productive individual who needed to be protected from the grabbers and the monopolizers.

But he did not have them and on election day he was chastened and politically destroyed. He was trounced by his Republican opponent, Julius Heil. NPA chapters had been set up in few other states, and some candidates in Iowa and California had been hardy enough to run under NPA banners. They, too, were snowed under. The dream was finished. Roosevelt wrote to an associate, a few days after the results were announced, "we have . . . eliminated Phil La Follette and the Farmer-Labor people in the Northwest as a standing Third Party threat. They must and will come to us *if* we remain definitely the liberal party."

Phil had written from time to time that the La Follettes knew how to take a licking, though he was hardly an example. He remembered how, when he was beaten in the 1932 primary, he had spent a sleepless night writhing in humiliation. This time the defeat was shattering. Gordon Sinykin, one of his helpers and associates in the thirties and later his law partner, said that Phil was never the same afterward, that he overreacted to this latest humiliation and would never again risk losing. He was only forty-one years old, yet he never again ran for public office despite his unmatchable experience, still powerful name, and many supporters who might be won back. It was "just a tragedy," in Sinykin's words, but it was not the only or the last tragedy in the La Follette family.[29]

"We all stand together"

Phil's political hara-kiri came at a time when his sisters were experiencing the worst of times. First there was Mary, who was deserted and subsequently divorced under circumstances that would have strained the imagination of a novelist.

When Mary was an infant and Old Bob was in the governor's mansion, one of his secretaries was Nellie Dunn, an Irish girl who had begun working in his law office as a pigtailed teen-ager. Bob had hired her because he knew and liked her immigrant family—that was the way things were done in small-town Madison. He quickly found that she was both skilled and energetic. He valued her so much that he took her along to Washington when he went to the Senate.

Nellie became a protegée and family member. She had a room of her own in the house at 1864 Wyoming Avenue in Washington where the La Follettes lived from 1909 to 1913. She watched the younger children grow and was their comforter, confidante, and occasional amanuensis. When the whole clan was assembled at the farm, she often helped out with the chores. She accompanied Phil on his trip to England in 1914. She was family, virtually a third La Follette sister. But she was an independent-minded girl, too, with friends and ideas of her own. She later wrote of the wonderful experiences, the sights, the attractions of Washington early in the new century, where great men, issues, and ideas were on almost daily intimate display in the home and office of her boss. He relied on her heavily and, when he published his *Autobiography,* wrote an affectionate and grateful acknowledgment of her help in the copy he presented to her.

In 1916 Nellie married Fred MacKenzie, a Madison friend and a member of the editorial staff of *La Follette's Magazine,* who at the same time quit his job for another in New York. The senator was furious. He expected loyalty from those nearest him as a matter of course, and this was double desertion. Phil had the nerve to stand up to him and defend Nellie; they had a roaring, fist-clenched argument that ended with Phil stomping out of the house and threatening to leave home.

The marriage lasted twelve years. There was one child, who died. Then, in 1928, Fred died too. Nellie continued to work at research and editorial jobs in New York. Bob, Jr., meeting her there on one occasion, asked if she would be interested in coming back to Washington to work for him. She was and she did, and the old friendly relationship was resumed with Bob, Rachel, Mary, and Ralph—Ralph Sucher, Bob and Phil's brother-in-law and Phil's best friend to boot.

Two days before Christmas 1934, Ralph left for Europe to do some stories for the Washington press bureau that he ran. He wrote Mary a letter from London on January 7 of the new year. It read in full:

Dear Mary:
   I sailed December 23 with assignments which will provide adequately for some months ahead and enable me, I hope, to work indefinitely on this side. Meanwhile I have seen Nellie. We love each other. In the hope that you will agree it is best for all concerned, I am asking you to divorce me. My address during the winter will be American Express Company, London, and the Washington office will be kept advised where I may be reached for the forwarding of mail. I shall write Bob.
                                                                                                    Ralph[30]

Sucher went on to marry Nellie. More than fifty years later, he was still professing warm and admiring feelings toward the La Follettes, but they never spoke to him again except for the coolest minimum required by business—the arranging of support and a divorce, which involved Phil, and some legislative contacts with Bob when Ralph was later employed by New York State's waterpower authority.

Mary was thirty-five and jobless and had two children, ten-year-old Bob and Joan, who was just three. The family closed ranks around her. "I'm asking around among my friends . . . about part-time teaching," Fola promised. "The *present* is cared for—we all stand together and neither you, Bob or Joan are going to be in any need either now or in the future."[31] It was a brave but not quite accurate promise. Fola, still the believing and protective big sister, begged Mary to avoid dead-end jobs and continue in New

York with art study to bring out her latent talents. But in time necessity and habit asserted themselves. Mary took a minor government job in Washington and worked her way through an uninspiring series of them for the rest of her unmarried life.

Meanwhile, Fola's generous offers to guarantee Mary against want were sincere but could not be fulfilled from her own resources. She and Mid had fallen on hard times. Studio cutbacks in the Depression had ended his job, and changing fashions in the theater made it impossible for him to find producers for his work. Savings accumulated in the fat years disappeared, some in the market collapse, some inexorably eaten away by living expenses. Basically discarded in his mid-fifties, poor Middleton struggled with depression. "I am in one of my useless feeling spells," ran a letter to Bob in 1934. "I get so overwhelmed with the futility of life at times." Reflexively, he kept on with his work—short pieces, an historical playlet that was staged once or twice by nonprofit "theater groups," and a gentle, engaging autobiography that was turned down by publisher after publisher until after World War II. "Why I keep writing is hard to say," he ruminated, but the answer was obviously that it kept him alive. Fola tried to cheer him up. "[T]here seems no way I can contribute constructively," she told him. "I can only go on loving you, knowing deeply that some way of work will come through for you."[32]

But her own courage needed all the bolstering it could get as their economic situation worsened. What kept Fola alive was completing the partly done biography of her father handed down to her by her mother. It became the absorbing and dominating task into which she now poured her life, as if from beyond the grave Old Bob was still dictating the terms of her existence.

Belle's part of the biography had reached only 1909 when she died, and the manuscript she had created, a patchwork of many researchers' drafts and her own, needed total reworking. After that Fola had to work her way through the mountain range of family papers, "like a mole, burrowing, burrowing." She burrowed devoutly, scrupulously, supplementing them with newspaper research and interviews, accumulating notebooks that still fill huge boxes in the Library of Congress Manuscript Division, sculpturing Dad's monument with unfamiliar tools. It would keep her busy for twenty-two years after Belle died.

Poor Mid again came second to the La Follette family's requirements. ("[T]his is such an absorbing family," Isen once observed, "that one is swept into it willy-nilly.") The couple moved back to New York for a while, but then Fola found there was no way she could manage the research except

to move to a small apartment in Arlington, Virginia, a Washington sub-
urb, in 1937. Mid stayed in New York for another few years, lonely and
still knocking on closed doors until he gave up and moved down to join
her. From 1937 onward a recurrent note in Fola's correspondence was
the need for money. An agreement was worked out with the brothers in
1937 under which each advanced her twenty-five hundred dollars against
a future share of the book's earnings, but two years later she was in
trouble again, and asking for more money to get to a point where she
would have enough manuscript to show a publisher in hopes of getting
an advance. They could only provide a few hundred dollars each. Later,
Bob "bought" the Maple Bluff home from the estate, and the rest of the
place was sold off, providing a small share on which Fola could continue
to live. Eventually there was a contract with Macmillan, but the book did
not see the light of day for many years after the lowest point in Fola's
fortunes.

Mary, once her own financial condition stabilized slightly after the divorce, sent Fola some money from time to time from her own share of the
estate's modest proceeds and from other savings. She needed little. "It would
give me pleasure to help in a small way," she said simply but insistently.
In her own adversity Mary showed an inner solidity that justified the family's faith in her. On her forty-first birthday in 1940, with the world in
flames, she answered a greeting from Fola. "Your wish for sunshine in my
heart is granted . . . I sense in you . . . a new power which in turn brings
me an inner peace and happiness. And the realization that despite the destructive forces about us, life is good."[33]

Belle would have been proud of her younger daughter.

"Modern war poisons democracy"

What was left of Bob's political career took a downward turn after 1938.
Starting in that year, foreign affairs and the buildup of the armed forces
became the absorbing passion of the president and, like it or not, the most
urgent business before Congress. Roosevelt's critics, Bob included, argued
that Roosevelt shifted the focus of concern from domestic affairs in order
to disguise his failure to end the Depression. Undoubtedly FDR profited
politically by the shift, but he was merely the beneficiary of events set in
motion by Germany. The countdown to war ran on steadily. Hitler an-
nexed Austria in February of 1938, came to the brink of war at Munich
in September, swallowed Czechoslovakia in March of 1939, and attacked
Poland that September, setting off World War II. Between the beginning

of April and the end of June 1940, his armies overran Denmark, Norway, the Netherlands, Belgium, and France and isolated Great Britain.

From the moment of the declaration of war, Roosevelt used what influence he could to help the French and British, and Bob La Follette fought against him as hard as he could. So did Phil, who was back in private law practice but still could get speaking engagements and newspaper interviews to express his isolationist convictions. But it was Bob who could try to mobilize anti-intervention sentiment in the place where it counted, the Congress.

He did try, in concert with other senatorial opponents of intervention, and they all failed. On every issue—the lifting of the embargo against arms shipments to France and Britain in 1939, the emergency transfers of "surplus" ships and weaponry to the British in 1940, and Lend Lease and conscription in 1940 and 1941—he and the isolationists were beaten. What was more, large groups of progressive followers in Wisconsin deserted him to support Roosevelt on these issues. "Midwestern isolationism," sometimes offered as the explanation for his course, was not as solid a phenomenon as it has sometimes been described.

The simplest interpretation of Bob's attitude is that he believed he was reliving his father's 1914–1917 antiwar struggle. Both he and Phil unquestionably wanted to keep the faith. Neither, of course, had any absolute certainty that Old Bob would have kept his opinions unchanged when confronted with a Hitler instead of a kaiser, and there is no way to know, no magic that allows history to read the minds of the dead. But both were probably right in their feeling that he would have been deeply worried about the impact of the war on the democratic order he cherished. "Modern war," said Young Bob, "poisons democracy." Whatever its purposes, it exalted the unbridled power of the commander-in-chief. And in the pursuit of industrial efficiency to build up the armed forces, antitrust actions and heavy taxes on excess profits were abandoned (over futile protests by La Follette) as dangerous obstacles.

In the long historical haul, the effects of World War II on American democracy, poisonous or otherwise, were too complicated to be summarized in a formula. The case can be made that by temporarily restoring life to the economy and bringing minorities and women into the work force the war laid the foundation for many postwar liberal gains that expanded the democratic base. Be that as it may, those developments were in the future in 1940 and 1941, and the immediate dismaying fact for anti-intervention progressives to absorb was that "Dr. New Deal," as Roosevelt himself later said, was replaced by "Dr. Win-the-War."

La Follette's role even as an opposition-party New Deal supporter therefore became irrelevant. He and Roosevelt had a brief truce in the summer of 1940. He endorsed Roosevelt as the lesser of two evils since the Republican candidate, Wendell Willkie, was as much of an interventionist as the president and less likely to sustain whatever was left of progressive-liberal policies. Roosevelt somewhat gingerly returned the favor. He was still angry at Phil and resentful of Bob's opposition on foreign policy. But in that summer's Senate campaign, Bob, on the Progressive ticket, was the only candidate with a chance to beat the stalwart Republican nominee, a blatant conservative named Fred Clausen. So Roosevelt permitted several members of the administration—including Henry Wallace, soon to be vice president—to speak for him in Wisconsin, to the visible and understandable outrage of Bob's Democratic rival, James Finnegan.[34]

Possibly that helped to swing some Democratic votes La Follette's way. He needed every one of them. The Progressives in Wisconsin were a shaken group since 1938, many of them joining or rejoining the Democratic fold, while the state's voters in general were caught up in a resurgence of "regular" Republicanism that returned Governor Heil to office. Bob had become battle-weary and at the same time more deeply rooted in Washington life. He was negligent in local fence-mending, all the more necessary after Phil's debacle, and showed a general distaste for campaigning at home. He appeared to think that he had made a record and that the Wisconsin voters could return him or not as they chose, without special entreaty on his part. Being a political realist, he therefore expected to lose, according to Isen's recollection, and "insisted . . . that he wouldn't care at all."[35] He barely won, coming in with 45 percent of the vote, just four points ahead of Finnegan. Though rejected by more than half the state's voters, he would return to the Senate.

His presence there would, as a practical matter, make no difference in important national policies. He would have work to do and a certain respected role among his colleagues. But for all practical purposes, the La Follette influence in American political debate came to an end between 1938 and 1940.

All the rest is epilogue.

Epilogue: The War and After

Eleven months after the beginning of Bob's third full term in the Senate, Pearl Harbor was attacked. The battle against isolation was ended. Phil, as he had done in the First World War, accepted the facts of life and went into service. He and Isen had only recently bought a farm—a long-cherished ambition of his, but not hers—in Roxbury, Wisconsin. "We're farmers," she quipped to Fola. When he took a captain's commission in the military police and left for active duty, she found herself alone with a job she hadn't bargained for. "[I]t is quite a change from my years of political activity to again become a hausfrau," she said.

Phil had probably assumed that he would have some role in military government of occupied territories. But he was quickly reassigned to a demanding post that he loved on the staff of General Douglas MacArthur. Nominally his job was public relations, though he undertook a large assortment of tasks. He spent two years in the Southwest Pacific, and saw at least one amphibious landing from a vantage point immediately behind the first wave. A photograph of him in helmet and fatigues shows an unshaven, grinning man who seemed for the moment to have found renewed purpose and energy in his life.

That made him somewhat the opposite of Bob, who showed increasing reluctance to come to grips with maintaining the fading Progressive Party of Wisconsin. He did not mind the routine of Senate work. Quite the contrary, he loved it. But he hated, in his son's phrase, "what one had to do to get there." He had bought a home in Virginia in the 1930s, and he spent less and less time in the state of his birth, to the increasing dismay not only of Phil but of his Wisconsin associates. Phil tried alternately cheering and scolding him. "Nothing that is happening or can happen in Washington is anywhere near as important as your relations with your state. Year after year has gone by and you have gotten further and further away from your constituents . . . [T]his is the Old Man's birthday, . . . the one thing he never did was to let ANYTHING in Washington interfere with his relations with the folks back home."[1]

But perhaps Bob had meant what he said in 1919 about Madison no longer being "home" to him. He returned to the state infrequently, and after one long visit there in 1943 caught pneumonia and went to the hospital for six weeks. After a long period of relatively stable health while he was actively engaged in the fight to beat the Depression, he now relapsed. In 1944 there was another hospitalization, in Washington, with a diagnosis of rheumatic fever. Defeat was gnawing at his body and spirit alike.

Without the nurture of either brother the Wisconsin Progressive party continued to languish. The political and economic composition of the state was changing. The strong farm base of the La Follettes was shrinking. Labor unions, never a major element of the La Follette constituency, were more inclined to turn their political attentions and support to the Democrats. They became even more alienated from Young Bob because of his increasing distrust and suspicion of the Soviet Union. By 1945 it was turning into a sinewy anticommunism, and this at a time not only when Communists carried some weight in the labor movement, but also when red-baiting was such a standard weapon in the conservative arsenal that honest liberals distrusted it and those who enthusiastically espoused it. Bob lost liberal union support that he had earned as the chairman of the Senate civil liberties committee that had thrown the blaze of light on union-busting.

It was unfair that labor votes should go to the Wisconsin Democrats, basking in the reflection of Roosevelt's name, rather than to him and his Progressives. But politics can be unfair. In the 1944 general election the Progressive party vote shrank to 6 percent of the state total. La Follette was no help, for he had spent less than a week in Wisconsin during the campaign. Party members complained that he had "personally laid down in this campaign."[2]

Nonetheless, in the spring 1945 debates over the foundation of the United Nations, Bob continued to flail away at the USSR, at Great Britain, and apparently at internationalism, though in fact Bob's views on that subject were undergoing modification. Nevertheless, his public stands isolated him further from what was then mainstream liberalism. By the middle of the year he was feeling depressed and told friends in Madison that he did not think he would run for another term in 1946. They persuaded him to change his mind. If you withdraw, one of them warned, "[you] will lose all of the respect you have built for yourself," but a fighting campaign ending in defeat would enable the La Follette name to "live on with honor." It is hard to think of a consideration that would have weighed more with the troubled senator.

So he came back to Wisconsin in March for a convention of the remnants of the Progressive party leadership. Everyone could see that the party was sinking in a sea of troubles. The choices were to cut losses and go over to the Democrats (as many like Tom Amlie had already done), or to merge with the Republicans, or to remain independent and struggle on, looking to the future. Bob's choice was to return to the Republican fold. That, he was convinced, would give him the best chance in the primary and the general election.

Phil, back from the wars, felt otherwise. Rendered combative again by military experience that he had enjoyed, he was prone to believe that the battle could be joined again under the Progressive label, and won in the long run. But Bob did not want Phil to make a fighting speech to the convention and reopen the wounds of 1938. He had their mutual friend Gordon Sinykin call Phil the night before the four hundred-odd delegates were to vote and tell him to stay away and avoid provoking a divisive debate. Later, and for the same reason, he asked Phil to stay out of his primary campaign. Phil had been away long enough to feel that he ought to defer. He had persuaded Bob to let him run for governor in 1934, but this time he yielded and followed instructions. Still, his letters told of hurt feelings and increasing dismay at the "apathy and indifference on the part of the public" all over the state. Better, in his view, to make a progressive battle against both old parties and take a beating than to leave issues unaddressed. Echoes of Old Bob still stirred in him.

The disagreement finally brought a coolness between the brothers that, by the evidence of the family letters, never thereafter thawed visibly. Phil had long since come to the conclusion that it was not good for Bob to have learned the senator's job from the top down instead of slogging through the trenches in the home state. Events of 1946 confirmed his conviction.[3]

With Bob's active support for the decision, the convention decided by a 284–128 vote to rejoin the Republicans. Bob entered the primary and went back to Washington to work on a congressional reorganization measure, the La Follette-Monroney bill, that would streamline the committee system, enhance support and research services for members, and give Congress a more informed voice in framing the budget and challenging the president's exclusive initiative. It was an important piece of legislation for the time, and won Bob national and congressional commendation. It did nothing special, however, for Wisconsin voters.[4]

But Bob had made up his mind. As in 1940, he believed that he served the people of the state as their senator conscientiously and well and deserved their support without having to court it back in the local arena that he had long left behind. He spent only eight days in the state before the voting, ignoring warnings that things didn't "feel" right to experienced Progressive associates on the ground. Bob lost, to an unknown challenger, an obscure county judge and war veteran named Joseph R. McCarthy who at that time was seen as being less of an anticommunist than Robert M. La Follette.

And so the dynasty was officially as well as substantively ended. Back in 1934 Alf Rogers, Dad's old law partner, had written a mordantly prophetic letter to Bob, advising him that he ought to think about getting out of the political game altogether after a victory, when his spirits were high. "If you don't," he warned, "the public will turn on you as sure as God, sometime, and your life will be behind you. It's different with Phil. He has his profession."[5]

Alf had been wrong about Phil, who was crushed by his own beating, but he was right about Bob. The Senate had been the center of his world for most of his life. He missed it more than he could express. He was offered a couple of minor posts by the Truman administration, but he turned them down. He did serve nominally on the [Herbert] Hoover Commission for Reorganization of the Government. We do not know if he smiled at the fortunes that had brought their names together again.

Like many other defeated senators he opened an office in Washington to serve as a consultant to those who needed to do business with the government. He kept himself busy, "consulting" for firms like Sears, Roebuck, Hawaiian Steamship, and United Fruit—another old political enemy turned associate. Life was not unkind. It offered leisure and a getaway "farm" in Virginia, travel, and a growing (though still modest) bank account that kept his two sons in private school and college. There were also bouts with bursitis, mild diabetes, diverticulitis, and, in 1948, an episode not formally labeled a heart attack but showing the beginning of coronary artery disease. We do not know what thoughts these brushes with still one more old adversary—illness—brought to La Follette's mind.

On February 24, 1953, some two weeks after his fifty-eighth birthday, he called Rachel from his office in the National Press Building and told her he was going home early. At home he went up to the second floor, took a .22-caliber pistol that he kept in his bedroom, walked into the bathroom, and shot himself through the roof of the mouth. Three days later he was buried in Madison, next to Dad. The family was there, together again for a funeral. First Old Bob. Then Belle. Now, by his own hand, "Bobbie."[6]

It was the very year that the biography, finally finished by Fola, was published.

The story should, perhaps, end there, but a few more notes are in order. The biography—two volumes and almost twelve hundred pages long—got respectful reviews, reminding Americans that it was the story of a politician of a time long, long ago. Then it disappeared into the libraries where copies still gather dust. Fola was not yet through; she spent another eighteen years—until her own death in 1970 at eighty-seven—cataloging and organizing the great mass of the La Follette papers now housed at the Library of Congress.

Mid finally escaped from the chill of the Depression and the loneliness of an artist without an audience. During the war he found work with the Alien Property Custodian, helping to deal with the literary and property rights of authors from enemy and occupied countries. He knew a great deal about copyright law, having been an organizer of the Dramatists' Guild, and he read several languages. He stayed on with the government after the war and finally retired on a small pension until he died in December 1967. They lived quietly and sparingly, occasionally visiting Mary or Rachel. Bob and Rachel's son Bronson recalls that his family had one of the early television sets and that Uncle Mid used to like to visit and watch Milton Berle.

Fola, Mary, and Rachel lived on as old women without their men, meeting now and then, remembering birthdays, occasionally trading notes —usually about family matters rather than politics—but probably communicating for the most part by telephone, the telephone that was responsible for a steadily shrinking number of La Follette letters. Rachel died in December 1961, then Fola in February 1970, and finally Mary in February 1988. Her obituary in the *Washington Post* described her simply as an "Air Force Editor" and said that she had worked for the Department of Agriculture before transferring to the Air Force in 1947. It made absolutely no mention of her having been a senator's daughter and a senator's sister.

Phil devoted himself to rebuilding his law practice, interrupted first for his governorships and then for the war. After Bob shut him out of the Progressive party's last struggles, Phil showed some interest in the abortive 1948 presidential candidacy of General Douglas MacArthur, whom he had come to admire as a great leader, perhaps the last on his lifelong list of models. He spoke on behalf of a slate of delegates pledged to the general in the April primary. It lost. In 1952 he contributed to the Eisenhower campaign.

In 1954 he made an abrupt change. He and Isen moved to Long Island, and he became the chairman of the Hazeltine Electronics Corporation. Whatever motive he had for leaving home, it spent its force soon. In 1959 they returned to Madison and tried to resume life there. Their old friends were dwindling in number—that is, those whose friendships had survived the political splits of the 1930s and 1940s. Isen organized a Women's Service Exchange that brought together retired, skilled women with employers who could use them. Phil would go to the law office where he and Sinykin were partners, then to the Madison Club for lunch. Then he would go to the State Historical Society, to which he had donated his papers, and work on his autobiography. (Isen wrote one too; his was published, hers was not.) Young scholars working there found him approachable and friendly. But he seemed lonely. Rumors persisted and persist that he drank considerably and sometimes had to be helped home from his research carrel. His nephew Bronson says flatly that "Uncle Phil" had a drinking problem. Phil himself acknowledged that he drank during the adjustment period after getting out of the service, and that "for some, the adjustment never ended." But whether he had a genuine alcohol problem or was merely a discouraged man who got through his days with a bottle's help, he had come to a curious finale for a La Follette.

He died on August 18, 1965, the exact date of Belle's death thirty-four years earlier. Isen outlived him by eight years. She went on with her work, painted a little, coped with widowhood as best she could. She quoted to Fola the comment of one friend: "You will get over it but you will never get used to it." In another letter she wrote, "Now I am not first with anyone."[7]

Phil's son, Bob III, a lawyer, never entered politics. Bob's son Bronson did. In 1964 he ran for attorney general of Wisconsin as a Democrat and was elected to a four-year term. In 1968 he ran for governor and lost. In 1975 he again became attorney general and held the post until 1987. His leaving office ended talk of a renewal of the La Follette tradition in the third generation. Interviewed in 1989, Bronson said firmly that he had no interest whatever in a political future.

And so Bob and Belle's children, raised in their unique surroundings, did not escape the usual ills of mortal flesh—divorce, drink, depression, suicide. They were an intense lot who asked much of themselves as well as their fellow countrymen. Their love for each other had been a strength, a challenge, and in the long run a burden as each one tried to cope with failed expectations and to live in a world never quite as sheltering as their childhood memories of home (which probably screened out long separations, debts, conflicts, and disappointments).

Family loyalty and political faith had been welded together in a supportive fashion hard to reproduce now. But was their joint belief that they were lone crusaders against the forces of evil in some way responsible for the midlife crises that they met with varying degrees of gallantry and surrender? Would they have ended up more contentedly if as children they had been left to follow their individual inclinations without indoctrination? Would they have become contented bankers or *avant-garde* artists or even just average citizens with marginal interest in politics? There is no answer, of course. It is not a bad idea from time to time to remember the words of Ecclesiastes that whatever we do, "all go unto one place, all are of the dust and all turn to dust again."

Still, in a more permissive day, it is wise to recognize, at least, and to respect the strength the La Follettes got from a common commitment to great goals. For them, family feeling grew out of a soil richer than mere shared pleasures or simple affections. It was forged in the heat of mutual dedication to something bigger than self-gratification. That is worth considering as Americans try to redefine "family values" on the eve of the twenty-first century.

On the other hand, it is risky for parents to dedicate their children on the altar of an ideal. Some can stand it, and some plainly can not.

Family was one pillar of the La Follettes' existence. The other was Old Bob's "religion" of democracy. We Americans in the 1990s show signs of believing collectively that if economic growth is assured, democracy somehow takes care of itself. He thought, on the contrary, that it involved "constant struggle." Of course he could be more casual about the rewards of prosperity because he grew up in an age that took economic self-sufficiency for granted and rarely had to confront what appeared to be a choice between economic health and freedom. His sons did face that bitter dilemma in the crunch of the Depression and they turned to remedies for the sick economy first. If that meant shrinking the scope of individualism by creating more bureaucrats or a dependent relationship to government it was too bad. First things had to come first.

The unexpected prosperity of the post–World War II era strengthened the national confidence that growth would nourish democratic gains. It seemed to do so in the areas of civil rights, as old barriers fell before advancing social mobility. And there was a tendency to take the universal popularity, the prevalence, the spiritual health of our democratic society for granted or to measure it by the generous yardstick of how much better it was than totalitarianism abroad, that is, to judge it by how much better it was than the alternatives and not by what it could be at its best.

I suspect Old Bob would not have shared that view. He was a prophet who lived, as we do, amidst great riches and great injustice existing hand in hand. Like a prophet, he told us that we needed to be saved from our worst selves by attention to the rules and sacrifices for the faith. It is a message that isn't terribly comforting, as prophetic messages usually are not. But it was distinctive and set La Follette apart.

I don't hesitate to say that it's worth listening to. I wrote this book so that we should remember La Follette. I want people to remember him not because he had a particular program or accomplishment or legacy. I want more of us to remember him because of his blazing courage and because he kept insisting and insisting that democracy was a life and involves continual struggle, and that we could do better.

It is. It does. And we *can* do better.

Notes

Bibliography

Index

Notes

In citing published works, personal names, and manuscript collections in the notes, short titles and abbreviations have been used, as follows:

Autobiography	Robert M. La Follette, *La Follette's Autobiography: A Personal Narrative of Political Experiences.* Madison, 1968.
Belle	Lucy Freeman, Sherry La Follette, and George A. Zabriskie. *Belle: The Biography of Belle Case La Follette.* New York, 1986.
GM	George Middleton
IBL	Isabel Bacon La Follette
LFP	La Follette Family Papers, Library of Congress
PFLP	Philip Fox La Follette Papers, State Historical Society of Wisconsin
RML	Robert Marion La Follette
RML, Jr.	Robert Marion La Follette, Jr.
RML	Belle Case La Follette and Fola La Follette. *Robert M. La Follette, June 14, 1855–June 18, 1925.* 2 vols. New York, 1953.
SHSW	State Historical Society of Wisconsin

A shortened form has been used to cite the location of letters in collections by series and box. For example, LFP A.5 refers to La Follette Family Papers, Series A, Box 5.

CHAPTER 1. BELLE AND BOB (1879–1905)

1. *Autobiography,* 5; *RML* 1:34–36. A full discussion of the sources for this book appears in the Bibliography, along with complete citations. However, a brief comment on the principal sources for each chapter also seems in order. Little first-hand material exists on La Follette's childhood and early development except for what he chose or was able to recall in his autobiography, which was intended as a campaign document for 1912. After Bob died, Belle La Follette began the "official" two-volume biography and carried it to 1909; after Belle died, their daughter

Fola completed it. Belle supplemented her own recollections by conscientious interviewing, but for the most part she presents the story of La Follette's life only as he himself saw it. The personal and family correspondence in the extensive La Follette Family Papers in the Library of Congress is scanty up to the twentieth century. The Robert Marion La Follette, Sr., Papers at the State Historical Society of Wisconsin, which document his gubernatorial campaigns and career, are almost entirely political and official, not personal. On the other side of the ledger from the *Autobiography* and *RML* is David Thelen's skeptical *The Early Life of Robert M. La Follette,* which stands alone among secondary works in close attention to La Follette's first thirty years of life. Though admirably diligent in unearthing primary sources, it is shaped by a "reappraisal" that aims to contest the proposition that La Follette was a rebel from the start and an innovator in Wisconsin progressivism—two claims La Follette himself did not advance. Thelen's account ends in 1884. The story of Wisconsin politics in the 1890s and of La Follette's 1901–1905 tenure as governor is thoroughly aired in a number of monographs. Those written before 1955 usually give La Follette and his allies a starring role in a battle for democracy. After 1955 they tend to be more detached and critical, part of a reworking of the whole field of Progressive historiography in less-than-admiring ways. Though I disagree with their premises, I found the most useful of these works to be Thelen's own *The New Citizenship: Origins of Progressivism in Wisconsin;* Robert S. Maxwell, *La Follette and the Rise of the Progressives in Wisconsin;* and Herbert F. Margulies, *The Decline of the Progressive Movement in Wisconsin.* I have used others as cited. The most complete and current source of Wisconsin history is the six-volume *History of Wisconsin* emerging under the auspices of the State Historical Society of Wisconsin, but the fourth volume, which will fall precisely between the early 1890s and World War I, is not yet available.

2. *RML* 1:52.

3. *Autobiography,* 6.

4. "Night Thoughts," LFP B.1.

5. *RML* 1:43.

6. Fola La Follette, "Robert M. La Follette, My Father," *Twentieth Century,* Apr. 1912, 515–18.

7. Details of La Follette's boyhood are found in *RML* 1:1–20 and in Thelen, *Early Life,* 4–20.

8. Belle's early life is described in *RML* 1:5–6 and in *Belle,* 1–6.

9. P. La Follette, *Adventure in Politics,* 7.

10. The material on Bascom and on the university up to and during his presidency is in volume 1 of Merle Curti and Vernon Carstensen's *University of Wisconsin: A History,* particularly 270–90 and 380–400. In *Early Life,* 21–50, Thelen does a thorough job of combing primary materials and synthesizing them with Belle's recollections in *RML* 1:21–41. There are some interviews and documents in LFP D.50–51. Belle and Fola kept all their materials for the biography—notes, documents, clippings, interview transcripts, correspondence, and so forth—and these are filed with their own papers in the family collection.

11. *Autobiography,* 12–13; *RML* 1:37–39.

12. Copies of the oration are in Belle's biography file, referred to in note 10 above.

13. *Autobiography,* 8.

14. *RML* 1:48; Thelen, *Early Life,* 51–72. Thelen devotes considerable energy to showing that Keyes himself was being forced out of power by party opponents (including La Follette's mentor, General George Bryant); that there is no hard evidence that he or any other "boss" opposed La Follette in 1880 and 1882; and that when he did contest La Follette's nomination for the House seat in 1884 he did so because of an intraparty feud rather than a desire to suppress a young crusader. Thelen implies that La Follette's story of the first interview with Keyes is a retrospective invention, a desire to create an "insurgent" past, when in fact La Follette was predictably "regular" as a beginning officeholder. But to imply is not to prove, and granting the impossibility of proving a negative—i.e., that the confrontation between La Follette and Keyes did not take place—I believe that La Follette ought not to be accused of outright falsehood without more substantial evidence. La Follette himself gave only a paragraph or two to the story and did not claim that in 1880 he was setting out to end boss rule in Dane County. His basic point is that the fight was forced on him. But in all of his work on La Follette, Thelen is so determined to rebut what he sees as a La Follette legend that he often becomes tendentious. See a more extended discussion below at note 31.

15. In his own words: "Boss Keyes did not know it but opposition of that sort was the best service he could have rendered me."

16. "Night Thoughts," n.p.

17. *RML* 1:55, 92.

18. Belle's claim to being the first woman to graduate was occasionally questioned because an alumni directory apparently erred in listing another woman in the student body of the law school in 1875. Edward J. Reisner convincingly validates Belle's priority in a brief essay in *Gargoyle: University of Wisconsin Law School Forum,* Winter 1991/92, 10–11.

19. Belle to Theodore Dreiser, then the editor of the magazine *Delineator,* May n.d. 1911, LFP D.24. "Letters Sent, 1898–1912."

20. *RML* 1:56.

21. *Autobiography,* 20–22; Thelen, *Early Life,* 66–70.

22. *Autobiography,* 23–57.

23. *RML* 1:86.

24. Ibid. 62, 66.

25. Ibid. 67; *Autobiography,* 30.

26. *RML* 1:70–73.

27. *Autobiography,* 25–26, 36–37; *RML* 1:88, 92. The Republican defeat in Wisconsin in 1890 was partly due to anger at a public-education measure, the so-called Bennett Law, signed by Governor Hoard, that Catholic and Lutheran immigrant voters perceived as a blow to their parochial schools and then stayed away from the polls in protest. Nationwide there was resentment against the high McKinley Tariff of 1890 (which La Follette had supported.)

28. *Autobiography,* 62–64; *RML* 1:97.

29. *Autobiography,* 65–70; *RML* 1:98–100; Nesbit, *Wisconsin: A History,* 404.

30. *Autobiography,* 65, 72. La Follette's claim that nothing in his life ever affected him in the way the bribe did leaves some of his biographers understand-

ably incredulous (see note 31 below). Surely, they argue, he cannot have been so naive, so easily shocked by the evidence of corruption among the bosses he claimed to have been fighting. But it is one thing to suspect outright lawbreaking through bribery, and another to be asked directly to take part in it. "One who has never been subject to an experience like that," La Follette said, "cannot realize just what comes over him." That votes and judicial decisions were bought and bartered for may have been common knowledge, but it is conceivable that La Follette, at the very start of the muckraking era, had not yet linked individual episodes of graft into a pattern; what he simply says is that he felt dirtied by the implication of Sawyer's offer and in the upheaval of his feelings began for the first time to see his past clashes with Sawyer not as separate incidents but as pieces in a puzzle he was now solving.

31. The remainder of the chapter rests mainly on the work of Thelen's *New Citizenship,* Maxwell's *La Follette and the Rise of the Progressives in Wisconsin,* and Margulies's *Decline of the Progressive Movement in Wisconsin.* While I am grateful for their research, I question their interpretation. They all quarrel, not unreasonably, with a story that puts La Follette at the center of the war to defeat the interests and bring good government to the state. But they tend—Thelen especially—to go beyond that and suggest that La Follette was something of an opportunist who wanted to take control of the Republican party in Wisconsin, found a progressive movement already taking shape, and saw in it a perfect instrument with which to mobilize other "outs" contesting the established leadership. He moved in to build a progressive coalition, supplant its originators, and wrap the takeover in the mantle of a struggle between the forces of good and the legions of the unrighteous.

Concede at the outset that La Follette had a liberal streak of self-righteousness, vanity, and paranoia. His capacity to polarize was great and remains so a century after he began his national career. Nevertheless, the attacks on him by the scholars cited miss some critical points, in my view. They must be seen as part of a general reexamination of the entire Progressive Era since Richard Hofstadter's 1955 work, *The Age of Reform from Bryan to FDR.,* Previous accounts of progressivism, such as they were, like Charles Madison's *Critics and Crusaders: A Century of American Protest* (New York, 1947) or Louis Filler's *Crusaders for American Liberalism* (Yellow Springs, Ohio, 1950), took seriously the claims of such men and women as La Follette, William Allen White, Frederic C. Howe, Lincoln Steffens, Ida Tarbell, Finley P. Dunne, Tom Johnson, Brand Whitlock, Jane Addams, Florence Kelley, Louis Brandeis, Theodore Roosevelt, and Woodrow Wilson (to name a representative few) that they were fighting to preserve the vitality of American self-government against the eroding forces of concentrated corporate power.

Post-1950s scholarship busied itself with deconstructing this professed aim. One after another, a number of historians—Samuel P. Hays, Robert Wiebe, George Mowry, Gabriel Kolko, Richard Abrams, Allen Davis, David Chalmers (again to name a sampling)—critically explored complexities that they found in progressivism. They were not all identical in purpose or in outlook, but the cumulative effect of their work was to paint a fairly unflattering portrait of the progressive generation. The "crusaders," it turned out, were genteel "old-stock" Americans; they were elitists who felt threatened by loss of status to the emerging cadres of business management and the urban and state machines of political management; they wanted regulation and conservation not so much to tame the railroads, the developers, and the trusts as to make them orderly and predictable in their dealings with the public; many of them were hostile to labor unions and immigrants; some were prohibitionists, others segregationists, most of them imperialists, and almost all were wedded to restrictive ideals of family life. In sum, whether intentionally or not, the new scholarship on progressivism simply dismissed as irrelevant if not imaginary the moral credentials of the entire movement. The progressives' invocation of the golden rule, the social gospel, the Declaration of Independence, the egalitarian rhetoric of the party of Jackson, the Free-Soil traditions of the party of Lincoln—these were all, apparently, rhetoric of the kind in which interest groups spontaneously, almost unknowingly, couch and attempt to universalize their own perspectives.

I will not quarrel with this overview here, except to say that it seems to me to demean and dehumanize the past; to trivialize the passions, appetites, reflections, and inner struggles of once-alive men and women; to turn a blind eye to the genuine and palpable evils that aroused them to action—simply because they ignored other evils currently considered more important. I do take note, however, that biographers working out of such a background cannot help finding La Follette a juicy target.

I have no intention of defending him against every and any criticism made of him, but many of them are mutually contradictory and some are sustainable only by selective reading. If, for example, he was purely opportunistic in 1890, he might well have stayed "regular." A brilliant and lucrative career at the bar—and political offices as well—were his for the asking if mere ambition was what goaded him. He most assuredly saw issues in moralistic terms, but that was hardly an original point of view in the 1890s, and there is no attack he delivered on the motives of his enemies that was not answered by them in kind. Nor did he rely on high-minded exhortation to make his points; he was distinguished for the enormous diligence with which he prepared his speeches and his uncanny ability to hold the attention of audiences with a recital of facts and statistics. Thelen also notes that he was approachable and well liked outside the political arena. Diligent research and personal popularity hardly fit the portrait of a ranting zealot.

Another charge by Maxwell, Thelen, and Margulies is that La Follette rewarded his friends with patronage like any other "boss," and expected their support in return, but the issue, it would seem to me, is whether his appointees were qualified and whether he expected or offered any material considerations in return. He never denied wanting to have in Wisconsin a solid supporting body of legislators and officials who thought as he did. It was what democratic politics, for him, was all about, and if he sometimes held the reins too tightly he was, all the same, always willing to submit his ideas to the test of popular judgment, to fight for them in open debate that assumed the attentiveness and intelligence of his audiences.

I have no wish to sanctify La Follette or his cohorts of a reforming generation. I do, however, believe that his and their righteous anger ought not to be lightly dismissed or patronized. Granting that there are two sides to every argument, it seems natural to me to use the term "wrong" to describe sweatshops, slums, the theft of public lands and resources, the deliberate ruining of competitors, or the purchase of voters, judges, and lawmakers to gain profit-making advantages. To interpret La Follette, as Thelen does in *Robert La Follette and the Insurgent Spirit,* essentially as a spokesman for consumers and taxpayers is to be overly reductive. At the heart of progressive thought in general were certain key beliefs in the necessity of principled action to preserve equal opportunity and representative government. Progressives like La Follette shared an ideal of public participation by informed *citizens* who settled their affairs on generally recognized principles of public justice and relied on conscience and reason to attain consensus on what kind of official conduct was good and what kind was wrong and deserved punishment.

Allowing for all the negatives—people are more complicated and less autonomous in their behavior than we believed a century ago, self-interest is not confined to any one group, some social benefits were produced by "the system" even unreformed—why should the progressives not have at least due respect? Is our performance as a democracy markedly better now? I do not mean to beat critics of the progressives over the head with those questions. I only suggest that a bit more humility is in order in the handling of the reformers of the past and that historians should not be arrogant in their supposed unmasking of the "myths" of yesterday.

32. *Autobiography,* 12.

33. RML to unidentified correspondent, n.d., LFP B.104; *Autobiography,* 10–12. La Follette is not very specific about early readings that shaped his emerging views in 1891, but he does report reading "one of Henry George's early books" in the 1870s and being affected by "this movement of the Grangers swirling about me."

34. Margulies, *Decline,* 3–81; Thelen, *New Citizenship,* esp. 290–312.

35. Above sources plus Nesbit, *Wisconsin,* 339–47; Newton Dent, "Senator Robert M. La Follette," *Munsey's,* Feb. 1907, 655–59; *Autobiography,* 84–85.

36. "The Menace of the Machine," *Autobiography,* 84–85; *RML* 1:119–20.

37. Margulies, *Decline,* 38; *RML* 1:124.

38. *RML* 1:113, 128, 146; *Autobiography,* 119.

39. Margulies, *Decline,* 44–51.

40. *Autobiography,* ix.

41. Margulies, *Decline,* 52–67; *Autobiography,* 98–158.

42. *Autobiography,* 115–16; *RML* 1:143.

43. *Autobiography,* 145; *RML* 1:172.

44. Lincoln Steffens, "Wisconsin: A State Where the People Have Restored Representative Government," *McClure's,* Oct. 1904, 563–79.

45. *Autobiography,* 153.

46. Ibid., 157, 159.

CHAPTER 2. BOB: ON THE ROAD AND ON THE RISE (1906–1911)

1. RML to J. Siebecker, Jan. 7, 1906, LFP A.5; *RML* 1:200. From this point on, the letters in the La Follette Family Collection in the Library of Congress, particularly the intrafamily correspondence in Series A, become the principal source of this book. Belle and Fola La Follette quoted from these letters extensively in their biography, so it is possible to find some of the cited passages both in the manuscripts and in their two-volume work. In all cases I went back to the unexcerpted and

unedited originals, which hereafter I will cite exclusively, to avoid redundancy. General readers who may wish to consult the excerpts in Belle and Fola's text will have little trouble in finding them, as they occur in strict chronology for the most part, and the context will make the location clear. Pages from both *RML* and the *Autobiography* are usually cited to furnish background commentary by Bob, Belle, or Fola.

2. The "dear old rotten Senate" is in RML to Belle, Jan. 19, 1907, LFP A.6. No matter who was the named addressee of most of the letters in this series, it was usually assumed that they were for general family consumption and close friends; therefore citations here may differ from those in the notes to *RML*. "The hole is prepared" is cited by Nathaniel Wright Stephenson in his *Nelson W. Aldrich* (New York, 1930) 265.

3. *Autobiography,* 160–61; *RML* 1:201.

4. *RML* 1:205; Belle to J. Siebecker, Apr. 24, 1906, LFP A.5.

5. Apr. 23, 1906, *Congressional Record,* 59th Cong., 1st sess., 5713–23.

6. Belle says (*RML* 1:206) that she wrote this to Fola, but it is in the letter to Siebecker cited in note 4 above.

7. *RML* 1:203.

8. *Autobiography,* 163–66.

9. RML to "My Dear Ones," Jan. 28, 1907, LFP A.6.

10. *Autobiography,* 166; *RML* 1:223; Roosevelt to RML, Feb. 19, 1907, in E. E. Morison, ed., *Letters of Theodore Roosevelt* (Cambridge, Mass., 1951–54), 5:594.

11. *Autobiography,* 166.

12. Roosevelt to White, Jan. 5, 1907, *Letters* 5:540; *RML* 1:223.

13. RML to Belle, Dec. 4, 16, 1906, LFP A.5; Belle to RML, Dec. 9, 1906, LFP A.4.

14. *RML* 1:223; RML to Belle, Jan. 30, 1907, LFP A.6.

15. RML to Belle, Feb. 9, 1907, LFP A.6.

16. Roosevelt to White, July 31, 1906, *Letters* 5:340; Roosevelt to Kermit Roosevelt, May 30, 1908, ibid. 6:1043–44.

17. *Autobiography of William Allen White,* 427–28.

18. RML to "Dear Little Mary," Dec. 11, 1906, LFP A.5.

19. *RML* 1:218–19.

20. Ibid. 1:212; RML to Belle, Jan. 20, 1907, LFP A.6.

21. *Autobiography,* 179.

22. *RML* 1:227.

23. *Autobiography,* 166–78, 177–79.

24. *RML* 1:243.

25. Ibid. 1:238–56; May 29, 1908, *Congressional Record,* 60th Cong., 1st sess., 7158–91; *Washington Evening Star,* May 29, 1908.

26. RML to "My Dear Girl," Feb. 9, 1907, LFP, A.6.

27. RML to Belle, July 4, 7, 19, 1905, LFP A.4.

28. RML to Belle (en route to Walla Walla, Wash.), Apr. 14, 1907, LFP A.6.

29. *RML* 1:214; RML to "My Dear Girl," Feb. 9, 1907; RML to Belle, April 23, 1907, LFP A.6.

30. *RML* 1:196.

31. Ibid. 1:266.

32. Ibid. 1:300.

33. RML to Belle, Jan. 16, Feb. 13, 1907, LFP A.6.

34. RML to "My Dearest Ones," Jan. 30, 1907, LFP A.6.

35. RML to Belle, July 30, 1907, LFP A.6.

36. RML to Belle, June 27, 1907, LFP A.6.

37. RML to Belle, Mar. 27, 1907, LFP A.6.

38. RML to Belle, Aug. 20, 1909, LFP A.8.

39. Belle to "Dear Papa," June 25, 1905, LFP A.3.

40. RML to "My Dear Little Girl," Apr. 22, 1896, LFP A.1; RML to "Dear Ones All," July 19, 1905, LFP A.4.

41. Aug. 4, Sep. 21, Sep. 23, Sep. 26, 1905, LFP A.4.

42. Oct. 19, 1905; RML to Fola, June 16, 1906; RML to Belle, Aug. 7, 1906, LFP A.4.

43. RML to Belle, Dec. 6, 14, 1906, LFP A.4; *RML* 1:225.

44. RML to "Dear Girl and Little Ones," Feb. 13, 1907, LFP A.6. There are many such homesick letters. One to Bobbie on August 29 speaks with unusual frankness to a little boy. "In the work which I am doing and in which I am putting so much of my life the hard thing about it is the way I have to give up being with you all. I feel that no amount of being together hereafter will take the place of the days which are passing just now. If my nights were not so hard I should surely have you and Phil with me a part of the time—but I declare—the way I have to sit round in the depots waiting for trains through the long weary hours of the nights keeps me from sending for you."

45. RML to Belle, Jan. 20, Mar. 4, Mar. 24, Apr. 26, Apr. 28, 1907, LFP A.6.

46. P. La Follette, *Adventure in Politics,* 8–9.

47. RML to "My dear Girl, Bobbie, Phil and Little Mary," Jan. 4, 1907, LFP A.6.

48. RML to Belle and the children, Oct. 31, Nov. 17, 1909, LFP A.8.

49. RML to "Bobbie," Dec. 9, 1906, LFP A.4; RML to Phil, Feb. 14, 1907, LFP A.6.

50. RML to "My Dear Bobbie," Feb. 5, 1907, LFP A.6.

51. RML, postscript to letter of Belle to J. Siebecker, Mar. 10, 1907, LFP A.5.

52. For the La Follette family version of these events, see *RML* 1:257–62; *Autobiography,* 203–8.

53. *Autobiography of William Allen White,* 423–27, 429–30, 454–55.

54. See note 31 in Chapter 1.

55. *Autobiography,* 220–22; RML to E. A. Van Valkenberg, Feb. 12, 1911; RML to Fremont Older, Apr. 18, 1911, LFP B.106.

56. William Kittle, "Robert M. La Follette: A Statesman after the Order of Lincoln," *Arena,* June 1906, 571–76.

57. Ray Stannard Baker, *American Chronicle,* 265.

CHAPTER 3. BELLE: A "NEW WOMAN" AND HER FAMILY (1891–1911)

1. *RML* 1:53.

2. Typescript citing the *Wisconsin State Journal* of Jan. 20, 1886, which credits the story to the *Transcript* of Jan. 8, in LFP D.52.

3. *Autobiography,* 134–35.

4. *RML* 1:111.

5. Ibid. 1:91.

6. Ibid. 1:12. See also, Frances Willard and Mary Livermore, eds., *A Woman of the Century: Biographical Sketches of Leading American Women in All Walks of Life* (Buffalo, 1893), and John W. Leonard, ed., *Woman's Who's Who of America, 1914–1915* (New York, 1914).

7. See biographical material in register of the Papers of Gwyneth K. Roe, State Historical Society of Wisconsin.

8. P. La Follette, *Adventure in Politics,* 9; *Belle,* 86–87.

9. Belle to RML, June 27, 1905, LFP A.3. See also Apr. 8: "We are very secure in our nest if the father bird is also safe."

10. July 3, 1905; Apr. 14, 1907, LFP A.5.

11. Aug. 16, 1905, LFP A.3.

12. Feb. 12, 1907, LFP A.5.

13. *Belle,* 68–69. Copy also in LFP D.24.

14. Belle to Fola and J. Siebecker, Apr. 24, 1906, LFP A.5.

15. Belle to RML, Jan. 2, 6, May 7, 1907, LFP A.5.

16. June 25, 1905; Oct. 23, 1909, LFP A.7.

17. Belle to "My Dearest One," Aug. 16, 1905, LFP A.3.

18. Ibid.

19. Nov. 15, 1905, LFP A.3; Jan. 9, 1907, LFP A.5.

20. Belle to "My Beloved Phil," Jan. 28, 1919, LFP A.24; Dec. 13, 1906, LFP A.5.

21. Oct. 5, 1905, LFP A.3.

22. Dec. 4, 1905; Jan. 27, 1907, LFP A.5.

23. Nov. 19, 1906, LFP A.5; Oct. 5, 1905, LFP A.3.

24. July 31, Sep. 22, Oct. 8, 18, 1905, LFP A.3.

25. Mar. 27, Apr. 8, 1907, LFP A.5.

26. Jan. 28, 1904, Sep. 22, 27, 1905, LFP A.3.

27. May 7, 1907, LFP A.5.

28. May 10, 1907, LFP A.5.

29. *La Follette's Weekly Magazine* (hereafter cited as *La Follette's*), Jan. 9, 1909.

30. *RML* 1:263–65.

31. Belle to RML, Aug. 3, 1903, LFP A.2.

32. Steffens, "The Victorious Mother," *The Progressive,* Belle La Follette Memorial Edition, Nov. 7, 1931.

33. *La Follette's,* Jan. 9, 23, 30, 1909.

34. *Belle,* 34.

35. Belle to Anton Oppegard, June 14, 1911, LFP D.24.

36. Belle to North American Press Syndicate, June 9, 1911, LFP D.24; Belle to Fola, July 1, 1911, LFP A.10.

37. "Clifton Fremont Hodge," *American,* June 1912.

38. Allon Gal, *Brandeis of Boston* (Cambridge, Mass., 1980), 8–9, 121; BCL to Evans, July 8, 1911, LFP A.10; Evans in *Springfield Republican,* Apr. 15, 1931, quoted in *RML* 1:281, Belle La Follette, "Interesting People," *American* Sep. 14, 1913.

39. Belle to Evans, May 18, 1911, LFP D.25; Belle to Fola, Aug. 10, 1913, LFP A.12.

40. Belle to Gwyneth K. Roe, Aug. 23, 1913, Gwyneth K. Roe Papers.

CHAPTER 4. FOLA: FROM ART TO ACTIVISM (1904–1911)

1. Almost all of the material in this chapter is based on Fola's letters, in most cases to one or both of her parents. Where the recipient is different, I have so indicated; otherwise I have merely shown the date of the letter, unless, as in this instance, it is already given in the text. I have cited direct quotations from the letters or specific events alluded to, but I have not tried to reconstruct itineraries letter by letter. In a few cases I take note of an especially affectionate salutation to convey the flavor of the relationship.

2. "My dearest Mama and Papa," Nov. 12, 1900, LFP A.2.

3. *Jubilee Badger,* 1905; see also "My dearest Mother," July 30, 1904, LFP A.2.

4. June n.d., July 18, 21, 22 (to "Mother, dear heart"), Aug. 5, 1904, LFP A.2.

5. July 30, 21, 25, Aug. 3, 1904, LFP A.2.

6. To "Dearest Papa," July 7, 1904; to Belle, June 19, July 4, 22, 1904, LFP A.2.

7. To "My dearest Mother," July 25, and to "Dearest Papa," Aug. 3, 1904; also to RML, Mar. 16, 1905, LFP A.4.

8. Feb. 25, 1905, LFP A.4.

9. Nov. 14, 29, 1904, LFP A.3. See also Benjamin McArthur, *Actors and American Culture, 1880–1920* (Philadelphia, 1984), 4–25, 27–30, 220–21; *Belle,* 101; George Middleton, *These Things Are Mine,* 163; *Actors Equity Golden Anniversary Journal, 1913–1963.*

10. Nov. 9, 1904, LFP A.3.

11. Sep. 20, 1904, LFP A.3.

12. Sep. 1, Oct. 19, Nov. n.d., 1908, LFP A.7.

13. Nov. 20, 1906, LFP A.5; Nov. 19, 1905, LFP A.4; May 9, 1906, LFP A.4; Middleton, *These Things Are Mine,* 86.

14. Feb. 7, May 22, Dec. 16, 1905, LFP A.4.

15. May 28, Dec. 7, 1905, Jan. 13, 31, 1906, LFP A.4; Dec. 8, 1904, LFP A.3; and see also Dec. 20, 27, 1905, LFP A.4, and Nov. 13, 1906, LFP A.5.

16. Oct. 26, 1906, LFP A.4.

17. Dec. 27, 1905, Jan. n.d., 1906, LFP A.4.

18. See Nov. 20, 1906, to "Darling Mother mine," LFP A.5; Nov. 23, 26, 1910, LFP A.9; Sep. 1, 1908, LFP A.7.

19. Nov. n.d., 1908, June 19, 1910, LFP A.9.

20. Nov. 15, 1907, LFP A.6.

21. RML to Belle, Oct. 19, 1909, LFP A.8.

22. A copy is available in Fola's papers, LFP E.145.

23. Jan. 4, 26, 27, 1910, LFP A.9.

24. RML to Fola, Jan. 29, 1910, LFP A.9.

25. Fola to family, Mar. 13, 1910, LFP A.9; Cleveland *Plain Dealer,* Mar. 13, 1910.

26. Fola to family, Apr. 3, 7, June 19, n.d., 27, 30, July 7, 1910, LFP A.9.

27. A flyer advertising the show is in Fola's 1910 correspondence.

28. Oct. 10, Nov. 13, 1910, LFP, A.9.

29. "A Hawthorne Fantasy Developed into A Play," *New York Times,* Jan. 15, 1911.

30. Middleton, *These Things Are Mine,* 1–82. Middleton says that his first meeting with the senator was at Fola's apartment early in La Follette's first term and that La Follette was unaware that "months before, I had asked his daughter to marry me," but "Fola hadn't seen it my way" (p. 90). There is not the barest suggestion of this in Fola's own correspondence prior to 1910, nor does Middleton himself seem to give it any great importance, leaving the exact development of the relationship before the autumn of 1910 a pleasant, minor puzzle.

31. The letters cited in this section — to the beginning of the story of how Fola broke the news to her parents — are all from a sheaf of them written by Fola to George between Dec. 13 and Dec. 26, 1910, LFP A.9. Some have a date, one or two do not, none is paginated, some have no salutation. In the next two notes I cite specifically dated letters from the packet.

32. Dec. 17, 1910, LFP A.9.

33. Dec. 20, 24, 1910, LFP A.9.

34. Jan. 5, 1911, LFP A.10.

35. Mar. 11, 12, 15 (two of that date), 17, 20, 1911, LFP A.10.

36. Fola to Belle, Mar. 14, 1911; Belle to Fola, Mar. 17, 1911, LFP A.10.

37. Belle to Gwyneth Roe (on childbirth), May 31, 1907, Gwyneth K. Roe Papers; to Fola, July 25, 1911, LFP A.10.

38. Apr. 3, 1911, LFP A.10.

39. Belle to Fola, Mar. 28, Apr. 3, 12, July 26, 1911; Belle to E. Evans, Sep. 28, 1911, LFP D.24.

40. Fola to GM, May 7, 1911, LFP A.10.

41. Fola to GM, May 21, 1911, LFP A.10.

42. Fola to GM, May n.d., 29, 31, June 20, 22, 1911, LFP A.10.

43. Fola to family, Aug. 2, 19, 18, July 10, 23, 1911; Fola to GM, July 24, 1911, LFP A.10.

44. June 27, Sep. 1, Sep. 18, 1911, LFP A.11.

45. Belle to GM, Sep. 7, Nov. 21, 1911, LFP A.10.

46. Fola to GM, Oct. 27, 1911; Fola to Belle, Oct. 9, Nov. 6, 1911, LFP A.11.

CHAPTER 5. TRANSITION TIME:
THE FAMILY COMPLETED (1912–1916)

1. The entire story of the battle for the nomination is told from the La Follette point of view both in *RML* 1:352–443 and in *Autobiography,* 204–341.

2. *RML* 1:354.

3. *Autobiography,* 320.

4. RML 1:350–55.

5. Ray Stannard Baker, "The Meaning of Insurgency," *American,* May 1911, 59–64.

6. See *Autobiography,* esp. 213–35.

7. Mark Sullivan, *The War Begins: 1909–1914,* vol. 4 of *Our Times: The United States, 1900–1925.*

8. Ibid., 415.

9. RML to Elliot S. Norton, Jan. 15, 1912; to Colony Club, Dec. 12, 1911; to Gil Roe, Dec. 14, 1911, *LFP* B.107; to Albert Beveridge, Jan. 29, 1911, LFP B.106; to Robert W. Lyon, n.d., LFP B.107.

10. The basic source for the story is the Philadelphia *Evening Bulletin,* Feb. 3, 1912. La Follette gives the banquet itself less than half a page in the *Autobiography* (259) while Fola, in *RML* vol. 1, covers it quite thoroughly, relying on the recollections of Middleton, who was there but barely mentions it in *These Things Are Mine.*

11. The complete text of the speech appears as an appendix in *Autobiography.*

12. RML to George Keenan, Feb. 12, 1912, LFP B.107; to Josie Siebecker, Feb. 15, 1912, LFP A.12.

13. Philadelphia *Evening Bulletin,* Feb. 3, 1913.

14. *RML* 1:409–12, 417–20.

15. Sullivan, *War Begins,* 475.

16. RML to Roe, Feb. 6, 1912, LFP B.107; to Josie Siebecker, Feb. 15, 1912, LFP A.12.

17. To Keenan, Feb. 12, 1912, see note 12; Sullivan, *War Begins,* 472–75.

18. RML to Hiram Johnson, Nov. 3, 1911.

19. *RML* 1:420–40 tells the story from La Follette's viewpoint. He never forgave McGovern, who was a Milwaukee-based lawyer and represented a different progressive constituency and outlook. The two fought each other in 1914 and later (see text), with bad results for progressivism in Wisconsin.

20. RML to Alf Rogers, Feb. 13, 1912, LFP B.107.

21. *Autobiography of William Allen White,* 451.

22. Baker to RML, Sep. 9, 1912, LFP B.71.

23. RML to Roe, July 8, 1912 (from internal evidence), LFP B.107.

24. RML to Spreckels, July 12, 1912, LFP B.107.

25. Arthur Link, *Woodrow Wilson and the Progressive Era,* 24; *RML* 1:453.

26. Evans to RML, July 17, 1912, LFP B.71; RML to J. A. Littlemore, July 17, 1912, LFP B.107; *RML* 1:452.

27. *RML* 1:451, 454, 460, 464.

28. RML to Josie Siebecker, Mar. 6, 1913, LFP A.13; *RML* 1:482. The entire Wilson–La Follette honeymoon is covered in *RML* 1:458–83.

29. Ibid., 462.

30. Entire story in *RML* 1:521–36. See Hyman Weintraub, *Andrew Furuseth, Emancipator of Seamen* (New York, 1959).

31. RML to RML, Jr., Sep. 19, 1913; to Belle, Oct. 24, 1913, LFP A.13.

32. RML to Josie, May 7, 1913; to RML, Jr., Sep. 19, 1913, LFP A.13.

33. *RML* 1:506–8, and with somewhat more objectivity in Nesbit, *Wisconsin,* 431–32.

34. RML to Fola, July n.d. 1914; to "Dearly Beloved Ones," Aug. 12, 1914, LFP A.16.

35. To "Dear Ones," May 27, June 13, Aug. 5, Dec. 28, 1915, LFP A.18.

36. Belle to RML, Jr., Feb. 2, 1915, LFP A.17.

37. *RML* 1:490–91.
38. Ibid. 1:580–84; RML to Belle, Oct. 29, 17, 1915, LFP A.18.
39. Belle to RML, Jr., Oct. 14, 1913, LFP A.13.
40. *RML* 1:452–53.
41. *RML* 1:476.
42. Middleton, *These Things Are Mine,* 124.
43. Belle to "Beloved Netha," Aug. 23, 1913, Gwyneth Roe Papers, and Belle, "Letters Sent, 1898–1912," LFP D.24.
44. Fola to Belle, June 29, 1913; Belle to Fola, July 7, 1913, LFP A.13.
45. *Belle,* 133; *La Follette's,* Aug. 23, 30, 1913.
46. RML to "My Dear Girl and Kiddies," Nov. 10, 1913, A.13.
47. *Belle,* 130.
48. Belle to family, Apr. 14–May 1, 1914, LFP A.13.
49. Belle to family, July 6, 19, 20, Aug. 1, 4, 23, 1914, LFP A.13. See also letters of July 26, 28.
50. Belle to family, July 19, 20, 1914, LFP A.13.
51. Aug. 4, 1914, LFP A.13.
52. *Belle,* 145.
53. Fola to GM, Jan. 3, 1912; GM to RML Jan. 30, 1912, LFP, A.12; Fola to GM, July 10, 1914, LFP A.14.
54. Fola to GM, Jan. 9, Mar. 26, 27, 1912, LFP A.12.
55. Mar. 27, 28, 30, 31, 1912, LFP A.12.
56. Apr. 3, n.d., 12, 1912, LFP A.12.
57. Middleton, *These Things Are Mine,* 93–94; Fola toBelle, n.d. 1912, LFP A.12.
58. GM to "Mater," Aug. 15, 1912, LFP A.12; *These Things Are Mine,* 95–109.
59. Ibid., 116.
60. Ibid., 110–14.
61. Fola to Belle, June n.d., 1914, LFP A.14.
62. Fola to GM, July 26, 27, 1914, LFP A.14; Aug. 2, 1914, LFP A.15.
63. Fola to GM, Aug. 2, 1914, LFP A.15; July 17, 26, 23, 27, 1914, LFP A.14.
64. Fola to GM, Aug. 20, 19, 13, 1914, LFP A.15.
65. Fola to GM, Aug. 3, 30, 1914; to Belle, Sep. n.d., 1914, LFP A.15.
66. GM to Fola, Aug. 22, 1914, LFP A.17.
67. RML, Jr., Jan. 5, 9, 21, 1906; Phil, Apr. 6, 1906, LFP A.5.
68. RML, Jr., Jan. 26; J. Siebecker to Belle, Feb. 7, 1906, LFP A.5.
69. RML, Jr., to Phil, Sep. 24, 1913, LFP A.13; to Mary, Aug. 9, June 21, 1917, LFP A.20.
70. RML, Jr., to Fola, Aug. 1, 1911, LFP A.11.
71. Belle to RML, Jr., Feb. 20, 1915, LFP, A.17; RML, Sr., to RML, Jr., Oct. 14, 1915, LFP A.18.
72. RML, Jr., to Belle, Aug. 30, 1911; RML to RML, Jr., Sep. 2, 1911, LFP A.11.
73. RML, Jr., to family, Feb. 23, 1914, LFP A.15.
74. RML to "Bobbie," Aug. 20, 1911, LFP A.11; Belle to "Dear Ones All," Oct. 11, 1910, LFP A.9; RML to "My Dear Boy," Mar. 31, 1914, LFP A.16.
75. Belle to "Beloved Boy," Sep. 30, Oct. 30, Nov. 10, 1913; Fola to RML, Jr., Nov. 12, 1913, LFP A.12; RML to RML, Jr., Nov. 7, 1913, LFP A.13.

76. RML to "Bobbie," Sep. 22, Oct. 1, Nov. 9, 1914, LFP A.16.

77. Belle to RML, Oct. 23, 24, 30, 1914; to "Bobbie," Oct. 24, 1914, LFP A.14; RML, Jr., to "Dear Ones," Feb. 9, 1915, LFP A.18.

78. Belle to RML, Jr., Nov. 11, 1914, LFP A.14; RML to "Bobbie," Nov. 9, 18, 1914, LFP A.16.

79. Fola to family, n.d., with June correspondence for 1914 but probably later, LFP A.14.

80. RML, Jr., to RML, Sr., Mar. 22, 1915; RML, Sr., May–Oct. 1915, passim, LFP A.18.

81. RML to Belle, Oct. 16, 1915; to "My dear Bobbie," June 4, 19, 1915, which concludes, "Boy, you don't know how I love you." See also May 27 ("It is simply wonderful the way he has met it all. He has great stuff in him") and July 6 ("It is just great the way he keeps his grit"); see also June 13 and July 27. LFP A.18.

82. RML, Jr., to Belle, July 25, 1914, LFP A.15; RML to Josie Siebecker, Sep. 6, 1915, LFP A.18.

CHAPTER 6. THE CATASTROPHE: ALONE AND AT BAY (1917–1919)

1. LFP, A.16. The primary sources for this chapter continue to be the family letters and the first volume of *RML*. These offer the fullest day-by-day account of the family's wartime ordeal, but of course exclusively from the La Follette perspective. General histories of the war period are numerous and mostly adequate. For a quick overview, Arthur Link's chapters on World War I in *American Epoch* (New York, 1973) are satisfactory, and the most detailed information of the moves toward war from the White House view can be found in the volumes of his biography of Wilson. Biographies of the few senatorial war resisters are scarce, but I profited by Richard Lowitt's biography of George Norris, and to a lesser extent by Norris's disappointingly flat autobiography, *Fighting Liberal*. I got valuable insights into Wilson's and Theodore Roosevelt's reactions to the war from John M. Cooper's *The Warrior and the Priest* (Cambridge, Mass., 1983). The classic formulation of the 1914–1917 "isolationist" point of view is found in the writings of Charles A. Beard, particularly in *The Rise of American Civilization* (New York, 1942). Walter Millis's *Road to War* (New York, 1935), still holds up as a readable journalistic summary (though it embarrassed Millis somewhat in 1940–1941, when World War II isolationists—including Philip and "Young Bob" La Follette—used it as a cautionary text even though Millis himself had become an interventionist, rightly arguing that the situation was very different). For the frenzy on the home front and the general progressive rush to war, David Kennedy's *Over Here* is thorough and reflective, though the subject still requires a great deal of explanation.

2. Mark Sullivan, *The War Begins,* 123.

3. *RML* 1:495.

4. P. La Follette, *Adventure in Politics,* p. 32.

5. RML to Phil, Aug. 24, 1914; to Belle, Aug. 14, 1914; LFP A.16; Phil to RML, Sep. 14, 4, 1914, LFP A.15.

6. RML to Phil, Aug. 28, 1914, LFP A.16; Fola to GM, Aug. 30, 1914, LFP A.14; GM to Fola, July 13, 1914, LFP A.17.

7. *Belle,* 143.

8. *RML* 1:518.

9. Ibid., 540–42.

10. RML to "Dear Mama," Nov. 26, 1915, LFP A.18. For a fine overall account of the entire Ford expedition, see Barbara Kraft, *The Peace Ship* (New York, 1978).

11. *RML* 1:551–52.

12. Ibid., 558–60.

13. *La Follette's,* May 1, 1916; also *RML* 1:565.

14. RML 1:574–77.

15. Ibid., 589.

16. RML to family, Jan. 31, 1917, LFP A.20.

17. Feb. 2, 1917, LFP A.20.

18. *RML* 1:595–96.

19. RML to Belle, Feb. 8, 1917, LFP A.20.

20. The complete story of the armed ship filibuster that follows is primarily drawn from *RML* vol. 1; Norris, *Fighting Liberal;* Robert C. Byrd, *The Senate, 1789–1989* (Washington, 1991), 2:118–24; and *New York Times,* Mar. 2–5, 1917.

21. *RML* 1:626; RML to Belle, Mar. 5, 1917; Belle to RML, Mar. 5, 1917, LFP A.20.

22. *RML* 1:626.

23. Ibid., 629–32.

24. Ibid., 628; Byrd, *The Senate,* 2:124.

25. Rauschenbusch to RML, Mar. n.d. 1917, LFP B.81; RML 1:633.

26. Ibid., 1:645.

27. Ibid., 1:651, 654.

28. Ibid., 1:657–65.

29. Ibid., 1:667.

30. P. La Follette, *Adventure in Politics,* 47; Kennedy, *Over Here,* 109–110.

31. *RML* 2:751–52, 759.

32. Steffens to RML, Oct. 7, 1917, LFP B.82; RML to Fred Holmes, n.d. 1917, LFP B.111. See also RML to Belle, July 7, 1917 ("I suppose they are laying for a chance to put us out"), and Aug. 25 ("We must be careful not to let anything in which will ban the magazine").

33. *RML* 2:761–69.

34. For the attacks on RML see *RML* 2:731–931 passim, but some specific examples are in 779–91, 795–99, 814–16, 838–39, 868–69, 875–86, 898, 910–12, 915–17, 928–31. The TR, Taft, and Butler remarks are at 771–72.

35. Ibid., 783–89; RML, Jr., to "Dear Ones," Oct. 7, 1917, LFP A.20.

36. Debs to RML, Oct. 15, 1917, LFP B.80; RML to Debs, Nov. n.d. 1917, LFP B.111.

37. Belle to G. K. Roe, Aug. 23, 1913, Gwyneth K. Roe Papers; Belle to RML, Jr., Nov. 5, 1914, LFP A.14; Belle to family, n.d. 1918, LFP A.22.

38. Kennedy, *Over Here,* 54–80.

39. *RML* 2:847.

40. Kennedy, *Over Here,* 92.

41. RML to Belle, Mar. 8, 1917, LFP A.20.

42. RML to Belle, Mar. 20, June 19, Sep. 6, 1917, LFP A.20; GM to RML, Jr., Oct. 3, 1917, LFP A.22; RML to family, Aug. 28, 1917, LFP A.22; diary of Clara (Suzanne) La Follette, LFP A.21; RML to family, June 20, July 2, 1917, LFP A.20.

43. P. La Follette, *Adventure in Politics,* 42; see 42–61 for entire story of Phil's campus experiences during the war.

44. Phil to RML, Jr., Mar. 20, 1916, LFP A.19.

45. P. La Follette, *Adventure in Politics,* 38; Phil to RML, Mar. 10, 1917; to Belle, May 7, 1917, LFP A.20.

46. Phil to RML, Jan. 19, 1917; to Belle, Apr. 9, Apr. 14, 1917, LFP A.20.

47. Phil to "Dear Ones," Dec. 11, 1917; to family, Oct. 15, 1917, LFP A.20.

48. RML, Jr., to Belle, July 14; to Mary, June 21, 1917; Mary to RML, Jr., Oct. 30, 1917; RML, Jr., to Mary, Nov. 3, 1917, LFP A.20.

49. RML to Phil, Oct. 21, Nov. 16, 1917; to Belle, Oct. 10, Sep. 4, 1917, LFP A.20.

50. RML, Jr., to RML, Aug. 6, 1918, LFP A.23.

51. RML to Phil, May 21, 1918, LFP A.23; Belle to RML, June 24, 1917, LFP A.20.

52. RML, Jr., to RML, Jan. 20, 1917, LFP A.20.

53. Phil to Belle, Mar. 28, May 15, 21, 1918, LFP A.23.

54. *RML* 2:889; RML, Jr., to RML, Oct. 7, 1918. Belle's reaction to learning that Phil owed money (a past-due notice from a bank, addressed to him at La Jolla, had fallen into her hands) is in a letter from her to him, Jan. 28, 1919, LFP A.24; she says: "All my life I have been discovering that we owed more money than I had known about. Daddy had not told me because he thought it would worry me. To this day he does not understand how the *uncertainty* wears me." He answered on Feb. 3, 1919 (LFP A.26), assuring her that he had by then paid off the note, owed nothing at the moment, and would, if in need of extra money for books and tuition, borrow thirty dollars from her instead of from a bank.

55. See Phil to Belle, Nov. 17, 1917[?]; Mary to Belle, Nov. 1917; Belle to Mary, Oct. 19, Nov. 4, 1917; Belle to Phil, Dec. 14, 1917, LFP A.20.

56. Belle to Phil, Aug. 7, 1918; to RML, Nov. 6, 1918, LFP A.22.

57. Fola to family, June 19, Aug. 12, 1917, LFP A.20.

58. Fola to family, Oct. n.d., 16, Nov. 6, 20, 1918, LFP A.22.

CHAPTER 7. IN ANOTHER COUNTRY: OLD BOB'S LAST CAMPAIGNS (1919–1925)

1. *RML* 2:905; RML to family, Nov. 7, 1918, LFP A.24.

2. RML to family, n.d., 1919, LFP A.26.

3. RML to family, Jan. 13, 1919, LFP A.26.

4. RML to family, Mar. 14, 1919, LFP A.26.

5. RML to family, Nov. 26, Oct. 26, 1918; RML to "Loved Ones," Jan. 20, 1919, LFP A.26; letter to Brandeis quoted in RML to family, Nov. 26, 1918; Nov. 27; 1918, LFP A.24.

6. RML to family, Jan. 28, Feb. 25, Jan. 9, 1919, LFP A.26; Apr. 16, May 12, 1919, LFP A.27.

7. RML to "My Loved Ones," Apr. 20, 27, 1919, LFP A.27; quoted to *RML* 2:957; RML to family, Feb. 10, 1919, LFP A.26.

8. *RML* 2:910–12, 928–31; RML to family, Nov. 30, 1918, LFP A.24; RML to Belle, Jan. 20, 1919, LFP A.27; Belle to RML, Jan. 21, 1919, LFP A.24.

9. *RML* 2:918; RML to family, Dec. 24, 10, 1918, LFP A.24.

10. RML to family, Feb. 22, 24, 1919, LFP A.26.

11. *RML* 2:943–47; RML to family, Mar. 10, 1919, LFP A.26; Mar. 1, 1919, *The Congressional Record,* 65th Cong., 3d sess., 4711.

12. RML to family, Mar. 18, Feb. 14, Mar. 17, 25, 29, 1919, LFP A.26.

13. RML to family, Apr. 24, 22, Mar. 29, May 12, 1919, LFP A.26; Belle's being left with only $3.50 described in *Belle,* 187.

14. RML's objections to the Versailles treaty can be found passim in his letters of 1919; see also RML 2:960–84; see particular letters to RML dated June 29, Apr. 7, 1919, LFP A.27; RML 2:1156. None of La Follette's objections were uniquely his, and some of them were at least strengthened, if they did not actually originate, in his rage against Wilson. He was part of a curious antitreaty alliance of conservative nationalists, stalwart Republican partisans, disillusioned pro-war liberals, and consistent antiwar radicals, whom it is misleading to lump under the catchall label of isolationist.

15. RML to family, May 2, 16, June 29, 1919, LFP A.27.

16. Phil to RML, Feb. 7, 1919; RML to family, Jan. 7, 1919, LFP A.26.

17. RML to RML, Jr., May 6, 1919; to Phil, May 31, 1919, LFP A.27; for changing Wisconsin scene see Paul Glad, *War, a New Era, and Depression, 1914–1940* (1990), vol. 5 in the six-volume *History of Wisconsin* in process by the State Historical Society of Wisconsin, especially chapters 1 through 7. Early in 1990, before the volume was in print, Professor Glad was kind enough to furnish me a manuscript copy for use in preparing a paper (see Chapter 8, note 1, below).

18. P. La Follette, *Adventure in Politics,* 66. My perception of the La Follette "machine" is based on the various La Follette memoirs and letters, modified by the Glad volume cited in note 17 and Nesbit's *Wisconsin.*

19. *RML,* 2:995; Phil to "Dad," Apr. 20, 1920, LFP A.28.

20. *RML* 2:997.

21. *RML* 2:999–1010; for election results, see U.S. Bureau of the Census, *Historical Statistics of the United States, Colonial Times to 1957* (Washington, 1960).

22. P. La Follette *Adventure in Politics,* 69–70; *RML* 2:1025.

23. Middleton, *These Things Are Mine,* 173 (but Middleton erroneously dates the "all the rest is velvet" remark to 1920); P. La Follette, *Adventure in Politics,* 71–72; *RML* 2:1061.

24. Belle to RML from La Jolla, Jan. 27, Feb. 23, Apr. 14 (to Phil), Feb. 6, 1919, LFP A.24.

25. Belle to "My Precious Phil," Feb. 23, 1921; to "My Loved Ones," Jan. 25, 1921; RML, Jr., to Phil, Sep. 21, 1921, LFP A.29.

26. Belle to Mary, Oct. 26, 1923; to family, May 30, 1923; to Mary, May 7, 1923, LFP A.29.

27. RML to family, Feb. 2, 1919, LFP A.26; Fola to "Bobs," June 25, 1919, LFP A.25.

28. Fola to "Bobs, darling," June 30, 1919; to Belle Aug. 16, 1919; to "Mary, darling," Sep. 19, 1919, LFP A.25.

29. Fola to Belle, Mar. 10, 1923; to Mid, May 22, June 6, 1924, LFP A.30; P. La Follette, *Adventure in Politics,* 61.

30. RML to Bob and Phil, May 30, 1919; to Mary, July 26, 1919, LFP A.27; RML, Jr., to "Dearest Mary, dear," Mar. 15, 1919; Phil to Mary, July 30, 1919, LFP A.26.

31. Mary to Belle, Apr. 11, 1919; to Phil, June 11, July 29, 1919, LFP A.25.

32. Ralph G. Sucher, interview with author, Apr. 30, May 1, 1988.

33. Belle to Mary, Mar. n.d. 1921; to family, Mar. 8, 1921; Fola to Belle, Feb. 1, 1921, LFP A.29.

34. Frederic C. Howe, "Where Are the Pre-War Radicals?" *Survey,* Apr. 1, 1926.

35. RML to RML, Jr., Feb. 6, 1919; RML, Jr., to RML, Feb. 12, 1919, LFP A.26; Belle to Fola, Apr. 5, 1919; RML, Jr., to "Dad," Apr. 10, May 11, May 4, Mar. 25, 1919, LFP A.24.

36. RML, Jr., to family, May 21, June 29, 1919; to Phil, June 2, 1919, LFP A.24.

37. P. La Follette, *Adventure in Politics,* 114; RML, Jr., to Fola, June 16, 1919; to RML, Apr. 30, May 26, July 30, Aug. 3, 1919, LFP A.26; RML to RML, Jr., Aug. 6, 1919, LFP A.27.

38. Belle to RML, Feb. 6, 1919, LFP A.24.

39. Maney, *"Young Bob,"* 31–32; RML, Jr., to Phil, Mar. 21, 1923; RML to RML, Jr., June 16, 1923, LFP A.30.

40. Phil to RML, Apr. 30, 1919, LFP A.26. Some letters in the family papers in Washington are duplicated in PFLP; in such cases I use the copy in LFP. Therefore, citations to PFLP indicate that I have not found duplicates of those letters in LFP.

41. Belle to Phil, Feb. 2, 1919, LFP A.24; Phil to family, Feb. n.d., Feb. 26, July 21, Apr. 21, 1919, LFP A.26. Memo of aims on twenty-third birthday in PFLP 2.131.

42. Phil to self, May 8, 1921, PFLP 2.131; to Belle, Jan. 3, 1919, LFP A.26; see also Phil to Belle, Mar. 18, Apr. 19, 1921, LFP A.29; Phil to Belle, July 24, 1919, LFP A.26.

43. P. La Follette, *Adventure in Politics,* 62–64; RML, Jr., to Phil, Jan. 29, 1921; Phil to Belle, Mar. 18, May 8, 1919, LFP A.29.

44. P. La Follette, *Adventure in Politics,* 68, 71–77.

45. IBL commencement [?] address, May 11, 1916, PFLP 3.160.

46. IBL to "Dearest Family," n.d., 1918; "Sunday night," and Apr. 11, 1919, PFLP 3.160.

47. P. La Follette, *Adventure in Politics,* 78–81; Phil to IBL, Sep. 27, 1921, PFLP 2.131; Belle to IBL, June 6, 1924, LFP A.30; IBL, "If You Can Take It" (autobiography), typewritten manuscript, 11–32; PFLP 3:165.

48. Phil to IBL, July 13, Aug. 8, Oct. 11, 12, 1921, Mar. 23, 1922, PFLP 2.131; to IBL, Mar. 23, 1922, LFP A.29; IBL, "If You Can Take It," 22.

49. The entire trip abroad is covered in *RML* 2:1075–87.

50. *RML* 2:1082, 1083, 1086.

51. RML, Jr., to Fola and Mid, Oct. 11, 1923; RML, Jr., to "Dear Ones," Nov. 17, 1923, LFP A.30; P. La Follette, *Adventure in Politics,* 89.

52. The preconvention material is from *RML* 2:1096–1109. Independent ver-

sions of the 1924 campaign include Kenneth MacKay, *The Progressive Movement of 1924,* and Arthur M. Schlesinger, Jr., Fred Israel, and W. P. Hansen, eds., *The History of American Presidential Elections, 1789–1984* (New York, 1986) 4:2459–585. The La Follettes' view is summed up in RML 2:1107–47; in P. La Follette *Adventure in Politics,* 86–99; and, of course, in the letters. David Thelen offers interesting analysis in *Robert M. La Follette and the Insurgent Spirit,* 179–94. Thelen's view of these final days of La Follette's career is somewhat mellower than that in his *Early Life of Robert M. La Follette,* but he continues, in my judgment, to view the entire course of early twentieth-century United States politics in the context of a perceived struggle between "modernizers" and their opponents, in which contestants are pigeonholed without appropriate attention to their own sense of motivation. I sampled contemporary magazines and newspapers extensively but have cited only those actually quoted.

53. *New York Times,* July 6–8, 1924; *RML* 2:1109–16.

54. *RML* 2:1116.

55. The platform is printed in various sources; see note 53, above.

56. F. Frankfurter, "Why I Shall Vote for La Follette," *New Republic,* Oct. 22, 1924, 199–201.

57. *RML* 2:1126, 1136.

58. See *Baltimore American,* Oct. 12, 1924; *Belle,* 218–19.

59. Belle to "Loved Ones," July 11, 1924, LFP A.30; Phil to IBL, Aug. 30, 1924, PFLP 2.132; RML, Jr., to Rachel Young, Oct. 23, 1924, LFP A.31.

60. *RML* 2:1121, 1147; P. La Follette, *Adventure in Politics,* 98–99. No third party or independent candidate exceeded La Follette's 16.5 percent of the popular vote until the presidential election of 1992, when Ross Perot received between 19 and 20 percent.

61. *RML,* 2:1149.

62. RML to Josie Siebecker, Dec. 27, 1924, LFP A.32; *RML* 2:1160.

63. *RML* 2:1152; RML to "Dear Ones," Apr. 28, 1925, LFP A.32; RML to family, Jan. 26, 1919, A:26.

64. *RML* 2:1167–74; *Belle,* 226–28.

65. *Belle,* 229–31; Maney, *"Young Bob,"* 38–39.

CHAPTER 8. THE SUCCESSION THAT WASN'T (1925–1941)

1. LFP C.16. The major sources for this chapter other than the family letters are P. La Follette, *Adventure in Politics,* and Maney's *"Young Bob,"* which is thoroughly researched, though its story line is sometimes lost in details. For Young Bob's Senate career I sampled newspapers and periodicals as indicated in the notes. I find it hard to recommend any particular volume among the many general histories of the New Deal, but the two on which I relied heavily were William E. Leuchtenburg, *Franklin D. Roosevelt and the New Deal,* and Joseph Lash, *Dealers and Dreamers* (New York, 1988). Young Bob's important role as chairman of the Senate Civil Liberties Committee investigating anti-union activities is dealt with in Jerold Auerbach, *Labor and Liberty,* which repays reading as a close portrait of the senator at work and why the work mattered. For the period from 1939 through 1941 see note 34, below. This chapter was prepared originally as "Political Prob-

lems of an Heir-Apparent: Robert M. La Follette, Jr., and the New Deal," and presented as a paper at the 1990 annual meeting of the Organization of American Historians. I have borrowed freely from that version where I felt the need. For Phil's career as governor, the principal scholarly source has been Glad's *War, a New Era, and Depression, 1914–1940.*

2. *"Young Bob,"* 47–48; RML, Jr., to Phil and Isen, Jan. 25, 1927, LFP A.35.

3. RML, Jr., to "Rachel, dear," Mar. 2, 1925; to family, Feb. 17, 1925, LFP A.32; to "Dear Ones," Feb. 28, 1929, LFP A.38.

4. RML, Jr., to Belle, May 7, 1929, to Rachel, July 26, Aug. 9, 1929, LFP A.38.

5. Fola to Mary, Nov. 7, 1924, LFP A.30; to Mid, July 24, 1928, A.36; to "Mary, darling," Aug. 26, 1930, LFP A.39.

6. Belle to Fola and Mid, Sep. 26, 1928 (see also to "Beloved Mary," Aug. 25, 1928, LFP A.36); to Mid, Mar. 13, Apr. 14, 1929, LFP A.37; for further struggles with the book see Belle's letters of Jan. 29 and Mar. 10, 1929, and Jan. 22, 1927, to Isen, LFP A.34; RML to Fola and Mid, Nov. 14, 1928, LFP A.36; see also RML to Fola and Mid, "Mother is somewhat tired of her work," Dec. 30, 1930, LFP A.40.

7. RML, Jr., to Phil, Aug. 22, 1929, LFP A.38; a copy of the agreement creating *The Progressive* is in the same box; Phil to Bob, Aug. 30, 1939, LFP A.38. Isen's column was called "A Room of Our Own." The name may be not only a paraphrase of Virginia Woolf's book about the needs and problems of women (which appeared in 1929) but a reference to Isen's own liking, expressed elsewhere in her writings, for a "room of our own" (preferably with a good fire) where she and Phil could talk informally in privacy and comfort about the issues on their minds.

8. Phil to family, May 7, 1929, LFP A.38.

9. On 1928 election see Fola to RML, Jr., Oct. 28, 1928, A.36; RML, Jr., to Fola, Nov. 4, 1930, LFP A.40; RML, Jr., to Belle and Mary, Apr. 14, 1931, LFP A.41. Bob's comment on the cities and states not being responsible for the crash are in an interview with William Hard, broadcast over NBC stations on January 11, 1932; "The city governments did not pass any ordinances which erected prohibitive tariff barriers, or any legislation affecting the credit policy of the banking system." LFP C.556.

10. *"Young Bob,"* 85, 90–92; RML, Jr., to Fola, May 15, 1931, LFP A.41; Phil to Belle, Dec. 21, 1930, LFP A.39.

11. P. La Follette, *Adventure in Politics,* 162; see 126 for debate on future of progressives; IBL, "If You Can Take It," 70–100.

12. *Adventure in Politics,* 125–26; Phil to Fola, Nov. 4, 1930, LFP A.39; drafts of 1930 platform are in PFLP 1.1; Phil to Bob, Dec. 15, Apr. 18, 1931, LFP A.41.

13. Brandeis to "My Dear Bob and Phil," June 19, 1925 (date is written as 1926 but clearly in error), LFP C.1.

14. Meditation by Phil on Feb. 12, 1920, in PFLP 2.131 and also in LFP A.28; Fola to Mid, Oct. 29, 1931; RML, Jr., to Fola, Oct. 23, 1931, LFP A.41. The doctor's excuse is repeated in a letter from Ralph Sucher to Phil, Sep. 18, 1931, PFLP 2.135. Three months after Belle's death, poor Young Bob suffered another personal disaster when the first child born to him and Rachel died a few hours after birth. His letter to Fola and Mid says: "As I see it, life is only a test of one's stamina and it only differs in that some appear to have the thumb screws twisted down a little harder than others. It is this struggle to find the courage to meet the impacts

of life which seems in one sense to make it an experience of sufficient magnitude to justify enduring it." Nov. 11, 1931, LFP A.41.

15. RML, Jr., radio address, Apr. 5, 1935, LFP C.551; "For Rodney Dutcher's Column," n.d., but 1937 from internal evidence, LFP C.559; Scripps quoted in Alfred Lief, *Democracy's Norris* (New York, 1939), 375–78; James Causey to RML, Jr., Sep. 19, 1939, LFP C.17; *Adventure in Politics*, 153.

16. "*Young Bob*," 95–103; RML, Jr., to Fola, Mar. 4, 1932, LFP A.42; *Adventure in Politics*, 184–203; IBL, "If You Can Take It," 151–211. For Phil and Isen's view of their 1939 trip to Europe (one marvels at Phil's knack for being there at precise moments of historical significance), see *Adventure in Politics*, 257–59, and IBL, "If You Can Take It," 356–65.

17. Fola to Mary, Nov. 9, 1932, LFP A.41; RML, Jr., to Phil, Feb. 7, 1933, LFP A.43; *Adventure in Politics*, 204–07; "*Young Bob*," 106–7. What FDR actually did was to tell Bob, while Phil was still in Europe, that he would offer either Phil or Felix Frankfurter the attorney generalship if Thomas Walsh declined it. Walsh didn't decline it, but he did die of a heart attack before the appointment was made. Thereupon FDR gave the job to Homer Cummings.

18. "*Young Bob*," 110–30; RML, Jr., to Fola and Mid, Apr. 3, 10, 1933; to Rachel, Nov. 8, 1933, LFP A.43; speech at Bridgeport, May 5, 1933, speech to Wisconsin Federation of Labor, July 20, 1933, both in LFP C.557; radio talk, Apr. 5, 1935, LFP C.558.

19. *Adventure in Politics*, 209–13; "*Young Bob*," 132–42; Glad, *War, a New Era, and Depression*, ch. 10, "Cries of Protest," 398–447, and ch. 12, "Controversies along the Middle Way," 483–523, for general view from non–La Follette standpoint.

20. Belle to RML, Jr., Aug. 8, 1931, LFP A.41.

21. Statistics on the WPP victory are from Glad, *War, a New Era, and Depression*, 436–45.

22. *Adventure in Politics*, 217–24; Glad, *War, a New Era, and Depression*, 468–74.

23. "Why We Lost," *Nation*, Dec. 3, 1938, 586–87.

24. Elmer Davis, "Wisconsin Is Different," *Harper's* 165 (June–Nov. 1932): 613–24, and "The Wisconsin Brothers," *Harper's* 178 (Dec. 1938–May 1939): 268–77; Marquis Childs, *I Write from Washington* (New York, 1942), 20–21; Tugwell quoted in Arthur M. Schlesinger, Jr., *The Politics of Upheaval*, 330.

25. "Democrats Talk La Follette Boom," *New York Times*, Mar. 23, 1935; "Copeland in West Urges a Coalition," *New York Times*, Sep. 22, 1937; "President Invites La Follette on Cruise Amid Rumors of Strained Relations," *New York Times*, May 14, 1938; *The Secret Diary of Harold L. Ickes* (New York, 1953–54), 2:395; "*Young Bob*," 197–202.

26. Auerbach, *Labor and Liberty: "Young Bob*," 170–88.

27. Phil to Bob, Dec. 5, 1937, LFP A.45.

28. *Adventure in Politics*, 217–45, which naturally tells the story from Phil's viewpoint. Davis, "The Wisconsin Brothers" (see note 24 above), has a judicious but brief summary.

29. Glad, *War, a New Era, and Depression, 1914–1940*, 499–506, 510–33. Phil's version of the NPA disaster is contained in very brief compass in *Adventure*

in Politics, 246–54, in which he claims that he did not want to run for governor in 1938 but was forced into it by lack of another viable candidate and, knowing he would lose, "took his medicine." It does not sound convincing. Isen, in "If You Can Take It," loyally supplements his story. See also Davis, "The Wisconsin Brothers," and an interesting interview between Phil and Max Lerner in *Nation,* May 14, 1938. *Time,* May 4, 1938, reports on the grand launching rally. Gordon Sinykin's assessment of Phil's withdrawal from candidacies of any kind after 1938 is from my interview with him on Sep. 1, 1987; Phil's memory of writhing in humiliation after his 1932 loss is in *Adventure in Politics,* 178. FDR's triumphant comment is in *"Young Bob,"* 209.

30. Information on Nellie Dunn MacKenzie is from the descriptive material in the Papers of Frederick William and Nellie Dunn MacKenzie in the State Historical Society of Wisconsin; *Adventure in Politics,* 38; Ralph's letter to Mary is in LFP A.44.

31. Fola to Mary, June 5, 1931, LFP A.44; see other Fola to Mary letters of 1935, especially July and August, for encouragement.

32. Mid to RML, Jr., n.d., "Sunday," 1934, LFP A.43; to RML, Jr., Dec. 27, 1936, LFP A.44; Fola to Mid, Dec. 3, 1938, LFP A.46. Her entire correspondence with him at this period contains frequent attempts to cheer him up.

33. Fola to Mid, Dec. 5, 1938; Fola to Phil and Bob, with proposed agreement, Apr. 29, 1937, LFP A.45; Mary to Fola, Apr. 26, 1939, undated, and Aug. 17, 1940, LFP A.47.

34. Phil gives short shrift to his isolationism, 263–65 in *Adventure in Politics.* Bob's course in 1939–1941 is covered in *"Young Bob,"* 226–50; his reluctant campaign of 1940 and narrow victory are particularly dealt with on 242–45. A good general overview of "isolationism" is found in Wayne S. Cole, *America First.*

35. *"Young Bob,"* 245.

EPILOGUE: THE WAR AND AFTER

1. Maney, *"Young Bob,"* 260; *Wisconsin Magazine of History,* Winter 1980–1981, cover; IBL, "If You Can Take It"; interview with Bronson C. La Follette, Nov. 2, 1989.

2. *"Young Bob,"* 262–63.

3. *"Young Bob,"* 268–71; interview with Gordon Sinykin; *"Young Bob,"* 287–88; P. La Follette, *Adventure in Politics,* 274–79.

4. *"Young Bob,"* 288–304.

5. Alf Rogers to RML, Jr., Feb. 4, 1934, LFP C.12.

6. *"Young Bob,"* 305–14.

7. *Washington Post,* Feb. 12, 1988; *Adventure in Politics,* 272; IBL to Fola, May 19, 1967, Jan. 7, 1968, LFP A.54.

Bibliography

Some bibliographies guide the reader to further research or an overview of all the materials conceivably related to a topic that may have shaped the author's views. Other bibliographies list the materials actually drawn on for the work at hand and cited in the notes. This bibliography is of the latter variety. Some of the general works listed in it—particularly existing biographies of the La Follette family members—would be useful to those who want to learn more about any of the subjects touched on here.

MANUSCRIPTS

As the notes make clear, the basic source of this book is the La Follette Family Papers in the Library of Congress, which has prepared an excellent register of the papers it holds. The mass of material is enormous, numbering approximately 414,000 items in nearly 1,400 containers, but the heart of it for me was in the 56 containers in Series A, predominantly consisting of correspondence among the family members. Series B and C comprise the papers of Robert M. La Follette and Robert M. La Follette, Jr., including considerable documentary and otherwise official material accumulated or created by them and their staffs during their combined forty-one years in the United States Senate. Their files of outgoing and incoming personal correspondence are richly rewarding. Series D and E include the papers of Belle Case and Fola La Follette. Again, there is gold for present and future historians in their public writings and personal correspondence, particularly in the "biography" files of clippings, interviews, and memorabilia that they accumulated during their work on the two-volume life of Old Bob. Two very small series (three containers in all) contain papers of Philip and Mary La Follette. A 19-container series of the papers of Gilbert E. Roe and a one-container set of papers of Alfred T. Rogers represent these two onetime law partners of Old Bob and lifelong friends of the family. Finally there is Series J, 140 containers of the National Progressive Republican League, organized to support La Follette's 1912 presidential bid. I did not consult these last, or other related collections of La Follette associates and fellow progressives (such as Louis Brandeis and Ray Stannard Baker), also in the Library of Congress.

The other principal collection that I used was the Philip Fox La Follette Papers in the State Historical Society of Wisconsin at Madison. These are in three series, the first of them devoted to public papers and the second and third, in which I did my work, consisting of Phil's personal correspondence and that of other members of his family—many of them, but by no means all, duplicates of those in the Library of Congress. I also found good personal material in two other sets of papers at the State Historical Society, those of Gwyneth K. Roe, Gilbert Roe's wife, and of Frederick W. and Nellie D. MacKenzie. He was for a time the editor of *La Follette's Weekly Magazine* (later simply *La Follette's Magazine* and after 1929 *The Progressive*), and she was secretary to Robert La Follette, Sr., from 1901 to 1916, and to Robert, Jr., for a brief period in the 1930s.

The State Historical Society of Wisconsin also has a collection of Old Bob's pre-1905 papers (available at other libraries on microfilm), which are primarily political and which I did not use, as well as several collections of papers of La Follette political colleagues and friends which I likewise did not use because the focus of my book was the immediate family rather than the ups and downs of progressivism in Wisconsin. I hope that others may be spurred to pick up where I leave off.

In summary, then, the principal manuscript collections were: La Follette Family Collection, Library of Congress; Philip Fox La Follette Papers, State Historical Society of Wisconsin; Frederick W. and Nellie Dunn MacKenzie Papers, State Historical Society of Wisconsin; Gwyneth K. Roe Papers, State Historical Society of Wisconsin.

The reader will note that the book is primarily a record of the world as seen through La Follette eyes. I make no bones about that; it was precisely what I wanted to convey, but I hope it is clear in the text that I am aware of the boundaries of that conscious approach and most decidedly hope that I have not had the last word.

PUBLIC DOCUMENTS

Congressional Record

PERIODICALS AND NEWSPAPERS

I have listed below only those papers and magazines from which I actually quoted material. It will be noted that I have not used Madison or other Wisconsin journals, and have therefore not given a sense of the enormous hostility that the La Follettes could provoke. I could have done so and likewise found materials that illustrated the passionate loyalty of their adherents. But again, this was not quite my purpose: the La Follettes *believed* that they were part of a happy few fighting the massed powers of reaction, and how they responded to those beliefs is the central theme of this story. I would be greatly interested if someone of goodwill and objectivity would do a study on the intense feelings about the La Follettes in Wisconsin and what they revealed.

The newspapers I consulted include *New York Times, Washington Evening Star, Philadelphia Evening Bulletin,* and *Chicago Tribune.*

Of the magazines I used, *La Follette's Weekly Magazine* (see above for various name changes) was indispensable in following the political reactions of two generations of La Follettes to changing events. I also consulted these magazines: *American, Arena, Harper's, McClure's, Nation, New Republic, Survey,* and *Wisconsin Magazine of History.*

INTERVIEWS

I was able to interview one man who knew and remembered the senior La Follettes, Ralph Sucher, who became their son-in-law in 1921. All of the La Follette children are dead; I was able to interview two of their six surviving grandchildren: Mary's daughter, Joan, and Robert, Jr.'s son Bronson. I was also gratified to get interviews with two Madison friends and associates of Philip and Isen La Follette: Mary Sheridan, who was managing editor of *The Progressive* for many years (her husband, Morris Rubin, was editor); and Gordon Sinykin, who was Phil's law partner and political adviser. The interviews took place as follows: Mary Sheridan, Aug. 28, 1987; Gordon Sinykin, Sep. 1, 1987; Ralph Gunn Sucher, Apr. 30, May 1, 1988; Joan La Follette Sucher, July 5, 1988; Bronson Cutting La Follette, Nov. 2, 1989.

BOOKS

As I indicated in my notes to Chapter 1, Robert La Follette's life story is inseparable from the history of the Progressive movement, and in the last thirty-five years, historians have been subjecting that movement to sharp critical scrutiny. I have not attempted to list here the various works, old and new, that I consulted, but I would recommend to the reader who wants a summary of the trends the article "In Search of Progressivism," by Daniel T. Rodgers, in *The Promise of American History: Progress and Prospects,* edited by Stanley Kutler and Stan Katz (Baltimore, 1982). It focuses on changes in the way historians see and describe the movement, starting mainly in 1970. It does not do full justice to the "revisionism" that began fifteen years earlier with Richard Hofstadter's *The Age of Reform from Bryan to FDR* (New York, 1955), but it is a good overview and offers a fine bibliography. I disagree strongly, however, with its central point, that historians have failed to find any central essence of progressivism and have concentrated instead on what disparate interest-groups supported "progressive" measures, how they interacted and communicated, and what various kinds of rhetoric they employed. Rodgers concludes that this trend toward dissection and microscopic analysis (in which ideas such as progress, honest government, and citizenship disappear totally or become quaint slogans) does not blur our understanding of a political phenomenon; rather, he says, to "abandon the hunt for the *essence* of the noise and tumult of that era may not be . . . to lose the whole enterprise of historical comprehension. It may be to find it." To me, this is a bit like saying that if you spend time studying the physiology of the taste buds and the chemical ingredients of a peach (water, fiber, fructose, etc.) you will get closer to knowing why people enjoy eating peaches. I am, to put it mildly, unpersuaded, but Rodgers will inform a reader of where to look for contemporary studies of the era.

Getting down to the La Follette family itself, there are, first of all, family memoirs by Old Bob himself, by his son-in-law George Middleton, and by his son Phil.

345

The "big" biography of Bob is the one by his wife and daughter. A recent biography of Belle was prepared by her granddaughter (Phil's daughter) in collaboration with her husband and an outside writer. These are:

La Follette, Robert M. *La Follette's Autobiography: A Personal Narrative of Political Experiences*. Madison, 1968.
La Follette, Belle Case and Fola La Follette. *Robert M. La Follette, June 14, 1855–June 18, 1925*. 2 vols. New York, 1953.
La Follette, Philip. *Adventure in Politics: The Memoirs of Philip La Follette*. Edited by Donald Young. New York, 1970.
Middleton, George. *These Things Are Mine: The Autobiography of a Journeyman Playwright*. New York, 1947.
Freeman, Lucy, Sherry La Follette, and George A. Zabriskie. *Belle: The Biography of Belle Case La Follette*. New York, 1986.

To these might be added a volume of selections from his writings and speeches up to 1920: *The Political Philosophy of Robert M. La Follette*. Compiled by Ellen Torelle. Madison, 1920.

The next category of books consists of biographies of La Follettes by nonfamily members. Surprisingly, there are only two "regular" biographies of La Follette, Sr., quite brief:

Thelen, David P. *Robert M. La Follette and the Insurgent Spirit*. Boston, 1976. Reprint. Madison, 1986. Thelen has a good bibliography, especially rich in works on progressivism dating from the 1960s.
Greenbaum, Fred. *Robert Marion La Follette*. New York, 1975.

In addition, there is a complete, if not exactly sparkling biography of Robert La Follette, Jr.:

Maney, Patrick J. *"Young Bob" La Follette: A Biography of Robert M. La Follette, Jr., 1895–1953*. Columbia, Mo., 1978.

The following primary and secondary works were also valuable to me:

Ashby, LeRoy. *The Spearless Leader: Senator Borah and the Progressive Movement in the 1920s*. Urbana, Ill., 1972.
Auerbach, Jerold S. *Labor and Liberty: The La Follette Committee and the New Deal*. Indianapolis, 1966.
Baker, Ray Stannard. *American Chronicle*. New York, 1945.
Cole, Wayne S. *America First: The Battle against Intervention, 1940–1941*. Madison, 1953.
Curti, Merle, and Vernon Carstensen. *The University of Wisconsin: A History, 1848–1925,* 2 vols. Madison, 1949.
Glad, Paul W. *The History of Wisconsin*. Vol. 5, *War, a New Era, and Depression, 1914–1940*. Madison, 1990.
Graham, Otis. *An Encore for Reform: The Old Progressives and the New Deal*. New York, 1967.
Howe, Frederic C. *The Confessions of a Reformer*. New York, 1925.

Johnson, Tom L. *My Story*. New York, 1911.

Kennedy, David M. *Over Here: The First World War and American Society*. New York, 1980.

Leuchtenburg, William E. *Franklin D. Roosevelt and the New Deal, 1932–1940*. New York, 1963.

————. *The Perils of Prosperity, 1914–1932*. Chicago, 1958.

Link, Arthur S. *Woodrow Wilson and the Progressive Era, 1910–1917*. New York, 1954.

Lowitt, Richard. *George W. Norris: The Persistence of a Progressive, 1913–1933*. Urbana, Ill., 1971.

MacKay, Kenneth. *The Progressive Movement of 1924*. New York, 1947.

Margulies, Herbert F. *The Decline of the Progressive Movement in Wisconsin, 1890–1920*. Madison, 1968.

Maxwell, Robert S. *La Follette and the Rise of the Progressives in Wisconsin, 1890–1928*. Madison, 1956.

Nesbit, Robert C. *Wisconsin: A History*. Madison, 1973.

Norris, George W. *Fighting Liberal: The Autobiography of George W. Norris*. New York, 1961.

Perrett, Geoffrey. *America in the Twenties: A History*. New York, 1982.

Schlesinger, Jr., Arthur M. *The Politics of Upheaval*. Boston, 1960.

Steffens, Lincoln. *The Autobiography of Lincoln Steffens*. New York, 1931.

Thelen, David. *The Early Life of Robert M. La Follette, 1855–1884*. Chicago, 1966.

————. *The New Citizenship: Origins of Progressivism in Wisconsin, 1885–1900*. Columbia, Mo., 1972.

The Letters of Theodore Roosevelt. 8 vols. Edited by Elting E. Morison. Cambridge, Mass., 1951–1954.

White, William Allen. *The Autobiography of William Allen White*. New York, 1946.

Index

Actor's Equity: Fola La Follette early member of, xiv, 109

Adam and Eva: Middleton hit play with Guy Bolton (1918), 223, 246

Adamson Railway Labor Act: RML Sr. supports, 196

Addams, Jane (progressive activist): as first chairman of Women's Peace Party, 160; pacifist allies of, 188; in Peoples Council of America, 207; supports RML Sr. (1924), 268

Aldrich, Nelson (senator from Rhode Island): as conservative dominating figure in Senate, 46–47; in parliamentary duel with RML Sr. over currency bill, 56–57; retires in 1911, 57

Algonquin (U.S. ship): sunk Mar. 12, 1917, 203

Allen, William (professor at University of Wisconsin): influence on Belle, 13

Allison, William B. (senator from Iowa, important insider): 46; death noted, 73

American magazine: RML Sr. contracts with, for autobiography, 76; runs articles by Belle, 96

American Rights League: denounces RML Sr. (1917), 203

Amlie, Thomas (Wisconsin progressive pushes for Farmer-Labor party in 1934): settles for Progressive Party of Wisconsin, 295

Aquiden Lodge, Maine: Fola and Middleton vacation at (1919), 247–48

Associated Press: misquotes RML Sr. (St. Paul speech), 209; admits error, 230

Athenian literary society. *See* oratory

Baker, Bertha Kunz (drama coach): admired by Fola, 111–12; reads "revolutionary" play, 116; accompanies Fola to Europe, 127

Baker, Newton D. (progressive): elected mayor of Cleveland (1911), 134

Baker, Ray Stannard (progressive journalist): 75; helps RML Sr. prepare autobiography and becomes family friend, 76; describes progressive triumphs, 134; supports Wilson reservedly in 1912, 143

Ballinger, Richard (secretary of interior): involved in Taft controversy with progressives, 72

banking system: criticized by RML Sr. as supporting "system" of privilege, 55

Bascom, John (president, University of Wisconsin): early career and philosophy of, 10–11; liberal educational ideas and impact on students, 13–14; mentor of G. Stanley Hall, 80

Battle Creek (Kellogg) Sanitarium, Michigan: Bob and Belle take cure at, 246, 264

Berger, Victor (Wisconsin socialist): RML Sr. corresponds with, 236–37

Beveridge, Albert (senator from Indiana), 52; in insurgent bloc (1910), 75

Birge, Edward A. (instructor in biology at University of Wisconsin): influenced Belle's senior essay, 13

Bishop, Emily ("Aunt Emily"): organizes women's exercise classes, 79; and theories of education, 80; in New York City, 107–8; as parental surrogate to Fola, 112; lectures on suffrage and other re-

348

Eastman, Ellen (Buchanan) (half-sister of
RML Sr.): identified, 5; and marriage to
Dean Eastman, 6; husband takes over
farm in Primrose, 8
Eastman, Orville (RML Sr. nephew): runs
Dakota ranch for him, 79
Emergency Civil Liberties Committee.
See Civil Liberties Committee, U.S.
Senate
Emily Bishop League. *See* Bishop, Emily
Esch-Cummons Transportation Act of
1920 (returns railroads to private owner-
ship on generous terms): opposed by
RML Sr., 237
Espionage Act (1917): RML Sr. opposes,
207
Evans, Elizabeth ("Aunt Bunkie"): meets
Bob and Belle, visits and describes family
at Maple Bluff, 98–99; admired by Belle,
99, 101; Belle confides doubts about
Middleton to, 126; cautions RML Sr. on
hatred of T. Roosevelt, 144; notes RML
Sr.'s recovery in 1913, 145

Family: role of, in La Follettes' lives, xv–
xvi; RML Sr. sees, as refuge from struggle, 21; Belle's early ideas of, 22; wish to
raise children on farm, 60; RML's long
absences from, 64–66; his parental style
and exhortations in, 67–70; urges boys
to tenderness, 69, 70; La Follette, characterized by others, 76, 98; Fola's strong
attachment to, 110; Fola's problems in
admitting George Middleton to, 121–22;
1910 Christmas, celebrations, 122; RML
Jr. especially dependent on, 170; RML
Sr.'s particular need of, in 1917–18,
212, 214; wartime ordeal of, 212–24
passim; Phil's sense of obligation to, 215;
World War dispersion and reunion of,
226–27; RML Sr. repeats desire to have,
together, 227; Phil describes, as scarred
by war, 249; Phil on centrality of, in
their lives, 257; shattering impact of
RML Sr. and Belle's death upon children
of, 288
Farmer-Labor Party: left wing rebel part of,
runs Parley P. Christensen for president
in 1920, 241; spurned by RML Sr. in
1924, 266
Federal Reserve Act (1913): RML Sr. votes
against, 146

filibusters: RML's first, in Senate (1908),
55–57; against armed ship bill of 1917,
199–202; on mineral leasing bill (1919),
232
Ford, Henry: as sponsor of "peace ship," 192
Fourteen Points. *See* Versailles, Treaty of
Fox, Philip (family friend and physician), 35
Frank, Glenn (president, University of Wisconsin, 1926–37): ousted with Phil's assistance, 302
Furuseth, Andrew (president, International
Seamen's Union): meets RML Sr. in
1909, 146; friendship and collaboration
on La Follette's Seamen's Act, 146–48;
predicts RML Sr. "crucifixion" in 1917,
202; at nomination convention of 1924,
267

Gardner, Gilson (political correspondent):
doubts Taft renomination, 134
German-Americans: favorable image in
U.S. quickly lost in World War, 184;
question of, influence on RML Sr.'s neutralism, 186; confront violent hostility,
212
Goldman, Emma (anarchist, feminist,
friend of La Follettes): visits with Fola
(1912), 162
Gompers, Samuel (president, American
Federation of Labor): RML Sr.'s suspicions of, 241; endorses RML Sr. in 1924,
271
Gore, Thomas P (senator from Oklahoma):
and role in 1906 filibuster, 57; resolution
to bar American travel on ships of warring nations, 193
Greenwich Village: characterized, 164;
Fola and Middleton move to, 164
Gronna, Asle (anti-war senator from North
Dakota): in RML Sr. filibuster, 200;
"nay" vote on war, 205

Hale, Gardner: and vacations with Fola
and Middleton in 1918, 223
Hall, G. Stanley (psychologist, educator):
influence on Emily Bishop, 80
Hamlet: favorite play of RML Sr., 7; lectures on, 59
Hannan, John: as RML Sr. secretary, 48;
with RML Sr. at Philadelphia publishers'
banquet, 138–39; as go-between in dispute over RML Sr.'s withdrawal from